The Key Texts of Political Philosophy

This book introduces readers to analytical interpretations of seminal writings and thinkers in the history of political thought, including Socrates, Plato, Aristotle, the Bible, Thomas Aquinas, Machiavelli, Bacon, Hobbes, Locke, Montesquieu, Rousseau, Tocqueville, Marx, and Nietzsche. Chronologically arranged, each chapter in the book is devoted to the work of a single thinker. The selected texts together engage with two thousand years of debate on fundamental questions, which include: What is the purpose of political life? What is the good life, for us as individuals and for us as a political community? What is justice? What is a right? Do human beings have rights? What kinds of human virtues are there and which regimes best promote them? The difficulty of accessing the texts included in this volume is the result not only of their subtlety but also of the dramatic change in everyday life. The authors shed light on the texts' vocabulary and complexities of thought and help students understand and weigh the various interpretations of each philosopher's thought.

- Contains accessible interpretive essays on the greatest texts in the history of political thought, from Plato to Nietzsche.
- Includes key passages plus a succinct discussion that glosses the text, examines later-day interpretations, and guides students in forming their own interpretations.
- Allows students to learn from, rather than only about, each thinker, and to apply their thought to the present day.

Thomas L. Pangle holds the Joe R. Long Chair in Democratic Studies in the Department of Government and is codirector of the Thomas Jefferson Center for the Study of Core Texts and Ideas at the University of Texas at Austin.

Timothy W. Burns is Professor of Government at Baylor University.

T0381806

The Key Texts of Political Philosophy

An Introduction

THOMAS L. PANGLE
University of Texas at Austin

TIMOTHY W. BURNS
Baylor University

CAMBRIDGE
UNIVERSITY PRESS

CAMBRIDGE
UNIVERSITY PRESS

University Printing House, Cambridge CB2 8BS, United Kingdom

One Liberty Plaza, 20th Floor, New York, NY 10006, USA

477 Williamstown Road, Port Melbourne, VIC 3207, Australia

4843/24, 2nd Floor, Ansari Road, Daryaganj, Delhi - 110002, India

79 Anson Road, #06-04/06, Singapore 079906

Cambridge University Press is part of the University of Cambridge.

It furthers the University's mission by disseminating knowledge in the pursuit of education, learning and research at the highest international levels of excellence.

www.cambridge.org
Information on this title: www.cambridge.org/9780521185004

© Thomas L. Pangle and Timothy W. Burns 2015

First published 2015

A catalogue record for this publication is available from the British Library

Library of Congress Cataloging in Publication data
Pangle, Thomas L.
The key texts of political philosophy : an introduction / Thomas L. Pangle,
University of Texas at Austin, Timothy W. Burns, Baylor University.
pages   cm
Includes index.
ISBN 978-1-107-00607-2 (hardback) – ISBN 978-0-521-18500-4
1. Political science – Philosophy.   I. Burns, Timothy, 1958–   II. Title.
JA71.P3383   2014
320.01–dc23   2014015719

ISBN 978-1-107-00607-2 Hardback
ISBN 978-0-521-18500-4 Paperback

To Heather and Sophia, Daniel and David

Contents

vii

Acknowledgments

A section of Chapter 4, "The Bible," was previously published as "The Hebrew Bible's Challenge to Political Philosophy: Some Introductory Reflections" by Thomas Pangle, in *Political Philosophy and the Human Soul* edited by Michael Palmer and Thomas Pangle. We wish to thank Rowman and Littlefield Publishers for their kind permission to reprint. We also wish to thank the Earhart Foundation for providing generous summer funding during the composition of this book.

Introduction

What is political philosophy? Why is its study important? And why should political philosophy be introduced as it is in this volume – through a sustained encounter with a very few old books, whose authors lived in civic cultures profoundly unlike our own? Why do we not begin from books and thinkers of our own time? How will we get at the problems that are most important for us today through reading long-dead authors? Are not the important issues of politics those that are pressing, urgent, "the burning issues of the day?" What is in these old books that could be more significant?

The answer is simple. The books that we will be studying embody humanity's most powerful attempts to grapple with the truly fundamental and enduring questions about human existence. What are the ultimate ends or purposes of our lives, as individuals and as political communities? What constitutes human fulfillment and flourishing? Can security, health, prosperity, and entertainment be all that our existence is for? Or must not these goods be understood as, at best, a foundation and means or opportunity, for higher activities and concerns? To speak of the "higher" is to speak of that which has and bestows *dignity*; what is it that gives our existence dignity? What is it that makes this particular life-form – a human life – deserving of special respect or even reverence? What makes us different in rank from the other animals, so that we feel that we are free to eat and to enslave them, but not our fellow humans?

We express our respect for humanity by speaking of "human rights." Respect for human rights is a major dimension of what we call justice, or righteousness. What is the full meaning of *justice*? Most obviously, we discern two massive aspects: Justice means distributing to each and every person what is fairly due; including but going beyond the former – justice means caring for the *common good* of society as a whole. On what basis does justice, in both these senses, make a claim on us, as individuals, such that we feel obliged (and we think that others ought to feel obliged) to respect and to care for justice, even or especially when this entails substantial personal cost – sometimes even the ultimate sacrifice of one's life? Is not this distinctly human capacity, for deliberately subordinating one's personal good to what one believes to be right, a major dimension of what dignifies human life, as a life that is more than that of a very clever animal? Is justice not a *virtue* – an admirable quality of character, a defining trait of a truly good person and of a healthy soul? But does being just, then, involve not so much self-denial as, instead, self-enhancement: Is being just not a crucial component of one's own truly greatest personal good? Or is there not a puzzle here, at the heart of our conception of the value of justice – a puzzle as to the sense in which justice is good, and for whom it is good? Does not a similar puzzle lurk in our conception of the value of other moral virtues, such as courage and generosity or charity? Do not these virtues entail selflessness or self-transcendence, while yet simultaneously being essential to self-realization in full dignity? What exactly does each of these moral virtues entail, and how are they related to one another and to justice? To what extent should the civic common good entail the communal cultivation of these moral virtues?

We have brought into focus major dimensions of our humanity's self-transcending or self-transfiguring concern for what is beyond narrow self-interest. Yet the most passionate expression of such concern is found in love and friendship. How are the claims made on us by love, and friendship, and family, related to the claims of justice and the other moral virtues? Are there not grave tensions among and between these diverse claims and obligations? How ought we to contend with these tensions?

The self-transcending dimensions and claims of human existence, when they are experienced deeply, lead beyond themselves to a further vast field of questions. For we are aware that we are situated in a larger cosmic whole – of which we humans, as a species, are not the masters, and not necessarily even the peak. We experience an awe for nature, of which we sense that we are the custodians, and not the owners. What is the meaning, and basis, of this awe and sense of responsibility? What is the ultimate source and ground of nature as we thus experience and revere it? Is there a deeper level of reality behind or above what we primarily experience as "nature?" What other beings, deserving equal or even higher respect than us humans, may exist? Does divinity exist? Does it afford us the possibility of an escape from the limits of our apparent natural mortality or finitude? What is the evidence for, and against, the existence of higher, ruling and redeeming, divinity? If there is such divinity, what claims does that divinity make on us, and how are these claims related to the claims of justice, of friendship, of love and family? How should political life and human laws relate and respond to the possibility that there are supreme divine commandments or divine laws?

Up to this point we have stressed fundamental questions about our senses of dedication or obligation to what is beyond ourselves. But another key constituent of human dignity is personal liberty. What is *genuine* liberty? Is it merely freedom from physical and other constraints? Is it living as one pleases? How does one distinguish liberty from license? Does not full liberty require participation in republican self-government – taking on a responsible and meaningful share in shaping the common life of one's society? Is not civic liberty closely akin to the virtue of justice, as an intensely active virtue?

But is not the fullest human liberty a liberation of our *minds*, to and through *thinking*, for ourselves, and acting in accordance with our *independent* judging? Does this not entail a critical *questioning* of our society's beliefs, demands, customs, even its laws? But if so, how does this intellectual liberation fit together with political liberation, entailing law-abiding citizenship dedicated to the common good? How may one seriously question society's laws and customs and culture, while still remaining a loyal, dedicated citizen? What is the relation between such intellectual virtue and moral or civic virtue? Is there not here a gravely tension-ridden challenge? Can most people rise to this challenge – or is true freedom of the mind possible only for a few, very strong and unusually independent, even solitary, souls? Is this rare wisdom and strength of soul the truest meaning of *intellectual* virtue or excellence?

Yet *equality*, and respect for others as equals, is also a demand of justice. What exactly is the morally compelling meaning of equality, and how is this meaning of equality related to virtue and to liberty? Is it not very problematic to suppose that people are equal, in many important respects – in intelligence, in artistic talent, in capacity to love, in their moral care and civic zeal? In what sense then can everyone deserve equal respect, let alone equal treatment?

This leads on to another big set of questions: What kind of political order or regime most completely fulfills and lends dignity to its members? We have been raised in a mass liberal democracy, and of course have had had bred into us, from early childhood, the claim that ours is the best, or even the sole legitimate, form of government and society. But is that true? What are the proof, the arguments, and the evidence? Have not other, very different, forms of government bred citizens who believed with equal passion and conviction that theirs was the best, or even the sole legitimate, form of government and society? Have not other forms of government implicitly or explicitly claimed to be based on notions of human dignity, of happiness, of excellence, of divinity, of love, and of justice or the common good that are decisively superior to our notions? What are the arguments for those claimants, and how do they measure up against the arguments that can be marshaled for the rightness and goodness of our liberal democracy? Until we hear or engage in such debate, will we really have more than a merely dogmatic, inbred opinion as to the superiority of our democracy?

In raising these last questions, we begin to sense what is so controversial about political philosophy. Authentic political philosophy, as the sustained pursuit of questioning of the sort we have begun to sketch, is an unsettling and disturbing enterprise. Political philosophy was initiated by Socrates, who was tried and executed by the Athenian democracy as an impious corrupter of the young. And this was no accident, Plato teaches, in the first work that we shall examine. For citizens naturally become upset when they hear these fundamental questions pursued seriously and relentlessly. All human beings, not only citizens of democracies, are born and raised in one or another specific political and social culture that inculcates fundamental opinions that give the official answers to life's most basic questions. These answers tell citizens what they are supposed to think about all the important issues: what is right and wrong, just and unjust, good and bad, noble and base; who and what they ought to love; what friendship is, what a good family is, what divinity is; what one ought to admire and to strive for. The official answers constitute the very foundations of each society, and of its people's attachments – to their families, to their jobs, to their religions, to their friends, to their country. Political philosophy arises out of the awareness that these authoritative answers, until they are critically scrutinized, are held as mere opinions: They, and the culture or way of life they constitute, can be questioned, doubted, challenged to give a justification. Political philosophy began in earnest when Socrates became the first philosopher to make his central focus the striving for genuine *knowledge* about these most important matters – about what is truly right, good, noble, and just; about what constitutes true love and friendship; about what god or the gods might truly be. But when his fellow citizens sensed that these questions were being pressed and pursued intransigently, and that this meant that the respectable, traditional answers were being severely interrogated, the citizenry became – for understandable reasons – alarmed.

In every age and culture where it has appeared, political philosophy has meant questioning what is sacred, doubting what one is not supposed to doubt. This means that the questioning that is at the heart of political philosophy is a dubious and even a dangerous enterprise. It can do vast harm; it can undermine society; it can leave individuals bewildered and weakened. We are thus confronted with one of the most agonizing problems of human existence: There is no simple harmony between what is good for social or personal stability, for civic commitment and attachment, and what is good for genuine freedom of the mind.

This problem persists in our own, liberal democratic, society and culture, but the problem takes on a distinctive new character. Like every other culture, ours has its own set of authoritative answers to all the big questions of human existence. Our civic society stands or falls with respect for tolerance, for freedom of religion and of expression, for the free market, for majority consent as the sole legitimate basis of government, for human rights – conceived as each individual's freedom to pursue happiness as he or she wishes, so long as this does not prevent anyone else from enjoying the same freedom. Yet as the adjective "liberal" connotes, our civic culture, more than any that ever came before, prides itself on being open to, and in some measure encouraging of, critical and even radical questioning or doubt. How far, and how truly philosophically, we ought in public life to press this doubt is a very big, very serious, very fraught question.

But we cannot today avoid political philosophy in some form and degree. We are spurred toward the radical self-doubt, the self-critical questioning, that is political philosophy by more than simply our liberal ethos. For we are haunted by the awareness that there are many reasons for viewing our present-day civic culture with unease, not to say alarm. To be sure, we have major sources of satisfaction and pride. At least in North America and Europe, modern democracy has achieved unprecedented security, prosperity, technological power, rule of law, and liberation from oppression. These benefits have been spread to more and more previously subordinated or exploited groups, including, notably, women and all sorts of downtrodden or marginalized minorities. But it is much less clear that we have progressed in virtue, civic or moral or intellectual; and in our efforts to continue our progress in more basic respects, we constantly encounter the obstacles thrown up by a grave deficit in our civic and personal virtues – and more generally, in the spiritual elements of culture. Our lives are largely given over to working for a living, in jobs that have little civic dimension; to attending to our immediate families; and to relaxing or entertaining ourselves in rather mindless ways that allow escape and recuperation from the toil or narrowness of our jobs. The concept of true "leisure," communal and personal, has almost disappeared from our consciousness. The concept of true leisure is developed by Aristotle at the end of his *Politics*. Aristotle contrasts "leisure" with both work and play (as relaxation or entertainment). Entertainment and relaxation are unserious and restorative, even escapist: They give us pleasures that afford recuperation from, and for, the burdensome work that we make the serious business of life. Business (work) and play (entertainment) thus form a life cycle of seriousness without pleasure and pleasure without seriousness. Leisure breaks out of that cycle. Leisure is *serious pleasure or joy*. Leisure means the energetic, passionate, and freely chosen engagement in spiritually enlarging, uplifting, and fulfilling activity, reaping the profound joys of the soul. In our culture, however, the time and effort spent on studious reading, thoughtfully reflective conversation, religious worship, philosophic inquiry, artistic production, and, last but not least, sustained political participation, has not grown in any proportion to the growth in our more basic achievements. Is this the way it has to be? Does modern democracy have to purchase its manifest, basic benefits at the cost of a populace that tends toward becoming politically apathetic and childlike, socially atomized, and spiritually shallow? We are forced to wonder: Could there be something truly defective about, something important that is missing from, our liberal democracy's basic principles? Or, on the other hand, could it be that our culture has developed historically in such a way that it has lost sight of major rich dimensions of what our original liberal principles mean or imply? Have we as peoples over time forgotten key aspects of the spiritual depths and aspirations belonging to liberal republicanism, properly understood?

These daunting questions intensify, for us here and now, the centuries-old needs to which authentic political philosophy is the response, in all times and places. We today experience, if in a distinctive way, the age-old hunger to liberate our minds from simple submission to our present civic culture and its breeding of us. We are impelled in our own way to ask: What are the cogent reasons for, the decisive justifications of, the underlying aims or purposes that animate our form of government and cultural way of life? Is there no need or possibility for far-reaching reform of what we have been given in the way of answers to these basic questions about our historical existence?

Can any serious person living in today's liberal democracies *not* feel the need to engage in such critical questioning, challenging, and testing of the outlook that has been instilled into us? But as soon as we respond to this felt need by seeking the path to philosophic questioning, we confront a massive obstacle. It is doubtful whether anyone, in any time and place, can really understand the meaning of the compelling arguments that validate "our" form of government and way of life unless one hears those arguments tested by searching questions and strong *counter*arguments from *alien* viewpoints – from intelligent advocates of contrasting or opposed forms of government and ways of life. If we are to partake of political philosophy, we need to encounter, and to listen to, and to argue with profound, articulate thinkers who do not share, who dispute, our fundamental assumptions about morals and politics. But where and how can we encounter such bracing challenges? How can we avoid remaining trapped, often without fully realizing it, in the mind-set of the culture in which we grew up? Won't all our questions be formed by, won't they in one way or another simply echo, this culture that we and everyone alive today around us has been brought up in? How can we obtain a radically critical perspective, one that is truly outside modern culture? The answer is not to be found in mere trips to the exotic, either vicarious or actual. What we need is to encounter deeply thoughtful critics who challenge our most basic civic and moral assumptions by confronting us with radically contrasting civic and moral arguments.

It is at this point that there comes into sharp relief a key reason why genuine political philosophizing today begins from protracted meditation on a few old books. It is only through studying and wrestling with the sort of books that will be introduced in the following pages that we today are enabled to encounter the profound sort of challenges that can liberate our minds from servitude to contemporary dogmas. It is only in the sort of books that we will be discussing that we can find articulate, deep political thinkers who do not share, who pose radical alternatives to, our inbred basic assumptions about morals and politics.

We start from classical republican political philosophy, founded by Socrates and fully elaborated by Plato and Aristotle. These thinkers draw us into sustained reflection about participatory republicanism, grounded in a strongly communal civic culture. Such an "illiberal" political order proves to be, paradoxically, the matrix out of which emerges the idea of philosophy as a distinct and superior way of life – the way of life, highly individual or self-sufficient, and even somewhat iconoclastic, lived by Socrates.

In Part II we turn to the very different, but by no means hostile, civic and moral thinking rooted in obedient fidelity to biblical revelation. We focus first on key political dimensions of the Hebrew and Christian Scriptures, and then on Saint Thomas Aquinas's grand project of subordinating classical political philosophy to Christian theology through the conceptual framework of "natural law."

Part III introduces successive versions of the "modern" rationalist and humanist political philosophizing that arose in the Renaissance and culminated in the Enlightenment of the eighteenth century. What unites these thinkers is their shared rejection and critique of both classical political philosophy and the medieval Christian natural law synthesis. What individualizes them are the diverse, original, comprehensive, political theories that they devised as replacements for the classical and medieval frameworks. In studying the "moderns," and especially Locke and Montesquieu, we will be engaging the theorists who laid the philosophic and moral foundations for our own liberal democratic constitutionalism and free market economic system. We will be analyzing the grounds for our own society – in the light of the challenges posed by classical and medieval political theory. We will begin to reenact, by and for ourselves, the great debates and arguments that the founders of our way of life and thinking undertook as they brought into being for the first time the ideas that we now take for granted. We will thus no longer take those ideas for granted. Instead, we will think them through in the way that they were thought through by the thinkers who could not possibly take them for granted because they were arguing for them for the first time, in a skeptical and even hostile culture shaped by a previous classical and Christian tradition.

Finally, in Part IV, we will come to grips with subsequent thinkers who rebelled against the Enlightenment's ideas of liberal constitutionalism and the free market, doing so in the name of competing visions of altogether different and – these thinkers argued – superior ways of organizing human society. We will thus put our way of living and thinking to another radically thought-provoking test. At the same time, we will begin to understand why and how our culture today is riven with deep divisions and antagonisms: For the critical ideas of Rousseau, Marx, Tocqueville, and Nietzsche have had a continuing powerful impact, putting into question, but also supplementing and enlarging, Enlightenment political theorizing and practice.

Our overall aim in this book has now become clearer. We seek to help readers, through their study of these texts, to begin to move toward a position from which they can freely judge for themselves whether and to what extent they should embrace, or should take a critical distance from, the principles underlying and animating our civic culture. We hope to stimulate and to respond to a thirst in readers to confront and to wrestle with the most fundamental questions, to reenact the titanic controversies that animate the history of political philosophy and that cannot ever cease to underlie civilized existence. The thinkers and works of the past are studied here not as dated museum pieces or objects of antiquarian curiosity; they are confronted as powerful voices that challenge us to join in searching debates. The point is not to learn *about* these thinkers and texts, but *from* them.

This overall aim has dictated our highly selective choice of texts. We have certainly not surveyed or summarized the entire history of political thought. Nor have we provided a full synoptic epitome of any single thinker or vision. Each chapter seeks to be no more and no less than a provocative invitation and guide to the reader's own further, ever-deeper encounter with each alternative way of thinking. In full awareness that our choices are contestable and that we have been constrained to leave aside crucial works and towering thinkers, we have sought to provide, within the limits of a manageable volume, sustained examples of how to interpret key texts that are both accessible to beginning students (of all ages) and that introduce most clearly and profoundly the major alternative visions and axial turning points in the history of political philosophy.

PART I

CLASSICAL POLITICAL PHILOSOPHY

1

Plato's *Apology of Socrates*

The history of political philosophy may be said to begin with the courtroom drama that led to the execution of the thinker who founded the enterprise. Socrates (469–399 BC) wrote nothing for publication. In his own lifetime he was made notorious as the central, dubious character in Ancient Greece's greatest comedy, the *Clouds* by Aristophanes (446–386 BC). After his execution, Socrates was portrayed much more favorably and seriously in numerous dialogic dramatizations by his students, above all Xenophon (431–355 BC) and Plato (427–347 BC). None of these depictions of Socrates purport to be histories. They are products of the dramatic art. Their purpose is not to preserve an exact record of what Socrates actually said, but rather to convey what it was like to encounter Socrates – and thereby to be aroused to intense, perplexed, and critical thinking about profound and abiding problems of human existence. All of Plato's Socratic dialogues, and not least his *Apology of Socrates*,* are rich in deliberately provocative puzzles meant to stimulate probing detective work – through repeated rereading, with alertness and with dogged and even suspicious questioning. The Platonic dialogues are meant to constitute a kind of training ground for becoming a human being who goes through life truly awakened, by Socrates and Socratic questioning, to life's depths and challenges.

---

* We recommend the translation by Thomas G. and Grace Starry West, in *Four Texts on Socrates*, revised edition (Ithaca, NY: Cornell University Press, 1998). Our translations, referring to the text by standard Stephanus pagination, are from this edition, with minor emendations. Our focus will be on Socrates' speech prior to the vote of the jury to convict him.

The Challenge to Our Way of Thinking

Plato's *Apology* presents Socrates delivering his sole public account of his life as a whole and what he lived for. But the account takes the form of a defense in a criminal trial that culminates in Socrates' death sentence. Plato thus provokes a number of questions: What is it about Socrates, and his way of life, in relation to the political society around him, that leads to so dire a clash with the legal authorities? Is this not a blamable, avoidable crime on the part of the Athenian democracy? Or at least a terrible accident, the result of a deep misunderstanding? Or is there something essential to Socratic political philosophy that makes it unavoidably threatening to lawful society, and hence always in danger of lawful punishment? What answer does Plato mean to teach us?

The most eligible place to start our search for clues is the official indictment, which Socrates recites (24b): "Socrates does injustice, by corrupting the young, and by not believing in the gods in whom the city believes, but in other divine things [*daimonia*] that are novel/strange." Now *our* first reaction to this, coming as we do from a liberal democratic culture, is that the very charge reveals a decisive and pervasive flaw in Athenian democracy: The indictment expresses an arrant denial of the basic human right to freedom of speech and freedom of thought, including freedom of religious belief. We see at once that the direct democracy of the Greeks was emphatically not *liberal* democracy. Classical republicanism lacked our notions of freedom of thought, speech, and religion. We are tempted to rush to the judgment that *this* is the problem of Socrates, and that the solution is to live as we do. Socrates would never be put on trial in our liberal democracy, with our Bill of Rights.

But is this the way Plato understands and presents the problem of Socrates? Does Plato have Socrates make a plea for freedom of speech? Or are we not simply imposing on the text our viewpoint, our cultural assumptions about what really matters?

If we look at the text with inquiring and open minds, we see that in fact Plato never has his Socrates argue for freedom of speech, or freedom of thought, or religious freedom. In fact, Socrates never once criticizes the law under which he is indicted; he never once says that the law, penalizing with death anyone who does not believe in the gods of the city, is an unjust or a bad law. (Plato has Socrates show that he is quite willing to criticize a law he does regard as bad [37a].) Instead, Socrates defends himself by saying that he did not commit the crime with which he is charged. He insists that he never broke the law, that he always conformed to belief in the lawful gods of the city, and that he did not ever lead any of the young to doubt or to question such belief. Here at the start we encounter an enormous challenge to our way of thinking. We are forced to ask: Why doesn't Plato have his Socrates plead for freedom of thought and freedom of speech and freedom of religion? What are Plato's and his Socrates' reasons for not seeing things the way we have been brought up to see them? What is the radically different view of healthy political life that Plato's Socrates has that is so alien to our own? We need to keep these questions before us, as the spurs to our own liberation from uncritical conformity to our inherited current beliefs.

The Peculiar Opening of Socrates' Defense

Plato has Socrates begin, not by responding to the formal charges, or to the arguments and evidence introduced by the prosecution speeches, but instead by a blanket attack on the veracity of the prosecution speakers: "They have said, so to speak, *nothing* true" (17a, our emphasis). The most amazing of their lies was a warning that Socrates is a cleverly deceptive speaker. This lie is most shameless, because it will immediately be seen that "I am not a clever speaker *at all*." Swearing an oath by Zeus, the highest Greek god, Socrates proclaims that he will tell "the whole truth," without beautiful adornment, speaking "at *random*, in the words that I *happen* upon" (17c, our emphasis). This is the way of speaking, he claims, that he usually employs in public. What is more, he claims that he is as totally unfamiliar with Athenian court proceedings and the manner of speaking in Athenian trials as a "foreigner" would be. He puts forward this claim as a seventy-year-old citizen in a participatory democracy, where (as we see vividly from this trial) juries of five hundred are regularly empanelled, day after day, to decide cases tried before large crowds. Has Socrates in his long life really never served on a jury or witnessed a trial?

The preposterousness of what Socrates is claiming about himself becomes plain in the speech that follows. Like all Socratic speeches portrayed in Plato, it is obviously anything but unplanned, uttered at random, and poorly delivered by a simple old man who is unfamiliar with courts and is not good at well-thought-out, clever courtroom speech (just consider the way Socrates ties his accuser Meletus in knots in the cross-examination!).

In other words, Plato has his Socrates make it fairly easy at the outset, for anyone who stops to think critically, to see that Socrates is far from speaking the plain truth: That he is in fact being slyly jesting or "ironic" – pretending comically to know much less than he does (and doing so while making a solemn oath, by the highest God, part of his joking).

We are thus confronted with a big initial puzzle: Why does Plato have his Socrates begin with such transparent irony? One reason that soon suggests itself, as we proceed further, is that Socrates thus immediately provokes the thoughtful in the audience to wonder what might be his strange rhetorical strategy. This prepares the alert listeners to realize that the entire speech unfolds as elusively ironic. Plato has Socrates begin in a way that prompts one to see that to understand what Socrates is going to convey, one must take everything with a grain of salt and try to figure out the sly point of the irony at every turn. An important relevant fact, which we learn a bit later, is that a number of young followers of Socrates are in the audience – including Plato (33e). From the outset Socrates provokes especially these young followers, making them wonder what he is trying to teach them, by his example, about how one ought to speak in public, in defensive explanation of the life and enterprise of political philosophy.

The "First Accusers"

Immediately after this provocative beginning, Socrates provokes more wonder by suddenly making the whole case infinitely more complex – declaring (18a, our emphasis) that the official charges and accusers are only the tip of an iceberg, as it were. "More dangerous" are certain "*first* false charges and *first* accusers," who have generated long-standing "slander," beginning years ago when Socrates was a younger man.

What were these "first" and more dangerous accusations? Socrates states them as if they were formalized in an indictment: "Socrates does injustice and is meddlesome, by investigating the things under the earth and the heavenly things, and by making the weaker speech the stronger, and by teaching others these same things" (19b; cf. 18b). Socrates is further accused of being a practitioner of deceptive, tricky rhetoric and of being a teacher of all this. What does all this mean? The answer becomes vividly clear if we read Aristophanes' *Clouds* and its depiction of Socrates, to which Socrates refers us. In that play Socrates is portrayed as living a life dedicated to scientific investigation of nature, on the basis of which he teaches that beliefs central to Greek piety are untrue: the belief that under the earth is a divine place named Hades, where the spirits of the deceased go, and the belief that in the heavens dwell the Olympian divinities ruled by Zeus, who sends the thunder and lightning as part of his punitive providence. Socrates is depicted in the *Clouds* as "making the weaker argument the stronger," and teaching others how to do so.

It is not difficult to see why these older, unofficial charges are "more dangerous." They make it clear that Socrates is not being condemned as some sort of religious dissident, but instead as an atheist: "Those, men of Athens, who have scattered this report about, are my dangerous accusers; for their listeners hold that investigators of these things also do not believe in gods" (18b–c). As is said in another work of Plato's, people "think that those who busy themselves with such matters, through astronomy and the other arts that go with it, become atheists, having seen that, as much as possible, actions come into being by necessities and not by the thoughts of an intention concerned with fulfillments of good things" (*Laws* 967a). The Athenian citizens think that scientific investigations lead to disbelief in Zeus's and the other gods' rewards and punishments that support justice. The citizens think that this leads to or goes with the replacement of civic virtue, with its stern demands for self-overcoming, by a corrupt outlook that no longer sees good reason to subordinate or to sacrifice personal profit and pleasure. The Athenians think that those who are thus corrupted by natural science turn to the study of tricky rhetoric (lawyers' skills), especially for courtroom use, but also for employment in the assembly, in order to defend or to hide their corrupt, exploitative activities. The teaching of such deceptive rhetoric is associated with the famous itinerant "sophists," who make large sums of money teaching techniques of self-advancement through clever rhetoric, especially courtroom rhetoric. Socrates repeatedly stresses (18b and c) that these first and more dangerous accusations, associating him with atheistic natural science and tricky rhetoric, were lodged, and took root in the jury members, years before – when the jury members were impressionable youths or children, and hence unable to judge the truth about what he was actually doing.

How does Socrates defend himself against these "first and more dangerous" charges, which he himself has injected into the trial? He vigorously denies that he ever was such an investigator into the religiously crucial aspects of nature. To establish the truth of this denial, he introduces only a single, massive piece of evidence: He calls the jurymen themselves as his witnesses. "Many among you" have "heard me conversing"; "teach and tell each other if any of you ever heard me conversing about such things" (19d). This appears to be impressive testimony; what witnesses could be more convincing to the jury than the jurymen themselves?

There is only one unobtrusive but decisive flaw. A moment before, Socrates had said repeatedly that most of the jury members were children at the crucial time, and were hence unable to judge what the truth was about what he was doing! Yet this is the sole evidence Socrates provides to refute the charge lodged years ago that he was an investigator of the natural phenomena relevant to religious belief. What Socrates presents as conclusive evidence for the untruth of the accusation proves on inspection to be a tricky lawyer's maneuver that begs the decisive question. Perhaps Socrates has not *recently* been *openly* pursuing such investigations into nature, but he himself has insisted on spotlighting the question whether such investigations were not his preoccupation when he was a *younger* man, perhaps laying the foundation for his philosophic life. What is more, Socrates says here emphatically (at 19c) that he does *not* dishonor this "sort of science" – indeed, that he hopes no one will ever charge him "with such great lawsuits as that." He speaks as if he regards being charged with dishonoring such investigations as being charged with a crime more serious than that of not believing in the gods of Athens.

What of the charge that he practiced tricky rhetoric? Socrates never explicitly denies this and offers no evidence whatsoever to refute it.

As for the accusation that he was a teacher, Socrates responds by strongly denying that he has ever taught *for pay*. But this is a red herring; the first accusations, as Socrates recited them repeatedly, never charged him with teaching *for pay*. Socrates has trickily substituted, and responded to, a different charge from the charge that he ascribed to the "first accusers."

Socrates has introduced into the trial, only to leave looming, these large questions about himself and his life: Is he not in fact a teacher? And if so, of what? What has been his real attitude toward tricky rhetoric and the practice and teaching of it? Is he not showing, in this very speech, that he is a master of tricky rhetoric? What has been his real posture toward, and relation with, the sophists? Above all, what has been his true involvement with the investigations into, and the teaching to others of, the scientific truth about what is under the earth and in the heavens – and all the radical religious implications that flow from such investigations?

The Delphic Oracle Story

At this point Socrates conjures up someone in the audience who is suspiciously dissatisfied and who demands an account of how these slanders could ever have arisen if Socrates was in fact not at all involved in such things (20c–d). In effect, Socrates shows how he expects or hopes an alert listener will react to what he has said: With doubting, critically suspicious questioning. Socrates responds by telling an amazing tale about how he learned, through the Delphic oracle (the most authoritative voice of divine revelation in Greece), that he possesses "human wisdom" – in which "probably I really am wise." Socrates predicts that some listeners are going to think he is "joking" or "being playful" (*paizein* – 20d). But he promises that the story will provide "the whole truth" about the source of the "slander" by the first accusers (20d, 21b).

But *does* this story that Socrates proceeds to tell explain what he was doing years ago? No, not at all! In fact, the story has the enormously clever effect of lulling the listener into forgetting the question that the story is supposed to be answering. The story fixes our attention on what has been taking place in *recent* years in Socrates' life, or, as he puts it, "even now" (23b): The story tells what has happened *since* the pronouncement of the Delphic oracle, not what happened *before* – not what made Socrates so famous that the most authoritative religious voice in Greece proclaimed that no one was wiser. As Socrates says at the end of the story (23d–e), it has explained where the *present* accusers – including, above all, Meletus, Anytus, and Lycon – come from, and why *they* "say the things that are ready at hand against all who philosophize," about "the thing aloft and under the earth." Yet, after finishing the story, Socrates reminds his listeners of the distinction he began by stressing: He says that he has been making a defense speech "about the things which the *first* accusers accused me of" and that he will turn *next* to "Meletus" and "the *later* accusers" (24b, our emphasis). Socrates thus again pretends that he has been explaining the first accusations, and thus prods his thoughtful listeners to wonder: What *is* the explanation, and why is he *avoiding* giving it? What was he doing *before* the Delphic oracle spoke? What way of life was he leading? What was it about that way of life that made the chap named Chaerephon go all the way to Delphi to ask the god such an amazing question – whether anyone was wiser than Socrates?

In another dialogue, the *Phaedo* (96), where Plato presents Socrates speaking in private to close friends on the day of his execution, we hear Socrates explain at length that as a young man he was an enthusiastic scientific investigator of nature, and that he became a student of the works of Anaxagoras (whose denial of the existence of the lawful gods Socrates cites later in the *Apology* [26d]). What is more, Socrates tells his close students that when he turned away from studying nature in the *manner* of his predecessors, he never abandoned the study of nature – but rather developed a new and more effective mode of studying the whole of nature, a study he has continued to carry on all his life, as he demonstrates in his final conversation with them.

Once we recognize that Socrates has called attention to his reputation as an investigator of natural necessities that draw into question core beliefs of Greek piety in order to hint that there is an important measure of truth in that reputation, we are in a better position to recognize what the story of the Delphic oracle signifies. The story is manifestly Socrates' way of conveying, as best he can when on trial in public, the deep and decisively crucial *change* that occurred in his philosophic life: the turn to the *refutative* dialogues with *non*philosophers, centered on their opinions about *morality*, which constituted his distinctive activity as the first *political* philosopher, the first philosopher concerned with "human wisdom" – which is wisdom about justice, nobility, and the good, about the most fundamental norms that define how one ought to live.

As Socrates' story goes, when the oracle was asked whether there was anyone wiser than Socrates, the god replied that there was no one. "When I heard these things," Socrates says, "I pondered them like this: 'What ever is the god saying, and what riddle is he posing? For I am conscious that I am not at all wise, either much or little'" (21b–c). Socrates already knew for certain that he was not wise. He did not need the god to learn that. But precisely this knowledge of his lack of wisdom impelled him to take the enigmatic revelation of the god with the utmost seriousness – to ponder and to puzzle "for a long time" over what message the god might be conveying. For Socrates stresses that he also knew, in the second place, that the god could not be lying, "For that is not lawful [*themis*] for him" (21b). In other words, Socrates also knew that purported divine revelation is inseparable from some conception of moral law that is believed to bind even divinity itself to truthfulness, in its solemn revelations.

If we put this together with what Socrates has previously provoked us to surmise, bolstered by what we learn from the *Phaedo*, we arrive at the following. Socrates began his philosophic career actively involved in the investigations that seemed to uncover the truth about the necessitated nature of the cosmos – and that thus seemed to show the untruth of core religious beliefs. But at some point in his early maturity, Socrates became convinced that the investigations into nature encountered major limitations that rendered them inconclusive. He became impressed and perplexed by the incapacity of science to dispose of the possibility, powerfully testified to by apparent religious experiences (some of which Socrates himself may have undergone [33c]), that all existence is governed by supernatural divinity intervening to administer with rewards and punishments a somewhat mysterious moral order that transcends and drastically qualifies what appears to reason to be "necessities" of nature. And Socrates confronted the severe implications for any attempt to acquire independent wisdom through merely human reasoning. If suprarational divine revelation is true, then what would seem to be called for is a humble submission to guidance by that higher divine authority, as delivered through oracles and diviners and inspired poets. As Socrates says after he has recounted his elaborate reaction to the oracle, "it is likely that" the god through the oracle "is saying this: that human wisdom is worth little or nothing" and that the god "made use of my name, making me an example, as if he would say that 'this one among you, humans, is wisest, who like Socrates knows that he is in truth worth nothing as regards wisdom'" (23a). This statement tempts us to think that Socrates' story tells how he abandoned any attempt to guide his life by his own rational lights and sought instead authoritative guidance from conduits of the gods – the inspired poets, diviners or prophets, and oracles.

But when we consider the Delphic oracle story as a whole, we see that this is not at all the picture painted by the story. To begin with, Socrates refused to accept the authority of the Delphic oracle. Reluctantly but firmly, he insisted on launching an "investigation" of the oracle's statement, with a view to "refuting" it and proving, to the oracle's face, that its revelation was wrong (21b–c). Of course, as the story unfolds, it turns out that what Socrates has proven is that there really can be found no one wiser than he. To this extent the story has him vindicating the oracle. But the story does not have him doing so in a way that relies on, or that leads to, faithful obedience or reverent hearkening or submission to any religious authority or personally experienced divine guidance. Instead, the story has Socrates establishing his own superior wisdom through public, rational refutations of civil society's authorities – political leaders, poets, and craftsmen. Through direct questioning and conversational argument, Socrates demonstrates that "all those reputed to know something," and first and foremost the statesmen or civic leaders, do not "know *anything* noble/beautiful-and-good" (*kalos kagathos*, the formula for conventional gentlemanly virtue [21c–d, 22a, our emphasis]). In his dialogues with the poets, the voices of divine inspiration, the carriers of Greek religious tradition, Socrates says, "I soon recognized that they do not make what they make by wisdom, but by some sort of nature and while inspired, *like the diviners and those who deliver oracles* – for they too say many *noble/beautiful* things, but they know *nothing* of what they speak" – that is, they understand nothing of the noble or beautiful (22b, our emphasis). Socrates shows his interlocutors to be incapable of articulating a coherent account of their most basic normative principles, by which they guide their lives and lead society.

At first, Socrates' tale gives the impression that his ongoing refutations of all the respected opinion leaders aroused in onlookers nothing but hatred, and that this hatred is the source of his being accused (21d–e; 22e–23a). But this turns out to be misleading, for the tale suddenly takes a dramatic new turn (23c–e). Socrates says that the crowds before whom he carries out his public refutations include many *young* people, who enjoy what they see, to such an extent that they are in large numbers imitating Socrates, publicly refuting "a great abundance of human beings" all over Athens. What has caused him to have accusers, he explains, is *not* the hostile reaction to his *own* refutations, but the fact that adults all over Athens are being refuted by the *youth*, who are known to be doing this in imitation of Socrates. At the end of the story, Socrates admits that he has had a deep and widespread spiritual impact on the youth of Athens, converting many to imitation of his iconoclastic life-activity, and that *that* is the source of his troubles.

How is this project, with its vast influence on the youth, something that the oracle ordered or advised him to do, even by implication? After all, the only thing the oracle said was that no one is wiser. Socrates *claims*, to be sure, that his amazing project has all been "in accordance with" the god (22a, 23b), "helping" (23b) the god, carrying out an act of "pious devotion" (*latreia* – 23c). But beneath these claims we can discern that Socrates *reads into* the oracle his own imperative project of inducing in the young critical skepticism, an educational project that was never even hinted at by the oracle. In effect, Socrates takes over the oracle. A kind of peak in this regard is reached when Socrates tells how he asked questions *on behalf of the oracle* – as if he, Socrates, really is the oracle: "I asked myself *on behalf of the oracle* whether I would prefer to be as I am, being in no way wise in their wisdom or ignorant in their ignorance, or to have both things that they have. I answered myself *and the oracle* that it profits me to be just as I am" (22e1–4, our emphasis). These last words make it clear that Socrates' knowledge of his own ignorance of "the noble-and-good" entails knowledge, rather than ignorance, of what is truly profitable or beneficial, for himself. Socrates later makes it even clearer that his Delphic oracle story and its pretense of "obedience to god" is his "ironic" way of conveying in public the distinctive kind of dialogic examination through which he achieved with confidence his own (and his followers') very great good. After he has been convicted, and when he is asked to propose a counter-penalty, he conjures up another questioner: "Someone might say, 'by being silent and keeping quiet, Socrates, won't you be able to live in exile for us?'" Socrates replies: "If I say that this is to disobey the god, and that because of this it is impossible to keep quiet, you will not be persuaded by me, on the ground that I am being ironic." And, "on the other hand, if I say that this even happens to be a very great good for a human being – to make speeches every day about virtue and the other things about which you hear me conversing and examining both myself and others," and that "the unexamined life is not worth living for a human being, you will be persuaded by me still less." But "this is the way it is, as I affirm" (37e–38a).

Socrates thus discloses that his Delphic oracle story is an image, expressing how and why his mature philosophizing became largely defined by a distinctive project of justifying and grounding, through refutative argument, the life of independent, critical, rational examination – in the face of the challenge posed by the claims of suprarational divine revelation and authority, and given the absence of an adequately complete or self-justifying scientific account of nature as intelligibly necessitated. However baffled Socrates initially was by the challenge of revelation, he eventually responded by conducting refutations centered on civic opinions as to the "noble-and-good" – the supreme societal moral norms that are believed to be sanctioned and commanded by suprarational divinity. Evidently a key dimension of Socrates' pre-Delphic knowledge of his own ignorance was his having arrived at the conclusion that what was generally opined to be "noble-and-good" was something that he could not rationally understand. Upon close examination, his reasoning detected in the accepted moral opinions specific, deep puzzles, ambiguities, vacuities, and contradictions. These conceptual difficulties were of such gravity that when he laid them out clearly to himself, he could no longer be governed by such opinions. What is more, he discovered that, as a momentous consequence, he could not seriously entertain any longer the possibility that he received communication from any divinity standing behind such norms, sanctioning and commanding or inspiring his obedience to them. He was impelled to ascend to rationally coherent norms, and a rationally intelligible conception of their cosmic basis, entailing a major rational reinterpretation of the divine. Yet he realized that this ascent was open to serious question, above all because he did not know whether in all this he was not idiosyncratic. He did not know whether this whole unfolding experience was not a manifestation of something wrong with him (a hypertrophy of rationalism), something condemned in the eyes of radically mysterious and demanding, all-powerful divinity. Socrates therefore set out to test whether others could (or could not) be brought, by rationally analyzing their received moral opinions, to the same transformative moral and theological experience to which he had himself been brought – or at least to partial but manifest versions or adumbrations of such experience. Ceaseless experiments with interlocutors have confirmed over and over again at least two very important facts. First, a number of young people (presumably those, especially, with strong, deep hearts and sharp, still flexible minds), having grasped what Socrates is showing about the generally accepted notions of the "noble-and-good," have been converted to his way of thinking and living. Socrates has thus found repeated strong evidence that his transformative moral-theological experience was by no means idiosyncratic. Second, the elders whom he cross-examines and, what is more, the many adult onlookers, have been deeply pained and antagonized by his cross-examinations; this is not only or primarily on account of his conversions of numerous young onlookers. The elders' pain and hatred are in immediate reaction to Socrates' own success in manifestly compelling them, as his interlocutors, and the audience as a whole, to recognize gross conceptual confusions in their opinions about the noble-and-good. The story suggests that the elders' passionately hateful reaction gives evidence of their undergoing the experience of having their deepest commitments and beliefs truly shaken, at least temporarily. This reaction that Socrates produces in the adults by his own refutations is repeatedly confirmed by its reproduction in the reactions to the refutations executed by his young imitators. Socrates thus has gained a second and broader (though less completely clear or unambiguous) kind of strong evidence – this time from people who were not candidates to join him in his life and outlook – that his own moral-theological reaction to the discovery of the conceptual difficulties in the opinions about the noble-and-good is by no means peculiar.

Yet the hatred on the part of the elders that is the result of all these Socratic refutations is dangerous for Socrates and for his youthful imitators. Moreover, the hatred is understandable and even to some extent justifiable. For the Socratic refutative activity as depicted in the Delphic oracle story portrays Socrates as having a widespread subversive effect on the youth of Athens, who all over the city are refuting in public their elders. And it is noteworthy that neither Socrates nor his many young followers are portrayed as refuting the sophists or other philosophers. The Socratics and Socrates are not defending the city's views or religious tradition against sophistic or philosophic criticism. Does not the story in effect admit, and indeed make vivid, how severely Socrates has been undermining the moral and religious foundations of Athens, especially among the young? Plato's Socrates thus provokes the question: How can this be a responsible thing to do? How can a civic republic be sustained on the basis of the young becoming Socratic skeptics, spending their lives questioning and refuting their society's leaders?

At this point, Socrates leaves these questions hanging. What he does next gives us evidence that helps us to begin to answer another big question that we have been provoked to by the preceding: What are the Socratic conversational refutations actually like? That is, what exactly are they about? In the next part of the defense speech, we get to watch Socrates refuting an authority – one of his accusers. We get a glimpse of what a Socratic refutation looks like and what topics Socrates focuses upon.

The Cross-Examination of Meletus

The refutation of Meletus has three parts, on three different topics, each requiring and provoking reflection. First (24d–25c), Socrates asks and forces Meletus to answer the question of who really *educates*, rather than corrupts, the young. As he had already shown in his first report of a dialogue, with the father Callias, a primary question that Socrates pursues is: What would one need to know, and who can claim to know, what it means truly to educate young people so that they acquire the "virtue of human being and citizen" (20a–b). Socrates calls into question the claim that Meletus advances in response, that "everyone" knows – which is a claim that society makes, insofar as it turns over to parents the main responsibility for educating morally their own children. Socrates casts doubt on parental authority as regards moral education; he insists on asking what *qualifies* parents to be able to educate their young to become truly good human beings and citizens. Isn't the case that as regards moral and civic education, as in all very complex and difficult enterprises, the truly qualified are very few? Through Meletus's responses we see exposed the fact that society tends not to stop to think much if any about this question.

The second or central refutation (25c–26a) is the most revealing about the radical questions Socrates raises concerning the coherence of widespread, basic moral beliefs. Socrates argues that if he – or anyone else – were in fact corrupting the young, then he or anyone doing that would necessarily be doing so *involuntarily*, since it would be out of *ignorance* of what he was doing. The law as well as everyone agrees that wrong done out of genuine ignorance of what one is doing does not deserve punishment. Instead, the proper response to such ignorance is education.

To see the full significance of this central Socratic refutation, one must start to think through the radical implications. Socrates is prodding us to ask: What do we necessarily mean by saying someone is *responsible* for his or her choice and action? Must we not mean that he or she acts *deliberately* – as a being with known options, among which a choice is made according to what consciousness sees to be better, and action is carried out executing that consciously deliberated decision? But this implies that when people are responsible for their actions, they are always choosing what seems or appears to them, at the moment of choosing, to be what is best to do. If or since crime and injustice are in fact truly very bad – if being a criminal makes one a much worse person, vicious and sick in one's very character and personality and soul; if becoming criminal is like getting cancer, but of the spirit not the body – then becoming a criminal must always be the result of *not realizing* this terrible, true meaning of crime and injustice, for oneself, for one's life and very soul. How then can we blame the criminal, or say he deliberately, knowingly, did wrong? Still worse, how can it possibly make any sense to seek to inflict on such a terribly ignorant and damaged person more suffering or hurt, to intensify his already bad condition of ignorance?

Someone might try to escape this Socratic conclusion by arguing that the criminal *does* know clearly that, and how, the crime is bad, for himself: That the criminal embraces injustice knowing that it will make his personality and life much worse. But this implies that committing crime is like someone drinking an awful poison, or being an addict who knows he is destroying himself but can't stop. Can that mean anything except that the criminal is no longer able to guide himself by his consciousness of what is best and most choice worthy for himself? Does that not mean that he is suffering from a terrible psychic sickness, in which he somehow cannot do what he knows to be best, like a person spiritually paralyzed? Doesn't this mean that the criminal is even more sick than if he were ignorant – even more pitiable, and not at all a responsible agent? How can we possibly say the criminal deserves to suffer more for being in such a pathetic condition, of mental paralysis and compulsion?

An alternative way of trying to escape the Socratic conclusion is to contend that crime is voluntary because it is a deliberate choice of what really *is* the best thing for a person to do at that moment. And it does seem that something like envy of criminals lurks in all retributive justice, or in all societies' ways of talking and thinking about the punishment of crime. For why otherwise do we say that the criminal who has not suffered punishment "gets away with it"? If crime or injustice is truly bad – if being a criminal is a deformation of one's personality – how is a criminal who is not caught "getting away" with anything? Isn't such a criminal like someone "getting away" with cancer? For crime is cancer in one's very soul, not in one's body. But why, similarly, do we say that when the criminal is punished, he "pays his debt to society"? Does this not presume that he truly profited from his crime – that prior to being made to suffer, he is well off, or in a good condition, as a successful criminal – rather than being sick or confused or in a terribly unwholesome inner condition? Does this not betray the fact that somehow we think that being just, or being law-abiding, is bad for the person who is so – unless he or she gets some reward? But what can this mean? That criminality is becoming a better human being, and not a worse one? That crime and injustice are good for one's core being? That being a just person is being a worse person? But is not justice a virtue, an excellence, something admirable; are not injustice and criminality despicable?

The issues Socrates has raised obviously require and call for a much more extended, painstakingly precise analysis and self-critical soul-searching. But Socrates here points to his characteristic bringing to light of deep confusions, radical incoherence, in our commonest, most passionately held convictions about justice, crime, responsibility, and punishment. These are convictions deeply connected to the notions of guilt and sin – and of divinity that punishes people for their sins. Socrates begins here to indicate how radical a gulf separates his coherent conception of justice from the incoherent notion that predominates in civic life, and especially in criminal law and traditional religion. Thus at the center of his cross-examination, we get a momentary glimpse of one major paradoxical Socratic thesis, namely, that all vice or crime must be a product of some deep ignorance, and hence not voluntary; that there is no guilt in the way common sense and all traditional religion assumes that there is; that retributive punishment makes no sense.

In the third refutation (26a–27e), Socrates presses the question of whether the indictment and charge addressed to him are coherent in their understanding of what lack of faith (and therefore faith) in divinity must mean. Socrates shows that Meletus gives expression to unresolved confusion in society's notion of what is meant and understood by "divinity" and thus by "belief in divinity." Here we get a glimpse of another kind of questioning Socrates engages in: He asks the deceptively simple question, "What is a god? What is meant by 'divinity'?" We cannot help noting that in this last part of the cross-examination, Socrates is especially playful. In a slyly comic way, he shows how he can assert that he believes in what the city believes in, while yet leaving his beliefs radically ambiguous; he can do this because the city's beliefs are themselves radically ambiguous or unclear.

The Puzzling Longest Section

With the end of the cross-examination of Meletus, Socrates appears to have completed his defense. He declares that what he has said is "sufficient" as an answer to the charges (28a). But his speech goes on, and in fact we now get the longest portion of the speech (28b–35d) – whose purpose or function Socrates never makes explicit. Plato sets us the challenge of figuring out what Socrates is up to.

Socrates introduces this part as he introduced the Delphic oracle story – by conjuring up a hostile questioner. But this time the challenge is of a very different character: "Perhaps, then, someone might say, 'Then are you not ashamed, Socrates, of having followed the sort of pursuit from which you now run the risk of dying?'" (28b). Now this question is in itself ambiguous, or susceptible of more than one meaning. But Socrates replies by giving the question a base interpretation. He takes the questioner to mean that Socrates should be ashamed of ever having to risk his life for anything. Socrates replies by taking very high moral ground. After attacking the baseness of the questioner, Socrates launches into what he calls "the just speech" or "the speech of justice." The leading point of this speech is that one must be prepared to die heroically for justice, as the heroes of Homeric poetry died in the Trojan War. Socrates thus commences a new, heroic self-portrait. He now claims that the model for his own life-activity has been the traditional Greek hero, Achilles, as portrayed by Homer – the authoritative poetic source of Greek religious and moral views. Socrates now quotes with approval Homer's authoritative poem, the *Iliad*, as his own guide in life. In other words, Socrates now presents himself in highly traditional terms. And throughout this whole longest part of the speech, Socrates shows his enormous concern for his own and for his city's manliness, and manly "reputation" as champions of justice. Indeed, he now speaks as if his chief concern in life were for "distinction" (as he puts it), as a courageous, just, and thus pious man. He makes this overriding concern for his reputation especially clear at the end of this long section, which concludes his defense speech as a whole. He again conjures up someone questioning from the audience, this time moved by indignation because Socrates is not begging for mercy. Socrates replies: "Why, then, will I do none of these things? Not because I am stubborn, men of Athens, nor because I dishonor you. Whether I am daring with regard to death or not is another story"; but "as to *reputation*, mine and yours and the whole city's, to me it does not seem to be noble for me to do any of these things." For "I am old and have this *name*; and whether it is true or false, it is reputed at least that Socrates is *distinguished* from the many human beings in some way. If, then, those of you who are reputed to be distinguished, whether in wisdom or courage or any other virtue at all, will act in this way, it would be shameful" (34e–35d, our emphasis). Socrates then ends with a ringing affirmation of his pious faith in the gods (35d).

The picture of himself that Socrates paints, in this part of the speech, stands in striking contrast to the picture he gave in the first part of his speech, through the Delphic oracle story. There, we recall, he portrayed himself as a radical moral skeptic, who spends his life proving before crowds (which include many young people) that neither he nor any of the political, religious, and craftsmen authorities of society know anything "noble and good." Now, Socrates speaks as one who knows for sure what is noble and good: What is noble and good is imitating the traditional hero Achilles, in being obedient to one's lawful commanders (28d–29a). Socrates now gives a new and different account of what he has been showing in his refutations. His purpose, he now says, has been to make these people feel "ashamed" because they care for money, and reputation, and honor, rather than or prior to prudence and truth and how one's soul will be the best possible (29d–e). He now says that in his conversations he tests people, not for knowledge but for virtue. And his test works; he now says that he has the knowledge that allows him to tell who has virtue of soul and who does not have it (29d–30a). He then goes on to make the following astonishing claim, directly contradicting the Delphic oracle story: "I go around and *do nothing but* persuade you, both younger and older, not to care for bodies and money before, nor as vehemently as, how your soul will be the best possible. I say: 'Not from money does virtue come, but from virtue comes money and all of the other good things for man beings both privately and publicly.'"

And "if," Socrates adds, "someone asserts that what I say is other than this, he speaks nonsense" (30b–c, our emphasis). As part of this new portrait, Socrates limns himself in the famous "gadfly" image, through which he proclaims his philosophizing to be a divine mission to wake up the city, which is like a sleepy horse – to wake it *not* to moral skepticism but to concern for virtue as the good of the soul, and hence the source of money, safety, and fame.

Further contradicting the Delphic oracle story, Socrates now claims that he never examined anyone in *public*, or before audiences, but always in private and discretely: "going to each of you *privately*, as a father or an older brother might do, persuading you to care for virtue" (31b, our emphasis). He now says that he did not ever "dare" to speak up in public: "It might seem to be strange that I do go around counseling these things and being a busybody *in private*, but that in *public* I do not dare to go up before your multitude to counsel the city" (31c, our emphasis). In the Delphic oracle story, we recall, he repeatedly stressed how *public* his refutational activity was, carried out before "many" (21d, 21e; see also 22b, 23a) including many young people (23c).

Now, within this new and different portrait, there is a subtle, rather comic paradox, which points us once again to Socrates' playfulness. Socrates first proclaims himself an imitator of Achilles – and he quotes the famous lines that vividly remind us that Achilles won glory by dying *young*, in battle, fighting to avenge his friend. But why, if Socrates modeled his life on the heroic Achilles, is he still alive, as a very old man? How did this Socrates, as a hero, manage to live so long? Well, Socrates explains, he had a special "daimonic voice" that always ordered him to avoid public actions that would endanger his own life. Even as he paints himself so heroically, Socrates rather comically lets alert listeners see something quite different just beneath the surface. He led a cautious, private, retired life as much as he could: "Do you suppose, then, that I would have survived so many years if I had been publicly active and had acted in a manner worthy of a good man, coming to the aid of the just things and, as one ought, regarding this as most important? Far from it, men of Athens; nor would any other human being" (32e). He does proceed to tell of how he refused to do *in*justice, and by this refusal risked his life, both under the oligarchy (when the oligarchs tried to force him to help them with their oppression) and similarly under the democracy (when he was required by law to preside at a famous trial of admirals and resisted the populace's demand for illegal proceedings). So Socrates did behave justly, in the sense that he refused, even at risk of his life, to do injustice or act unlawfully. But he was not active in public or in politics (because, he says, his private god told him not to be). He does finally admit that he has had an impact on the young, but only after insisting that he was never anyone's teacher, and therefore that he has no responsibility for whether any of his listeners has become just or unjust (33a–b). Yet he goes on, at 33d–34a, to give a rather long list of prominent young men who have been deeply influenced by him.

The massive question that confronts us is: How are we to put this new account – of Socrates as gadfly, privately preaching and promoting traditional civic virtue – together with the previous account, the Delphic oracle story of Socrates as public spreader of radical moral skepticism? As we have seen in detail, the two accounts are sharply contradictory, in a number of fundamental ways. Which account is true? Or are both false? Are both partial truths? Are they each a kind of comic exaggeration of one side of Socrates' life – which was in truth complex and had in fact two sides, or even many sides? What is Socrates' rhetorical strategy? What is he trying to accomplish by telling two such different and contradictory stories in the same speech?

It has become evident that Plato is having his Socrates speak on different levels to different people. The defense speech as a whole leaves many listeners and readers thinking of Socrates more in terms of the last account – as the heroic gadfly exhorting and waking the city up to manly civic justice. But the speech provokes more thoughtful and questioning listeners and readers to wonder how in the world this fits with the earlier Delphic oracle story's much more radical picture of Socrates' moral skepticism.

We must look to other Platonic dialogues to see what the Platonic Socrates was like, as portrayed in those dialogues, and then to compare those other dialogues with the two very different stories Plato has his Socrates give here in the *Apology*, when on trial, in his one and only public speech. But if, or as soon as, we do turn to the other dialogues, such as the *Republic*, the mystery deepens. For in none of the other thirty-two Platonic dialogues showing Socrates do we ever see Socrates behaving in *either* of the two ways he portrays himself as behaving in this sole public speech of his. Against the depiction in the Delphic oracle story, Plato's Socrates only very rarely cross-examines statesmen or poets, and never any craftsmen. He does not cross-examine anyone before large audiences – except poor Meletus in the *Apology*. As we will see in the opening pages of the *Republic*, Socrates *does* carry out *private* cross-examinations and refutations, which leave people aware that they do not know what they thought they knew – especially about justice. He *does* question, radically, the wisdom of Homer and the goodness of the heroes and heroic virtues Homer depicts. He *does* question the wisdom of political leaders and the educational system of the city. But he does this in very small groups, behind closed doors, often with sophists and with youths attracted to sophists (with whom Socrates never indicates he speaks in the *Apology*). On the other hand, Plato also does not show Socrates to be the gadfly: Socrates is not a private preacher of or exhorter to virtue – though by his questions, Socrates does evince a deep concern to understand virtue, and especially justice, and promote in young interlocutors a similar deep concern. He does try to get young people to think seriously, critically, about virtue, and especially justice – to begin to understand the different aspects of justice and the tensions between those aspects. He does always evince great respect for justice, combined with puzzlement about how all its aspects fit together.

Beginning to Piece Out the Puzzle

If we step back to take a reflective, synoptic view of the defense speech as a whole, we can make some progress toward an understanding of what Plato wants to teach by proceeding along the following lines.

In the last and longest part of his speech, Socrates indicates that republican and family life demand five specific virtues of character – which Socrates evokes and promotes in this part of the speech. First, civic life needs manly courage, including readiness to die in battle for one's republic. Second, civic life needs moderation – as habitual control over one's appetites and subordination of the love of money and luxury to the love of public service. And so, in the third place, civic life needs justice – meaning primarily obedience to law and to one's lawful rulers, along with willingness to forgo or to sacrifice one's personal interests for the common good. Fourth, civic life needs prudence or practical judgment, rooted in long practical experience in politics and in heartfelt attachment to one's civil society. Fifth and finally, civic life needs piety, as faith in gods who support and sanction the other virtues by promising some kind of immortality after death, and divine judgment leading to rewards and punishments. (In his last words in this dialogue, speaking to those who voted to acquit him, Socrates gives a vivid picture of a hoped-for afterlife.) Socrates realizes that these essential civic virtues are not mainly brought about by critical thought and doubt and questioning and argument. Education in civic virtue depends, first and foremost, on cultivating a sense of shame or a concern for reputation, a respect for the opinions of one's fellow citizens and a desire to be respected by them. It depends in the second place on a reverence for tradition and for shared traditional heroes – a sense of a past to be lived up to, and a sense of responsibility to pass that tradition down to future generations. This means, in the third place, that civic education needs to be centered on the enchanting beauty of poetry and the arts, which can inspire, in the hearts of citizens, the passionate attachments and concern for the common good that are central to a healthy republic. This importance of civic poetry, and music, and fine arts, indicates that the civic virtues need to be rooted in the emotions more than in reason. The forming of the heart, of the passions, is what constitutes a vigorous *civic* education, which must be contrasted with, and even opposed to, a *philosophic* education rooted in radical questioning and doubt and opening the mind to awareness of ignorance.

Socrates discovered, in and through his own life, by his own experience, and not merely as a matter of speculation, that the life of political philosophy is not simply or unqualifiedly good for most humans. While his own inquiry into the divine, through engaging citizens in the dialectical examination of their moral and political opinions, permitted him to conclude that the unexamined life is not worth living for a human being such as himself, he at the same time discovered the danger and potential destructiveness for most people of philosophic doubt and skepticism, especially about the divine. This, we may say, is the massive reason why he masks his own activity in various conventionally pious disguises – first as service to the Delphic oracle, and then, more completely, by delivering the last long part of his speech, in which he claims to show the perfect compatibility between his life and the heroic ideals of Homer's Achilles, and of traditional Athens. Socrates discovered that the life of radical inquiry is in severe tension with the requirements of a healthy republican society. Republican government and the family life that is its cornerstone require dedication, trust, commitment, patriotism, even love, among the fellow members of the community. A healthy republic requires an exclusive and to some extent intimate mutual care that is not skeptical, or tentative, or provisional, or exploratory, but instead solid and deeply set in the soul, in the emotions. One can also put the key point this way: Socrates discovered a bifurcation in human nature. Human beings are not simply, and certainly not primarily, philosophic beings. They are first and foremost political beings, social beings, family beings. Humans are in great measure fulfilled, emotionally and mentally, by participating in collective self-government, in the life devoted to the civic virtues that are essential to a strong republican society – and these are passionate, emotional virtues. The bonds or foundations of political society are only in small part rational, and they are *not* rooted in critical thought. Those bonds are mainly faith, passion, and emotion, which are educated through habit and custom and artistic imagination. But humans are also, and even more deeply, rational thinking beings, whose truest fulfillment is that of maximal self-consciousness, requiring full liberation and development of the mind; this requires a relentless questioning and doubt of all society's basic moral and religious opinions. This is the dilemma of human existence that Socrates tries to convey through his strangely contradictory speech: the inescapable tension between, on one hand, the political nature of humans – the requirements of a truly self-governing, fraternal republican political society – and, on the other hand, a higher, purer, intellectual nature and need for clarity, even in uncertainty.

Socrates, and his student Plato, responded to this fundamental tension or dilemma in human existence by developing a new philosophic rhetoric, or a new kind of communication. Since genuine philosophy's radical questioning is destructive of the spiritual foundations of any healthy republican society, that questioning must be kept under a veil, by which the political philosopher makes himself seem to be much more in conformity with tradition than he ever really is. The massive lesson Plato's Socrates teaches in the *Apology* is that the philosopher must learn to hide and to mute the skeptical core of his life of questioning, in order to protect the city from the corrosive effects of intransigent and radical philosophic questioning and doubting – and in order to protect himself, and his fellow philosophers or potential philosophers, from the city's inevitable, naturally defensive, and indignant punishment or persecution. The philosopher will recognize that the city as a whole can never be made philosophic. Civil society can be only *somewhat* elevated and enlightened, made *somewhat* more thoughtful, induced to have *some* respect for a *disguised* version of the philosopher (and only thus can a healthy republic be induced to tolerate philosophy). Socrates' whole posture implies that to try to enlighten the city, in the sense of exposing it directly to philosophic skepticism, is profoundly mistaken. To try to base citizenship and statesmanship on skeptical philosophy would destroy the essential moral foundations of the city and, in addition, would make people less thoughtful, less serious, less caring for the truth about their souls and their fulfillment. Such an attempt at philosophic enlightenment of society as a whole would debunk the rather fragile directedness of the city toward civic virtue, and would allow the ever-present and blinding concern for physical security, comfort, and money or material goods to swamp social existence.

We here take note of the momentous fact that today's American and European society and culture is based on a profoundly different attempt to solve the problem made so vivid in Plato's *Apology of Socrates*. When we turn in later chapters to Machiavelli, Bacon, Hobbes, Locke, and Montesquieu, we will study the diverse philosophic originators and sources of our distinctly "modern" conceptions of both the nature of the philosophic life and the nature of a healthy political society. Socrates would likely say that this modern philosophic outlook, on which our contemporary society is based, is not a solution but instead a contortion of both the philosophic life and healthy republican civic life; Socrates would probably contend that our type of republic entails a lowering and a narrowing of both civic life and the life of the mind. As we get further into the writings of the modern political philosophers, we will have to begin to judge for ourselves this titanic debate between the "ancients" and the "moderns." But first we will explore more fully the classical Socratic position, as elaborated by Plato and Aristotle. To begin with, we will examine the first book of Plato's *Republic*, with its vivid portrait of what Socrates was like characteristically – as a dialectician, exploring with specific individuals the nature of justice, when he was not on trial and forced to orate defensively before a vast crowd.

2

Plato's *Republic*, Book One*

Plato's longest and most famous Socratic dialogue consists in an uninterrupted narration by Socrates, to persons unidentified, of remarkable events and conversation that took place the previous night. Socrates begins by relating that he and a companion named Glaucon "went down, yesterday, to the Piraeus" – and it is there, in the port of Athens, that the entire subsequent dialogue is set, mostly inside the home of a resident alien named Cephalus. No other Platonic work is placed in this setting, with its specific atmosphere. The port is situated eight miles from the city of Athens and is a site appropriate for discussion involving radical civic and religious thought experimentation. Like most busy ports, it is rife with foreigners and alien ways, and even strange new gods. Indeed, this last is what Socrates says drew him there: He went to "pray to, and out of a wish to observe the festival of," a goddess whose festival was being introduced "for the first time." Socrates' piety comes to sight as attracted by "novel divinities" (recall the formal criminal charges lodged against him: *Apology* 24b–c).

Having prayed and observed, the pair headed back to the city: Socrates makes it clear that they did not intend to visit old Cephalus and his family. But they were compelled to wait, first by the command and hand of a slave, sent by Polemarchus, the son of Cephalus, and then by a jovial little gang led by Polemarchus. At the start of the Platonic dialogue on justice and the best regime we are lightheartedly reminded of the austere truth that society is controlled chiefly by force (including enslavement), and by the strength of numbers, especially the numbers of the younger males.

---

* We recommend the translation by Allan Bloom (New York: Basic Books, 1968). Our quotations, referring to the text by standard Stephanus pagination, are from this edition, with minor emendations.

But one member of the gang, Adeimantus, spoke up to mediate, offering a persuasive attraction: "Don't you know that at sunset there will be a torch race on horseback for the goddess?!" Polemarchus was then inspired to add other incentives: The gang has a party planned for the night. After a big dinner, there will be a magnificent religious spectacle, to which they must all go and where they will encounter many other younger men with whom to talk. When Glaucon acceded to this, apparently charmed by the prospect, Socrates – with manifest reluctance – followed him.

Yet as the whole subsequent dialogue makes clear, Socrates managed to derail totally the big plans. They never have any dinner, they never get to the torch race, they never leave the house, and they never meet anyone new. Instead, Socrates enchants them into spending the entire night, without sleep, food, or even a sip of wine, following him as he explores the nature of justice and of the best conceivable civic life. We are shown vividly how seductively demanding, how ascetic, and how private Socrates is, especially when talking about the themes of justice and philosophy.

We can suspect that Socrates also managed, through this all-night conversation, to accomplish what he was intending to achieve if he had been able to spend time alone with Glaucon. But this points us back to the big question posed by the opening words: Why is Socrates so interested in Glaucon? We find a big clue in the *Apology* (34a), where we learn that although Adeimantus was not himself a student of Socrates, he was ready to stand up in court to defend the influence Socrates had on his brother – who is none other than Plato himself. And we soon learn in the *Republic* that Adeimantus is also the brother of Glaucon. So the *Republic* is the long dialogue that shows us (among other things) how Socrates impressed favorably Plato's two older brothers, neither of whom ever became a philosophic student or follower of Socrates.

When they entered the home of Cephalus, they met also the brothers of Polemarchus, and, much more surprising, the famous sophist Thrasymachus – accompanied by his followers, Charmantides and Cleitophon. This means, of course, that Polemarchus and Adeimantus hoodwinked Socrates. They never hinted that they were inviting him to a dinner party with this famously feisty rival teacher present, together with a couple of his students. Polemarchus and Adeimantus set Socrates up, rightly hoping, it seems, for a debate, without asking Socrates if he wished such a challenge. Plato indicates that Socrates is not himself inclined to keep company with Thrasymachus, who turns out to be a violently outspoken critic of justice.

The Refutation of Cephalus

We need to ask – as we need to with any Platonic dialogue – why Plato has chosen to immortalize a dialogic encounter between Socrates and *this particular* character: What does Plato mean to teach by showing this human type interrogated by Socrates? What type of person is Cephalus? We see at once that he is *the* father figure, in a situation where he wields maximum patriarchal power – presiding in his own wealthy home over his sons or heirs and their guest-friends. What is more, Cephalus is *the* embodiment of patriarchal *piety*; we find him crowned with the sacred wreath and in an interval between performing sacrifices. At the outset, Plato sets vividly before us an exemplar of the class of people in whose hands traditional authority rests: the old, rich, priestly fathers. So long as such a figure is present, the conversation has to revolve around him, and it must remain deferential and conservative. What happens, however, is that after only a few minutes of conversing (at the start of which, the old father stresses that he wishes for more talk with Socrates), Cephalus returns to his sacrifices, never to reappear, not even to invite the company to the dinner that was planned! This is a major dramatic event, and Plato prods us to watch carefully to try to understand all that is implied in how Socrates, through urbane but incisive questioning and argument, moves the father to depart permanently, thus liberating the gathering from the direct sway of ancestral authority.

The conversation begins with Cephalus sounding much like a typical old man, gently chiding Socrates for not coming to visit him. Cephalus expresses how much he now enjoys conversation – but gives a revealing reason. The desire for the pleasure of conversing has increased as he has lost the capacity to enjoy the bodily pleasures. Socrates replies by politely voicing an eagerness to learn from the very old. But Socrates expresses what he seeks to learn in a rather disquieting fashion: What is life like when one is "on the threshold" – of Hades? Plato impels us to wonder: Why should the dialogue on justice begin with this question? Does Plato want us to consider the possibility of a deep connection between the concern for justice and the human confrontation with death and a possible passage to another life?

Cephalus begins his reply with a strong oath – "by Zeus!" Plato thus alerts us to the fact that the nature of divinity will loom in what ensues. Cephalus relates what it's like when old men get together: They sit around complaining about how old age causes the loss of sensual pleasures. But Cephalus says that he does not agree with his old pals; he presents himself as above such complaints, and he invokes the authority of the aged Sophocles, the great tragic poet, who, when once rudely asked if he could still have intercourse with a woman, cursed erotic passion as a "frenzied and savage master" from whom old age finally lets one "escape." Cephalus not only agrees but goes further: Old age brings, he says, "peace and freedom" from "very many mad masters." But, drawing a gentlemanly conclusion, Cephalus declares that what counts in life is character: If one has good character, then one handles well even old age; if one lacks good character, both youth and old age give trouble.

Socrates says to his anonymous listeners, "I was full of wonder at what he said," prodding us to look to see exactly what is so amazing about the statement of Cephalus. On inspection, the response given by Cephalus appears tension-ridden. If it is good character that allows him and some others to bear old age gracefully, why is there such relief at being freed from the frenzied and savage master *eros*, as well as from many other very mad masters? Cephalus betrays the fact that he, like many men, never achieved real control over his erotic lusts. Indeed, Cephalus seems still somewhat obsessed with those lusts; after all, Socrates did not ask him about erotic passion, but about living in the imminence of death. Again Plato provokes us to wonder why he has the dialogue on justice commence in this way – with an old patriarch who parries a Socratic question about living in the face of imminent death by confessing how he and other men live most of their lives enslaved to erotic lusts, invoking as an authority Sophocles (who, as a great poet, presumably knows the human heart). In the light of the severe repression of *eros* that will characterize the envisioned best regime that will be elaborated later, we may wonder: Could Plato be pointing us to the thought that erotic passion (as a kind of profound distraction from awareness of mortality?) is *the* wild card in human nature – that which above all makes doubtful the possibility of a rationally ordered society?

Socrates reports to his listeners that he next "stirred up" Cephalus – not by pointing out the tension or evasion in what Cephalus had said but by raising an admittedly somewhat vulgar objection that challenged the stress Cephalus had laid on good character. Socrates says that "the many" (*hoi polloi*) would not believe Cephalus's claim about the decisive importance of character. What counts, they would say, is wealth: It's his money that enables Cephalus to bear old age gracefully. Socrates thus made money or material property the theme.

This evoked another revealing response. Continuing to insist, as a gentleman, that "decency," not money, is the most important thing, the patriarch nevertheless conceded a lot to the vulgar view: You do have to possess wealth in order to live well. Without realizing it, Cephalus thus indicated a gulf between common opinion, with which Cephalus partly agrees in this key respect, and Socrates. We have learned from the *Apology* (23c, 31c, 38a–b) that Socrates lived in "ten-thousand-fold poverty" but was nonetheless confident that his is the life worth living for a human being. The figure of Cephalus shows, however, that the conventional gentlemanly life, of *non*philosophers, *does* need wealth. Next, however, Socrates went on to bring out the complimentary fact that Cephalus is gentlemanly in that he is not *overly* fond of his own wealth. Socrates averred that the reason is that Cephalus's wealth is mainly inherited; Socrates drew from this a momentous general principle: People who inherit tend to be less attached to their property than people who make their own money. For humans love excessively whatever they have brought into being as their own product – as poets love their own poems and parents their own children. We see, then, that a second large problem with love has emerged, this time with the love of one's own, especially one's own work. While perhaps not so disorderly as is sexual love, the love of one's own work is, Socrates suggests, a source of deluding and unjust attachments. This foreshadows a grand theme of the rest of the dialogue, and a leitmotif of classical republican thought: A maximally just society would have to minimize love of one's own, and in a healthy society, where money and material property is to be kept subordinate, it is necessary to prevent moneymakers from having a predominant role.

Socrates next asked a still more profoundly revealing question: "What do you suppose is the greatest good that you have enjoyed from possessing great wealth?" This question prods Cephalus, but also us, to confront the fact that wealth is not an end in itself but must be judged by the good that it procures. This question really stirs Cephalus up, for he has given some profound and original thought to it. Cephalus, it turns out, is deeply concerned with his approaching death, and with fear and hope regarding divine judgment, entailing reward or punishment in the afterlife. He avoided Socrates' question about what it is like to be facing imminent death, we now see, precisely because it is so emotionally charged for him and because he realizes that his view will sound strange to the younger fellows present. For when he was younger, Cephalus all but confesses, he was not a pious believer in the sacred tales about divine judgment in the afterlife. But as one gets old, he says, one begins to fear and to care about such things. And as a result, Cephalus now counts money as most beneficial because it contributes a great deal to a decent person's not having to commit the injustices of cheating or lying to any man, or of departing for the next life still owing some sacrifices to a god or money to a human.

This is how justice is introduced as *the* theme of this longest Socratic dialogue; this is apparently how Plato suggests that one should approach the Socratic investigation into the meaning of justice. We start by listening to an old patriarch, who was once overmastered by erotic passion and was largely untroubled by fear of the afterlife, who now, in his closeness to death, and release, by decrepitude, from erotic passion, has become convinced that he has acquired insight into divine judgment after death – and has *therefore* become deeply concerned with justice – with how his own life has been characterized by justice or injustice. Because or insofar as Cephalus thinks that he can and has made the sacrifices entailed in giving away his money to avoid and to remedy any injustice, he has great *hope*, as he says, for the afterlife, for a deserved salvation. This justice-based hope is beautifully articulated and thus strengthened by the wise poet Pindar, whom Cephalus quotes. Does not Plato ask us to ponder whether this or something like it is not a deep, if often hidden, psychological root of the human passion for justice? For the young, Cephalus testifies, all this is obscured – by (Plato suggests) strong erotic passions, with their attendant dazzlingly vital exhilarations.

Plato does not have Socrates directly examine or test the validity of Cephalus's possible experience of superior insight into the divinely transcendent. Instead, Socrates asks questions that bring to light contradictions and ignorance in what Cephalus opines to be *justice* and its requirements. Socrates proves to Cephalus the untenability of the principles of justice that Cephalus believes to be commanded and sanctioned by the gods. And Cephalus finds this discovery of his ignorance about justice to be disturbing enough so that he, who stressed his enjoyment of conversation and wish for more conversational visits with Socrates, does not remain at or return to the Socratic conversation inquiring into the truth about justice, but instead exits, never to reappear – though with a laugh at the jest of his son, who steps in claiming to defend, on the authority of a great poet, the refuted conception of justice held by his father. Does Cephalus absorb himself in religious ritual, as an escape from the Socratic dialogical inquiry into justice, because he experiences the ground of his faith and hope for the afterlife to be shaken by Socrates' questioning of his conception of justice?

But what specifically is the Socratic refutation of Cephalus, and what are its most obvious implications? Socrates asks Cephalus: Are your implicit principles – that one ought always to tell the truth and that one ought never to fail to return what belongs to someone – strictly valid? Are there not situations in which it is in fact unjust to tell the truth and to return someone else's property: situations in which, what is just, or one's moral duty, is to lie and to refuse to give someone his property when he asks for it? Socrates gives a vivid concrete example that proves this to be so, in a way that "everyone" would agree, as Cephalus himself admits.

What Cephalus at first believes that he believes is that there are certain laws or rules that define what justice is. Socrates shows to Cephalus that what he more truly believes is that everyone believes that for an action to be just, it must be evidently good, that is, beneficial, or at least not harmful, for the persons involved. Therefore every rule or law can and must be critically judged in each particular set of circumstances. Whenever following a rule or law brings more harm than good, it is unjust to follow the rule or law. Acting justly requires weighing the benefit and harm involved for the parties in every choice in each and every situation – which is always in some sense unique. Laws or rules can be at best moral guidelines, not categorical imperatives.

Yet in defense of Cephalus's outlook, one might question whether Socrates' counterexample, involving the deposit of property that is dangerous weaponry and the loss of the owner's soundness of mind, is not somewhat far-fetched, or at least one of those extreme "hard" cases that are misleading, or maybe even the "exceptions that prove the rules." To this, however, Socrates might well reply that *all* substantial property is *always* dangerous, because it can do great harm as well as good, often much more than weapons can (and thus, in the following exchanges, Socrates ceases to speak of property in weapons and speaks of property in general and of money); whether property does great harm or not depends on whether the owner or the one who controls the property *knows* that it is dangerous, and *knows how to use* it safely and beneficially. The fact that most owners of property fail to reflect on the pregnant truth that their property is as dangerous or more dangerous than weaponry shows that they are lacking in competence – and maybe even in soundness of mind.

This helps us to understand the far-reaching implications of Polemarchus's joke at this juncture (331d). When he comes to the defense of his father, who says, "I hand down the argument to you," Polemarchus playfully responds, "Am I not the heir of what belongs to you?" And Socrates addresses him as "you the heir." Part of what is at stake and being challenged in the Socratic refutation includes the justice of all inheritance and inheritance laws. Socrates is beginning to raise this subversive question: If or since the just use of property must maximize good and minimize harm for those involved, does not justice demand that all property be controlled, if not owned, by people who know how to use the property most beneficially? Is the truly just title to all property not wisdom about how best to use property?

The First Refutation of Polemarchus

What kind of person is Polemarchus? And why is the refutation of such a person important as the second stage in Plato's teaching on justice? The opening drama showed that Polemarchus is a leader of his young peers. Now we see that he is a loyal and spirited defender of his father. But as soon as his father has departed, it becomes clear that Polemarchus has accepted the Socratic refutation of his father and means to defend his inheritance on a new footing. With a passionate oath ("by Zeus!"), Polemarchus responds to Socrates' quizzical question by insisting that what the great poet Simonides meant when he asserted that "it is just to give (or to give back) to each what is owed," is that justice is owing and doing some *good* to *friends*, and *nothing* bad (332a). Polemarchus's father had never mentioned friends or friendship, or the good, but Socrates had introduced friendship as well as the good in his counterexample challenging Cephalus's principles of justice; this seems to have rung a bell with Polemarchus. Whereas his father's conception expressed more the transactional outlook of a businessman, thinking of justice primarily in terms of dealings between independent individuals involving mutual respect for private property, Polemarchus thinks of justice in the richer terms of a sense of community or fraternity: To be just is to be a good friend, a good family member, a good citizen, who is dedicated to benefiting and defending his fellow community members.

Socrates shines a revealing light on what Polemarchus has in mind by immediately asking him about *enemies* (332b). Polemarchus answers that one owes to enemies what is fitting, which is harm. Socrates thus brings out the fact that Polemarchus sees the world very much in terms of "us" versus "them," friend versus enemy. Such thinking bulks large in the primary civic, or loyal citizens' and family members' and friends' outlook: Justice obviously entails and evokes our defending our country, our family, our friends – against foes. But a big problem in this emerges as Socrates proceeds to compel Polemarchus to realize that he cannot articulate what is the distinct and rich *positive good* that friends share, in being just, *above* and *beyond* the negative good of mutual defense and offense against outside enemies.

But first, Socrates completes the articulation of Polemarchus's definition of justice in a strange way. He gets Polemarchus to conceive of justice as an *art*, a practically beneficial skill, analogous to the arts of medicine and cooking: Even as doctoring is the art that knows how to distribute good medicines and nourishments to various bodies, so justice can be defined as the art that knows what to distribute, as good or beneficial, to friends – and as bad or harmful to enemies (332c–d). Thinking of justice in this way, as skilled practical knowledge, is obviously not the way Polemarchus (or anyone) usually thinks of justice, especially in friendship. We may be inclined to protest that friendship or community, and therefore justice as friendship, consists more in the bonds of *affection* that tie people together. That Socrates is deliberately exaggerating, or is not being entirely serious, in his focus on justice as *artfulness* is indicated when he finally formulates Polemarchus's definition, and in doing so drops any mention of art (at 332d). But by forcing justice into the mold of art, Socrates spotlights an important aspect of friendship and justice that our emphasis on feelings of affection obscures – a dimension of friendship and justice that Polemarchus is intelligent enough to acknowledge. We understand justice and true friendship to mean doing or bringing about some *good*, for and with, our friends and community – and not *merely feeling* good about and to and with them. But this implies that in order to be a just friend, or a just member of the community, one must *know what is good* to do for and with our friends and community. Socrates now makes this good a question, illuminated by analogies. As regards the bad of sickness and the good of health, it is the doctor who can best help friends and harm enemies; in a ship in a storm, it is the artful pilot. Now in what specific actions and works is justice, and the artfully just friend, supremely effective? In other words, what is the precise expertise concerning the common good that constitutes the practical wisdom of justice, as friendship? This is the challenge that Plato's Socrates poses to Polemarchus – but that Plato thereby also addresses to us.

The first and clearest answer Polemarchus can think of is: The wise action of justice takes place in battle, where just friends are good allies in defending one another and doing harm to enemies. We see how strongly Polemarchus is drawn to think of collective defense as the primary good for a community. But does this mean, Socrates asks, that justice or friendship is useless in peacetime? Polemarchus replies, "Of course not." He wants to articulate the significance of justice and friendship in the more important part of life, in peacetime. When Socrates presses, again with vivid analogies, the question of what is the peacetime activity that justice artfully undertakes, Polemarchus answers, "Contracts." He agrees when Socrates asks whether he does not mean "partnerships." But Socrates points out that a good partner for playing "draughts" (the ancient version of checkers) is someone who *knows how* to play that game well; a good partner for house building is a carpenter who *knows how* to build a house; and a good partner for harp playing is someone who *knows how* to play the harp. So again: In partnership with a view to achieving *what specific good*, is justice and the just person needed as knowledgeable? "In money matters," Polemarchus answers – and we see that Polemarchus when pressed moves back toward the outlook of his businessman father. But Socrates immediately asks a question reminiscent of the most revealing question he pressed on Cephalus. Money cannot be the good as an end. If justice is the art that makes one a good partner in money matters, then what about when money is to be used, that is, spent, by the partners? Obviously, what is needed *then* – when money becomes truly useful or good – is someone who knows the good and bad concerning what is to be purchased. In what regard does justice possess such knowledge? Polemarchus can merely respond, lamely, that a partner who knows justice does most good when money needs to be deposited and kept safe. Yes, but this means, Socrates points out, that justice is really good only so long as you do not want actually to use money, or any other good thing. And this implies that justice is rather secondary, or, as Socrates says in conclusion (333e), addressing Polemarchus as his friend, that "justice wouldn't be anything very serious."

Now this conclusion, to which Polemarchus has been led inexorably as a necessary consequence of the clearest idea he can come up with as to the value of justice as friendship, obviously contradicts radically a dimmer but deeper dimension of his conception: For he evidently holds justice as friendship to be something *very* serious, something far more important than money and any goods money can buy. Polemarchus's stress on battle and its dangers as the primary locus of the deeds of justice as friendship makes it clear that he is an admiring defender of justice conceived as demanding that one be prepared to risk the *sacrifice* of one's money and of those other goods money can buy, such as houses and horses and games; that one be ready to risk heroically even the good of life itself. Yet Polemarchus is unable to articulate what is the *greater* good thereby enacted or brought about by justice as devotional friendship (and Plato in effect presses on us the question whether we do not share this incapacity, and the need to remedy it in ourselves). What rich positive good does a wisely just friend and community achieve, over and beyond, and even at the cost of, money and other substantial goods, and even life itself?

But Socrates proceeds to show that the conclusion to which Polemarchus has been brought in his conception of justice as friendship has a much more troubling implication. If justice as friendship is only a means to our community's possessing securely money and other such goods, through the knowledge of how best to guard those goods from others, and since knowledge of how best to guard against stealing includes the knowledge of how best to steal, does not true concern for our community's good and its enhancement require that we go on the offensive so as to increase and not merely maintain the communal good? Is not an intelligently just friendship a wise partnership in robbery? Are not those who remain merely defensive, who merely guard what they have and fail to take from non-friends so as to increase the goods of friends or community members, worse friends, worse citizens, worse community members, less just? Socrates indicates how deeply and widely spread this undertow of thought is by associating it with Homer.

Swearing by Zeus, Polemarchus shows that he is revolted by this conclusion to which the critical examination of his articulation of his conception of justice has led; yet he will not and cannot abandon that conception – of justice as helping friends and harming enemies (334b). The simple but fundamental question Socrates has forced upon Polemarchus (and that Plato has forced upon us) is: How and why, exactly, is robbery intrinsically bad, and thus unjust, for the community of robbers, if or when its outcome is to increase the good things for the community? Or *is* robbery good, but justice demands that one do what is *bad* for one's community and friends? Is justice then *hurting* one's friends? Is justice as friendship sheer communal sacrifice of the good things in life? For the sake of *what*, exactly? Or is there not some greater common good to be found in or achieved by justice as friendship, a greater good that Polemarchus cannot yet articulate and whose achievement requires excluding robbery and such? If so, what, exactly, *is* that greater good? And how and why does that greater good require severe limitations on our pursuit of other specific goods?

Polemarchus is suddenly and vividly aware that he does not know what he thought he knew: what justice really is. Admitting that Socrates has indeed brought out the true implication of what he has said, Polemarchus also and more strongly believes that belonging to a gang of

shrewd and effective thieves is unjust and repellent. He realizes that he
has contradicted himself. He has discovered that he holds two opinions
as to the meaning of justice, both of which cannot be true, since each
entails that the other is necessarily false.

The Second Refutation of Polemarchus

Socrates turns (at 334c) to a second refutation of Polemarchus and his
thesis, asking now not about what the common good is that is achieved
in and by justice as friendship (a good that excludes robbery and such),
but instead about what a *good friend* is. Are friends individuals who *seem* to
be "worthy" (*chrestous*), or those who "really are" (*tous ontas*) worthy? And
are enemies those who *seem* to be not worthy, or those who *really* are not?
Polemarchus replies, with a slight note of hesitation, that "those whom
one believes to be worthy, one loves as friends, and those whom one
believes to be wicked one hates." But then Polemarchus must admit that
in "many" cases we all make big mistakes in these "beliefs." But from this
admission it necessarily follows, Socrates points out, given Polemarchus's
definition of justice – as helping friends and harming enemies – that it
will often be an obligation of justice to benefit the wicked and to harm
those who are good. Still worse: Since Polemarchus agrees that by "the
good" we mean the just, who do not commit injustice, it further follows
that in many cases justice obliges one to harm just people, who have
done no injustice (334d).

   In light of this implication, Polemarchus now strongly condemns as
"wicked" (*poneros*) his own thesis. He then agrees with Socrates that what
is just is to harm the unjust and to benefit the just – because this thesis
is finer or "nobler" (*kallion*). In other words, justice makes a claim of
nobility, of what is fine or high (*kalon*) that goes beyond and trumps
what is cared for or loved, or what one likes. And this becomes clearer as
Socrates now observes that this nobler argument necessarily entails that
for everyone who is mistaken about friends (and that means an awful lot
of people), what is just is to hurt friends and to help enemies! So once
again Polemarchus has grossly contradicted himself. Or (as Socrates
politely puts it) Polemarchus has contradicted the definition of justice
he derived from the poet Simonides (334e). Polemarchus emphatically
agrees. He proceeds to say that he wants to go back to change the definition of who a friend and an enemy really are – in order to say what is
both "correct" and "noble" (335b1). And here we see that Polemarchus
is not merely learning from Socrates that he does not know something

very important that he thought he knew. Now Polemarchus is showing that he is capable of learning, from being refuted, that he can and must change his fundamental outlook about the most important things in his life – that he must change what he thinks a friend or friendship means, and thus what justice means. Polemarchus now defines a friend as someone who not only seems but truly is worthy; someone who seems to be, but is not, is not truly a friend – and similarly for who is and is not an enemy. From this Socrates concludes (to the emphatic agreement of Polemarchus) that justice means doing good to the friend who is good and harm to the enemy who is bad.

Now this means that justice as friendship requires not only knowledge of a common good, which Polemarchus has been unable to articulate (the first refutation), but, in addition, justice as friendship requires knowledge or wisdom about the goodness and badness, the true worth, of those whom one loves and hates. Putting together these two requisite forms of wisdom about the good brings to view a major question that runs through and is repeatedly provoked by this second refutation: What does Socrates (or what do Socrates and Polemarchus) mean by "worthy" (*chrestos*) and "good" (*agathon*) when these terms are applied to people? The only explicit clue Socrates gives is that he gets Polemarchus to agree that "good" means "just" – but of course we are also trying to figure out what "just" means. What is most strictly consistent with the thesis of Polemarchus (that justice is benefiting friends and harming enemies) is that the goodness or worthiness, as justice, of an individual whom one loves as a true friend consists in that individual's being truly beneficial for the one who loves him. Yet is this notion of goodness or worthiness not insufficient, because it makes the goodness of the friend, and one's love for the friend, too utilitarian? When Polemarchus, following Socrates (at 334c1) repeatedly identifies the good person as the "worthy," and when he says that it is "manifestly nobler" to hold that it is just to benefit those who are just (334d), doesn't Polemarchus have in mind that justice obliges us to benefit, and in some cases also to love or to care for as friends, not only those who benefit us but, even more, perhaps, those who are *intrinsically* good and just and worthy, whether they benefit us or not? Does not a person who is good, worthy, and just have a claim on others that goes beyond the benefit that person gives to others? Yet this would mean that the definition that Polemarchus has thus far clung to – that justice consists in being beneficial (to friends) and harmful (to enemies) – is radically incomplete, or fails to articulate the most important dimension of justice (as Polemarchus himself experiences justice). This would also mean that, in order to know who is truly good, worthy, and just – and thus eligible to be a true friend – one would need to know what exactly is that goodness that is *inherent* in a just person that transcends (though it includes) such a person's being beneficial to another – and why such *intrinsic* goodness gives to the person who has it such a powerful claim on being benefited by others, even when they are not benefited, and even when they incur cost.

Polemarchus primarily understands and articulates justice to mean the mutual benefiting, including on a high and fulfilling level, of those who share in a community of friendship. But he also understands himself and his friends or community as good, worthy, and just in a nobler sense – expressed in their subordinating or even sacrificing their own benefit to some higher good inherent in people or causes other than themselves. But these two meanings of justice are at some tension; how can a just community be defined as one whose chief end is *both* mutual benefit *and* transcending or sacrificing mutual benefit for the sake of something else? Will or would a clear-sighted and noncontradictory understanding of justice lead Polemarchus (and us) finally to realize that the concern for benefit must ultimately be understood as subordinate to a transcendence of concern for benefit? *Or* is the contrary the case: That the apparent concern to transcend self-interest is in fact subordinate to or even a way to a concern for a truer, because more elevated or purer, self-interest and self-fulfillment? To put it another way: Are the truly good persons and communities, when they become fully self-conscious, truly concerned above all for themselves and their own good, or truly *not* concerned above all for themselves and their own good?

The Third Refutation of Polemarchus

In the last refutation of Polemarchus, Socrates introduces the possibility that there is a kind of self-interest, individual and collective, that is nobler or more admirable than the mundane goods procured by the ordinary arts and by money. Socrates turns to this refutation by asking (335b) if Polemarchus is sure that a just man ought to harm anyone – to which Polemarchus replies that "the wicked, and enemies, ought to be harmed!" In reply, Socrates asks: If a being is harmed, does it become better, or worse? Polemarchus replies that of course, if it is injured, it becomes worse. Socrates then asks if isn't the case that when a particular being – say, a dog – becomes worse, it is lessened with respect to the "excellence" or "virtue" (*arete*) of that being. When Polemarchus agrees,

Socrates applies this principle to human beings, and Polemarchus agrees: A harmed or injured human is made worse with respect to the excellence or virtue of a human being (335c).

This is a paradoxical implication of what has immediately preceded, and depends in part on a tricky or sophistic aspect of what Socrates has previously brought Polemarchus to agree to. For it is far from obvious that everything we would call an "injury" or "harm" to a being is a diminution of that being's virtue or excellence. Some things we would call injuries may actually enhance excellence or virtue, by bringing out capacities for endurance and self-control. Punishment may educate or help reform and improve a being. And we do not usually think of the injured victims of crimes, or of accidents, as having necessarily become worse people, in the sense of less virtuous, as a consequence of the harm they have suffered. Socrates is clearly being playful in this part, but here as ever, the playfulness has a serious point: Socrates is moving Polemarchus (and us) to see that the *most truly serious or damaging* harm is that which makes one a worse person, which diminishes or cripples one's virtue or excellence or flourishing as a human being. And now (335c4) Socrates takes an apparently obvious but momentous step: "But," he asks, "is not justice human virtue?" Polemarchus emphatically agrees. Socrates here makes explicit an aspect of our understanding of what we mean by justice that has been powerfully implicit all along: Justice is virtue, and that means justice is required for, or may even constitute, the excellence – the flourishing inner or spiritual condition – of a human being. To be a complete and excellent or flourishing person is to have the virtue of a human – this is, to be just – while to be unjust is to be an incomplete or mutilated person. From this there follows a famously paradoxical Socratic thesis: To engage in criminality is to suffer much worse damage than to be the victim of a criminal. Victims of crimes are not made unjust; they are not made worse people, in the most important respect, and so they are not injured in the most important respect. And Socrates leads Polemarchus to see next (335c6–7) that the worst harm, or the truest injury, perhaps the only complete harm or injury, that anyone could suffer would be to be rendered less virtuous – less just, more unjust.

But this aspect of Polemarchus's (and our) notion of justice does not fit easily with the other two major aspects of our understanding of justice, which have been in the foreground up until now. In the first place, if being just, as virtue or excellence, is itself the greatest good, then the good of justice is *not* so much in the benefits it procures others – as in the case of the arts – but in the activity of the just person, as fulfilling for himself. And in the second place, if justice is self-fulfillment, then it is not selfless. For if justice is virtue or human flourishing, then justice itself, or being just, is the greatest good for the just person and could not, in the final analysis, be a sacrifice or something selfless or even self-overcoming. Any sacrifices would be merely apparent, or would be the giving away or giving up of less important goods in return for the acquisition or exercise of far more important goods – the health and vigor of one's very being.

By bringing all this out at this point, Socrates indicates how incoherent or confused and contradictory our conception of justice is. We somehow think that justice is *both* self-sacrifice, or devotion to something beyond self, *and* self-realization or self-fulfillment. Socrates forces us to wonder, moreover, what passion or longing or hope it is in the human heart that ties us so strongly to this self-contradiction or absurdity.

Socrates forges ahead (335c–d) to make a very bad argument claiming to show that since justice is human virtue, justice cannot possibly mean doing bad to anyone. He claims that even as heat cannot cool, and wetting cannot dry, so good cannot do harm – as if goodness were like the physical properties of heating or drying, or as if it were physically impossible for the harmful to ever be a result of doing good! Then he concludes that since the just is good, it follows that the just can do no harm. By this sophistic argument, Polemarchus is refuted or proven self-contradictory a third time, since he holds that it is just to harm enemies – but has now agreed that the just can never harm anyone.

One has to wonder, of course, why Socrates has at this point engaged in such arrant sophistic trickery. And the clearest dramatic reason immediately appears: Socrates has succeeded in completely infuriating Thrasymachus – a great sophist who knows sophistry when he sees it – who comes roaring in, after having been restrained several times (336b–c). But Socrates has also succeeded in having several salutary effects on Polemarchus. First, he has compelled Polemarchus to begin to see the deep and puzzling implications of our understanding that justice is a virtue, or at the core of human excellence. Second, he has begun to make Polemarchus gentler, by leading him to doubt his confident belief that it is right to harm enemies. As we saw from the start, Polemarchus is a pugnacious young man, full of spirit and loyalty and a sense of dignity. Socrates has taken the first big step in taming and redirecting that passionate concern with dignity and that loyalty; he has begun to convert Polemarchus to a new object of loyalty – Socrates, and philosophic self-knowledge pursued through peaceful, friendly question and answer.

At the end of this refutation, Socrates playfully declares that the two of them will do battle, or wage aggressive war, against anyone who claims what Polemarchus claimed a few moments before – that Simonides or any other wise man asserts that justice is helping friends and harming enemies. Polemarchus emphatically agrees. "'I for one,' he said, 'stand ready to be your partner in the battle.'" Polemarchus has begun to throw in his lot with Socrates. And in another dialogue, Plato's *Phaedrus* (257b), we learn that Polemarchus did become philosophic. So here we have the privilege of watching the first big steps in a true Socratic conversion.

But the jesting about the two of them going to war against those with whom they disagree points to another dimension of the comedy underlying this third refutation. Socrates has left the surface impression that the just person would never do anything that hurts another person in any way – that the just person would never fight and kill, even to defend himself or a loved one. Yet by concluding with talk about fighting battles for the truth, Socrates prods us to see that this is a misleading impression. It is true that the argument implies that the just person would never seek to make another person unjust or less just. But the argument does not in fact imply that the just person might not inflict great suffering on someone – *if* it were reasonable to suppose that the suffering would make the wicked person more just, or even merely less unjust. Socrates' argument does not exclude the possibility of severe punishments and even of capital punishment – and war aimed at punishment – *if* or insofar as this violence can be understood as deterrence or prevention of further injustice or as education for the unjust. Still, the surface impression Socrates gives is of a sort of pacifism, according to which the just person would never seek to make anyone else suffer anything. And it is this impression that is a major part of what evidently provokes the wrath of Thrasymachus, and the next, longer dramatic episode.

The Opening Drama of Thrasymachus

As ever, we need to try to see who Thrasymachus is, and what type of person he represents, in order to figure out why Plato thinks it is necessary to show Socrates refuting this type, as the next stage in Plato's teaching about justice. Thrasymachus is emphatically presented here as a famous sophist, that is, a professional teacher of the art of rhetoric, including the art of debate and courtroom advocacy, as well as other skills and insights necessary to political success. Thrasymachus's success as an educator enables him to claim and to expect, as his deserved compensation, large sums of money. But it appears that he values much more the honor and admiration that he claims he deserves – and that he values the big pay as in large part a mark of honor; for he is eager to teach even without being paid, once he is assured that he will thereby win honor (337d–338b). His prowess as a teacher is further highlighted by the presence of two of his students, one of whom, Cleitophon, soon speaks up in loyal support of his teacher. Socrates points out that young Glaucon, and others present, are potential students for Thrasymachus (338a). It seems not unlikely that Thrasymachus has come "fishing," at the house of Cephalus, for new students among the sons of the wealthy. But, because Socrates has managed to get him extremely irritated, and because this is a private, closed-door session outside the city of Athens, with no mature citizens present except Socrates, Thrasymachus turns out to be amazingly (and we may suspect unusually) frank about the cynically amoral or even immoral implications of his teaching.

But in the course of the drama that now ensues, something quite astounding and unexpected happens: While Socrates describes Thrasymachus entering like a roaring wild beast (336b), we eventually hear of Thrasymachus blushing (350d) and then refusing to continue with more than perfunctory replies to any questions Socrates may ask. Somehow, Socrates taps into and renders acute a sense of shame in Thrasymachus. This provokes the big question: How and why did this happen to Thrasymachus? What did Socrates do to Thrasymachus in the conversation that finally made the latter ashamed of himself; and what does this reveal about the problematic character of Thrasymachus's understanding and life, and all that he represents?

From the very outset there is evidence of a contradiction within Thrasymachus. For if he is truly such a cynical amoralist – if he truly holds that the strong should take advantage of the weak – then why is he so indignant at Socrates for doing exactly this? Why does Thrasymachus proclaim that Socrates "*deserves* to suffer" if it can be shown that his teaching about justice is misleading the younger men (337d)? Why, as the argument goes on, does Thrasymachus repeatedly accuse Socrates of wrongdoing (340d, 341a–b)? Why does Thrasymachus not quietly congratulate Socrates for having the strength and wit to pull the wool over the younger and inexperienced men's eyes, winning honor by pretending to teach them the truth, while purveying to them a lot of nonsense? Thrasymachus assumes that Socrates, like Thrasymachus himself, aims to win the younger men's admiration, and it outrages Thrasymachus that Socrates is doing this on false pretenses. But again, why is this not exactly what an intelligent person who thinks as Thrasymachus thinks should endorse – the deception of people, whenever necessary, in order to win their benighted admiration and support? *Or,* if this *is* a mistake, if this is somehow *not* in Socrates' self-interest, if it is harmful, then why is it not something that Socrates should be *pitied* for, and even taught to correct, before he does himself more harm (as Socrates repeatedly suggests – 336e, 337d)?

The First Refutation of Thrasymachus

When Thrasymachus finally delivers his answer to the question of what justice is, it turns out to be amazingly brief and hence puzzling: "Justice," he declares, "is nothing other than the advantage of the stronger" (338c). After Socrates asks for clarification (by posing an irritating question), Thrasymachus angrily makes much clearer what he has in mind above all: Might makes right, where might is the dominion of "the ruling group" (*to archon*) in each city or political society, and right is what the ruling group commands for its own advantage. Thrasymachus is the first to give an emphatically political definition of justice; he is the first to mention "democratic rule," along with "tyrannical rule" and "aristocratic rule." He is also the first to mention *law* as something closely associated with justice. But law, he makes clear, is derivative from the advantage of the ruling group. Every political society, Thrasymachus teaches, is divided into rulers and ruled, and the ruling group or class makes the laws and does everything else in its ruling with a view to its own advantage. "Justice" is simply the name given everywhere to the commands, including especially the laws, that the rulers promulgate for their own advantage; "injustice" is the name given to failing to obey those commands, and hence becoming subject to the punishment that the rulers apply and threaten in order to enforce their selfish hegemony (338d–339a).

Socrates refutes this Thrasymachean conception by showing that when viewed in the context of Thrasymachus's overall conception of ruling, it is incoherent or self-contradictory (339a–e). For while Thrasymachus has declared that the just is the advantage of the stronger, he has also clearly implied, and in answer to Socrates' question confirms that he holds, that the just is to obey the rulers. That these two are mutually contradictory for Thrasymachus becomes evident on the basis of his answer to a simple but penetrating Socratic question: Are all rulers infallible, or do some make mistakes? Thrasymachus responds that rulers are "entirely" capable of making mistakes, and often set down laws "incorrectly," in the sense that they make laws that are to their disadvantage. But from this, Socrates points out, it necessarily follows that obeying the rulers and their laws is in many cases the contrary of doing what is to the advantage of the rulers or the stronger!

Thrasymachus is at first bewildered, and when Socrates patiently explains how Thrasymachus is trammeled in self-contradiction, Polemarchus delightedly seconds Socrates: "Yes by Zeus, Socrates, most clearly!" (340a) – and then Cleitophon speaks up for his teacher, to counter Polemarchus. But Polemarchus retorts by showing that he has really grasped the refutation that Socrates has executed. Polemarchus is a clear thinker. Cleitophon seeks to find solid ground for his teacher by claiming that what Thrasymachus meant by "the advantage of the stronger" is "what the stronger *might believe* (*hegoito*) to be his advantage." Polemarchus retorts, accurately but polemically, that this is not what Thrasymachus said; but Socrates says that it makes no difference, if that is what Thrasymachus really did mean and what he now wishes to say. Socrates is not interested in winning debater's points but in examining what Thrasymachus really believes and lives by.

Thrasymachus, having been given a few moments to think while the others joust, utterly rejects, with contempt, the position that his student Cleitophon has attributed to him. (Cleitophon falls silent, never to speak again; he has learned suddenly how drastically he has misunderstood his teacher's lessons!) "Do you suppose," Thrasymachus says to Socrates, "that I call a man who makes mistakes '*stronger*,' at the moment he is making mistakes!?" (340c). But Socrates points out that Thrasymachus did agree that the *rulers* do make mistakes. And did not Thrasymachus identify the rulers with the stronger? This provokes the first long speech from Thrasymachus, explaining his position – which previously he did not state clearly or precisely, despite his having insisted from the outset on "clear and precise" speech (recall 336d).

Thrasymachus now makes a very big point of precision in speech. In precise speaking, he insists, a craftsman, as craftsman, does not make mistakes, but does so only insofar as he departs from being a true crafts-man. A doctor in the precise sense is not someone who makes a medical error, nor is a calculator someone who makes a mistake in calculation; errors signal a slippage away from craftsmanship and from being a true craftsman. And ruling is, above all, an artful craft. True rule is not stu-pid or incompetent domination, but intelligent, crafty knowledge of dominating a society by commanding what is *truly* "best for oneself" (340d–341a). Thrasymachus now makes it clear that he has very high standards for what a *truly* "strong" person is and what a *true* ruler is; he apparently regards very few regimes or individuals, among those who happen to hold political sway, to be true rulers or to be truly strong.

We need to consider why it is that Thrasymachus takes this momentous step of abandoning the simpler path or position that Cleitophon tried to get him to adopt. Why not stick with the thesis that might makes right, that the good or advantageous is whatever anyone in power *thinks* is his advantage – especially since the rather extreme position Thrasymachus now adopts, that the true ruler is an artist who does not make mistakes, leads to his eventual downfall? But Cleitophon's suggested position entails grave difficulties. Can anyone who knows anything about politics really think that the advantageous for a ruler is whatever a ruler *believes* is advantageous for him? Is there not validity to the insistence that ruling in the full sense requires a certain wisdom? But more than that: Thrasymachus is an exemplar of an unusual but unusually revealing kind of person – who may only in this conversation with Socrates come to realize fully who he is and what he lives for. Thrasymachus dedicates his itinerant life to understanding, and to teaching the politically most promising young in many cities, the difficult and demanding art of rule – and he claims to deserve, in return for such generous and arduous educational dedication, vast compensation in money and honor. His whole life, his wealth, but more important, his self-esteem and sense of his own great deserving, depend on his conviction that there is indeed a difficult art of ruling, and that his rare capacity to teach that art, and to win deserved fame on that basis, makes him a very strong human specimen indeed. As a teacher, Thrasymachus does not himself exercise the art of political rule directly; instead, he sees himself as in an important sense above politics. He is the intellectual orchestrator, and in that sense "ruler," behind the scenes. He is the shaper or creator of his students who actually enter politics and rule successfully. It is the deep ambiguity in this self-understanding, and the deeply ambiguous human concern and ambition that this self-understanding reflects or expresses, that Socrates now focuses on, leading to a second and more thorough refutation of Thrasymachus and his outlook on life.

The Second Refutation of Thrasymachus

All right, Socrates says, let us speak of the ruler as craftsman "in the precise sense of the term" and not in the loose usage of common parlance (341c). Socrates then proceeds to draw out what is implied by questions – as usual, with concrete examples: Is the doctor in the precise sense a moneymaker or one who cares for the sick? Thrasymachus declares that the doctor is one who cares for the sick. He further answers Socrates that the pilot as pilot is ruler over the sailors; the pilot is not defined by being a sailor, even though he too sails in the ship. Thrasymachus likewise agrees that each craft is "by nature" concerned with seeking and providing the advantageous in or for that craft. But Socrates then asks: Is there anything else advantageous to the art as such, other than that the art be as perfect, or as perfectly practiced, as possible (341d)?

This question understandably puzzles Thrasymachus, who wonders what Socrates is getting at. In response, Socrates develops a very strange (and dubious) two-part thesis. First, he asks if Thrasymachus does not agree that the medical art or science is needed because the body by itself is defective, and its advantage consists in the medical art's remedying of the defect (341e). Thrasymachus agrees. Now, the fallaciousness of this proposition Socrates indicates by mentioning that one implication of what he is saying is that eyes are unable to see and ears are unable to hear without the help of some art such as medicine. In other words, this thesis abstracts from nature, or the natural powers of things, beginning with the body. (Later, at 353c–d, Socrates emphatically remarks that eyes have their own proper virtue or excellence.) Socrates conspicuously ignores the fact that the arts, starting most obviously with medicine, take their standards from and are thus governed by nature: The art of medicine follows nature or tries to secure the health dictated by the nature of the body. Plato thus forces us to ask: Why does he have Socrates present such a strange argument, whose obviously erroneous character Socrates quietly indicates even while he presents it?

The answer begins to appear when we consider what is implied in Thrasymachus's ready agreement: This strange argument brings out a key aspect of Thrasymachus's peculiar view of the world – a view that exaggerates the importance of art and overlooks the importance of nature (Thrasymachus never even uses the word "nature" or its derivatives – cf. 341d, 352a, 358e, 370a–b). This strange Socratic argument is a kind of mirror in which we see Thrasymachus's soul. (This is very common in the Platonic dialogues: We often see Socrates elaborating very bad arguments, or sometimes myths, that delight or find agreement with his interlocutor – and thereby reveal what is in the heart of the interlocutor, for us to ponder.) But then of course the puzzle becomes: Why is it important for us to reflect on someone such as Thrasymachus, who has this peculiarly distorted way of seeing the world? The answer is that in and through Thrasymachus, Plato asks us to follow an exploration of an outlook that can become quite prevalent among sophisticated intellects (and that has mushroomed in modernity): the view that conceives of human art (*techne*), science – today we would say "technology" – as responsible for most if not all of the ordering of existence that is beneficial for humans, overcoming a nature (including human nature) that is not ordered in a way beneficial to humans.

In the second place, Socrates asks Thrasymachus whether each art or craft is also inherently defective and in need of another art to remedy its defect and thus "provide what is advantageous" – and then this remedying art has need of another remedying art, and this goes on and on. Or, whether it is not the case that every art, in the precise sense, is without defect and hence does not need remedial advantage, and hence "it is not fitting for an art to seek the advantage of something other than that of which it is the art – being correct, without injury or taint." Thrasymachus again agrees – and we see still more clearly how Socrates is bringing out the high rank in the order of things that Thrasymachus accords to art and artfulness.

Socrates goes on to draw out a momentous necessary implication of this outlook (an implication that he reports Thrasymachus resisted but could not finally deny). The advantage that each art is directed to, and works to procure, by giving its orders, is *not* the advantage of the art itself – since that comes in the flourishing practice of the art, which itself needs no remedy. The advantage that the true craftsman works to procure in his ruling and ordering is the advantage of the matters that the art heals or cares for and rules over. Medicine works for the advantage of the sick, not the advantage of medicine (which inheres in the activity of doctoring); the pilot works for the advantage of those sailing on the ship, not the advantage of the piloting art. But then it follows that the goal in action of every art in the precise sense is the advantage of the *weaker*, who are ruled and need help, *not* the advantage of the stronger or rulers, who are perfect as practitioners of the art. And everyone could see, Socrates reports, that the argument, as agreed to by Thrasymachus, about the just, in relation to the art of rule, had turned out the contrary of what Thrasymachus had originally contended.

At this point, Thrasymachus reacted the way people often react when they have been refuted or shown to be maintaining a self-contradictory thesis, especially in front of an audience. He again became angrily abusive, calling Socrates a naive big baby (343a–b). When Socrates asked in what particular way he was being charged with this, Thrasymachus launched into his longest and most impassioned speech (343b–344c). Socrates, Thrasymachus charged, is speaking as if he thinks that shepherds and cowherds care for and fatten sheep and cattle for the good of the animals, rather than for the benefit of the masters and themselves. But in fact rulers in cities look upon the ruled in no way other than shepherds and cowherds look at sheep and cattle – to be cared for so as to be used and exploited. In order to clarify what he thinks he believes, Thrasymachus says for the first time that ruling is injustice, and that *injustice* is what is truly advantageous for the person who possesses it. Justice, Thrasymachus now says, is truly disadvantageous for the person who possesses it. The one who obeys the laws is exploited by the rulers, and also by contractual partners, and by others who avoid obeying the laws. The one who *justly* rules or takes part in ruling is penalized, if only because he neglects his own property, and incurs the resentment of his friends and family. One sees the superiority of injustice most clearly if one looks at the most perfect injustice, which is tyranny, by which the tyrant becomes most happy – and those who suffer his injustice most miserable. The tyrant is the total thief, who takes everything away from one and all – not only all their property but even their freedom and their very selves, turning all others into his slaves. And when the tyrant is truly successful, he wins all the prestige and glory too, being congratulated by his own slaves as well as by everyone else who hears of his accomplishments. The praise the tyrant wins is not mere flattery, since people really blame only the suffering of injustice, not the doing of it; in their hearts they admire someone who exploits everyone he rules over.

Having delivered this blast, Thrasymachus got up to leave.

But the company compelled Thrasymachus to stay to defend what he had said; Socrates appealed to Thrasymachus's care for them all *as a teacher*, as well as a learner – about most important matters. Thrasymachus responded by expressing his frustration at their inability to *learn* those most important matters from him (344d–345b).

In other words, Thrasymachus's vocation as a teacher here comes to the fore. He emphatically agrees that he takes very seriously teaching others the truth about what way of life is most profitable. But we see then what Socrates brings out here: Thrasymachus himself does *not* live a life of exploiting others; Thrasymachus himself lives a life of trying to help others, and he *prides* himself on living such a life. He is a *dedicated professional* teacher. Thrasymachus's previous long speech praising injustice and even tyranny does not express his own way of life in its deeds or what he really lives for in practice; the beliefs he thinks he has, and that he has expressed in his long speech, are not the beliefs that his life is actually based on, and Socrates is trying to bring him to a deeper self-knowledge, by showing him the profound contradiction with which his existence – and his teaching – is riven. (And Plato asks us to reflect on whether some version of this self-contradictory self-understanding is not shared by others.)

Now as the wide scope of this whole conversation about "art in the precise sense" indicates, in his "professionalism" as a teacher Thrasymachus exemplifies a more general, profound, human aspiration or concern. Human beings do generally wish to express in action, and to have recognized, their own excellence and dignity in dedicating or devoting themselves to practicing a craft well – and that means necessarily benefiting, making life better, for those they take care of or serve through their art. This human concern to be good at, and to have a good reputation in, some public craft, may serve as a key basis of justice in an important social or civic sense. Such professionalism becomes a cornerstone of the justice that is found in the best imaginable regime that Socrates constructs in speech in the later books of the *Republic*. The best regime turns out to be a society of dedicated craftsmen, where justice means each performing his own craft well (370a, 406e–407a, 433a–b, 441d–e) – with the ruler-guardians being the "public craftsmen of the city's freedom" (395b–c). The desire to be conspicuously good at one's job extends emphatically to the job of ruling – and this comes out when we reflect more, under Socrates guidance (345c–e), on the analogy Thrasymachus drew between ruling and shepherding. For is it so obvious that shepherds do not, as shepherds, really care for the welfare of their sheep? True, the welfare of the sheep is not *all* that the men who are shepherds care for; they also expect some pay or recompense for their shepherding. But isn't that because the shepherds realize that their shepherding in itself is caring for the sheep, and not just exploiting them? Don't shepherds demand pay precisely because they think that they have not, in practicing the art of sheep herding, been caring mainly for themselves? And do not the shepherds want to think of themselves, and be known by others, as good, competent shepherds – whose sheep are healthy and safe?

Socrates insists on the applicability of the shepherding analogy, in this sense, to political rule. There are indeed rulers who behave as Thrasymachus described in his long speech: rulers who enslave and impoverish their subjects and reduce their societies to a kind of slave plantation (e.g., various ancient Greek tyrants; the Somozas in Nicaragua; King Farouk in Egypt; Battista in Cuba). But are these the rulers who become glorious and respected? Are these the sorts of rulers Thrasymachus wants his students to become? Does he not rather want to be famous for producing students whose rule makes their countries free, prosperous, strong, stable, lasting – with citizens in future generations who look back and say, "Ah, when that student of Thrasymachus ran things, those were great days!"? And as Socrates stresses, an amazing feature of Thrasymachus's long speech, indicating its gross incompleteness as an expression of his viewpoint, is that nowhere in it did he mention the *art* of rule, or indeed any art whatsoever – even though a moment before he agreed that he thought art was sovereign in life.

Socrates insists on their previous agreement, about art in the precise sense, but now suddenly Socrates takes a strikingly new tack, bringing out more radical implications concerning the big differences between himself and Thrasymachus (345e). Socrates asks Thrasymachus if he thinks that rulers – in the true or precise sense, those "who rule truly," inasmuch as they understand the art of ruling – rule willingly. When Thrasymachus answers that he doesn't merely think so, he knows so, Socrates brings out the fact that this is a key part of their disagreement. Socrates holds that no one who really knows or understands the political art practices it willingly, or indeed practices any art willingly. The clearest evidence, Socrates submits, is that every craftsman wants to be paid wages for practicing his art: The craftsman of rule does not regard ruling itself, or the practice of any art, as in itself sufficiently advantageous for the practitioner. But what defines each craftsman, as the craftsman that he is, is not his moneymaking, since he shares that with all the other crafts, but rather the particular capacity his art gives him to procure a specific and unique sort of benefit for his clients or subjects. And Thrasymachus is once again compelled, reluctantly (346c–d), to agree that the craftsman as craftsman of any ruling art does not, in practicing his craft, seek his own advantage. Hence, Socrates concludes (346e–347a) that since the one "who is to do anything fine [noble] by art never does what is best for himself nor does he command it," but "rather what is best for the one who is ruled," no one ever willingly chooses to rule, except for some kind recompense beyond the ruling – money, or honor, or avoiding a penalty.

It seems that Thrasymachus's practice of his teaching craft has been deeply ambiguous, and that prior to this confrontation with Socrates he has never felt the need to sort out precisely – even or especially in his own mind – first, whose good is his ultimate goal in his teaching and, second, whose good he is teaching his students to think is the ultimate goal of their rule. But Socrates is compelling Thrasymachus – and the onlookers – to confront this question of the good (meaning, "whose good," *cui bono?*).

At this point the refuted and self-contradictory Thrasymachus either falls silent or is given no opportunity to answer, because the puzzled Glaucon intervenes to ask what Socrates means by "the penalty" that may be avoided by ruling. And when we consider what Thrasymachus says when he comes back a few pages later into the argument (at 348c), we are forced to conclude that while Thrasymachus may have been refuted in speech, he has not, up to this point, been convinced or refuted in his heart or in his beliefs. He is likely at this point still to think that he has been outmaneuvered by some sort of sophistic tricks. He still does not fully grasp or feel in his bones the contradiction Socrates has in fact revealed in his outlook, the contradiction between the conviction that ruling is exploiting and the conviction that ruling is an art, benefiting the ruled, an art of which Thrasymachus is the generously dedicated and beneficial, and therefore richly deserving, teacher.

Socrates has indicated that he is convinced that it is the latter outlook that is the deeper, though less obvious, basis of Thrasymachus's life, and Plato prods us to consider whether what motivates noble political ambition generally may not be a version of the latter outlook – the quest to become meritorious on the basis of public service. But Socrates draws a conclusion that moves in a challenging and even troubling different direction. He answers Glaucon that the "most decent" (*epieikestatoi*) rule willingly not out of any conviction that ruling is good for them, or from any ambition to win deserved money or honor for public service, but only when they have to rule in order to avoid the penalty, for themselves, of being ruled by someone "more wicked" – or (Socrates corrects himself) because they don't have any who are better than or similar to themselves to whom they can turn over the task. Socrates goes on to make a striking pronouncement that brings to an end his refutation of Thrasymachus's thesis that justice is the advantage of the stronger: "I am afraid that if a city of good men came to be, there would be a fight over not ruling, just as there is now over ruling"; "there it would become manifest that in reality a true ruler does not by nature look to his own advantage but rather that of the one who is ruled." From this "it follows that everyone who is a knower would choose to be benefited by another rather than to take the trouble of benefiting another. In this way, then, I in no way agree with Thrasymachus that the just is the advantage of the stronger" (347d). Without giving Glaucon a chance to respond to, or to question, this remarkable statement, Socrates says that they will investigate it some other time, and insists that they turn to another question raised by Thrasymachus, namely, whether the unjust life is superior to the just. Socrates had a little earlier (at 345a) declared emphatically that he does *not* think that injustice is "more gainful" (*kerdaleoteron*) than justice – and Socrates had said he was sure others present felt the same. Socrates did not there make it clear what he meant by justice, although he certainly implied justice meant not cheating or oppressing through violence. Now (at 347e) Glaucon immediately and emphatically says he rejects Thrasymachus's claims and stands on the side of those who say the just life is "more profitable" (*lusitelesteron*) – and we see that Glaucon is a strong partisan of justice, even when or though he doesn't yet quite understand what it is. Socrates does not here declare his own opinion; instead, he proposes that they try to persuade Thrasymachus that he is wrong. As Socrates confesses at the end of book one, however, there is something very inadequate about the argumentation that now follows.

The Just Life Is Superior to the Unjust

The first of Socrates' next arguments refuting Thrasymachus proves, on the basis of the premises of Thrasymachus, that justice is *virtue*, or excellence and wisdom. This constitutes a refutation of Thrasymachus, for at the outset the latter affirms "the opposite" (348c) – that it is injustice that is virtue, since injustice is more profitable. But if injustice is virtue, then, Thrasymachus agrees, he means that injustice is fine or noble as well as mighty. Thrasymachus goes even further – he agrees that, in understanding injustice to be virtue, he invests injustice with everything that Socrates and Glaucon ascribe to justice. And Socrates says that he thinks Thrasymachus now really is speaking with "daring" and expressing what he truly believes, without any joking (349a). Socrates thus underlines the fact that Thrasymachus really does think that he *admires* injustice, as a *virtue*, and prides himself on having injustice, as virtue – and prides himself on being a teacher of injustice, as virtue.

Socrates next asks Thrasymachus whether it is not the case that the just man does *not* try to get the better of another just man, but does claim to *deserve* more than the unjust man and considers this *deserving* to be just, a just claim of desert for his virtue (349b). Thrasymachus agrees emphatically. But, Socrates asks, what about the unjust person? Does he not claim to *deserve* to get the better of the just man? Thrasymachus says that he of course does, since the unjust man claims to *deserve* to get the better of everyone. Socrates next gets Thrasymachus to agree that since the unjust man is wise and good, he must resemble the wise and good, or all other sorts of wisdom and goodness; and if he resembles them, he is exactly like them (349d). Then Socrates reintroduces the arts, along with wisdom and goodness in the arts – adducing as examples first music and then medicine. He forces Thrasymachus to admit that the wise and good musician does *not* seek to do better at tuning his instrument, and hence to *deserve* more, than another musician, but the same. So too for a doctor: A truly skilled doctor seeks to prescribe the same food and drink as another truly skilled doctor – in the practice of his art, he does not compete to do better than another skilled practitioner but better than someone unskilled or less skilled. And in every science or art, Socrates forces Thrasymachus to agree, the expert seeks to do and to get the same as another expert, and to do better and to get more than the nonexpert. Only nonexperts seek to do better than the expert as well as another non-expert, or claim to deserve more than an expert – presumably because they do not really know or appreciate what expertise is and deserves. But then it is the just man who resembles the experts, the knowers or the wise in the arts, and it is the unjust who, in seeking to get more and in claiming to deserve more than everyone, resembles the unskilled. And it was agreed that whatever something resembles, it is; so the just man is wise and prudent, the unjust man the contrary.

Now Socrates says at the end (350c–d) that, in fact, the argument did not proceed as easily as he has just told it, but Thrasymachus was very resistant, and sweating, and finally blushing – which Socrates had never seen him do before. And this provokes us to ask: What exactly is it that has finally made a man who is so hardheaded and sophisticated sweat and blush? What painful defect has he seen detected in himself? Does he not finally see that Socrates has shown him to be in fact a kind of moralist, even or precisely in his praise of immorality, of injustice? Socrates has brought out, first, Thrasymachus's belief that injustice is a virtue, admirable because centered on knowledge, and, second, that knowledge as science or art has standards, to which the craftsman adheres, with an expectation of desert. The artist or knower prides himself not on getting the better of everyone but on conforming to the standards all knowers share – and on being superior to the non-knowers. On account of that dedication, the skilled craftsman claims to *deserve* a recompense, above all honor and respect – implying that sticking to the art is not in itself simply profitable, but involves risk and sacrifice, for the good of others.

Having blushed, having thus disclosed that he has begun to realize how deep is the contradiction within himself, Thrasymachus in effect throws in the towel; he says he still has something to say, but only in a long speech, *not* in answers to questions – and since they won't let him deliver an oration, he will answer only perfunctorily.

Socrates takes advantage of this lack of resistance to present two further brief arguments showing that justice is stronger than injustice, and concludes his encounter with Thrasymachus with very strong praise of the life of justice versus the life of injustice. But at the very end of book one, Socrates criticizes himself for having failed to finish the first investigation, into what justice is, before rushing to the second, the investigation into whether justice was more profitable than injustice. The result, he declares at the end (354b–c), is that he knows nothing from the conversation, for how can one know whether justice is a virtue, or that it is more profitable than injustice, if one doesn't first clarify what justice is? Certainly the last three arguments in book one are, as Socrates himself stresses (at 348b), very rhetorical. In them Socrates shows himself to be a defender of justice. But does not this suggest that Socrates knows a lot about what justice is, or that he exaggerates at the end insofar as he suggests that he is totally ignorant of what justice is? Is it possible that Socrates thinks that through careful reflection on the refutations in book one of the *Republic* the answer to the question of what justice is can be descried?

However that may be, the confessed inadequacy of Socrates' arguments provokes the passionate protest and eloquent intervention of Glaucon, seconded by his more measured brother, Adeimantus, thus ushering in the third and longest portion of the *Republic*. In the dialogue with Glaucon and Adeimantus, Socrates enlarges the inquiry into the meaning of justice by constructing as a thought experiment the best imaginable city, and looking for justice within it and within the souls of its citizen-rulers. Space does not permit our following the elaboration of this thought experiment. We stress only that it leads to Socrates declaring, in no uncertain terms, that it is not possible for him to conceive how the city he has imagined could ever come into being in actuality; the elaboration of the imagined republic is truly a thought experiment, like a painting of some mythic figure (472c–473b; see also 592a–b). As Plato has the philosophic spokesman in his longest dialogue declare, "the most beautiful and best way of life," insofar as it can be imitated by the best political regime, "is really the truest tragedy" (*Laws* 817b–c). One may say that classical political philosophy as a whole is tragic wisdom, inasmuch as it is wisdom about the insuperable tensions, and thus limitations, of all civic life. Yet Socrates taught that "he who is by art a tragic poet is also a comic poet" (*Symposium* 223d). Life is redeemed from tragedy and even partakes in some measure of a divine comedy insofar as it can become philosophic life, which is lived "looking away toward the god" and thereby transcending the inevitably tragic tensions and thus limits of civic existence (*Laws* 804a–b).

We turn now from Plato and his Socrates to the greatest student of Plato, Aristotle – who embarked in his *Politics* on the more practical project of showing how the political philosophy originated by Socrates and Plato can address itself to political men directly, to illuminate what they are doing, or aspiring to do, in actual political life.

3

Aristotle's *Politics*

Aristotle (384–322 BC) published dialogues, but they have all been long lost, except for small fragments. What survives of his writings are treatises, based on lecture courses that he gave at his school in Athens called the "Lyceum." Lectures are of course orations, exercises in rhetoric, and Aristotle's treatises constitute a magnificent new version of the art of civically responsible philosophic teaching that we have seen displayed and taught by Plato and his Socrates. We have learned from Plato that *the* first principle of such rhetoric is the realization that the philosopher's radically skeptical moral questioning is dangerous for lawful society. Aristotle himself stresses that "law has *no* strength, as regards being obeyed, *except* habit; and this does not come into being except through length of time" (*Politics** 1269a20–21; consider the context). Philosophic questioning essentially challenges the moral habituation that is the sole strong basis of lawful society. Responsible public expression of philosophic questioning must therefore be cautiously muted and muffled.

Accordingly, Aristotle begins his *Politics* in a tone that is anything but skeptical. He starts out making a number of very big claims on behalf of the nobility and the supremacy in rank of politics, as lived in the self-governing, republican city – the *polis*. He asserts that that city is a "community" (*koinonia*) whose aim is *the* most authoritative good, encompassing *all* other goods of all other communities. (He gives no indication, at the start of the *Politics*, that the philosophic life and friendship might transcend the city – as he suggests near the end of his *Nicomachean Ethics*.)

---

* We recommend the translation by Carnes Lord, second edition (Chicago: University of Chicago Press, 2013), and the translation by Peter L. Phillips Simpson (Chapel Hill: University of North Carolina Press, 1997), even though he rearranges the order of the books as that order has come down to us. Translations in this chapter (and emphases within quotations) are our own, and all citations are by standard Bekker page and line numbers.

No one before or after Aristotle has ever commenced a book by making such enormous claims for the scope and supremacy of politics.

But Aristotle feels compelled to bring to the reader's attention the fact that there are thinkers who do not share his elevated conception of politics. Going on the attack, Aristotle criticizes these thinkers as expressing an understanding that is "not *noble*" or "not *beautiful*" (*kalon*). More specifically, Aristotle criticizes these unnamed thinkers for confusing political rule with other types of rule, and especially with household management. These unnamed opponents make the mistake of conceiving political rule as paternalistic, like the rule of a parent over children. Hence they claim that monarchy is a kind of political rule, whereas Aristotle denies that monarchy is political rule. Still worse, these opponents suppose that there is no qualitative difference between political rule and mastery over slaves. Now of course, by attacking these views at the outset, Aristotle draws attention to them. He provokes his readers to see that what he is claiming about politics is controversial. He prods us to think for ourselves about what the arguments might be for these opposing views that he attacks.

Then Aristotle does something strange. He declares that the truth of his view, and the untruth of his opponents' views, will become clear "if we carry out our investigation in the usual way" – which is to analyze a whole into its smallest indivisible parts. This would mean that we should start our study of the political whole by studying the individuals who make up the city: the citizens. But in what immediately follows, Aristotle does *not* proceed in this way. Instead, he declares that the "noble" or "beautiful" way of studying the city is to assume that it is something that "grows" – like a plant or an animal. Hence he does not start with individual citizens, but with the family, and assumes that the family is the embryo out of which the civic organism grows, over time. This approach rather conspicuously avoids (and provokes readers familiar with Plato to ponder) the sort of question pressed by Thrasymachus and Glaucon in Plato's *Republic*: whether the city or civic association is not artificial, a product of human convention or contract entered into by essentially antagonistic individuals.

The Human Is by Nature a Political Animal

Aristotle will indeed hint at this line of questioning as needing investigation, but in chapter two he proceeds on the initial assumption that the city is an organism that grows. Yet he at once makes clear that the city is a very odd kind of naturally growing community. It is not like other natural animal societies – beehives, ant colonies, wolf packs. Those other natural animal communities have forms that are unvarying, whereas the city does not emerge except after a long time, out of earlier social forms. Still more provocatively, Aristotle soon reminds us that more often than not, the independent city utterly fails to emerge, and what emerges instead is the large-scale "nation" (*ethnos*).

The first stage in the process of growth of the city is the household, based primarily on sexual coupling. Sexual coupling, Aristotle says, is the ever-present manifestation of human sociability, without which the species would not survive, and it results not from choice, but from a natural drive shared with other life-forms. Aristotle immediately adds that the *human* household also entails *slavery* – at the least, the enslavement of animals. This, he notes, involves foresight and intelligence (unlike sexual coupling): It is through mastery over slaves that humanity, in its distinctively *intelligent* sociability, first clearly manifests itself. Instead of addressing the question of the justification for human slavery, Aristotle moves immediately to a different question: that of the relation between slavery and women. Can or should women be treated as slaves? No: This is contrary to nature, Aristotle answers. And at this point, he begins to speak of nature in an amazing way – as a female personality, having intentions, who has purposefully crafted the various beings in nature with specific, unique functions: "the female is distinguished by Nature from the slave." For "Nature [fem.] makes nothing in an economizing spirit," but "one thing with a view to one thing; and each instrument would perform most nobly if it served one task rather than many" (1252a34–b4). Here we see that Aristotle is *the* philosopher of intelligent design – by a female divinity in, or identified with, Nature. Is Aristotle serious? Or is this his responsible religious rhetoric?

Aristotle leads from Nature's intention regarding the non-slave status of women to a political point: It is characteristic of "barbarians," Aristotle observes, to fail to obey Nature's intention in this basic respect; "barbarians" treat women as slaves. So the primary distinction between civilization and barbarism, for Aristotle, is whether or not women are regarded as slaves, as property. Aristotle explains the reason why barbarians treat women as property: The male barbarians are themselves lacking a knowledge of, or capacity for, truly free human rule. Being free as a human requires being able to rule as a human, and human ruling requires the recognition that women – mothers, wives, sisters – are also free, and should be ruled as free.

At this point Aristotle takes another big step: "This is why," he says, the *poets* assert that "it is fitting for Greeks to rule barbarians" – "the assumption being, that barbarian and slave are by nature the same thing" (1252b8–9). Aristotle makes it sound as if the Greek poets assume that peoples whose men rule over the women as slaves are unfit to rule themselves and ought to be dominated, as slaves, by the civilized Greeks. Now this is the first quotation from any poet in the *Politics*. We recall how very important the poets are in Greek cultural life and education; they are the bringers of the inspired word from the gods. Does Aristotle agree with the poets? Does he accept their authority? He here seems to. But one of the most important rules for beginning to catch on to Aristotle, or to any careful philosophic writer, is this: Whenever a philosopher quotes a sacred text, one must always check the original source to discover, and to mediate on, the context. One will often discover that the philosopher is quietly indicating his dissent from the sacred authority. In this case the quote is from Euripides' famous play *Iphigenia in Aulis*. The play is about human sacrifice, to the female goddess Diana, of a daughter, Iphigenia, by her father. The line Aristotle quotes is spoken by the daughter just before she is burned on the altar. Iphigenia is claiming that it is all right for fathers to burn their daughters as human sacrifices to the gods, because all Greeks agree that women are worth very little in comparison with men.

What is Aristotle quietly asking the reader to think about here? We suggest two things. First, the Greeks may not be so far removed, in Aristotle's eyes, from the barbarians. Second, there is an enormous difference between Aristotle's philosophic understanding of divinity, of Nature as divine – and the traditional Greek poetic conception of the gods and the sacrifices those gods demand.

The subtle critique of the Greeks and their traditions, their poetic authorities, continues with the immediately following poetic quotation, from Hesiod's *Works and Days*: "From these two partnerships, then, the household first arose," says Aristotle, and "Hesiod's verse is rightly spoken: 'first a house, and woman, and ox for plowing'" (1252b10–12). When one looks up the context of this quote, one finds that in the next line in the poem, Hesiod advises that one ought to buy the woman as a slave. This verse of Hesiod's is obviously *not* "rightly spoken" in the philosopher's opinion. Aristotle again implicitly provokes his thoughtful readers to ask: Have the Greeks yet fully transcended their own barbaric past? In other words, we begin to see that while Aristotle elevates and praises the city and its *apparent* culmination among the *Greeks*, he more quietly but acutely raises some very big doubts about the city, and especially its Greek version.

From sexual coupling, and enslavement, of animals and then of humans, emerges the household and, from the union of many households, the village (1252b15ff). Aristotle notes that the village tends to be ruled in the way that the family originally is ruled – by a patriarch, monarchically. Aristotle goes on to make it clear that in a sense this is the stage most human societies never get beyond. Humans remain always in families, which tend to be ruled monarchically, by the patriarchal father; as humans come together in larger and larger societies, these bigger societies tend to remain rooted in the family mode of thinking, under patriarchal-monarchic rule: They are ruled by a king, or a "premier," or a "president" who is a kind of father figure. "This," says Aristotle, "is why *cities* were at *first* under kings, *and nations are even now.*" *Nations* represent a kind of short-circuiting of the natural maturation of human civic development. Nations leaves their inhabitants in the primitive condition of being ruled monarchically, like children, by some central authority in which the inhabitants do not participate. The truly natural, if rare, culmination of human maturation is the independent republican city, where a large portion of the inhabitants can and must participate directly in the highest sovereign decisions, without being led by any single fatherlike figure.

What is even more remarkable about this passage is that Aristotle quietly indicates that *all religion* is a kind of throwback to the patriarchal forms of human society: "And this why *all* assert that the *gods* are under a king – because they themselves are still under kings now, or were in antiquity." For "even as human beings assimilate the looks of the gods to themselves, so they do with their ways of life as well" (1252b24–27). Here Aristotle quotes Homer, *the* supreme poetic authority.

Independent urban life, Aristotle goes on to say, is the stage that is truly complete, self-sufficient. The city is a form of society in which humans are not compelled to devote almost all their attention to daily needs. The city is a form of society in which humans have *leisure.* It is the use of leisure that constitutes the city's most important claim to true, that is, spiritual, self-sufficiency. In this leisure, the higher – the truly human – spiritual needs and capacities, which before lay dormant, can emerge: "The city possesses the limit of entire self-sufficiency, so to speak; and while coming into being for the sake of living, it exists for the sake of living well" (1252b28–30).

The city, Aristotle goes on to say, is that for the sake of which the earlier social forms came into being. This is quite a radical statement when we consider what it implies about the family. The family exists for the sake of the city, for the sake of the political community – not the other way around. Aristotle then makes still clearer what he means, in perhaps his most famous statement: "By nature the human being is a political animal." For "the human alone among the animals has rational speech" (*logos*), which "serves to reveal the advantageous and the harmful, and hence also the just and the unjust, and other things [of this sort]; and partnership in these things is what makes a household and a city" (1253a2–19). The humanly social is the living together that actualizes the human capacities for collective self-government based on rational discourse, debate, and collective action guided by reason. Humans discover, in and through the life of a republican *polis*, that the development and employment of their capacities for collective, rational self-government is something more than merely a means to other ends, such as prosperity, security, family, and empire. They discover the joyfully fulfilling character of these civic capacities and experiences as the very ends of life, as involving the challenges that make life truly worthwhile and complete. This is why *only* a small, participatory republican society is a *fully* human society.

Aristotle proceeds to bring out some of the controversial implications of his thesis that the human is a political animal by nature. First, human beings are fulfilled by being *parts*, of the larger natural whole that is the city. The *individual*, as such, is naturally incomplete, spiritually as well as physically; the individual is to the city as the hand is to the whole body (1253a19–27). Aristotle, one might say, speaks emphatically as a communitarian rather than as an individualist. He will not speak much of *individual rights*. Instead, his focus will be on the fulfillment the individual finds through dedication and even devotion to the city, through the noble civic *virtues*. Yet Aristotle adds a striking qualification: "One who is incapable of participating, *or who is in need of nothing through being self-sufficient*, is no part of a city, and so is either a beast *or a god*" (1253a28–29, our emphasis; cf. 1267a8–12). Aristotle thus tacitly points off toward the philosophic life, the life of radical spiritual independence, which he shows that he is going to present as divine or godlike, and thus, in a religious fashion, as transcending political life and community.

Aristotle adds another large qualification to his thesis on the naturalness of the city. We must, he says, bless the man who first *put a city together*, and hence caused these great goods (1253a29–30). The philosopher discloses here that the city is a *construct*. To be sure, the construction is not artificial but is rather in accordance with nature. But this presents a paradox: Politics is natural, but it arises from human choice, thought, and construction, and hence not automatically. Humans express their social nature very differently from the other animals. Humans do not follow instinct or a program but follow reason or thought or opinion, and hence must discover and work out for themselves what is best for their nature. Unlike the other animals, therefore, humans make many mistakes, they often distort or fail to express their nature, and the truly natural society is therefore rare and fragile.

What is more, this entails that humans are by nature capable of going *very* bad: "Even as the human is the best of the animals when completed, when separated from law and adjudication he is the worst of all"; indeed, "without virtue, he is the most unholy and most savage" (1253a38). Humans need justice not only to fulfill themselves but, more primarily and massively, to prevent themselves from falling into hideous abuse of one another. Hence humans need not only republican participation but the rule of law – law limiting what humans can do in politics; law narrowing the range of discretion; law forcing everyone to follow the same or similar rules, and not allowing themselves what they will not allow to others. Aristotle thus shows that he is in no way sentimental or "optimistic" about the human potential. Most of the time, humans abuse their potential. Much of political life is trying to prevent the bad rather than to realize the good.

Moral Virtue and Political Rule

In the rest of book one, Aristotle examines the household, which remains in some sense the cornerstone of civic life. While it represents an earlier, less fully human, stage in mankind's natural development, the household is not superseded by the city. It persists within and as a part of the city. But this means that the private family looms as a rival focus of the citizen's attachment, concern, devotion, and hopes for fulfillment. In chapters three to eleven, which we do not have space to examine, Aristotle shows how problematic, how much in need of subordination, are the two mundane concerns that tend to preoccupy household management – the employment and acquisition of human slaves and the acquisition and employment of other material property. Here again, Aristotle presents Nature as a beneficent, purposeful being who "provides" and "does nothing in vain," but he quietly raises doubts about this even as he presents it. For example, by pointing out that slaves are needed for both production and action, and that only those who are severely deficient in intellectual ability would justly be called natural slaves, Aristotle allows us to see that there are in fact no humans who are natural slaves, just as he quietly shows that nature in fact "provides" only for those who work for their living.

In the last few pages of book one, Aristotle turns to the higher aspects of family life. The chief focus of a fully human household should be not property, but rather the education in virtue of human beings, and especially the free human beings – the spouses and children (1259b18–21). Aristotle here lays out the famous four cardinal virtues: *courage*, or rational governance of one's fears and anger; *moderation*, or rational control of one's desires for pleasure; *justice*, or rational subordination of self-interest to the common good; and *prudence*, or practical judgment about how to implement the other three virtues in all sorts of specific situations. Aristotle makes clearer here what he has repeatedly indicated throughout book one, about the kind of virtue that politics and the family should be mainly concerned with: *moral* virtue, the virtue of *practical* life, which, though it includes prudence, is quite different from *intellectual* virtue, as the virtue of science or philosophy. *Intellectual* virtue is the excellence of deep critical thinking, questioning, analyzing – the activity from which Aristotle's treatise sprang, and that is needed in readers if they are to learn the most important lessons in his treatise. *Moral* virtue, by contrast, is the virtue of the emotions, the passions, in action. The virtue of healthy, well-educated emotions is *obeying* practical reason's persuasion – like subjects obeying a king, or children a parent. The virtue of practical reasoning (prudence) is excellence in being the patriarch or king of one's own emotions. The education that produces such virtue is acquired or instilled *not* through reading books, or going to school, or thinking and debating, but through practice, practice, practice. Learning moral virtue is much more like learning to play a musical instrument than it is like learning to question and to argue thoughtfully. Moral education requires giving to young people repeated and increasingly difficult emotional challenges in actual experience – of dangers in war and in peace, of adjudications between conflicting claims to justice, of exposure to temptations of pleasure and pain.

But to understand fully the proper cultivation of the four cardinal virtues in wife and children, Aristotle says, we must understand the specific kind of rule that is to be exercised over children, on the one hand, and wives, on the other. We must always contrast both types of rule, as rule over free persons, with the mastery over slaves. Children are non-slaves but also not-yet-fully-free; they have *potential* virtue that requires and deserves monarchic rule. But wives, Aristotle says, are adults who should *not* be ruled as children, still less as slaves; wives have a fulfilled capacity for virtue that requires and deserves republican governance. Aristotle here illuminates what he means by republican or truly political rule, by contrast with despotic and monarchic rule – which contrast, we recall, was a major point he insisted on at the beginning of the whole work. The husband's rule over his wife is *the* paradigm of truly political rule (1259a41). From this we learn that political rule has four defining characteristics. First, unlike the rule over slave or over child, political rule is effected through adult, rational, shared deliberation and consent, in which those being ruled contribute something to the deliberation and must have their concerns taken seriously. Second, political rule is primarily for the good of the governed, not the governor. Third, political rule, no less than monarchic rule, always means hierarchy – the rulers have the final say and issue commands. But fourth – and here is where the peculiarity of the husband-wife relationship appears – in most political rule, commanding offices *rotate* among the citizens; the citizens take turns being the ruler, because, Aristotle says, political rule "wishes by its nature to be on an equal footing and to differ in nothing" (1259b5). Now this brings out a deep paradox in the concept of true political rule. Such rule by nature seeks to be *both* hierarchical *and* equal. In fact, Aristotle notes how the ambiguity of political rule manifests itself in actual political customs in republics. Where citizens are in fact pretty much equal in virtue and ability, they strive to *hide* that equality through rituals and customs that make the one temporarily ruling *seem* somehow superior. Does Aristotle not begin to bring out here a tension in the very concept of political rule? Aristotle stresses that the political rule of the husband avoids this tension: The wife is always ruled, rather than ruling; the hierarchy of husband over wife is fixed. But what is the justification or reason for this fixity?

Aristotle gives a strangely ambiguous set of reasons. First, he says (1259a43) that the husband or male is by nature more "hegemonic" or "expert at leading." Aristotle notes, however, that this natural superiority of male over female does not always hold. This of course provokes the question: In these cases, where the female is not inferior at leading, ought not the wife to lead, some or all of the time? In the next chapter, Aristotle pursues the question. It is a puzzle, he says, why women don't deserve a turn at ruling (1259b32ff.). He goes on to give a justification based on female psychology, and hence virtue: Whereas "the slave is wholly lacking the deliberative element," and "the child has it, but it is

incomplete" (*ateles*) the female "has it, but it is *not in control*" (*akuron*)
(1260a10). What do these last words mean? Does Aristotle mean that
in the male soul, deliberative reason has better control over the emotions? Or does he mean that men do not allow women to be in control?
His only hint of an answer is something quite strange: He mentions
Socrates for the first time, and points out that Socrates insisted that a
woman's courage and justice are the same as a man's. Aristotle says that
the position he is here defending is "contrary to what Socrates thought."
Then Aristotle calls in an authority, over and against Socrates – the
poet Sophocles; he quotes a line from his famous play *Ajax*: "Silence
brings adornment to a woman" (1260a28). The context of this line is
of course crucial to gauging Aristotle's point. The context turns out to
be quite extraordinary. In the play, the hero Ajax goes raving mad, in
the middle of the night. Just as he does so, and is starting off to murder his fellow leaders in the Greek camp, his wife wakes up and tries
to persuade him from going off to commit mass murder. The words
Aristotle quotes as his authority for the correctness of the permanent
rule of husbands over wives are part of the speech that the insane Ajax
gives in rejecting the entreaties of his prudent wife. In this rather lurid,
tongue-in-cheek-fashion, Aristotle leaves us to figure out for ourselves
the extent to which he endorses, and the extent to which he questions,
the conventional view as regards the permanent and universal subordination of wives to husbands.

In the second book of the *Politics*, which we are compelled to skip,
Aristotle surveys and discusses critically all the greatest previous attempts
to articulate what would be the best form of political regime. We note
only this: The discussion makes clear that the actual existing regime that
Aristotle admires the most is that of Carthage – a non-Greek city, run
by Africans. Aristotle quietly indicates that it is *not Greeks* who have succeeded best at politics.

The Contest over the "Political Regime"

Book three, the heart of the *Politics*, opens on a note of remarkable puzzlement: "For one investigating the *political regime* – what each sort is
and what its quality – virtually the first investigation concerns the city,
to see what in the world the city actually is" (1274b32). The city comes
to sight as problematic as soon as one begins to investigate the *regime*
(*politeia*). Aristotle begins from a perplexity that constantly emerges in
actual politics, in times of crisis or revolution and fundamental political

change – especially, he indicates, when there is a change to democracy from oligarchy or from tyranny. The new democracy asks: Was the previous government or ruling group really the city or the country? Must we keep the commitments, pay the debts, remain allies with the friends, of the city under the *previous* regime? What Aristotle had given in book one, we now see, was an overly harmonious picture of the city or the political community. In actual fact, Aristotle now stresses, politics is riven by disputes among quarreling partisans of alternative, competing answers to a fundamental question: Which "regime" or form of government truly speaks for, truly is, the city or country?

This is a problem that characterizes not just the *polis* known to antiquity. It is a basic problem that is endemic to all mature political life everywhere. And throughout book three we will see that Aristotle is speaking not simply about the ancient *polis* but about the fundamental alternative claimants in all political life, in all times and places.

To make clearer what is at stake in this fundamental controversy, Aristotle turns to the question of who is a *citizen* – who really belongs, that is, who has a right to participate. He immediately shows that this question is also disputed, or is a big part of the dispute over the regime. The argument over which regime is the true city is an argument over who truly belongs. Aristotle asks: Just what is at stake in this question of citizenship? What does it mean to be a citizen? The word is used, he notes, to designate a range of lesser and fuller degrees of belonging. Citizenship is not just being an inhabitant of a country, and not even having some judicial rights. Moreover, citizenship is for some persons only partial or incomplete, as in the case of children, or the retired who can no longer hold office, or those convicted of crimes and incarcerated or exiled. But by considering what these *partial* citizens *lack*, we can see what *full* citizenship means. A citizen in the complete sense is one who fully and truly shares in decision making and in office (1275a22).

But Aristotle proceeds to question this first definition. Some high offices are held only for a term, and one cannot hold them twice. Are we going to say that only people who are holding these offices are citizens? Aristotle responds that there are also offices that are open to many and that are held indefinitely: the jury and the sovereign assembly. He therefore proposes a revised definition: Let a citizen in the full sense be one who participates in both the sovereign assembly and the juries.

But then Aristotle immediately notes that this also is too restricted a definition. For there are many regimes that do not even have sovereign assemblies or juries. Aristotle now stresses that there are many regimes, some having "priority" and others being "*incorrect* and *deviant*" (1275b1). And the definition that we have arrived at works only for democracies. Aristotle therefore gives a more loose definition, in order to cover all regimes, including the nondemocratic. A citizen, he now says, is one who is entitled or has a right, and hence a potential – not necessarily ever realized – to *perhaps* become, from time to time, a magistrate (1275b4–20).

But does all this not suggest that democracy is the "prior" or correct regime, and that nondemocratic regimes are "deviant"? Isn't citizenship in a direct democracy both fuller or more intense, for each person who is engaged in the democracy's sovereign assembly, *and* more inclusive, of more inhabitants? Aristotle points to this conclusion, but he does not draw it. We are forced to wonder why not. Is there some good reason why such democratic intensity and inclusiveness are not in fact sound?

Aristotle next raises two big questions about the definition at which we have arrived. First, he reminds us that in every society, whatever else citizenship means or however intense and inclusive it is, whether one is a citizen is to a large extent determined by the accident of birth – where one is born and from whom. Aristotle reminds us, in other words, of something rather arbitrary, something merely conventional or legal, that is decisive in determining who belongs and who does not. In the second place, Aristotle confronts an even bigger question, a question raised by what happens after revolutions, when people raise the question of *justice* concerning citizenship. People question whether the law determining citizenship, or determining who really belongs, is a *just* or an *unjust* law. Aristotle gives the example of a democratic revolution that occurred in Athens, where some slaves and aliens were elevated to full citizenship. Opponents of that democratic revolution apparently said that these new citizens were not *justly* citizens – that they had no *right* to citizenship, presumably because they were *unqualified*. Aristotle brings out the implication of these objectors: A question can indeed be raised whether someone who is not *justly* a citizen is *really* a citizen, even if the law happens to say that he is. If we consider ruling, Aristotle argues, we see that the same issue arises: One can ask whether even the *lawful* rulers are *justly* rulers and therefore *really* rulers. The answer that Aristotle first suggests, the answer that reflects political reality, is that even those who are *un*justly citizens, and *un*justly rulers, if they are *legally* citizens and rulers, are still the *real* rulers and the *real* citizens. Do justice and injustice, then, not affect political reality?

At the start of the next or third chapter Aristotle makes it clear that the point we have reached is still problematic. And by this time we are seeing more clearly how our philosophic teacher is proceeding. He poses a fundamental question about political life, and then presents evidence from the way people speak and think about the matter, in order to come to an initial answer. He then questions that answer, on the basis of other, contradictory opinions also voiced by people involved in actual politics. He shows how the dispute can be seen to lead or point to a more refined and complete answer – about which he then raises new questions. In other words, Aristotle is proceeding dialectically and seeking to draw the reader into the inquiry with him. His purpose is not only or primarily to give us the answers but rather to help us to understand and to think for ourselves about the full problems, or the fully problematic character, of politics.

At the start of chapter three Aristotle reminds us of the big question with which he started: Partisans of one regime often say that another regime cannot and did not or does not really speak for or express the city. But now he has made it clearer that in effect what these complaints are expressing, in each case, is the view that the legal rulers and citizens, and the legal standards or qualifications of rulers and citizens, are *not just.* People are expressing their conviction that *justice* is more important than sheer power. And what they mean by justice is first and foremost the *common* benefit – the benefit not of a part, but of the whole. But then Aristotle adds a critique also of democracy, on this basis. If the majority, when it dominates, does so in the interest of the majority, *exploiting* minorities, then it too fails the test of justice as service to the common good.

We see now more clearly the most important dimension of what is at stake in the most fundamental dispute that defines all political life – the dispute among the competing regimes. All the competing regimes – for example, democracy, monarchy, aristocracy, oligarchy, and different subtypes of each and mixtures of them – *claim* to be just. And by this they mean first and foremost that they understand and aim at the true common good. They are quarreling over competing conceptions of what it means to serve the common good; each regime claims that its competitors are misguided or deceitful in *their* claim to promote the common good. Each regime claims that the *other* regimes are in *this* way deviant, to a greater or lesser extent.

Aristotle takes this conflict over justice seriously, and spends the rest of book three exploring all that is involved in it, and how it can best be resolved, in principle and in many diverse sets of circumstances. The refereeing of this controversy among regimes over justice is the central theme of Aristotle's *Politics*.

Before launching this enterprise, however, Aristotle pauses, still in chapter three, to make clearer the supreme significance of the regime and of the dispute among the regimes, and to reject an alternative way of conceiving human society or of the city – a way that he calls "most obvious," but that he sees as superficial (1276a17ff.). He raises or confronts the question: May it not be the case that the political regime, the arrangement of who are the rulers and who shares in eligibility to rule, is *not* what is most important in shaping the life of a society and defining what a society is? Some say, after all, that it is not politics, not who rules and who is a citizen, that is most important. Rather, they claim, what are most important are the land and the people – meaning the population's shared ethnicity, blood ties, family, language, and historical traditions over generations.

In response, Aristotle argues that the land and its inhabitants are indeed the necessary *matter* of political society – the clay, if you will. But the *character* of the society depends decisively on the way this matter is *formed* or organized. What gives a society or city its defining character is what *type* of person rules, with what *specific* conception of justice and other virtues, embodied in a distinct *way of life*. The kind of people who rule, and the ends for which they rule, set the direction of the whole society, determining which human qualities are to be encouraged and fostered, and which human characteristics are to be discouraged and condemned. A change in regime changes the way of life of everyone in the society. To make vivid his point, Aristotle uses the analogy of a drama, as well as of a musical composition. The very same persons may be actors in totally different plays, comic and tragic: What gives the dramas their specific characters are the *scripts*. Again, the very same notes may be employed in totally different musical compositions: What defines the composition is not the notes but the score. Politics writes the "script" or the "score" of social existence. Each regime will embody in its ruling personnel, and cultivate in others, certain basic notions of what is respectable and what is disgraceful, what is admirable and what is contemptible. And if not immediately, then over time, nothing is as influential in shaping the young and the people living in a society as these public, lawful moral standards. To be sure, there always are dissidents, opponents of the prevailing regime; no regime can dominate totally. But the qualities the regime promotes will still tend to dominate until it is weakened or undermined or overthrown.

The Standard for Judging the Contest among Regimes

Aristotle's manner of proceeding in the next two chapters is surprising and puzzling. He does not, as one might expect, raise and pursue the question as to what the true common good is. Instead, he raises another kind of moral question: He asks what the relation is between human virtue or excellence simply, that is, the virtue or excellence of a good human being, and the virtue of a serious citizen. Why does Aristotle at this point raise this question? How is it related to the question of the common good? The answer would seem to be that we expect or hope or assume that the common good includes or culminates in the fulfillment, the excellence or flourishing, of the humans who partake of the common good. We recall Aristotle's definition of a city or political society, back in chapter two of book one: The city comes into being for the sake of mere life, but it exists for the sake of the good life – meaning, the life of fulfillment, excellence, virtue.

Aristotle begins by showing, to our disconcertion, that the virtue or excellence of a fulfilled human being *cannot possibly be* the *same* as the virtue of a serious citizen. For the virtue of a serious citizen is, he points out, *relative* to the regime. The good citizen is dedicated to the particular goals and particular notion of the common good or good life held by that type of regime to which he is loyally dedicated. And these goals and notions of the good life are in conflict among the competing regimes. What one regime says is the good life, and the type of person who ought to rule and predominate, contradicts what another regime says. It necessarily follows that the serious or dedicated citizen of one type of regime will have goals and principles opposed to the goals and principles of other types of regimes. A good citizen in a democracy would be a bad citizen, maybe even a revolutionary, in a monarchy or oligarchy and vice versa.

But is there not *some* regime, Aristotle asks, that truly fulfills its serious citizens? Big problems become evident, Aristotle argues, even or precisely when we try to think about such a best regime (1276b36ff.). In the first place, won't there necessarily be vast inequality in political capacities – even or especially in the best conceivable society? In other words, won't there be a very few Lincolns, or Washingtons, with the vast majority having lesser civic capacities – and ranked accordingly? In the second place, in any regime, there are vastly different jobs needing to be done, requiring vastly different and unequal talents and capacities. Above all, Aristotle stresses, we must never forget that politics means *rulers* and *ruled.* If we think concretely, we see that only a few of the civic positions will be *supervisory* or *architectonic*, while most positions and tasks will be more or less subordinate.

But won't there be *someone* in the *best* regime, Aristotle next asks (1277a13), who is excellent, and completely fulfilled, as a human being? Yes: Those who *rule*, who supervise, and direct, and take fullest responsibility – while the others, those who are subordinate citizens, do not enact such complete practical wisdom. Good ruling, Aristotle adds, requires not only special qualities of heart and mind but also a special *education*, a long and difficult training and gathering of experience.

Aristotle somewhat obliquely raises, however, a further serious set of problems. He suddenly quotes a famous *tyrant*, who always *hungered* for rule – so much that he could never be happy or fulfilled as a private person or as one who is ruled (1277a23). The troubling question Aristotle thereby puts on the table is this: If ruling is what fulfills a human being, then is not the society that allows a human who is best qualified the fullest and most unrestricted rule the best? But then, doesn't it follow that monarchic rule – of the wisest and most benevolent individual – is the best, for each individual who has the capacity? Can ruling, then, be a *common* good at all?

Aristotle responds to this big difficulty as follows. He appeals to what all people have in mind when they praise truly admirable rulers. While the virtues of leading and of giving orders and direction are superior to the virtues of being led or ruled, nevertheless we also, or at the same time, praise and honor in each person, even in rulers, the proven capacity to be ruled, to obey. It is this dual capacity – to be ruled as well as to rule – that is held to be "the virtue of the citizen" (1277a26–27), and *this* virtue is held to be truly *noble.* This, Aristotle says, highlights the difference between "despotic" rule and "political" rule. Truly political rule is exercised over persons who are free and similar to the ruler, and who are themselves also potential or future rulers. In contrast, despotic rule, even when it is benevolent, is rule over slaves, or over people who are not regarded as having the capacity or expectation of ever ascending to rule.

In order to know how to rule over free persons, Aristotle argues, it is necessary first to have the experience of being one of the ruled. A key part of the education and preparation for ruling, in a truly *political* fashion, is having spent a considerable time in one's youth as a subordinate, learning to obey orders in a free fashion, or as a free human being whom the leaders are preparing and testing for a future where the ruled becomes the ruler (1277b6–13).

Yet if one reflects on this answer and what it suggests about the spirit of the best regime, one sees that this leaves some big *un*answered questions. The problem becomes clear when Aristotle concludes the chapter by stressing how very great a difference there is between the virtues and responsibilities, and therefore the fulfillment, of the ruler, on one hand, and the much more *limited* virtues and therefore the much more *limited* fulfillment of the ruled, the subordinates, on the other. Only the ruler, Aristotle points out, exercises full practical reason. The ruled are guided decisively by the ruler's reasoning: The ruler in a republic, Aristotle says, is like the flute *player*, while the ruled are like the flute *makers*. It is the ruler who plays the music, while the ruled are in a profound sense instrumental to the ruler's art. Aristotle thus quietly compels his thoughtful reader to ask: Why would it ever be good for, in the interest of, someone who is nobly exercising rule to surrender rule and return to the ranks? If rotation of rule is good for the one *ascending* to office, isn't it bad for the one *descending* or retiring? Can all those who have the capacity to rule really enjoy rule at the same time, or to the same extent, even or especially in the best conceivable regime? It is noteworthy that Aristotle does not conclude by saying that in the best regime, rule should *rotate*; he says only that in the best regime, the ruler should first have had the experience and virtues of being ruled and should look upon the ruled as potential rulers.

In the next (fifth) chapter, Aristotle brings out additional grave and troubling puzzles. He shows that we have now proven that the best regime cannot possibly be a democracy: For dedication to ruling, and preparation for ruling, requires a very time-consuming special education, and this presupposes *leisure*, freedom from having to work for a living. Therefore none of the working class can be full citizens in the best regime. In any regime where citizens are from the working class, the very meaning of citizenship and rule must be drastically diluted and debased, since members of the working class, when children, can't afford to spend years acquiring the long necessary experience in office and public service in many different departments, and, when adults, lack the time and energy for full-time political activity. Where the working class is a major power in the regime, its members are inevitably led by a few, who must drastically simplify everything for them in a demagogic fashion, speaking for an audience that is usually tired, with little time and less knowledge. The best regime is "aristocratic" (1278a16–21).

This means, though, that the best regime is also not oligarchic; Aristotle draws a profound distinction between aristocracy and oligarchy.

Oligarchy is based on wealth; in oligarchies, what is honored, what qualifies a person for full citizenship and rule, is the capacity for managing property well or for making money. Oligarchies allow businessmen – merchants, bankers, and so on – to be citizens and to predominate. But such people are also un-leisured; they spend their lives in business. They may get a *kind* of education and experience, but it is not a *liberal* or *civic* education. They do not get an education and experience in government service, in the military, in the foreign service. Even when businessmen retire from business and finally get leisure, *it is too late.* Their minds and spirits and habits have already been formed in the moneymaking enterprise, and they lack the experience, knowledge, and habits required of good leaders who will take responsibility for the whole city as something much more than an economic organization.

By the end of Aristotle's discussion of the qualifications for citizenship in the best regime, we begin to see that the best regime is something that can almost never be realized; it is by no means a practical proposal. It is instead an invaluable standard, in the mind, for judging and arbitrating the great debate among the various actual competing regimes. It is a vision that allows one to see the imperfections, the rather drastic limits, on all actual regimes – and especially the limitations of all democracy as well as all oligarchy. Near the end of this radical chapter, Aristotle remarks on something that shows the deepest reason for the impracticality of the best regime. Citizenship, he observes, connotes dignity, honor; those who are not citizens, who are excluded, are like aliens. As such, they are likely to get angry; Aristotle quotes the angry Achilles from the *Iliad* (1278a35–39). He thus makes more vivid how very doubtful it is that the excluded, who will likely be the vast majority – both the rich and the poor – will tolerate their exclusion.

This prepares us for what happens in the next (sixth) chapter – which Aristotle begins with a strange question: "Is there only one regime, or are there many?" Our first response is likely to be, "Is it not obvious that there are many regimes? Have we not been learning that their conflict is the heart of the political problem?" But Aristotle means to prod us to see the following question: Have we not now learned that there is only one *true* regime, the best – "aristocracy" – the only regime that would really live up to the claim that all regimes make, namely, that they promote the full human good and excellence? After pointing to this troubling thought or doubt, Aristotle returns to acknowledging that there are many regimes, and, in particular, he stresses here democracy and oligarchy.

To make clearer the deepest reason why there are many regimes, Aristotle suddenly takes us back to the beginning of the whole book, or "the first discourses," to examine (as he puts it) "the purpose a city is constituted to serve" (1278b15–16). He restates the definition of the human as a political animal by nature. But he does not simply repeat what he said at the start. He spells out *three different dimensions* of the proposition that humans are political animals (1279b19ff.).

First, humans spontaneously group together: "Even when they need *nothing* in the way of *assistance* from one another, Aristotle observes, "they are in *no less degree* aimed at living together." Humans have a strong natural impulsion to live together in community, apart from any other need or further benefit or calculation.

Second, though, "it is also the case that common advantage joins in the attraction." The need to work together to achieve goods that can be obtained only cooperatively also brings humans together. But in this regard, Aristotle proceeds to add a massive qualification: "*to the extent, that a share in living nobly falls to each: this is especially the goal for all, both* in common and apart." The common advantage that humans seek is above all a share in nobility, in dignity, and it is this that is above all the end, for each and all.

Third and finally, humans join in communities for the sake of collective preservation or security: "They also come together for the sake of living itself, and they hold together the political community for this." But then Aristotle adds that this too – life itself – is seen as something *noble*: "For maybe there is a portion of the *noble* even in merely living, provided there is no great excess of hardships in living." In other words, even in their concern with mere preservation, humans (unlike other animals) are never free of a concern to preserve themselves in or with *dignity*.

In thus *re*stating and further elaborating the fundamental presupposition about human nature, Aristotle has spotlighted the human concern for nobility or dignity as the heart of the concern for the common good. He thus makes even sharper the massive difficulty seen in his elaboration of the best regime (aristocracy) as the regime in which the few finest human specimens would be completely fulfilled as political animals. For insofar as *all* humans have the profound natural need and longing to share in nobility, they are longing to be *rulers* and not only ruled. How can aristocracy ever satisfy this natural need and longing in the vast majority – in the working class and the business class? Does not republican rule, as Aristotle said back in book one, chapter twelve, "tend to be on an equal footing"? He reminds us of this in the next paragraph of chapter six, and he adds that political rule is characterized by *rotation* of rule (1279a7–9). Aristocracy, precisely because it completely fulfills the political nature of some, but only of some, cuts most off from sharing in that fulfillment and dignity. Yet if one gives up on aristocracy and broadens political life, then one not only harms those most capable of full human flourishing but debases the very meaning of the common good for all. For on behalf of aristocracy it may be argued that all the inhabitants living under a true aristocracy would have some share in dignity insofar as they could admire and support their ruling elite as people who are really admirable – excellent human specimens and not demagogues or people whose prestige is rooted in wealth. The lives of even the humblest denizens of a true aristocracy would be adorned and influenced and educated by the example set in public life by the predominance of rare human beings of real courage, moderation, justice, generosity, and prudence – who were dedicated also to enhancing as much as possible the spiritual as well as the material welfare of those governed. The public festivals and fine arts would reflect the actual presence of human greatness, leading the society. Those excluded from office and citizenship could take pride in the awareness that their labor contributed the economic basis that is essential to making possible the leisure necessary for rulers whose lives are wholly dedicated to fulfillment and to setting a noble example through virtuously generous ruling.

But, on the other hand, this means that by far the greater good would be realized and enjoyed by the governing elite. And in the second half of chapter six, Aristotle very strongly reminds us that central to our understanding of healthy or sound political rule is the thought that such rule is chiefly for the good of those who are ruled, and only incidentally for the good of the rulers – or indeed, even at the expense or sacrifice of the rulers' good. And all of a sudden Aristotle brings to the fore the deep tension that is thus revealed at the heart of our conception of political rule (1278b37–1279a16). Until now, Aristotle has mainly followed the high opinion of politics that conceives political rule as noble because it is fulfilling, as the enactment of human excellence or virtue that is the richest and most complete good for those who share in ruling. Now Aristotle spotlights the contrary opinion, which conceives political rule as chiefly serving the good of the others who are being ruled and advancing one's own good only incidentally, if at all. Aristotle reminds us that we *also* conceive of virtue as noble *in the sense* that it is or ought to be *selfless*, or even self-*sacrificing*. Rotation of rule is called for and justified on *this* basis *not* because ruling is good for the one doing it, but because it as a "burdensome service" (*leitourgia*) entailing the severe cost of the ruler's neglecting his own truest well-being. Aristotle thus put before us a profoundly puzzling ambiguity at the very heart of the highest aspirations of politics: Rule or the virtue of ruling is conceived as *both* self-fulfillment, and hence entailing the greatest good for those ruling, *and* self-sacrifice, and hence entailing decisive loss for those ruling. And both these incompatible opinions are bundled together as essential ingredients in what we now see is the deeply perplexing attractiveness, the exalted and inspiring character, the "nobility" (*kalon*), of great leaders and of political life at its peak. Yet Aristotle here makes the momentous suggestion that one who thinks through this puzzle and thereby arrives at a clear and consistent conception of ruling, in accordance with the *nature* of things, will recover an older outlook that sees ruling as public service and hence as not attractive, and indeed as something to be avoided as much as possible. Aristotle goes so far as to imply that the quest to rule betokens some sort of pathology: "Previously, as accords with nature, they claimed to merit doing public service by turns and having someone look to their good, just as when ruling previously they looked to his advantage"; however, "now, on account of the benefits from the common funds and also the benefits from the office, they wish to rule continuously, as if health would result all the time to those ruling, who are sick – for it is thus that they probably seek the offices" (1279a10–13). Aristotle hints here at the deepest perplexity (*aporia*) that he wants to stimulate, the puzzlement that can culminate in the vindication of the superiority of the private, nonpolitical life of the philosopher, who perfects his rational consciousness through intellectual virtues that are not mainly or essentially virtues of political rule or action – but whose vindication absolutely depends on a thorough clarification of the deepest tensions and contradictions or perplexities in humanity's primary conceptions of the virtues of the political life. Yet Aristotle does not here mention philosophy or the philosophic life. Instead, he clothes his indication of the superiority of a private life over the public life of rule in an appeal to an old-fashioned gentlemanly perspective, one that sees political ambition as vulgarly grasping – marking one as a busybody rather than a self-sufficient gentleman who minds his own business. Aristotle can responsibly allow himself to question political ambition here at this point in his instruction because he has reached a juncture where his analysis of aristocracy as the best regime has made clear the need to dampen or to seek another outlet for the ambition and zeal of potential aristocrats – the best of the young – who, in order to try to establish their own envisioned regime, might be seduced into oppression of the majority and thereby a severe contamination of their virtuous ambition.

What we have just learned to be the tension-ridden, pre-philosophic conception of the goodness of rule becomes the basis for the classification, in the seventh chapter, of all regimes into three "correct" regimes (kingship, aristocracy, and polity) and three "deviant" regimes (tyranny, oligarchy, and democracy). The correct regimes look to the common good, while the incorrect regimes look to the good of the rulers. But when, in spelling out a bit more the character of each of the six basic regimes, Aristotle gets to aristocracy, he subtly indicates the deep ambiguity or contradiction that is at work in the opinions he is here illuminating: "We are accustomed to call" the correct rule by the few, "aristocracy – *either* because the best are ruling, *or* because they are ruling with a view to the best for the city *and* for those participating in it" (1279a34–37, emphasis added).

If we survey Aristotle's sixfold typology of regimes, we see at once that he has broadened and loosened the standard that he sketched in the thought experiment of the one best regime. We now have a threefold standard; aristocracy is only one of three "correct" regimes. And this confronts us with two big puzzles. First, how and in what sense might *kingship* be a regime at all, since Aristotle started the whole work by loudly proclaiming on the first page that kingship was not even a form of political rule? Has our study of rule in an aristocratic republic helped us to see why kingship necessarily emerges as an eligible correct regime? Second, how can a correct regime be based on majority rule, given what Aristotle said in chapter five? How, that is, can the majority, who are the working class, have the genuine leisure to spend their lives acquiring and practicing and promoting civic virtue in any full sense? To this second question we immediately get the start of an answer, when Aristotle states the distinguishing characteristic of what he christens "polity": When "the multitude governs with a view to the common advantage, it is called by the term common to all regimes, "polity." This, Aristotle explains, "happens reasonably." For "it is possible for one or a few to be distinguished in virtue, but when more are concerned it is difficult for them to be proficient in virtue as a whole; they can be proficient in military virtue, for this does arise in a multitude; therefore in this regime the warrior element is the most authoritative, and those possessing heavy arms share in it" (1279a37–b4). Aristotle here makes concrete how drastic a dilution of moral standards is required in even the noblest or most virtuous form of majority rule: When or insofar as a regime ruled by the majority *does* care for and foster virtue, it will be military virtue that will predominate. For that is the virtue that everyone can understand and that many can partake of, without any very subtle education or consuming political experience.

Democracy vs. Oligarchy

With the scheme of regimes laid out, we are next confronted with yet another surprising turn in the argument. In chapter eight and the start of chapter nine, Aristotle ceases to focus on the correct regimes, let alone the best regime, and narrows his focus to two of the three "deviations" or incorrect regimes – democracy and oligarchy. Democracy is the regime in which the majority aims mainly at its own good, at the expense of minorities, and without an overriding concern for virtue, even military; oligarchy is the regime in which the minority aims in similar fashion at its own good, at the expense of the majority. Why do these deviant regimes now become the focus? At this point, Aristotle for the first time explicitly states that he is "treating the subject matter philosophically." He thus brings gently to the fore his perspective as superior to that of the nonphilosophic citizen or statesman. What this seems to mean in the first place is that the political philosopher – precisely because he has thought through so carefully what would be required to have the best or correct regimes – recognizes that in actual political life, one rarely deals with such regimes or their partisans. In actual political life, political science has to try to make the best of the contest between partisans of two fundamentally deviant or selfishly exploitative regimes, democracy and oligarchy, without ever losing sight of the high and tension-ridden standards that clarify how very limited and in need of mitigation is this nigh-ubiquitous state of affairs.

To clarify "philosophically" the natures of oligarchy and democracy, Aristotle now stresses that it is not so much numbers that define the true characters of these two regimes. It is rather their contrasting economic statuses. He thereby deflates or demystifies the claims of both the oligarchs and the democrats. For "oligarchy," by its very name, claims to be the "rule of the few" – of an, or the, elite; the philosopher insists on the truth that oligarchy is the regime of the few *rich* – that it is money or property, and not virtue or excellence, by which they truly define themselves. On the other hand, democracy by its very name claims to be the "rule by the people" (*demos*); the philosopher insists on the truth that democracy is the regime of the *poorer*, the working class that is needy and hence lacks leisure.

Yet Aristotle does not leave it at revealing the economic basis that shapes the two regimes. He turns in chapter nine to listen to and then to articulate the highest arguments each side makes, for the *justice* of its cause – or what he calls "oligarchic and democratic justice" (1280a7). He does not treat these claims of justice as mere ideology or propaganda; he takes them seriously and shows that he thinks the arguments are intended seriously – and, what is more, have some partial validity. Even the selfish regimes, he makes clear, are not simply selfish. Every regime claims, and wishes to believe, that it stands for something more than its ruling class's selfish interest. As Aristotle has previously stressed, human beings seek dignity in politics, and what they mean by dignity includes transcendence of narrow self-interest, through some sense and capacity for justice as service to the common good. We see here what is so characteristic of Aristotle's political science; he is never cynical, but also never starry-eyed. He articulates the highest standards and then, in that light, gives the most clear-eyed appraisal of the moral claims advanced by the competing factions in the political arena. Only if one has articulated in one's mind's eye a clear picture of the truly best regime, Aristotle implies, can one begin to see politics for what it really is, without the blinders and blunders of either cynicism or idealism.

What then is the moral argument between democracy and oligarchy; what sort of appeal to justice does each side make? In presenting these appeals, Aristotle articulates yet another dimension of justice that has so far not been so explicit. We recall that justice first came to sight as equivalent to the common good. Then, in the second place, we have seen that the highest human good is the virtue or excellence that is enacted and fulfilled in generous ruling; thus justice is also a key part of such human virtue or excellence. Now at the beginning of chapter nine Aristotle speaks of justice in a third sense: as "equality" in the sense of "fairness." This is what he calls in his *Ethics* "distributive" justice. The fair and thus just distribution of good and bad things that must be parceled out in any community is one that gives to each person a share equal to that person's merit or desert. Shares in the good things, and in particular rule and honor, should go to those who have shown – by past performance and by future promise or potential – that they can use the good things, and especially ruling office, well. By the same token, shares in the burdens, such as taxes, should go to those who can bear the burdens well. Shares in the simply bad things, such as punishments and dishonors, should go to those who have shown that they abuse the good things.

Aristotle suggests that when the two class competitors, rich and poor, make their respective claims to rule, each claims to deserve to hold sway because of certain meritorious qualities. The rich say: We deserve to rule because being rich makes one a better citizen, or is a sign of one's being better. The poor majority says: We deserve to rule because all citizens are free, and being free makes one equal in civic merit to every other free person (and the majority principle – of one equal vote for each person, with the most votes predominating – expresses this equal merit). Aristotle responds by criticizing both – saying that neither side speaks of the most important and valid claim of merit or desert. But he concedes that there is something to the argument of the rich. Their argument might hold if or insofar as property or moneymaking were *the* chief purposes of the political community. For then those who put up more money, and who proved that they could manage money better, should have more of a say.

Now strangely, Aristotle does *not* turn and specify the strength of the democratic argument. He leaves the task to us readers, and prods us to ask ourselves: What *is* the argument? Why is being free a *qualification* for *ruling?* What capacity for governing is developed or exhibited, what contribution to rule does a person make, simply by being free? The most obvious answer would seem to be that a free person is ready to fight to defend the community from foreign as well as domestic domination or enslavement – in other words, military virtue, as Aristotle suggested back in chapter seven. Aristotle thus moves us to think through the way the democratic argument, at its highest, points to the rule of citizens who conceive themselves as members of a citizen army or militia and police.

But Aristotle rejoins that both sides, in talking about either wealth or freedom, fail to refer to (as he puts it) the "thing that has most authority" in the light of the true ends of political life. The civic community exists not for mere preservation in freedom from domination, and not for mere economic prosperity and security. The city exists for "living well," for the good life, and that means human fulfillment, in complete virtue or excellence. Aristotle thus restates the case for aristocracy, but this time, on the basis of distributive justice, justice as fairness or fair equality – and in a direct confrontation with the moral claims of democracy and oligarchy. Here, in a passing but pregnant passage, he raises and rejects an alternative conception of political life, which he associates with a sophist, Lycophron: He argued that politics must be understood as a social compact, a kind of deal made by independent individuals with a view to the mutual satisfaction of individual material interests, and thus concerned *only* with one another's individual *rights* as partners in the contract, and not caring about one another's character but only about everyone's obedience to the rules of the contract (1280a34–b13). Aristotle shows that he is aware of the idea of trying to understand politics in this way. It is precisely this conception of politics that becomes, through Thomas Hobbes and John Locke, the foundation of modern constitutionalism. But Aristotle retorts that this outlook expressed by Lycophron is a base and mutilated, and even untenable, conception of political life. A genuinely human civil society cannot be made up of people who do not care whether or not their neighbors are virtuous, fulfilled, and happy: "Partnership in a place and for the sake of not committing injustice against each other and of transacting business" are things that "must necessarily be present if there is to be a city, but not even when all of them are present is it yet a city"; a city is "the partnership" of "households and families," for the sake of "a complete and self-sufficient life." This "will not be possible," to be sure, unless people "inhabit one and the same location and make use of intermarriage," as well as "clans, festivals, and the pastimes of living together." This sort of thing "is the work of affection; for affection is the choice of living together." But it is "living happily and nobly" that "is the end of the city, and these things are for the sake of this end." The "political partnership must be set down, therefore, as being for the sake of noble actions, not for the sake of living together" (1280b29–1281a3). Aristotle here brings out very explicitly another key implication of his thesis on the political nature of the human being, centered on a concern for dignity or nobility or virtue. The overarching concern of the good life is not mutual affection or love, or friendship and fraternity, or even religious worship. It is rather excellence and noble deeds. Affection, friendship and fraternity, and religion are important avenues for the expression of noble deeds; however, the purpose of civic life is a shared dedication to virtue or excellence.

The Case for Democracy

At this point, at the end of chapter nine, Aristotle seems to have intransigently returned to the case for aristocracy. But in chapter ten Aristotle surprises us once again: He goes through all the claims, of all the six types of regime, and says *none* of them is satisfactory! Why not? In particular, what is wrong with aristocracy? Chapter ten introduces yet another, fourth dimension of the meaning of the virtue of justice: "[V]irtue assuredly does not ruin what has it, nor is justice destructive of the city" (1281a19–21). All the other and higher aspects of justice depend on the civil society continuing to exist, as a place not destroyed by civil strife. Therefore, whatever seriously threatens the existence of the community cannot be just. This is not to deny that justice may demand that we some-times risk the city's survival in a fight with enemies. But it cannot be that justice demands something that practically guarantees extinction, social breakdown, or collapse of the society. And what is it about this dimension of justice that tells against aristocracy? Aristotle writes: "Should the decent rule and be sovereign over everything? In this case, all the others are necessarily deprived of honors, since they are not honored by hold-ing political offices. For we say that the offices are honors," and "when the same persons always rule the others are necessarily deprived of hon-ors" (1281a27–31). Aristotle now makes more explicit the difficulty we saw implied in the reference to Achilles and his anger at the end of chapter five. A few lines previously in this tenth chapter, when Aristotle attacked the claim of the majority, or of democracy, he did something very strange but very revealing (1281a17–18): When giving the major-ity's response to his criticism of their confiscating the property of the rich, he started cursing! This is the only place (here and a little later, at 1281b18–20) in all Aristotle's many volumes of writings that he curses. Why here? He is reporting the response of the majority to criticism of them and of their democratic injustice, and he means to make vivid the fact that when criticized, the democrats do not argue reasonably. They express their anger by starting to curse. In actual politics, and hence in realistic political theory or philosophy, anger must be listened to, and even bowed to, when those who get angry are strong. And the majority tends to be strongest because it is most numerous.

On this implicit basis, then, Aristotle takes the momentous step of submitting to the democrats or the majority. He accepts the brute fact that the majority, because they are the strongest, and because they are likely to get angry if left out, must have participation in governing, and, indeed, the predominant role. The claim of merit based on virtue must be drastically compromised in order to save the community from the destruction of civil war prompted by majoritarian frustration and anger and violence. But Aristotle goes on to try to build the most vir-tuous case possible for majority rule, or democracy. That is his leading task in chapter eleven and the task that he continues in books six and eight. Henceforth Aristotle's practical teaching is that the best one can hope for in most actual politics is democracy or the rule of the majority, somehow elevated and moderated, as much as possible. What we find in the eleventh chapter as a whole is that Aristotle's argument has two chief aims. First, he tries to bring out what is most virtuous, or potentially most reasonable and public spirited, about majoritarian dominion. Second, he tries to show how the rule of the majority – that is, giving the majority the *final* say – can be mixed with, and thus checked and balanced by, some strong oligarchic and aristocratic counterweights. In other words, he develops the idea of a "mixed regime": a mixture mainly of democracy with some oligarchy, moving in the direction of what he has christened "polity."

Aristotle begins the eleventh chapter by reminding us that a powerful case has been made against the rule of the multitude. But then he advances a surprising contention: Democracy or the rule of the multitude can actually be understood to be more virtuous than aristocracy. How so? Even though the multitude as individuals are not "serious men," when they "come together" and somehow pool or combine their scattered, fragmentary pieces of the virtues, then those fragments can cumulate to be equal to or greater than the virtues of the very best individuals. The obvious big question and difficulty here is how exactly one joins or pools or puts together, into a functioning whole, the incomplete fragments of virtue that are scattered among the various individuals who make up the mass so that, as a mass, they are more virtuous than an outstandingly virtuous statesman. Why will people of mediocre capacities, when brought together in a crowd, not act like a mob? Why will the crowd not become more vicious and stupid? Why won't they become *worse* as a crowd than when they were separate? Aristotle gives (1281b1–9) three analogies that, when one considers them, bring out the problems with his claim. First he says that dinners to which many contribute a dish are better than those hosted by a single person. Second, Aristotle says that the many can become one *being*, like a single human being put together out of different people's feet, hands, and senses. Third, Aristotle says that the many are better judges of music and of poetry, because one person judges well one part and another person another part of the work of art. Then, having mentioned works of art, Aristotle adds the observation that this is precisely how excellent individuals are distinguished; in their individual beings, the best qualities that are scattered among others are integrated in a single whole (1281b9–15). Does this reminder of what makes an excellent individual not show the weakness of the argument for pooling virtue to make a crowd that is more excellent than the best individuals? But Aristotle takes a key further step. He suggests that the same kind of unification of scattered good qualities that we see in an outstanding individual is what characterizes a good work of art. Does this not remind us that it takes a great artist to combine and to orchestrate the beauties that he sees scattered in many people? Is Aristotle not hinting that, in order for the pooling to work, in a mass assembly, you would need gifted popular leaders, to orchestrate the potential contributions of different people? It concurs with this suggestion that Aristotle next concedes (at 1281b15) that it is unclear whether every multitude can have its scattered good qualities pooled in this way – that is, like a work of art. He then reports the cursing response of someone (it sounds like a partisan of oligarchy) who angrily disagrees with this whole line of argument: "by Zeus, it is clear that in some cases it is impossible: the same argument would apply to beasts – for what difference is there between some [multitudes] and beasts, so to speak?" (1281b17–20). The rich, Aristotle reminds us, can get angry too, and their angry reaction to mob rule is also dangerous to the community. Certainly Aristotle concedes that the argument he has given holds only of a certain sort of multitude, prompting the reader to ask: "What sort?" Has Aristotle not quietly indicated that there is a need for a political artist, a virtuous leader of the *demos*, a Themistocles or a Pericles or a Lincoln or a Churchill, who will orchestrate and draw on the varying strengths of more limited assemblymen, while repressing or mitigating their diverse vices? One can imagine a crowd of not very generous people becoming as a group more generous, and a crowd of not very courageous people becoming as a group more courageous, and a crowd of not very fair-minded or public-spirited people becoming more fair-minded and public-spirited – *if* the crowd gets the right kind of leadership and inspiring guidance.

At this point, in a concessionary response, apparently to the cursing oligarchic opponent, Aristotle takes a big step back (at 1281b22ff.) qualifying the case he has started to make for democracy. The majority should not wield *all* the ruling power, and in particular not the important offices. Aristotle appeals to the authority of Solon, the lawgiver of democratic Athens, and one of the traditional seven wise men of Greece. Solon created a tempered democracy, where the multitude had a limited but ultimately sovereign power. Specifically, in Solon's constitutional system the many predominated in deliberation and judging – in the legislative assemblies and juries – but did not run the administrative offices, which were filled by persons of special qualifications selected by popular election and subjected to popular "audit" in the assembly. Aristotle in effect suggests that the many should not be allowed to discuss or to vote on day-to-day policy, but should instead elect a few who will conduct policy for them and will then be required to justify their conduct of office at the end of their fairly short terms, before the assembled mass of citizenry sitting as judges. He further suggests that the majority (who are, we must not forget, the poorer and therefore those without leisure for an elaborate civic education through experience) should not be free to elect themselves, or whomever they wish; in the best democracies there will be some easily recognized restrictive qualifications for eligibility for high office. Aristotle praises democracies where candidates for the highest offices – treasurers and generals in particular – must have a substantial property qualification. In a well-mixed democracy, the mass majority has the final say, but by reserving the highest offices for the rich and leisured, from whom the majority elects its preferred candidates, an effective stake in the regime is reserved for the fewer who are more wealthy. This can reassure the wealthier minority and reconcile them to the tempered democracy. Moreover, while the rich are *not* the same as the virtuous, they at least have the leisure that allows them to obtain civic education through experience in office. The wealthier, who use their leisure to pursue careers of public service, tend to be identified in the public mind with the virtuous. The wealthy can be a kind of avatar of the virtuous, and may even include some who are genuinely virtuous.

Aristotle concludes chapter eleven by saying that what has become especially clear is the need for the rule of laws, suggesting that in a democracy the majority should be limited by some kind of fixed fundamental laws. But he immediately reminds us that laws are only as good as the humans who make them, and that in each regime it is those who wield sovereign authority who have the final say in making the laws. In a democracy, the poorer majority will be the ultimate lawmakers. It is therefore not altogether surprising that in chapter twelve Aristotle seems as it were to take a deep breath and start all over once again. He is not satisfied with the democratic mixed regime under the rule of law as the resolution of the fundamental political problem, the question of who ought to rule.

Kingship vs. the Rule of Law

Yet what is so strange about the remainder of book three is that the discussion does not seem to advance toward a better *practical* solution to the basic question of how to settle the quarrel among the regimes. Indeed, in all the rest of the *Politics*, Aristotle never reaches a better practical solution than one or another version of the mixed democratic regime proposed in chapter eleven. And in the three subsequent books (four to six, especially six) it becomes clear in much more detail why and how various versions of a mixed or qualified democratic regime can be the best practical solutions. The discussion in the remainder of book three seems aimed rather at making more explicit and vivid the severe limitations of all republican political life. Aristotle indicates that the understanding of justice as equality requires a more emphatically philosophic investigation: "There is difficulty here and matter for political philosophy." The more explicitly philosophic discussion of equality culminates in an argument for absolute monarchic rule by the truly most virtuous individual, as the best regime simply – though this is at the same time shown to be a regime that is very risky and in almost every actual circumstance impractical.

In chapter twelve and in the first part of chapter thirteen, Aristotle restates the arguments for the various regimes, but now with a new stress on the standard of competence – or *knowledge* of the *art* of ruling. On this basis, the claim of aristocracy or the rule of the virtuous at first seems stronger and stronger. The biggest problem in the case for aristocracy appears to be the small number of the virtuous, which may render them insufficiently numerous to perform the tasks of government. Yet this problem seems to point only to the need for an aristocratic regime in which the virtuous would need to allocate many *subordinate* offices to the majority, rich and poor. Suddenly, however, Aristotle raises a new objection, to all republican regimes, even or especially to aristocracy (1283b13ff.). Whatever criterion of merit or qualification to rule one uses, if there arises a single extraordinary individual who is much more qualified in those terms than all the rest combined, distributive justice requires that that person rule, as king. Aristotle goes further. He contends that no republican regime can make a place for the truly outstanding, fully virtuous, and wise individual. All regimes, including aristocracy, must "ostracize" the truly best human being. Such a person simply cannot fit in, cannot enact and express his supreme virtue, in a regime where he is required to rule as part of a team with others; he is like a giant among dwarfs, like "a god among human beings." The outstanding individual cannot be included in a rule of law because law always presumes a basic similarity and commensurability in the moral and intellectual capacities of all the citizens under the law. "It would not be asserted," Aristotle writes, that the best regime, which most fulfills the aim of all political life "ought to throw out and remove such a person!" But "neither that it rule *over* such a person – that would be akin to their claiming to deserve to rule over Zeus, ruling in rotation!" "What is left – which is likely to be *according to nature* – is for all gladly to obey such a person, with the result that such be permanent/eternal (*aidious*) kings in the cities" (1284b17–35). Aristotle would seem to have in mind primarily titanic political leaders who come to be regarded as quasi-divine or are in fact worshiped as divine "heroes" – Brasidas, Peisistratus, Themistocles, Philopoemen, or, closer to us in time, Washington, Lincoln, Atatürk, Churchill, de Gaulle. But may not his opening emphatic reference to political philosophy hint that he is now thinking through the problematic place in republican politics of the wise political philosopher?

A new section begins, with a note of moral hesitation (1284b35–36): "Perhaps it is noble, after the arguments that have been uttered, to make a transition, and to investigate kingship." The hesitation reflects the fact that this monarchic line of analysis runs contrary to what appeared, from the start of the *Politics*, to be the noble and true outlook. We recall that the whole treatise began, on the first page, by asserting the ignobility, as well as the falsehood, of failing to distinguish, as distinct in kind, the art of political rule from the art of kingship, and the political ruler or statesman from the king (and the household manager). The rest of book one was a sustained polemic against those who collapsed these distinctions. Kingship was said to be primarily a patriarchal kind of societal rule belonging to primitive times, and to "nations." And Aristotle's discussion here, in chapter fourteen, reflects and even vibrantly echoes (through the quotation from the poet-statesman Alcaeus) the antipathy to princely government, seen as tantamount to barbarian slavery, or as belonging only to archaic times, that was a widely held conviction among the republican Greeks. Aristotle thus gives one of his signals that his investigation here is not meant as a practical proposal of kingship for Greek cities, but is rather a theoretical inquiry, meant to illuminate further the problematic conceptual basis of republican government.

Of course, the controversially favorable view now being taken of kingship was first very briefly indicated back in the seventh chapter, where Aristotle surprised and puzzled his republican readers by including kingship among the correct regimes – but without explaining how and why this could be, given the opening of the treatise. Here Aristotle reminds his readers of that earlier jarring surprise – "for we assert this to be one of the correct regimes" – and thus seems to indicate that now, finally, he is in the course of explaining and justifying that assertion. But he also lets us see that he is doing so as part of his ongoing provocation to his readers, goading them to puzzle over the basic question, of *whose* advantage political rule is conceived as serving. The first part of "what needs to be investigated," he says, is "whether it is *advantageous for a city and a land* that is going to be managed nobly to be ruled by a king, or not – but instead, by some other regime." Aristotle reminds us that the original criterion for correct regimes, stated back in chapter seven, where kingship was first included among correct regimes, was that the rulers not look to their own advantage but instead assume the burden of neglecting their own advantage in order to look to the advantage of the ruled. But now Aristotle problematizes this by adding (at 1284b40) another additional or alternative and open-ended question regarding kingly rule. For he goes on to ask: "OR, to *whom* (pl. – the pronoun may refer again to "cities") is it advantageous, and to *whom* (pl.) is it *not* advantageous?"

Aristotle soon announces as the grounding question the following: "whether it is more advantageous to be ruled by the best man or by the best *laws*" (1286a2–9). The question of the superiority of absolute monarchy is simultaneously the question of the superiority of the rule of law. A debate ensues, with the podium given first to "the opinion of those who believe that it is advantageous to be ruled by the king." Their initial criticism of the supremacy of law is that written laws by their very nature speak only in general terms, and are thus incapable of giving orders that fit the diversity, in reality, of all particular challenges, each with its unique needs. To this Aristotle gives, in his own name, a twofold rejoinder. First, rulers must grasp the relevant universal principles into which they need to fit the particular cases: Every situation must be judged not simply as unique but as an instance of rationally perceived generalizations (1286a16–18). Written laws impel rulers to bring to their regulation of particulars appropriate general principles that might otherwise be missed. Aristotle's second point is an appeal to the superiority of dispassionate rule, and the observation that law is uncontaminated by the passionate element, from which no human soul is free. But Aristotle immediately concedes that an opponent might assert that it is precisely the possession of the passionate element that helps make the wise man "deliberate more nobly about the particulars." The wise and virtuous king would be a man most perfectly in control of his passions, while yet enabled by his passions to judge sympathetically of individual human situations. What is more, the sage king would have a deep understanding of the passions, which the law lacks. The law's lack of passion implicates law's mulish and stony incapacity to make sympathetic as well as wise allowances for the agonizing diversity of human situations. The critics of law have thus reinforced their powerful opening criticism (including, by implication, the notion of "divine law," or of wise divinity conceived as ruling through laws).

At this point, when the case for the superiority of supra-legal sagacious kingship seems (to say the least) far from being refuted, Aristotle suddenly squelches the debate by co-opting the wise man to the side of the supremacy of law (1286a22–24): It has become "obvious," Aristotle tendentiously claims, that the wise man "must necessarily be the law-*giver.*" Yet Aristotle does not explicate the craft of the wise lawgiver. Instead, he immediately restates, though in a new and more republican and jurisprudential form, the problem of law. The sage lawgiver's laws "ought *not* to be sovereign where they apply erroneously, while they ought to be sovereign otherwise." Aristotle substitutes, for the argument over the advantageousness of kingship, a new and very different argument: Assuming wise law should be usually but not always supreme, who should rule as regards matters where the application of even or precisely the wise law would be unwise? Should the judge who is empowered to overrule law be the single individual who is truly wise and virtuous, or should it be everyone else (1286a24–25)? On reflection, we see that the opening point made by the critics of the rule of law has been in considerable measure tacitly conceded and incorporated: Even or precisely the rule of laws made by a wise lawgiver must be overruled by prudential judgment as to when the wise laws are to be suspended or contravened, and as to what ought then to be the extralegal, particularistic, sovereign commands. (This implies that no reasonable divine or natural law, no law of reason, could be categorically binding, a categorical imperative.)

Aristotle opens the new argument with the observation that in fact the *democratic assemblies* pass verdicts, and deliberate, and make judgments, on particular cases; he reminds us that in mature republics the most usual alternative to strict adherence to the rule of law is the sway, not of wise individuals, but of the lawless popular assemblies. Aristotle once again sublimates the mighty power of the multitude, by employing his ennobling argument: "The mob" (as he now calls it – 1286a31) "also judges many things better than any given individual," when its inferior, ordinary, individual capacities are pooled. He adds two new pleadings, which speak not for "the mob's" virtue but for its lesser susceptibility to vice: The many are harder to corrupt than are a few; the many are less likely than a single individual to be blinded, all at once as a group, by anger or some other passion (1286a26–37).

But Aristotle cannot leave it at this renewed evocation of the potential, in democracy, for a certain degree of wisdom and incorruptibility. He concedes that "it is not easy" for a multitude to remain restrained once it starts overriding constitutional laws (1286a38). He builds a new case, for bestowing the authority to override the constitutional laws on an "aristocratic" body composed of those "similar in virtue" – rather than on the one best individual. Are not the few, who are "all good men and good citizens," less corruptible than a virtuous individual? Granted, the few *are* susceptible to strife among themselves, while the virtuous individual is not, but this ought "probably" to be "countered" by stressing the moral seriousness of their souls. But this, of course (Aristotle has to concede), they share with their competitor – that single, surpassing individual. Aristotle is manifestly bending over backward to argue for the superiority of a republic to a virtuous kingship. He is intent on presenting his teaching on the limits of republicanism and the rule of law in a manner that is not subversive of republics. For, as is made still plainer in the digression that next ensues, virtuous kingship is all but impossible as a practical replacement for existing republics.

Aristotle abruptly provides a bird's-eye view of the history of Greek political evolution (1286b8–22), showing not only that the days of kingship are long past but that in the early epochs when kingship flourished there were not yet individuals of perfected political wisdom and hence complete virtue. "And since it has happened that the cities have become larger," Aristotle concludes, "perhaps it is no longer easy for any regime to come into being except democracy" (1286b21–22; compare also 1285a1–b33). The time at which absolute monarchy was acceptable does not correspond to the time at which a supremely virtuous individual will arise. This last consideration, together with the glimpse of history that underlies it, overshadows not only the discussion here but the entire treatise.

In the wake of this brief but telling history lesson, Aristotle switches back to arguments against "someone," who would persist in "setting down kingship as best for the cities." Aristotle gives the initial impression that he is piling more arguments onto the refutation of this defeated cause. In the first place, he raises what he claims is the baffling practical problem of succession. In the second place, he outlines the "perplexity" involving the extent of the power of the king's police. But then he suddenly comments: "It is probably not difficult to define" such a thing in the case of a king who governs under law; "it is concerning the king who does all things in accordance with his own will that the argument now has come to a stand, and that the investigation needs to be made" (1286b22–87a2). A reassuringly republican detour has wound up back where we started: at the most serious, as yet unresolved, debate.

Yet the terms of the contestation have subtly but profoundly shifted. Aristotle reopens the dispute by citing (at 1287a10–16) the opinion of some who oppose absolute monarchy on grounds of distributive justice or "deserving," and who appeal to what is right or just by nature, conceiving the distribution of honorable offices as analogous to the distribution of the food and shelter that bodies "by nature" need. This analogy indicates that ruling office is now once again understood to be an essential good, a natural need, *for the ones ruling* – their spiritual food, one is tempted to say. And so the issue for distributive justice, when or insofar as it is in accord with natural right or justice, is how to distribute rule in proportion to the various claimants' needs and capacities to flourish spiritually through or on the basis of their ruling. The good of the ruled is no longer the primary or even an explicit consideration. Aristotle seems to imply that in the final analysis the deepest motivation for those opposing absolute monarchy is not that they and others will not benefit in any way by being so governed, but rather that they and others will not get their fair share of the great good of ruling.

Arguing on this ground – of how the great good of ruling, for the rulers, ought to be distributed – the opponents of absolute monarchy contend (1287a12ff.) that among "those who are similar by nature" it is "just that no one rule more than be ruled, that they take turns"; "but this," they point out, "is already law – the ordering is law"; and "even if," among these similar people, "some are better at ruling, these ought to be set up as the guardians of the law, *and the servants* of the law." These "guardian-servants of the law" ought not to be conceived as empowered to act outside the law. The opponents now desperately deny that the rule of law can be supplemented by extralegal human prudence: "Whatever the law does not seem to be able to direct, a human being would not be able to know either." As for the evident necessity sometimes to change the law or to make particular rulings that appear to be outside or even contrary to the law, the opponents of kingship insist that such changes and rulings, when made correctly, are in accord with the law or with the deep spirit of the law, that is, with the wise intention discernible behind or within the law; such judgments, they say, are the result of having been "educated by" the law. For the law transcends all its human servants. The highest case for the supremacy of law is a case for the supremacy of unwritten, higher, *divine* law, and of *divinity* as legislative intelligence in its purity, underlying and informing the laws of the land. Here we glimpse the deepest issue in the debate over the rule of law. "He who calls for the rule of law is held to call for the rule of *god* and intelligence (*nous*) *alone*." The upholders of the supremacy of law experience law's majestic wisdom as the emanation from a superhuman, divinely legislative intelligence, uncolored and undiverted by passions – in contrast to the "beastliness" of human-all-too-human desire and anger that "perverts rulers even when they are the best men."

But this reverent defense of law as divine makes no reference to the *human* lawgivers or to the supreme importance of *their* decision as to what will be the *regime*. To put the problem another way: How do the reverent upholders of divine law understand divine law to be promulgated to us? The answer seems to be given in their proclamation that "yet more sovereign, and concerning more sovereign matters, than the written laws, are the laws of *custom*" (1287b5–6). So it transpires that the reverent case for the sovereignty of higher, unwritten law, as the expression of divine "intelligence" (*nous*), is a case for the sovereignty and wisdom of *inherited* legal traditions, that have come to be experienced as sacred. The pleaders for the rule of law wind up having moved far from what they gave as their initial impression – that among a citizenry of similar people all deserve an equal share in governing, as if all were competent and equally capable of fulfilling their excellence through governing; the reverent case for the rule of law culminates in upholding the rule of divine law on the ground that *no* citizens are sufficiently competent or reasonable to be trusted with rule. Law is presented as the divine ruler's antidote to ineradicable human irrationality and vice. This major component of the argument for law might at first seem to accord better with a stress on the view that ruling is a burdensome sacrifice, but Aristotle presents the upholders of the rule of law as unwilling and unable to abandon or to subordinate the view that ruling with its severe challenges is something good for the ruler – as the nourishment needed for a healthy and vigorous spiritual flourishing (even if humans cannot be trusted to attain this fully). After all, God Himself, as lawgiver, is a ruler; is not his legislative ruling conceived as constituting in large part his excellence, his flourishing? It seems that law, even or especially law as divine, cannot be seriously defended without this positive view of the goodness, *for the lawgiver*, of lawgiving as ruling.

Accordingly, the lofty positive case for the supreme rule of law is supplemented by more down-to-earth, negative criticisms of the proposal for absolute monarchy – no longer on grounds of the need to contain the human proclivity to vice, or even on grounds of equal distributive justice, but now on grounds of the limits of what is conceded to be the possible emergence of extraordinary individual human competence and wisdom (1287b8ff.). "The prayer of Agamemnon," the Homeric king favored by Zeus, teaches that it is hard for one man to survey everything; he will need many helpers. Two or more heads are better than one. But these sensible arguments about the superior prudence of a plurality of rulers are interwoven with a very big concession: Once the upholders of the rule of law focus on what the task of ruling really entails, "they do not dispute," Aristotle says, that "*to legislate about matters of deliberation is among the impossible things*," and therefore that "it is necessary for a human being to make the judgment on such matters." They retreat to insisting only that it should be "not one (human) but rather many." Even or precisely "monarchs," they finally plead, make "fellow rulers" of their friends, whom they can trust; however, a friend is an equal, so, when monarchs suppose they ought to rule with the help of friends, they are in effect conceding that rule ought to be shared among equals (1287b19–35).

Despite the considerable strength of all these arguments, the upholders of law and republicanism fail to address the massive truth that Aristotle made clear in his account of the reasons for the necessary republican practice of ostracism. The arguments of the upholders of law and republicanism do not face up to the existence among the human species of rare individuals whose political capacity and wisdom surpass those of all the other citizens combined: These individuals alone can be conceived to *fully* realize, by means of ruling absolutely, the virtuously and politically active "good life" that is the supreme conscious aspiration and aim of all politics, and that cannot in any other way be conceived as fully realized. Accordingly, in chapter seventeen, Aristotle restates the case for absolute monarchy in the very rare case of such superior human specimens, or a succession of them, arising among populaces who may be sufficiently docile to allow such specimens the complete authority they deserve in order to flourish. Aristotle reformulates his distinction between "deviant" versus "correct" regimes (which originally, back in chapter seven, made no explicit reference to natural right, and conceived rule as for the advantage of the ruled rather than, or even at the expense of, the ruler). He substitutes a distinction between "regimes that are deviant because they come into being *against nature*" versus "what is *by nature* justly and advantageously ruled despotically, and what in a kingly fashion, and what politically" (1287b38–41). Absolute kingship by the supremely virtuous is justified for two reasons. First, it accords with distributive justice, on which every regime rests its justification, insofar as the rulers in every regime claim to deserve to rule in accordance with some superiority. But now superiority and consequent desert is conceived in terms of the ruler's capacity for self-fulfillment. This becomes clear from the formulation of the second reason: "It is unfitting" not only to remove from rule a human being of such superiority but also to require him to rule taking turns with others; for it is against nature for the part to be superior to the whole, and this is what would happen if such a person were to have to take a place equal with the rest. The rest, as individuals and taken all together, are the parts, with subordinate functions as parts – to revert to Aristotle's earlier analogy, they are, as it were, the flute *makers*. The flourishing of the finest human specimen is the whole, in the sense of being that at which the whole of the city, indeed civic existence as a whole, ultimately aims as: The finest human specimen should be the flute *player*. It is on this basis that Aristotle declares completed the determination of what kingship is, in its different forms, and "whether it is not advantageous to cities, or whether it is, and to whom, and how."

Practical Advice to Lawgivers and Statesmen

In books four through six, Aristotle undertakes a more practical study. He begins by setting forth a complex account of the task of political science, viewed now as an emphatically therapeutic science or art, such as medicine or gymnastics: The political scientist has the responsibility of discovering what health and fitness are, in the various bodies politic. This means, as we have learned through our study of book three, that the political scientist differs from the citizen or partisan of any actual regime by the fact that the political scientist is the nonpartisan umpire who brings to the fore the nature of justice and virtue as the standards for political life, made vivid in the inquiry into the "best" regime. But this very notion, the "best," is more complicated than we have thus far recognized. In politics, the concept of what is the "best" is fourfold and points to a fourfold task. The political scientist must elaborate not only the best regime simply, the "regime," as Aristotle here says, "that one would pray for above all, with external things providing no impediment" (1288b21–22). The political scientist ought also to elaborate what regime is "best" in each of a wide variety of different sets of regime environments – for the best *simply* is almost always impossible. In the third place, the political scientist ought also to elaborate what is the best regime "given a basic presupposition," that is, what is the best, supposing that one is not going to try to change to another and better regime even if the circumstances might allow such an improvement. And in the fourth place, the political scientist ought to elaborate what is best in the sense of most likely to be suitable for many or most cities; since the best "simply" is a kind of utopia, we need also a notion of a regime that is a generally or frequently attainable object of aspiration – one that is not a utopia. What is more, regime reforms ought to be such that, in their existing conditions, people can be "easily persuaded of" and can readily partake of the reforms. Nor ought the nobly ambitious reformer to suppose that he will thereby abandon a greater task for a lesser: "It is no less an achievement to correct a regime than to found a regime"; "the statesman ought to be able to help the *existing* regimes." Stressing once again that laws are derivative from and expressive of the more fundamental phenomenon of the regime (1289a4–7), Aristotle calls for fresh study of the varieties of democracy and oligarchy – of the deviant but common regimes.

In the second chapter, Aristotle takes us back to the third book's typology of the three "correct" regimes with their three "perversions." But now, focusing on the three deviant regimes, he ranks them in a new way. Democracy is the "most measured" of the three (see also *Nicomachean Ethics* 1160b19–20), while tyranny, as the perversion of "the first and most divine," is "necessarily worst" – "being most removed from polity." Second worst is oligarchy, "from which," Aristotle adds, "aristocracy is far removed" (1289a40–b5). The underlying thought would seem to be that because the two best of the correct regimes concentrate governance in the few best and give to them the free hand appropriate to virtue, the perversions of these regimes give similarly unrestrained scope to the few vicious; by contrast, in polity, and in its perversion, democracy, the more "average" multitude hold sway, with some sense of their own limitations and less able to do either great good or great evil.

Aristotle next lays out (1289b12–26) an agenda of five tasks whose successive execution will structure books four and five. He will first clarify the diversity of subtypes of each of the six regimes, and especially of democracy and oligarchy. Second, he will clarify which regime is "most common, *and* which is most choice worthy after the best regime." But the third (and central) task will be to show "as regards the *other* regimes, which is choice worthy for whom: for probably democracy, rather than oligarchy, is a *necessity* for some, but the reverse is the case for others." Fourth, he will consider how democracies and oligarchies should be set up. "Finally," or as our "goal" (*telos*), an "attempt must be made to elaborate" what "destroys/corrupts" and what "saves" the regimes – generally, and in the case of each. This fifth item will turn out to be assigned by far the most space (all of book five). Aristotle's therapeutic political science comes to sight as having a strongly preservative aim or culmination.

Aristotle addresses the first task by examining in the next few chapters the character and the causes of the diversity among subtypes, especially of oligarchy and democracy. The chief cause is the economic diversity within both the rich and the poor classes. But there are also crucial non-economic distinctions among different rich and poor classes – especially whether and what types of arms are possessed. Finally, Aristotle considers variation in the moral quality of different rich and poor classes. All of these factors combine, in many different ways, to create many different types of oligarchy and democracy. Yet we must not lose sight of the fact, Aristotle stresses, that the fundamental distinction is that between the rich and the poor. The best of each of the two competing regimes, democracy and oligarchy, is that version that is least extreme, that is most inclusive of or gives the greatest voice and power to its opponents or to the subordinate class. The best oligarchy is the most democratic oligarchy, while still remaining an oligarchy, or a regime where the rich have the final say. The best democracy – the type of democracy whose character we have seen Aristotle begin to outline in chapter eleven of book three – is the most oligarchic democracy, while still remaining a democracy, or a regime where the poor majority has the final say but the rich feel secure, with their property protected and some of their rights and privileges as rich respected.

Aristotle points to two factors beyond the institutional setup that can especially affect the character and relative excellence of these defective regimes of oligarchy and democracy. First, he stresses at the end of chapter five that the spirit and character of the ruling class may be more important than the institutional structure. A regime that is constitutionally immoderate may be moderated by men of decent or moderate character in office, and vice versa. Second, and in another major paradox, Aristotle favors as a practical matter the regimes with the *least* leisure, the *least* political participation in quantity or amount. In most actual participatory republican regimes, he suggests, where the ruling groups are largely lacking in virtue and wisdom, the less they are active, the better. The less leisure they have, and the more they have to work and to attend to their own business, the less oppressive and self-destructive they are likely to be. We see here that Aristotle does not favor as wise an increase of leisure and civic participation simply, but only of *nobly employed* leisure and participation. It is the *quality*, and not the quantity, of leisure and participation that matters. Democratic citizenries are less likely to be swept up by the passions leading to unified mob-assemblies under demagogues if the democracies are dominated by a majority of small farmers and others possessing modest but independent property: "For they have to work for a living, and are unable to have leisure, with the result that they establish laws, and assemble in [only] the necessary assemblies" (1292b25–30). By the same token, the best oligarchies (1293a15ff.) are those where most of the rich do not have a great deal of time to participate in politics, because they have to manage their farms or businesses; under these conditions the wealthy are more willing to turn most offices over to a few who are wealthier, more experienced, and better educated – and whose political power the less wealthy want to keep checked and limited by the higher authority of the law.

In chapters seven through nine of book four, Aristotle glides into the second item on his agenda and turns finally to a fuller investigation of the regime he has designated "polity." At first Aristotle characterizes this regime as a good "mixture of oligarchy and democracy" (1293b33; 1294b1), and in chapter nine he describes a number of methods of arranging voting, and distributing office, so as to forge well-balanced combinations of oligarchy and democracy. But, after briefly treating tyranny in chapter ten, Aristotle returns to polity in chapter eleven, and develops a new possibility: a regime with a substantial *middle* class – a middle class that, while not in the majority, nevertheless is large enough and strong enough to compete effectively with both the rich minority and the poor majority. Aristotle here (1296a8) speaks for the first time of a great practical advantage of a *large* city: Larger cities, wealthier cities, are more likely to have a substantial middle class. Again we see how undoctrinaire Aristotle's practical wisdom is. Moreover, Aristotle now says that one of the chief advantages of *democracy* is that the democratic majority is more likely than the oligarchic minority to include as part of itself the middle class – for the poor majority tends to be more inclusive than the wealthy minority.

But what precisely is so good about the middle class (1295b)? First and foremost, Aristotle argues for the *moral* superiority of the middle class in contrast to both the poor and the rich. The possession of a moderate amount of wealth frees people from the dependence and grinding need and petty criminality that attend poverty, while at the same time avoiding the temptations and vices of luxury – immoderate self-indulgence, overweening ambition and arrogant pride, or refusal to share rule. In the second place, the middle class is prone to be preoccupied with its personal business, and hence "least likes to rule or wishes to rule." Third, the members of the middle class are especially "likely to be secure," because they have sufficient wealth not to envy and to covet, and thus to threaten, the wealth of the rich, and yet not so much wealth that they are looked at with envying covetousness by the poor. Fourth, the middle class tends to support whichever of the two rival classes of rich and poor is weaker at any time, and thus "prevents the coming into being of excessive extremes." The middle class is close enough in fortune to each of the other two classes to have some real sympathy with their hopes and fears in political life. The middle class can act as a mediating force between the rich and poor, shifting to support whichever is weaker and thus maintaining the balance. This mediating vocation of the middle class is enhanced by the likelihood that the middle class will be smaller and hence weaker than the poor majority, and poorer and hence weaker than the rich minority. Therefore, the middle class tends to feel more vulnerable and more defensive, which intensifies its tendency to be more desirous of peace and concord and compromise, than is either of the other classes. And the preceding is intensified by the fact that the other two classes see the middle class as more sympathetic and less hostile than each views its opponent as being. As Aristotle stresses a bit later (1297a4), the middle class can be an arbiter between rich and poor. In short, the larger and more powerful the middle class, the stronger is the class basis for a compromise, leading perhaps to friendship or community throughout the whole society of the city.

But in chapter thirteen Aristotle begins to add yet another consideration. Membership in the middle class, and hence the constitutional and other prerogatives that go with such membership, can be defined by the possession of heavy armor, or the equipment and leisure necessary for serving in the civil militia or for having been a veteran. In other words, the regime of the middle class can be a regime that favors the military virtues of a citizen army: courage, discipline, patriotism or public service of a basic sort, the willingness to fight for the freedom of the whole city, and a sense of esprit de corps or fraternity that grows up in the experience of the shared burdens and challenges of national defense. Aristotle now elaborates on the suggestion that he made back in book three, chapter seven, about the kind of military virtue one can expect in a regime dominated by the majority. He makes it clear that he is *not* thinking, in the best case, of a *bourgeois* middle class, but of a more militant, public-spirited class rooted in militia service.

In book five, Aristotle presents a treatise on revolution or civil strife and overthrow of the regimes, treating both the causes of revolution and the ways each regime may best prevent revolution. He provides much advice concerning the moderation of institutions and public policies in order to conciliate whatever is likely to be the most disadvantaged class in each type of regime. As is implied by the discussion in book four, Aristotle always counsels trying to moderate the regime, or to include as much as possible of the opposed faction. But he stresses also the need for civic education in each regime – an education of the young that will make them the best citizens for that particular regime. Each regime needs to instill in its young a love of that regime, of its principles, of its traditions and heroes and accomplishments. Each regime needs to instill in its young the habits and tastes and capacities that are needed to make that regime work well and remain stable. Yet Aristotle notes that the habits and emotions and capacities that are truly needed in each regime are not the ones that are most popular or well liked by the ruling class. Civic education is not what most partisans think it is (1310a12ff.). A good education will make the citizens aware of the dangerous vices to which that regime is prone, and will help citizens begin to correct or counterbalance those vices. In democracy in particular, the grave danger is an education that flatters democracy, flatters the majority, exalts freedom and equality without any reference to virtue and to the moral superiority of those who are wiser and more public-spirited, and that promotes envy of the rich. Such an education is all too typical of democracy, Aristotle indicates. That kind of democratic education is what rots civic spirit in democracy, and makes the citizens slavish individualists, easy prey to demagogues – rather than prudently active, self-governing citizens who see and feel the need constantly to temper and to balance the excessive democratic spirit with strong aristocratic and also oligarchic ingredients in institutions and civic education. In general, Aristotle teaches that each regime needs to counteract the proclivities, the drift or natural tendency, of the regime. The calling of the true statesman and political philosopher – as opposed to the sophist or demagogue or fool – is to identify and constantly to argue against what the ruling class, be it the majority or a minority, tends to think is "of course" right. Therefore, and as we saw vividly in the case of Socrates on trial, the political philosopher will usually not be one of the so-called right-thinking people.

In the sixth book, Aristotle reconsiders democracy. Up until now, he has focused mainly on democratic freedom as meaning a demand for participation in rule; this entails majority rule, and such rule, in practice, means the rule of the have-nots. But Aristotle asks us now to look with more equanimity on democratic freedom in the sense of "living as one wishes," or indeed, "*not being ruled* – by *anyone.*" It is from these two very different meanings of freedom, Aristotle now declares, that we must understand all the political practices characteristic of democracy to arise; he then rehearses most of the deplorable features (he omits demagogues) that lead toward or constitute extreme democratic government (1317a40–1318a2). Yet after leading us through this gloomy list, Aristotle returns to what he earlier designated the first and most measured form of democracy (recall 1291b30–38). He seems now to be pointing to a potentially constructive civic implication of the newly emphasized, *second* meaning of democratic freedom. Insofar as democratic politics (and leadership) focuses more on securing freedom in the sense of each citizen's maximum capacity to run his or her own life, not ruled by others, this might well give to the poorer majority a tolerant or even sympathetic recognition of the claim the wealthy have to be given the voting power that will protect them from being dominated by the unchecked or unbalanced majority.

Having planted this new seed of democratic theory, Aristotle asks us to reconsider his previous fourfold classification and ranking of the democratic regimes (1318b6ff.; recall 1292b24ff.). He reminds us that the best appeared to be the old rural-based democracy, because its farming populace lacked the leisure to assemble frequently. Now Aristotle introduces a major new consideration, akin to the previously stressed second dimension of the democratic idea of freedom: a hardworking poor majority "is more pleased by working than by engaging in politics and ruling, where no large profits accrue from the ruling offices; for the many seek gain, rather than honor." A sign of this, Aristotle adds, is that the many were willing to tolerate tyrannies in the old days, "and *they do tolerate oligarchies (at all times),* so long as they are not prevented from working and have nothing taken from them; for some of them quickly become rich, and the rest cease to be needy." "Besides," he continues, "if they do have some love of honor, their being sovereign as regards elections and audits fills the need." As evidence, he submits the observation that "in some populaces, such as that of Mantineia, the many are satisfied even if they do not share in the selection of ruling officers, except through some delegates chosen from all in rotation, so long as they remain sovereign as regards deliberation." Indeed, he asseverates, "this ought to be believed to be a model of democracy." From this he concludes that "it is advantageous and usual," in this model democracy, "for all to participate in election and auditing of officers, and in juries," but "for the greatest ruling offices" to be elected from candidates meeting substantial property qualifications, or even qualifications of capacity, rather than property. We see that Aristotle is providing the foundation for his earlier, and at the time seemingly overly hopeful, suggestion of the possibility of a "simultaneous democracy and [low-grade] aristocracy" (recall 1308b38–40). That suggestion now becomes more plausibly practical on the basis of a fuller (and not altogether flattering) understanding of the mentality, of the desires and ambition and conception of freedom, that typically characterizes a propertied democratic working class.

He then takes a further momentous step. The citizenry of this model democracy "must necessarily have a noble political life," and not only because "the ruling offices will always be administered by the best with the consent of the populace, who will not envy the decent"; what is more, "this ordering must necessarily be sufficient for the decent and notable." For "they will not be ruled by worse people, and they will rule justly *through the audit being in the hand of others.* For to be *dependent,*" and "not to be able to do everything according to one's own opinion, is advantageous": The "power to do whatever one wishes cannot defend against the baseness that is in each human being." The "necessary result (of such a democracy) is that there comes to pass what is most beneficial in the regimes – that the decent rule without falling into error, and the multitude are in no way at a disadvantage" (1318b32–19a4).

The need for a meaningful check on the political power of the conventionally "decent and notable" has become more and more evident in the preceding two books. Given this, the model democracy now being presented seems to be a candidate for an answer to the question Aristotle originally set as part of the second item on his agenda: "whether there happens to be *some other* regime (than the one that is most choice worthy after the best regime) that is *aristocratic* and constituted *nobly,* but harmonizes with the most cities – what it is" (1289b14–17).

Trans-Civic Leisure

In the last two books, Aristotle gives a more detailed elaboration of the simply best republican regime. At the outset, he raises and pursues the fundamental question that has been kept in the background throughout the book until now: Is politics, active engagement in political life, really the *most* choice-worthy existence, or is not the more withdrawn philosophic life more truly choice worthy? Aristotle answers with a pithy argument to the effect that the political life, though high or noble, must find its measure by taking second place to the philosophic life, which more completely engrosses, liberates, and fulfills our rational self-consciousness, our nature as rational animals (1323a14–1325b31).

But this brings to the table the question of how or to what extent and in what way an entire city's public life might somehow partake of or reflect this superiority of philosophy. Aristotle answers that the life of citizens of the best republic would be emphatically a *leisured* adult life, with concern for the education of the children toward *leisured* adulthood. Aristotle here articulates his key distinction between work, relaxation (or entertainment, play), and leisure (1333a31ff., and book eight as a whole). Work is painful but serious and necessary. Relaxation, play, or entertainment is pleasant but unserious, and related to work as a kind of restorative that enables people to get back to work. In contrast, true *leisure* is *serious* pleasure, the engrossing being-in-action (*energeia*) of our minds and souls in activities that are loved and pursued for their own sakes. Only true leisure, not work or relaxation, can satisfy the human longing for a meaningful purpose in life. A society as a whole can pursue true leisure by expanding its preoccupation with self-government to include a substantial communal engagement in literature, theater, and the fine arts, all aimed at provoking and encouraging deep reflection and heightened self-consciousness – and thereby providing for a civic or communal reflection of the much more private life of true philosophy.

This vision of the simply best, trans-civic republic remains utopian, but it is a vision that individuals can take as the polestar for their own lives as citizens, as family members, and as partakers of friendships, suffused with a deep awareness of and engagement in a rich leisure that enables them to transcend and to adorn the very inferior regimes allotted to them by fate. Aristotle's entire treatise, the *Politics*, is implicitly intended to foster and to contribute to – to become a textual focus and inspirer of – such trans-civic intellectual preoccupation of human being in all times and places.

PART II

BIBLICAL POLITICAL THEOLOGY

4

The Bible*

In turning from Athens to Jerusalem, we venture into a new realm. In a sense, we leave behind political philosophy, as it was originally founded by Socrates and carried on by his successors. We engage a writing that offers a radically alternative way of understanding and living human life. The Bible never refers to philosophy or to science, to "politics" or "the political." The Hebrew Bible (or Old Testament) and the Christian Gospels never speak of "nature" in general or of "human nature" in particular – or of "natural law," "natural right" or "natural rights," or "human rights." The Scriptures never refer to "democracy," "oligarchy," "republics" or republicanism, "statesmanship," "citizenship," "constitutions," "regimes," or "forms of government." The Bible elaborates a comprehensive, normative account of the whole of human existence – of righteousness or justice, of law, of cities and nations or peoples, of rulers and ruled, of family, of love, of education, and, above all, of divinity – without reference to, or apparent need for, many of the seemingly essential terms, categories, and concepts by which classical political philosophy sought to clarify the enduring meaning for human existence in all times and place of what the philosophers observed around them in republican practice. Starting with Socrates, the political philosophers claim that their unassisted human reasoning about empirical evidence available in principle to everyone makes decisive progress in uncovering the deepest permanent needs and problems of human nature from which one may derive lasting standards of good and bad. The Bible, in contrast, presents itself as the revelation to all mankind, through select

---

* Translations in this chapter are, with some emendations, from Robert Alter, *The Five Books of Moses* (New York: Norton, 2004); the Jewish Publication Society translation (1962–1982); and the Revised Standard Version.

inspired prophets, of authoritative guidance that humbles and shows the limitations of all merely human understanding and experience. The God who speaks through the Bible is a transcendent God, who as the creator of heaven and earth is not limited by any necessities, as his very name – "I will be what I will be" ("*Ehyeh-'Asher-Ehyeh*" – Exod. 3:14) – suggests. His only limits are those he imposes on himself by his unfailing promises or covenants that bespeak his adherence to and enforcement of justice: a justice that is intelligible to human critical thinking (Gen. 18:23–33; Deut. 32:4). He is known through the narration of his deeds and his commands.

Creation

"In the beginning," an unnamed narrator begins, "God was creating heaven and earth." The Bible presents the world as the creative work of a being Who calls beings – starting with light – into being out of darkness and the void. Whoever tells us this certainly wasn't there; it must, then, have been revealed to him. (By tradition, it was Moses to whom this was revealed, and to whom authorship of the first five books is ascribed.) The statement is a revealed answer to a question that arises of its own to any thoughtful human being, to one who asks: "How did this world in which I live come to be?" Before the one God created the world, there was nothing; there was a "void," welter and waste and darkness. God was not constrained in any way, it seems. There were no necessities that he had to manipulate, no preexisting beings that would limit His power. As subsequent theologians have put it, creation was *ex nihilo*, out of nothing; everything that is, is without a necessitating cause. It did not have to be, and could have been otherwise. According to philosophers, if anything could come to be without a cause, without a necessity, then the world would be unintelligible; according to the opening passage of the Bible, then, the world, created by God, is fundamentally unintelligible.

There is nonetheless a discernable order to God's creation, one that establishes in the reader's mind something about the intention of God in His creation. Three initial days of creation: of light, of the earthy, of the watery, of nonlife, and of plants, that is, of beings with no locomotion, no capacity to move or change – are followed by three days of creation of beings that move from place to place: first, sun and moon and stars, and then animals (with no fixed motion), and then humans. We are given a complete picture of the creation of the whole by a God who creates the whole merely by speaking – a distant God of awesome, sublime acts – an account that presents a rank ordering of the parts of creation; the heavenly bodies, which might otherwise appear to be divine beings worthy of worship, or (alternatively) evidence of unchangeable necessities, are deprecated: The sun isn't needed for vegetation, for example. But there is a commonsensical division that God has made of things into kinds, a "way" for each thing to live and move. The description of the first creation is, moreover, one of a clear ascent: We learn first of a homogeneous being (light), then of beings that have little motion, then of beings that have growth, then of living beings – animals – that have locomotion, and finally of the highest created being, man, that has a motion within him, an ability to rule the others, and who can move or change or go wrong in yet another way. But we don't learn of the last until we get, as we do next, a second account of creation.

The Second Account of Creation and the Fall

Humans are the center of the second story of creation. God makes man from the earth, and then plants a garden for him. Life is pleasant in the garden, and every plant that is good for food is there. It is fertile and well watered by four rivers. And God plants in this garden a tree of knowledge of good and evil, as well as a tree of life – from the latter of which, if he should eat, the man will live forever. Man is commanded by God on the other hand not to eat of the tree of knowledge of good and evil. He can eat of every other tree, but if he eats of this tree, on that day he shall die.

The second account calls to our attention, in the first place, the didactic character of the accounts: We have not one, but two accounts, each meant to unfold something significant about the world that we find ourselves in, something that cannot be captured or adequately conveyed by a single account. Second, the Bible presents contradiction as not something inherently troublesome to readers. The second account of creation, in which God is a kind of craftsman, working with given materials, tells us of God's plan for Man: Out of a rib of Adam (Man) God finally fashions a being suitable for Man, Woman (Eve). "This," declares Adam, "is at last bone of my bone and flesh of my flesh." And the narrator pauses, for the first time, to refer to a contemporary practice of readers: This, he says, is the reason that a woman shall leave her father's house and cling to a man. This, in other words, is the basis of sexual union and of marriage. This part of the account is given, then, explicitly, in order to explain human sexuality and marriage. We are then told how the two lived up to God's plan. And God walks in the garden and talks to Adam.

The commandment given to Adam is that he not eat of the tree of knowledge of good and evil. The commandment does not demand that he or the woman do something manifestly impossible; it is not like a commandment never to eat, for example. It is a commandment whose obedience is clearly within the realm of human possibility, freely to be obeyed. But it is so because, and only because, God has placed these first humans in a paradise, where their needs are easily met. That is, the perfect beginning of man's life on earth supports the argument that the defiance of God's commandment – the eating of the tree of knowledge of good and evil – was not an act compelled by, and so excused by, the harshness of their situation. Since the original situation of human beings was one of bounty, they were free to obey God's commands, and so are responsible for their deed. The account of the perfect beginning supports, and is meant to support, the moral understanding with which a reader approaches the text: Human beings are not compelled by their needs or self-interest to commit wrongs, but are free to do what is right.

A single creator God has made the world and made it a home for Man, who was to live happily in a state of childlike innocence but having an exalted place in creation, being a steward of God's creation, naming and having dominion over its other parts and recognizing the female of his species as the only fulfilling object of his longing.

But the cunning serpent tempts Eve, telling her that God has deceived her – that she shall not die but instead will know good and evil, like God. Eve sees that the fruit is good for food, and a delight to the eyes, and desirable for wisdom (she has already some knowledge of good); so she eats it, and gives it to Adam, who eats it, and suddenly they realize that they are naked, that is, that they somehow are not supposed to be naked. They have shame, which they did not have before. And that is the evidence that they now know good and evil. God states his punishments (Gen. 3.14). The first punishment is of the serpent, who will henceforth crawl on his belly (having somehow not done so before) and there will be enmity between himself and women; not just human beings but other parts of creation are affected by the Fall. The second punishment is of Woman, who will henceforth bear children in pain; the Bible thus explains why an apparently good (commanded) and ordinary part of a woman's life, childbirth, is so painful. Woman will also desire man and be ruled by him, as her punishment. The third punishment is of Adam, who henceforth will have to toil and sweat to live; God curses the ground so that it will produce food only through the hard labor of

Man. God then expels them from the garden before they eat of the tree of life and live forever. God is jealous of his knowledge combined with his eternity. And the humans, not knowing good and evil, had not given thought to the tree of life: They were not very aware of their mortality or its meaning. But human death now enters the world, with no possibility for humans to return to the garden. So while Adam and Eve, and their descendants up to Noah, live very long lives, reflecting their proximity to the original state of man – when God breathed his life into him – they will all eventually die. Yet God continues to care for man and to seek man's loving obedience and gratitude for that care, even as man continues to rebel against it.

The two accounts of creation disclose, then, a single God creating heaven and earth and all that is in it, a deprecation of heavenly bodies, and an account of our falling away from God's original plan. In the first account we are told that God's creation is in his eyes "very good," and in the second how it and in particular its peak, human beings, came to be not so good. Human beings, freely disobeying God, eating of the tree of knowledge of good and evil, drifting into disobedience, came to know good and evil, or to know it more fully, and were punished by God and expelled from the garden. Humans must now live with this knowledge and with a disrupted world. What they do with it determines whether or not they are good or evil.

Cain, Abel, and the Founding of Cities

The question of what humans do with the knowledge of good and evil forms the next part of the biblical narrative, which concerns the first descendants of Adam and Eve, the brothers Cain and Abel. Cain is a farmer, Abel a shepherd; each offers to God a sacrifice (which God clearly expects) from the fruits of their respective work. He is pleased with Abel's sacrifice but not with Cain's. God seems to prefer the offering of the nomad Abel, who relies upon God's bounty, more than that of the settled farmer Cain, who forces from the earth more than it would otherwise produce. God warns the angry Cain that he must rule over his wrath, or sin will result. But Cain murders Abel. God confronts Cain about the whereabouts of Abel, and Cain defiantly and with dissimulation answers with a question: "Am I my brother's keeper?" He seems unaware that God knows what he has done. "Your brother's blood cries out," says God. And God curses Cain: He will labor in vain to produce fruit from the earth and will become a fugitive and a wanderer, leading the very opposite of the settled life he had sought. Cain declares the punishment too severe; he will no longer see God, and wandering, he will be slain for his act. God assures him that he will not be, and puts a sign upon him. The punishment is in fact quite mild, reflecting the fact, perhaps, that there was no law laid down by God against murder.

Cain represents in his agriculture both settled life that relies on human art rather than on God and the desire to be first in esteem. His descendants are, we are told, the founders of cities and of the *arts* or *crafts* (musical instruments, cutting instruments of brass and iron, etc.). One of his descendants, moreover, Lamech, boasts that he as an avenger slays more men than does God. From the line of Seth, on the other hand – who replaces Abel – come no inventors or artisans or cities, but Enoch son of Jared, of whom it is said that he "walked with God" and not that, or when, he died, but simply that God "took him" (Gen. 5:24). Noah, too, is Seth's descendant, and becomes the very last righteous man in the world. Human arts, with which man would know and transform the given world, and cities, in which man would govern himself, are a movement away from reliance upon God and his provident care for men. They stand, we may say, for a proud autonomy. The Bible stands firmly against such autonomy through arts. What we would call "civilization" or "progress" or "development" is altogether different from the "righteousness" the Bible calls for.

So great is the difference, in fact, that by the time of Noah, the wickedness of everyone else on earth besides Noah causes God to repent of his creation of man. So evil does human life in cities become that there is left in the world only one righteous man. God saves Noah and his family and all animal species on the earth by having him build an ark and gather pairs of all living things into the ark. God then floods the earth and kills all living things on it.

Prior to the flood, then, mankind lives without law, in freedom from revealed law or restraint. But the result is disastrous. Man, now fully awake, knowing good and evil, knowing that he will die, lives unrighteously, in rebellion. God has to wipe out most of creation and start over. This time, He will give a law, but he will do so not as a mere imposition. He will do so in a covenant with Noah. When Noah emerges from the ark after the waters have subsided, he sacrifices many of the animals to God, who, after smelling the sweet sacrifice, declares the desire of man's heart to be evil from his youth. Yet God will never again destroy almost all life on earth. He is now prepared to make concessions to humanity's evil bent or to bring mankind back to Him in some way. He puts a rainbow in the heavens as a sign of his first covenant with men. So now the human condition, humanity's second chance as it were, is better. There is greater hope for man, with God realizing how this being is. But with that hope comes also an increase in punishment: A commandment for capital punishment of murder, as an indication of the dignity of human being (compare Gen. 9:2–6 with 1:26–30 and 2:15), and now the beasts fear and dread man. This is the first covenant that God makes. The second will be with Abraham.

Noah, the first man to have a vineyard and hence wine, gets drunk one night, and one of his sons, Ham, sees him drunk and naked. (Wine seems to remove the shame that knowledge of good and evil entails, or perhaps that very knowledge.) The other two sons of Noah, Shem and Japheth, cover their father's nakedness. The next day Noah curses Ham (who will become the father of Canaan) for having violated an un-promulgated law against seeing one's father naked. Noah blesses his other two sons. The land that Ham settles in, which became known through his son as "the land of Canaan," will be taken from his descendants, since God promises it subsequently to Abraham and his descendants. Mankind is now divided between the "cursed" and the "blessed."

We are also told of one of Noah's descendants, Nimrod, who becomes a "mighty hunter before God," a conqueror of beasts and of men, that is, a man who relies on himself and seeks glory through conquest. Nimrod founds a kingdom that includes a large city called Babel. It becomes the peak and emblem of the continuing attempt to rebel against reliance on God, or of proud autonomy. For its people seek to build a great city and a tower to the very heavens – the abode of God – lest they be scattered over the whole earth. They seek, that is, to remain together and to build a name for themselves. Their efforts have the opposite result. For God "comes down" to see what they are up to, and again speaking of himself in the plural, says: "'Behold, they are one people, and they have all one language; and this is what they begin to do; and now nothing will be withheld from them, which they purpose to do. Come, let us go down, and there confound their language, that they may not understand one another's speech.' So the Lord scattered them abroad from thence upon the face of all the earth; and they left off to build the city." The account thus explains how there came to be out of the single race that God had created, and then saved, various nations who cannot understand one another. God moves to thwart, through dividing men into nations, human accomplishment or human self-reliance and art.

Abraham and the Binding of Isaac

God calls Abraham to become the father of one of these nations, a new and blessed nation. Commanded by God to separate himself out from others in order to spawn this chosen nation, the childless Abraham is repeatedly promised, as he grows older and older, that he will be made that father. Abraham is commanded to circumcise himself and every male in his household as a sign of this new covenant. But besides this incisive sign, what characterizes Abraham and thus this chosen nation of which he is to be the father? We begin to learn this through three episodes: the birth of his son Isaac, the dialogue with God over the fate of Sodom and Gomorrah, and the Binding of Isaac. Through them we learn of a development that, though coming as a consequence of the Fall, represents an *ascent* from our original state. It is a deepening human awareness of mortality and a consequent deepening of human faith in and love of God.

"Isaac," Abraham's son, whose name means "he will laugh," is so named because of the laughter that his parents both expressed upon hearing the news from God that he would be born to them (Gen. 17:16–17, 18:9–15). Abraham was ninety-nine and his wife, Sarah, eighty-nine when Abraham was told by God that Sarah would bear him a son. Abraham's love of and trust in this wonder-working God, a trust that is the opposite of contemptuous laughter – which presupposes that there are things possible and impossible – makes him deserving of being the father of the chosen people.

We learn more of what it means for Abraham to trust in God and in his righteousness in the immediate sequel (chapter 18), which tells us God's plan for the cities of Sodom and Gomorrah. Their peoples are wicked, and God intends to kill them. Abraham intervenes, and appeals to God to spare the city of Sodom – if fifty, then forty-five, then forty, thirty, twenty, and finally ten righteous men are to be found in it. Or rather, he asks God if he will destroy the cities if ten righteous men are found. Abraham, that is, knowing better than his predecessors that he is going to die (see Gen. 18:27: "who am but dust and ashes") trusts that God is not a God who destroys the righteous along with the wicked. His hope or trust is that God rewards the righteous. He acts together with God; he acts as if he has a share in the responsibility for God acting righteously.

God has through a wonder given Abraham a son, and Isaac embodies Abraham's love of the chosen people, of his people who will trust in the Lord. But God says to Abraham: "Take your son, your only one, the one you love, Isaac, and go forth to the land of Moriah and offer him up as a burnt offering on one of the mountains which I shall say to you" (Gen. 22:2). It would appear that in making this demand, God is putting an end to the fulfillment of His promise and is violating the law He gave to Noah, concerning the shedding of innocent blood. Yet Abraham obeys; he is commanded to surrender to God, to give to God what is dearest to Abraham, to sacrifice his deepest hope to God, without expectation of any reward. Abraham loves not himself but God. God rightfully demands that he, and not oneself or even God's chosen people, be loved without qualification. Abraham obeys with a childlike trust in God, yet aware that he is mere dust or will die. And he is rewarded: God spares Isaac's life. God is a righteous God, not a tyrant God. But only by not presuming upon God's righteousness, only by accepting that God is an unfathomable God, does one come to merit a reward. In this way, by presenting God as unfathomable but just, as one who in His unfathomability makes possible the prospect of genuine sacrifice of one's own good, the Bible preserves the possibility of devotional, self-sacrificial love, just as it had begun to do in the story of Adam and Eve, with the clear indications there of human freedom and hence responsibility.

This unfathomability or fierce uncanniness of God, and hence the deepening of trust in and love of him, will become still more pronounced as God reveals himself to Moses, in Exodus:

> And Moses said to God, "look, when I come to the Israelites and say to them, 'The God of your fathers has sent me to you,' and they say to me, 'What is His name?' what shall I say to them?" And God said to Moses, "I-Will-Be-Who-I-Will-Be." And he said, "Thus shall you say to the Israelites, 'Ehyeh, I-Will-Be, has sent me to you.'"

God's very name bespeaks mystery or an unfathomable will. As God says later in Exodus, "I shall be gracious to whom I shall be gracious, and I shall show mercy to whom I shall show mercy" (33:19). Even the way in which He fulfills his promises – which are the only actions of His that one can predict – are unpredictable. "My ways are not your ways, neither are my thoughts your thoughts, says the Lord" (Isa. 55.8). God is accordingly said to dwell in a thick cloud or darkness (1 Kings 8:12), disclosing Himself unpredictably. What He does disclose of His purposes and His will is disclosed through the Torah, through the first five books and its laws.

Jacob/Israel, Joseph, Egypt

The people whom this mysterious God has chosen are to reflect His mysteriousness, and so are to be distinct from other peoples. Isaac's son Jacob, who comes to be named Israel and thus the Eponymous Patriarch, is perhaps most instructive in this respect. Jacob is easily the most deceitful character in the Hebrew Scriptures. Even his name means "crooked," like a heel – the heel of his brother, which he grasped when they were born, as if Jacob were trying to pull him back into the womb so that he would be first. Rebekah, the boys' mother, prefers Jacob to Esau, and sets up a wily scheme to have Jacob deceive his father and take his brother's blessing. So the question is, why does God permit this? Why does He prefer Jacob? Why are this man's deeds presented at such comparative length?

The account of how Jacob comes by his brother's birthright gives us some guidance (Gen. 25:27–35; cf. 38). From it we see that Esau is an impatient, impetuous, grunting, crude man of appetites, and while he is a clever hunter of animals, he is otherwise rather stupid. He has the appearance of a strong and spirited man but of one who is quite weak in understanding and self-control. Jacob is more delicate or gentle, but also clever with humans. God's preference may be said to be for the gentle but wily over the physically strong but slow.

After Jacob steals the final blessing that Isaac intended for Esau, he goes to Mesopotamia and eventually has an endogamous marriage to Leah and to Rachel, daughters of his uncle Laban. The two wives of Jacob and their slave girls have between them some ten children by Jacob before Rachel herself finally has a son by Jacob, Joseph. Jacob then manages by a trick to get all the healthiest of Laban's flock and heads back with them to the land of Canaan, secretly: Jacob is a timid man. One passage in the account of his exit from Laban's lands warrants our special attention. Rachel had stolen her father Laban's household gods, unbeknownst to Jacob. So when Laban comes to get his gods back, Jacob says that whoever should be found with them will die. Rachel has hidden them in a camel cushion upon which she sits in her tent. "Let not," she tells her searching father, "my lord be incensed that I am unable to rise before you, for the way of women is upon me." Rachel refers to her menstrual period as "the way of women," and her words provide a striking example of the Bible's manner of referring to what philosophers would call "nature." The Bible's word is "way." It is the same word used for "custom," as in "the way of the Philistines." No distinction is drawn between what is by nature and what is by law or custom. The way of birds is to have wings and feathers and to fly, the way of fish is to have scales and gills and fins, the way of Americans is to wear blue jeans, and the way of women is to menstruate. Or one could say "the custom of birds is to fly." The Bible goes to great lengths, that is, to ensure that since all the world is the work of the creator God, no distinction should arise between nature and custom that would call that creative work into question.

Jacob returns to Canaan to meet with Esau, but before he gets there he wrestles, in his dread of Esau's approaching men, all night long with some nameless being, God, and God renames him Israel, and Jacob is permanently lamed, made physically crooked, limping. (He will soon suffer also the loss of Rachel and, as he thinks, of Joseph.) The narrator pauses to explain a dietary law, the removal of the sciatic nerve, that results from the event: "Therefore the children of Israel do not eat the sinew of the thigh which is by the hip-socket to this day, for he had touched Jacob's hip-socket at the sinew of the thigh." This is the first time that the Bible refers to God's people as "the children of Israel," which became their name thereafter. Jacob, the eponymous ancestor, is clearly the model for that people – a timid, wily man who wrestled with God and was physically weakened by that event.

Jacob had sent news of his arrival in Canaan to Esau, but the latter had not replied; he has sent instead, ominously, his four hundred horsemen. The frightened Jacob attempts to placate his brother with many sheep and cattle before meeting him himself, and it works. The two are reconciled, with Jacob now calling him "my lord" and calling himself "your servant." He in effect gives up his claim to any worldly title to rule. And when his daughter Dinah is raped by the son of the local prince (Gen. 34), Jacob does nothing. Two of his sons, to avenge her honor, trick the whole tribe of men into circumcising themselves and then kill them all while they are recovering! Jacob, however, is angry at their deed, telling them that they have stirred up trouble in the land, while they are only a handful of men. The proud sons protest: "Like a whore should our sister be treated?" Keenly aware of his weakness, Jacob finds his sons' proud avenging of their sister's honor to be a mistake. (He says nothing about the terrible trick by which they accomplished it.) Then God appears again to Jacob to give him a way out, telling him to go to Bethel. Jacob rids his household of all other gods. "And the terror of God was upon the towns around them, and they did not pursue the sons of Jacob" (Gen. 35:5). A little later, when Rachel dies in childbirth, and Jacob's oldest son, Rueben lies with Jacob's own concubine, Jacob hears of it and does nothing. He apparently does not wish to make trouble. Such is the one whom God has favored, one with little sense of pride or honor, no desire to rule, and with a keen awareness of his worldly weakness and a strong reliance upon God.

In striking contrast with this account of Jacob, we are told next of all the kings who sprang up among the descendants of Esau, and explicitly told that Esau's land, Edon, had kings "before Israel ever did." This, our first indication that Israel will eventually have kings, comes by way of contrast: Israel will not, despite or rather because it is the people of God, emerge as a people through the rule of kings. The contrast continues as we learn next that Jacob loves his second youngest son, Joseph – a tattletale – born of Rachel, better than he loves Joseph's tougher, prouder brothers. When the brothers hear Joseph's prophetic dream of the sheaves – of how they will all bow to him one day – they have had enough of him, and throw him into a pit and then sell him as a slave, reporting to their father that he was killed by a wild beast. As a result Joseph ends up going to Egypt as a slave, is falsely accused by his master's wife of attempted rape, goes to prison, interprets well the dreams of a fellow prisoner who is a chief of Pharaoh, ends up interpreting Pharaoh's dreams, and becomes Pharaoh's right-hand man. During the seven years of famine that Joseph had correctly interpreted Pharaoh's dream to foretell, Jacob/Israel sends his sons into Egypt for food, setting the stage for the final, touching scenes in Genesis, and the last of its many accounts of deceptions, this time by Joseph, who does not disclose who he is and who plants a silver goblet on Benjamin in order to get his father into Egypt. (But whenever Joseph deceives his brothers, he weeps.) Once they are all there, Joseph discloses himself and is reconciled with them, and the people of Israel gradually flourish and prosper, so much so that the Egyptians consider them a threat to their rule, and enslave them. The people of Israel thus come to endure four hundred years of Pharaonic despotism, serving another people; they become a large people without experiencing any political rule of their own, with no great or proud leaders, no sense of proud independence, no military conquests, no participation in political deliberation.

Moses and the Divine Law

The Israelites are finally liberated from the Egyptians by their uncanny God and his wondrous works; Moses is the great prophet of God who leads them out. At every stage of their exodus and their forty-year journey to the promised land of Canaan, they are both reliant on God and rebellious against God, wishing to have a visible god like others, complaining about the lack of food, and then about the monotony of the very nourishing food that God provides them. For forty years Moses wanders in the wilderness with them, fighting off other tribes with God's miraculous help, and receiving from God on Mount Sinai the commandments by which his people are to live. Finally the promised land is in sight. But their leader, the prophet Moses, who spoke with God, is not even deemed worthy to lead God's people into that land. The people is God's people, not Moses' people.

Before we are given the account of their entry into the promised land led by the military leader Joshua – for whom God parts the rivers of the Jordan and knocks down the walls of the city of Jericho – we are given three books comprised largely of laws: Leviticus, Numbers, and Deuteronomy. And while these books lack the drama, the narrative enchantment, of the books that precede and follow them, they provide us with an understanding of the normative conceptions of authority in which the theocratic political thinking of the Bible is most deeply rooted. In stark contrast to classical political philosophy, neither the laws given in these books nor any other part of the Bible presents an explicit teaching on the "best regime." So what, if anything, takes the place, in the Bible, of the discussion of the best regime, or of the basic principles of legitimate government?

The Chosen People

The closest thing to an answer, as we have now begun to see, is that we find in the Bible a single, exemplary, chosen people, and an unfolding account of a succession of systems of authority under which that people lives. Each of these successive systems is blessed, or approved – though in every case with some severe reservations – and all of them are seen in vivid contrast to a *worst* system of authority: the Egyptian Pharaonic despotism. To begin with, then, we may say that the Bible appears to lay down as its clearest benchmark or standard what is worst, what is most to be avoided, as opposed to what is best, what is to be aspired to, in politics.

To better understand the biblical outlook, we need first to raise and seek an answer to the following question: *Why* is there a single chosen people, distinguished from the rest of humanity, given the fact that the biblical God is the one and only God, the creator of *all* mankind in His image? The elements of an answer appear in the parables of Genesis that precede and lead up to the designation of Abraham and his offspring as the chosen people. Humanity is created in the image of God, but out of the dust. Humanity partakes of divine intelligence and freedom, but in a subordinate capacity that requires a constant struggle to rule over the lower dimensions of human existence. When humans are left to themselves, they exhibit an overwhelming tendency to lose sight of this proper ordering. Mankind is prone to pervert its divine attributes in a proud attempt to escape, to replace or to usurp, the rule of God. Only through a long and painful process of humiliating and purifying education can the human race gradually recover a firm grasp on the strictly subordinate transcendence implied in its being created in the image of God. The chosen people is forcibly set apart and commanded to live as an image of transcendence that will be exemplary for all mankind because of the terrible tests to which this chosen people is put – tests recorded for all humans in the Scriptures (Isa. 42:6–7; cf. Lev. 10:3, 11:44; Deut. 28:10).

The Pre-Mosaic Biblical Forms of Human Authority

The testing takes political shape in a succession of what we may call biblical regimes. First, and in an important sense, perduring, is patriarchy – epitomized above all in the story of Abraham. The monogamous family, headed by the father but with a place of high honor assigned to the mother, is a cornerstone of any and every society favored by the Bible. The cultivation of familial kinship, of familial devotion, of familial responsibility, and of future hope centered on the family, remains always at the heart of biblical virtue. But patriarchy, though it begins as the sole form of Hebrew rule, and though it remains the kernel of Hebrew society, soon is shown to be inadequate as a mode of rule over a people of many families. As we have seen, Jacob, who so successfully procreates the large band of brothers that becomes the source of the twelve tribes of Israel, proves quite incapable of maintaining order or even peace among those brothers.

What is needed over and above the patriarchs, the Scripture teaches, is the rule of law. What Scripture means by the rule of law is the absolute rule of divine law – of a code made for, but not by, humans. In order to understand the character and the need for such a humbling, superhuman law, the people of Abraham – and we readers, vicariously – must first experience what human rule can become when it is un-humbled, unlimited by any such law beyond the human. We must experience the temptation such rule holds out – for the ruled even more than for the ruler. We must watch as the Israelites embrace the delusive comforts or pampering effected by efficient, untrammeled human administration. It is Joseph, the Pharaoh's right-hand slave (for all under Pharaoh are slaves) who starts the chosen people – and us – down this path. It is Joseph who brings Jacob to reside in Egypt and, what is more, it is Joseph who devises the abolition of private property among all Egyptians, thus completing the absolute character of the Pharaonic despotism (Gen. 41:39ff., 47:20–26).

Yet the Bible does not present this economic absolutism of Pharaonic rule in so pejorative a fashion as we today are inclined to view it; the Bible does not present Joseph in the dark light in which he appears in some contemporary analyses of Joseph as the arch-typical assimilating, and thus self-destructive, court-Jew. It seems characteristic of biblical political judgment, as opposed to our modern judgment, that what for the Bible seems to define the peculiarly monstrous character of the evil represented by the Pharaonic system, what sets the Egyptians apart from all other peoples, is their technological success in *mastering their environment.* The Egyptians are the one people who, the Scripture stresses, have almost no dependence on the weather: They have learned to use irrigation to master the Nile, and thereby to achieve apparent independence from forces beyond human control; the seventh plague, the plague that is the first to break the will of the Egyptians, is thunder and hail, which (the Bible says) "had not fallen on the land of Egypt since it had become a nation" (Exod. 9:24; cf. Deut. 11:10–12). The Pharaoh, one is inclined say, is presented as believing that he has realized what was sought in the construction of the Tower of Babel (Gen. 11:3ff.). The result is that the Egyptians, as depicted in Exodus, worship no gods (but cf. Gen. 47:22, 41:45, 50; Num. 33:4). They seem to substitute, for religion or worship of deities, a very powerful human magic (Exod. 7:11ff.). Pharaonic despotism, the Scripture suggests, is so limitlessly oppressive, so ruthlessly cruel, and so complete or all-embracing, because this despotism embodies and exemplifies the power of human contrivance constrained by no sense of a higher power that limits or would humble human arrogance.

Liberation from Human Despotism to Divine Law

The *third* political order, decisive for all the rest of biblical time, is of course the Mosaic liberation *from* Pharaonic despotism, *to* the divine law that puts an end, among the chosen people, to such unchecked human rule. Yet as we have foreshadowed, the biblical rule of law is something quite unlike what we have come to identify as the rule of law. Our conception of the rule of law is guided by the Lockean-Montesquieuian notions of law as the guarantor of pre-legal individual rights, and of government as a human institution that draws its legitimate authority solely from the consent of the governed. We need to try to free ourselves from these contemporary presuppositions in our effort to see clearly the authentically biblical conception of law, and to confront the challenge that conception poses to our ways of thinking.

Under God's close instruction, Moses wields enormous political power. He carries out purges of his opponents and thus occasionally overawes with terror the mass of the Hebrews, who are disciplined for forty grim and often frightening years in the desert. This fear and rigor are in service to a noble educative enterprise intended and required to transform a mass of demoralized slaves into a "kingdom of priests and a holy nation" (Exod. 19:6). The covenant between God and his people on Mount Sinai precedes the purging and training; and so what Moses most evidently is aiming at by his protracted indoctrination is the formation of a popular consciousness that can sustain and exemplify a covenantal and hence consensual form of divine as well as human authority. Yet it is important to see that the law delivered to the chosen people at Sinai is not the product of human wisdom, whether that human wisdom be conceived as arising from popular deliberation or from aristocratic or monarchic guidance; the law does not depend for its authority on the consent of those who are to live under it. The most that could be said is that the people's consent seals, by submissive acknowledgment and commitment, the unquestionable authority of the law for and over them. In other words, the consent of the people of Israel is solicited not in order to *validate* the law's wisdom or its authority but rather in order to elicit from God's people their solemn pledge to respect the divine law's *intrinsic*, and therefore permanent and noncontingent, authority and superiority, in wisdom and in rightness. Moreover, the people agree to obey God's law not for the sake of the rewards or benefits it promises, but for the sake of the law, and its lawgiver, and a life in obedience to the law, as supreme ends in themselves (Exod. 20ff.; Deut. 5–6). The covenant is thus radically dissimilar to the covenants later variously articulated by Hobbes and Locke and Rousseau and their successors.

By the covenant centered on the law given at Sinai, God continues and deepens that revelation of his character as ruler that he began in and by the previous covenants with Noah and Abraham. God's rule is that of a being whose power is total and whose authority is absolute, but who chooses in His grace to limit or to define His rule by unconstrained but unshakable legal commitments – and who demands from His chosen people a congruent solemn vow. God, however mysterious He may be, is a moral ruler: He rules, not with a view to some contingent self-interest or need or whim, but in accordance with solemn, unfailing promises based on immutable principles of lawful justice.

What is the substantive content and the spirit of the biblical law, conceived as a code of life whose regulative authority dwarfs all human pretensions to self-government?

In the *economic* sphere, we observe that the law of Moses protects private property, and especially private landed property, while imposing severe limits on the increase of such property. What we would call capital accumulation, as well as selfish enjoyment of the fruits of labor and investment, are not only limited but compelled to bow before the duties of *charity*. All property is conceived as owned ultimately, not by the community, and still less by the government, but rather by God, the Creator of heaven and earth (Exod. 21–13; Lev. 25; Deut. 15, 23, 26–27).

In the *erotic* sphere, sexual pleasure is severely limited to what conduces to the procreative life of the patriarchal family (Lev. 15, 18–20; Num. 5, 30; Deut. 21:15ff., 22:5ff.).

In the sphere of *penal* law, the principle of retribution prevails, with a grave sense of human responsibility and guilt. The Mosaic law codifies what we have learned from the book of Genesis about the terrible human proclivity to sin, the resultant condign divine punishment (tempered by divine mercy), and the desperate need humans have to seek divine forgiveness – as well as divine assistance in overcoming the constant temptation to sin. Especially if one compares the penal legislation of Plato's *Laws* with the letter and the spirit of the Mosaic penal legislation, it becomes clear that it is in this sphere that the Mosaic revelation most manifestly challenges the Socratic moral outlook, epitomized by Socrates' and the Athenian Stranger's oft-repeated and self-consciously paradoxical contention that virtue is knowledge, and that vice is therefore a form of ignorance.

Not only guilt but something more elusive and pervasive haunts and tarnishes human existence as well as other parts of creation: an *impurity*, an uncleanness, for which man is partly responsible, and that would seem to be in some measure a consequence of the incarnation of the divine "image" in the partly animal man. The law fully reveals to humans this uncleanness that haunts them (Lev. passim; Deut. 14:21, 23:10ff.).

The specific purgatory laws direct humans to the admission or full recognition of their impurity, as the first step to mitigating or perhaps even
overcoming that contamination – with God's help and through a vast
and complex array of rites. These rituals, and the spirit that is to infuse
them, are not merely negative or purgative. They are also, and perhaps
most fundamentally, directed upward, toward *transcendence* of human-
all-too-human weakness, and thereby toward a share in the godlike existence that is mankind's ultimate destiny as the creature created in the
image of God; God's words in Leviticus are: "you shall be holy, for I am
holy" (11:44–45, 19:2). God's holiness is inseparable from, though not
simply identical with, His righteousness or justice. That righteousness
is first and foremost His punitive law enforcement: "And exalted is the
Lord of Hosts by just judgment; the Holy God is proved holy by retributive justice," says the prophet Isaiah (Isa. 5:16). But retributive justice,
which after all comes into play only in response to human imperfec-
tion, has its source in a higher and purer aspect of justice: God's un-
needy, and therefore unqualifiedly and even unfathomably generous,
care and love for the common good of all His creatures. And the human
ascent toward holiness is an ascent from the uncleanness of unjust or
sinful selfishness toward justice in this rich, positive sense: toward not
merely respect, and compassion, but love – for one's "neighbor" and also
for "the stranger," as "oneself" (Lev. 19:18, 34) – and then, above and
beyond, to a self-forgetting love of God as the simply most lovable, and
as the source of everything else lovable (Deut. 6:5, 30:6). This indeed is
for the Scripture the most important purpose of the rule of law: loving
worship or adoration of God, and the purification and elevation of mankind toward assimilation to the radically transcendent "holiness" of the
deity. This ascent to holiness entails the constant struggle to rise above
everything selfish and ugly or disgusting and merely animal (especially
sexual – Lev. 15, 18–20; Deut. 22:5ff.), above the trammels of what is
material, mundane, and mortal – in order to ascend toward the realm of
that sublime spiritual beauty whose eternal, un-needy grace promises to
slake our soul's deepest thirst (Lev. 21). In the Mosaic regime, this ascent
is perhaps most vividly undertaken through the proper employment of
the fine arts in the gifts given to God, and especially in the joyful construction of the Tabernacle and execution of the priestly rituals associated with the Tabernacle (Exod. 25–31, 35:10–40:35).

From the point of view of political philosophy, the most obviously puzzling dimension of the divine law given through Moses is its lack of clarity regarding the organization of human rule or administration under

God's law. If we try to discern clues to the intended structure of human authority, we are struck, to begin with, by the absence of any democratic institutions in the divine law. The "assembly" – the heart of the classical democratic regime – is barely alluded to, and given no regular meeting time or place (Num. 35:24–25). What is more, there is no provision for popular election, let alone for selection of officers by lot (though see Num. 1:16 and 16:2). The one moment of nascent "popular sovereignty" is the attempt, on the part of the rebel Korah (leading "the whole community": Num. 16:19) to challenge Moses' singular authority in the name of widespread or even universally shared divine inspiration. That attempt meets with horrifyingly instructive divine punishment.

On the other hand, however, neither is there a king or a clearly defined political aristocracy, whether established on the basis of blood, or election, or divine anointment, or criteria of merit. (There is of course an aristocratic *priesthood*, administering the all-important rituals of worship.)

Instead of a governing assembly or an aristocracy or a monarchy, we are confronted with a number of appointed or anointed rulerships, whose lines of jurisdiction and authority overlap in what one is tempted to characterize as a maze. To begin with, there are the "Elders," whose authority antedates Moses and some of whom prove to have prophetic gifts (Exod. 3:16, 4:29, 17:5, 18:12, etc.); then there are the "Tribal Leaders" (who also antedate Moses, but are ratified by God – Deut. 1:13ff.) – but these are different from the Tribal Heads whom God commands to be appointed to lead the pioneers into the promised land (Num. 13). Then there are the new "Chiefs" who are also "Judges," appointed by Moses not through any divine inspiration but instead at the pertinent suggestion of his father-in-law Jethro, who comes to the aid of the apparently rather bewildered and overworked Moses (Exod. 18:13ff.). Then there are "Overseers" and "Scribes" (Exod. 5:6, 10, 14; Deut. 16:18, 20:5–9); last but by no means least, there is the divinely appointed warlord and successor to Moses, Joshua (Num. 27:15ff., 34:16).

From Joshua to David

The potential for turbulence that is implied in this constitutional jumble does not become evident in the first generation after Moses, that is, in the *fourth* regime, which carries out the conquest of the promised land. For the conquest requires disciplined military obedience to the warlord Joshua. On the whole, from the account in the book of Joshua, one may judge that this regime appears to be the most successful of all those described in the Scripture, not only militarily but, above all, in terms of the steadfastness of the people's *piety* (Josh. 24:31; Judg. 2:7, 3:10ff.). This might suggest that the pressure of external foes is required in order to maintain steady pious observance of the law. Yet even this regime-at-arms exhibits a decisive flaw, precisely in regard to pious obedience. On account of a combination of folly and softness (especially Joshua's pact with the Hivites – Josh. 9) the chosen people fails to extirpate entirely the idolatrous and abomination-practicing inhabitants of Canaan. The subsequent recurrent corruption of the chosen people, caused by intermarriage with the idolatrous native people, is the terrible price the Hebrews pay for this negligent disobedience of God's unambiguous commandment of pitiless exterminating conquest (Deut. 7:16ff.; Josh. 23:9ff.).

The persistence of Canaanite idolatry and of other Canaanite abominations contributes to the serious difficulties experienced in the *fifth* regime, the rule of the Judges that succeeds the generalship of Joshua (for whom God appoints no successor). Under the Judges, the full potential for disorder implicit in the bewildering Mosaic constitutional provisions becomes manifest. The epoch of the Judges is characterized by a nigh-anarchic fluidity and unpredictability, and by a tribal confederacy that proves woefully inadequate to deal with foreign threats. The recurrence of charismatic leaders – Deborah, Gideon, and Samson being the most notable – halts only temporarily a process of descent into lawless, internecine savagery.

The apparently obvious solution is the institution of a divinely anointed monarchy, the *sixth* and final form of biblical regime. Monarchy is repeatedly foreshadowed in the book of Judges, and earlier in the Deuteronomic prophecies of Moses himself (Deut. 17:14ff.). Yet the advent of monarchy is condemned by the prophet Samuel, apparently speaking for God as well as for himself (1 Sam. 8). Through this condemnation, Scripture compels us to wonder whether the Divinity does not look with considerable favor upon something like the regime and the world described in the book of Judges. The biblical God would seem to have good reason to prefer the turbulence, uncertainty, fragility, and vulnerability, the recurrent unexpected eruption of charismatic saviors, which characterizes the epoch of the Judges. The biblical God, one may be tempted to conclude, wants humans to remain unsettled, challenged by criminals within and by fearful enemies without, who keep alive the threat of becoming enslaved again, unless God sends charismatic savior-leaders.

Still, when all this has been said, it remains difficult to avoid the conclusion that monarchy at its best is depicted as the real peak of Israel's historical existence. For monarchy brings an unprecedented grandeur of biblical virtue, both intellectual and moral, even as it also brings, in the persons of the best as well as the worst kings, an enormity of biblical vice approaching at times the monstrosity of the Pharaoh. The peak that monarchy reaches in the Bible can be summed up in one name: David.

Certainly the Judges' deepening corruption – taking bribes, extorting choice cuts of meat meant for God, sexual liaisons with the women who come to offer sacrifices to God – makes the Judges become contemptible. Equally, if not more importantly, they are manifestly unable to lead the Israelites in battle against their Philistine neighbors, and a desperate, misguided attempt to use the ark of the covenant for this purpose ends in disastrous failure. Even the prophet Samuel's sons become corrupt. The elders of Israel therefore demand of the aged prophet Samuel, the only uncorrupt priest and judge, that they be given a king, "like other nations." Samuel, who has received revelations from God since his youth, is opposed to this demand. Samuel's reaction bespeaks his fear that acquiescing in the desire of the Israelites for a king will indeed make Israel merely "like other nations." But the elders persist, and Samuel therefore brings their request to God with a heavy heart. God's response is ominous; he tells Samuel to grant the request, so that the people will come to experience life under an earthly ruler, in all its selfish aggrandizement, corruption, and oppression (1 Sam. 8).

Yet the kingship that God proceeds to arrange does not bear out this grim warning. The man whom God directs Samuel to anoint as future king is Saul, from the humblest tribe (that of Benjamin) and its humblest house – but a man who is very handsome and tall. After his anointing, Saul briefly becomes a prophet, and through a lottery he is selected as king. When he hears of a horrible threat from one of Israel's enemies, the Ammonites, the spirit of God comes upon Saul; he becomes enraged, and issues a dreadful threat to any men of Israel who should fail to come out with him against the Ammonite. He wins a victory, which he attributes to the Lord, and is *then* solemnly made king (1 Sam. 9ff.). In selecting Saul, God certainly did not select a man lacking in royal capacities or in pious humility. By any ordinary human standards, Saul might well be judged a fine king. But Saul is nonetheless shown to be seriously flawed as a king of God's chosen people: And his specific failures are deeply instructive as to the difference between human and divine standards of excellence in human ruling.

For when the Philistines first threaten, Saul does not follow the commandments of God concerning burnt offerings, and Samuel tells Saul that God will therefore eventually replace Saul with another king, "a man after His own heart" (1 Sam. 13). The unsteadiness of Saul's obedience to divine commandment – his tendency to follow instead his own human prudential calculation of what is worth doing – becomes still more evident when Saul fails to follow Samuel's order from the Lord to destroy, as a punishment of the enemy Amalek, everything in Amalek's camp. Saul instead allows the people of Israel to keep "all that is good" and destroy only the "worthless" things (1 Sam. 15).

As the future replacement for Saul, God designates David, the lyre-playing youngest son of Jesse, a shepherd boy who is short and unprepossessing to behold: "For the Lord sees not as man sees; man looks on the outward appearances, but the Lord looks on the heart" (1 Sam. 16:6). The story of David's victory over Goliath, and of the aftermath of that victory, are among the most famous depictions of God's relation to his people, and are most revealing of the Hebrew Scriptures' implicit as well as explicit teaching about the kind of ruler and rulership that is best among humans. David is sent by his father to the Israelite camp with food for his oldest warrior brothers. When he arrives, he hears the challenge being made by the colossal, well-armed Philistine warrior Goliath, who seeks a battle of individual champions: Let one of the men of Israel come out to fight me, and the victor's people will enslave the people of the vanquished, without a battle of the whole armies. David asks what reward is offered for the man who will oppose this Goliath, and learns that it is great indeed. He then expresses open disdain in the Israelite camp for Goliath. "Who is this uncircumcised Philistine, that he should defy the armies of the living God?" (1 Sam. 17:26). His brothers take this as a taunt directed at them, and angrily tell David to go back to his sheep, accusing him of aiming at his own glory. But David is undeterred; he continues to ask his defiant question, and is eventually brought before King Saul.

Saul questions David: How can you, a mere youth inexperienced in battle, fight Goliath, who has been a soldier from his youth? David's words to the king are both frank and an implicit challenge: "The Lord delivered me from the paw of the lion and the bear, and He will deliver me from the hand of this Philistine." What is Saul to do? Can he openly admit that he lacks faith in the Lord, the God who is the very reason for the being of his people? "Go," Saul says, "and the Lord be with you." But in another failure of faith, Saul attempts to dress David in his own armor.

David takes it off, saying that he has no experience in it; David is not yet a soldier and will rely solely on God and what God has given him.

David then goes out to meet Goliath, who taunts him: "Am I a dog, that you come to me with sticks ... Come to me, and I will feed your flesh to the birds of the air and the beast of the field." David's response is telling: "You come to me with sword and shield and spear, but I come to you in the name of the Lord God of the hosts, the God of the armies of Israel, whom you have defied." "This day," David prophesies, "the Lord will deliver you into my hand, and I will strike you down, and I will cut off your head, and I will give the dead bodies of the host of the Philistines this day to the birds of the air and the beasts of the earth." Then David proclaims the purpose in all this: "That all the world may know that there is a God in Israel, and that all of this assembly may know that the Lord saves not with sword and spear." David places the outcome of the battle not in his own strength or capacity, or in any weapons of war, but squarely in the hands of God. And David declares his motive to be not his own glory but a manifestation to all the world of the glory of the God of Israel, and a reminder to his own people and the Philistines ("this assembly") of their need to rely on God rather than on human means of salvation.

David uses his shepherd's slingshot to strike a blow with a stone to Goliath's forehead, and the giant falls. David then rushes to him, takes Goliath's sword, and decapitates him. The narrator ensures that we realize that what has transpired is God's wondrous work: "There was no sword in the hand of David." The shepherd boy has won, against all odds, because of God – and the victory is God's. Yet do the Israelites fully understand? After the Israelites then put the Philistines to flight, they sing David's praises, explicitly over and against those of Saul: "Saul has slain his thousands, and David his ten thousands." Saul has lost the confidence of the people to David and will soon lose the kingship to him – despite his attempts to kill David.

After much bitter fighting, David marries Saul's daughter, Michal, takes the throne, and eventually conquers the city of Jerusalem, naming it the City of David. As he is bringing the ark of the covenant into the new capital city, David dances before the ark wearing only a loincloth, so as to display both his passion to subordinate his musical ability to the Lord and his own humble rank before God. This uncontrolled display of humility arouses the disdain of David's wife and queen. Michal finds her husband's behavior unbecoming a king. Michal is a lady, a woman of proud taste and propriety, who wishes her David to live up to his rank.

The Bible shows what God thinks of this: Michal is not merely brought low by God, but spends her life barren of children, while David loves and takes other wives. David is *not* a "gentleman" of the sort one encounters in classical political life, and he is not to have as his wife a high-class lady pulling him in the direction of gentlemanly pride and self-sufficiency (2 Sam. 6).

But a dark and sinful self-centeredness lurks even in the heart of David the anointed of God. He proves to be fundamentally flawed, fundamentally disposed to crime. David sees from his palace the beautiful wife of Uriah the Hittite, Bathsheba, bathing, and is overcome by desire for her. He takes her to bed and she becomes pregnant with his child, and he schemes to have Uriah killed by putting him in a chariot at the head of his armies against the Ammonites, so that he, David, can have Bathsheba as his wife. David succeeds in his scheme. Soon, however, David is visited by a prophet of the Lord, Nathan, who brings home to David his sinfulness and his desert – which David is led to passionately pronounce upon and against himself (2 Sam. 12:1–7). David has made himself publicly righteous but has been privately selfish, adulterous, and murderous. David's punishment is God's removal of his and Bathsheba's son, whom he loses despite his fasting and wearing sackcloth and pleading with God for mercy. Still, David and Bathsheba are granted a second son, Solomon. On his maturity, when asked by God for any gift, Solomon requests wisdom rather than riches and glory, and so is blessed by God. Solomon rather than David is authorized by God to build in Jerusalem a magnificent temple for the ark of the covenant and for sacrifices to God.

Nevertheless: Not despite but in a way because of David's profound acceptance of his guilty sinfulness, David stands as the Bible's peak paradigm of human rule. In all subsequent accounts of good kings, the highest compliment the Scripture pays is to say: "He was like David," and the Messiah, promised by the great prophets as the future, unprecedented, divinely anointed king of all the world, is promised as a new David. In David we seem to find the fullest expression of biblical humanity. He is at once the most profoundly and beautifully poetic, the most passionately erotic, the most heroic, and – as an essential foundation for all the preceding – the most effective *ruler* in the biblical narrative (the effectiveness and competence of David's rule is made most evident in the books of Chronicles). It seems necessarily implied or involved in these virtues that David is also the most spectacular (though of course not the most corrupt or degraded) *sinner* in the Bible. Through his sinning, prepared and made possible precisely by his spectacular talents and achievements, above all as a king, confronting the awesome challenges and temptations of full political responsibility, David comes to know what it means to *love God*, with a clarity and heartfelt eloquence and educative power that is unrivaled by any other human presented in the Bible. The proof and the product of David's unrivaled experience and articulation of love are the Psalms – which, the Bible stresses, are not the direct products of special revelation. (David is not a prophet, but a singer.)

It is true, of course, as we have indicated, that there is another monarchic peak, another king who rivals David for wisdom, and indeed for eroticism and for poetry: King Solomon, who is granted his wish or prayer of becoming wise. The proof of Solomon's wisdom, as well as his poetic power and capacity for love, is found in his Song of Songs, his Proverbs, and, above all, his Ecclesiastes. Yet a careful study of these amazing writings reveals, we think, that in the Bible's eyes wisdom in humans is a mixed blessing. Solomon is wiser than David; Solomon is all too wise. Solomon's wisdom reveals, by way of contrast, the superiority of David's more impassioned and less questioning insight. What is the problem in Solomon's wisdom? Solomon's wisdom outruns his love. His peak expression of love is his Song of Songs, a love song written by a young man, in whom love is directed to the enchanting beauty of womanhood. Such love of woman, Solomon writes in the culmination of the Song, "is as mighty as death." But in Ecclesiastes, written by an old or mature man, love has become eclipsed, and even chilled, by the prospect of death. Solomon seems never to have altogether realized what the Bible teaches to be the highest and truest love, the love given perhaps its most beautiful and moving expression in David's sixty-third psalm. This love of David's – this love of God that trembles between desperate personal need and self-sacrificial devotion, this love that David seems to have fully achieved only at rare, peak moments – is rooted in a faithful trust, not only in God's justice but in the divine love for man implicit in that justice. David's psalms sing of three great themes: love, death, and justice. Fully to understand justice or the law, and the demand of justice or the law, is also to understand what transcends even justice, and what alone fulfills the promise, the hope, embodied in justice and in obedience to the law. It would seem that full consciousness of God's mercy, of the mercy that justifies the hope that alone truly surmounts death, requires something like the ecstatic experience of love that is expressed in the Psalms. Solomon did not reach *that* ecstasy, perhaps because of his excessive wisdom, perhaps because (on account of that wisdom?) his love remained tethered to the tangible beauty and joy of the human-all-too-human. Solomon was indeed wise enough to glimpse his own limits; he concludes his Proverbs (31:30) with the wise teaching of a wise woman, the mother of King Lemuel: "The beauty of a woman is evanescent; it is for her fear of the Lord God that a woman is to be praised." Ecclesiastes gives the impression of being the most "philosophic" book in the Bible. But the Bible makes room for philosophy only on the Bible's own terms. Precisely because Solomon is shown in Ecclesiastes approaching something like the philosophic outlook, Solomon is there revealed as a man verging on despair – at the power of death, in light of the weakness or inscrutability of divine justice and providence. The wise and quasi-philosophic Solomon is overshadowed, in the Bible, by the passionate and poetic David. At the peak of biblical politics, we may conclude, is not the philosopher-king but the poet-king.

From the Old to the New Testament

Under the increasingly decadent successors of David, the people of God is eventually subjected to another enslavement, at the hands of the Babylonians, who destroy Jerusalem and its temple. But the Hebrews are promised, and finally given, a restoration to their homeland. They rebuild the temple and are commanded to live in the promise of a far greater restoration, under a new David, the Messiah, who will come – after generations of troubles – to elevate Israel to unprecedented power and glory infused with righteousness, presiding over the entire earth filled with universal obedience to divine law (Isa. 2:1–5, 11, 35:5–10, 52–53, 60, 65:17ff., 66:12ff.; Jer. 23:5–8; Mic. 4–5; Zech. 9:9–17). The Christian Scriptures present Jesus as the true, if paradoxical, fulfillment of these prophecies.

The son of Mary is revealed to be God's own son (Matt. 3:17). This does not signify, however, that the Christ has been sent to assume any sort of political rule. The devil offers to Jesus "all the kingdoms of the world and the glory of them." But the devil makes clear that this political power comes at a price: worship of the devil. In rejecting the bargain and the temptation of political rule, Jesus quotes the authority of the law of Moses: "You shall worship the Lord your God, and Him only shall you serve" (Matt. 4:1–11; Deut. 6:13).

For what, then, has the Son of God come into the world? What is the new revelation embodied in Christ? After Jesus has preached and taught in the synagogues, has gathered his disciples, and has practiced widespread healings of mental as well as physical illness, along with exorcisms of devils, he delivers his most famous sermon, the Sermon on the Mount (Matt. 5). Its central passages, the "beatitudes," proclaim eight human types who are "blessed" – who are, that is, not cursed but instead can expect something beyond any and all merely worldly happiness. The beatitudes thus circumscribe Jesus' vision of the right way of life.

In the first place, the "poor in spirit" are blessed – those who do not grasp at wealth or power but are content with what is given, who are neither greedy, nor angry, nor envious, nor resentful. "Theirs is the kingdom of heaven": They are promised, that is, an eternal life.

In the second place, "those who mourn" are blessed. Jesus blesses not those who laugh or exult (Jesus himself is never said to laugh), but those who suffer, those who feel in their bones that life is a vale of tears (Jesus is twice said to weep). Those who mourn shall, Jesus promises, be comforted.

In the third place, Jesus blesses "those who hunger and thirst for righteousness": They, he promises, shall be satisfied. Through Jesus, justice will somehow finally and fully prevail. We note that Jesus takes the necessities of the body, hunger and thirst, and, instead of promising to satisfy these physical needs, turns them into a spiritual metaphor: True hunger and thirst should be for righteousness, for being righteous oneself, seeking it as one would food and drink, day in and day out.

"The merciful" are blessed: They shall, Jesus promises, be shown mercy. Mercy is a virtue. For Aristotle, in his *Nicomachean Ethics*, mercy or pity is a passion, requiring direction by a sense or appreciation of the noble, so that actions following from it are done in the right way at the right time to the right people; mercy or compassion is not in itself a virtue, and when misdirected it becomes a vice. It may, for example, prevent the necessary harshness entailed in the punishment of crime and the fighting just wars. Christ elevates mercy, or compassion, to a major virtue.

"The pure of heart" are blessed; they shall "see God." This signals that what is important is not so much what one accomplishes as the spirit in which one strives; one's motives ought not to be mixed.

"The peacemakers" are blessed: They will, declares Jesus, "be called sons of God." There is a special affinity between Christ, *the* Son of God, and those who strive to make peace. Jesus indicates no close affinity between himself and warriors, however heroic or noble they may appear to mankind.

"Those persecuted for righteousness" are blessed: "The kingdom of heaven is theirs." Jesus thus signals that justice will not soon prevail on the earth. Closely connected is the final beatitude, pronounced on those "persecuted and reviled for my sake." Here at the end Jesus brings himself to the center of things; he does so in signaling that it will not be easy to follow him in this life that he is describing; it will bring persecution. But it will not be worthless: There is reward (and punishment) in a life to come.

How does this new teaching stand with respect to the Hebrew Scriptures, and in particular to the laws, the commandments, revealed to Moses, and the direction given by the subsequent prophets? Jesus answers this directly: "Think not that I have come to abolish the Law and the prophets; I have come not to abolish them but to fulfill them" (Matt. 5:17). All the commandments, it seems, are to be kept; nothing is to be relaxed. Jesus then makes explicit that his commandments demand even more than was demanded by the Mosaic law. In Matthew 5:21–48, he takes various Mosaic commandments and intensifies their difficulty, repeatedly using the expression, "You have heard that it was said … but I say.…" Not only murder but insults, contempt, and anger are condemned as what came to be called "mortal sins," that is, deadly to blessedness. The Mosaic law condemned adultery; Jesus condemns even adulterous desire, even lusting "in your heart." Similarly, whereas the Mosaic law made provision for divorce, Christ permits no divorce except on grounds of adultery. Swearing by oaths is forbidden, since such expostulation draws a distinction between big and small lies, both of which are to be condemned. In every way, the fullest moral purity, as the logical conclusion of the law, is commanded.

Most striking is the new disposition toward the wicked, which may be said to sum up and clarify the rest of Christ's moral teaching: The wicked are not to be resisted in their deeds against oneself. "If a man strikes your right cheek, give him the other also, and if any one would sue you and take your coat, let him have your cloak as well; and if any one forces you to go one mile, go with him two miles." Coming to the aid of *others* who are suffering evil is certainly still demanded, but for evil against oneself, Jesus counsels a surrender of one's own pride and material good, an offering of oneself to the evildoer in an attempt to change his heart. Finally, Jesus says, "you have heard that it was said, 'You shall love your neighbor and hate your enemy.' But I say to you, love your enemies and pray for those who persecute you." As we saw in the Polemarchus section of the *Republic*, the distinction between friend and foe is central to the life of the good citizen. Jesus condemns this distinction as something like a collective, worldly self-interest. His command is to seek one's enemies' good, to convert one's enemies to righteousness, rather than being taken up by the desire to inflict harm upon them or to demonstrate one's superiority over them. The law of Jesus aims at the securing of a heavenly rather than earthly reward: Eternal life, which had been dimly present as a promise in the Hebrew Scriptures (see, e.g., Gen. 5:24; 2 Kings 2:10; Pss. 16:10, 37:37–38, 49:16, 61:7, 68:21, 86:13, 88:11, 107:20, 116:8; Ezek. 18:4ff.; Dan. 12:2), now becomes fully explicit. And the new command is an explicit attempt to have the people of God, by aiming at this end, ascend above the practice of other nations: "If you salute only your brethren, what more are you doing than others? Do not even the Gentiles do the same? You, therefore, must be perfect, as your heavenly Father is perfect." But if the people of God is to surrender itself in this way to its enemies, will it not disappear as a distinct political entity? Does the new revelation not point, from the start, in the direction of an end to the traditional distinction between Gentile and Jew, even as it presumes that distinction?

This question is perhaps most clearly addressed when Jesus is asked by an expert in the Mosaic law what he must do to inherit eternal life (Luke 10:25). The questioner means to tempt or to test Jesus – to show that what Jesus is teaching is not orthodox but instead a corruption of Mosaic law. Jesus therefore responds initially with a question of his own: "What is written in the law? How do you read it?" The expert in the law gives a standard summary of the law (from Deut. 6:5 or Lev. 6:19): "You shall love the Lord your God with all your heart, with all your soul, with all your strength, and with all your mind; and your neighbor as yourself." Jesus tells him that his answer is correct (*orthos*), and that if he does this, he will live. But then the expert in the law, aware that Jesus has been attacking the experts in the law and claiming that the true wisdom has been revealed to him and thence to his uneducated disciples, presses him, in order to "justify" his own claim of the need to know the law. "Who," he asks, "is my neighbor?" Jesus replies (as was his wont) with a parable – of the Good Samaritan (Luke 10:30–37). In this parable, a priest and then a Levite (from the tribe of Moses), in careful observance of the Mosaic law concerning the need to avoid the ritual defilement that would result from touching a dead body, steer clear of a victim of robbers lying by the side of a road. But a Samaritan, that is, a member of a nearby people claiming to be descendants of Joseph and following a more ancient version of the Torah, acts out of compassion and proves himself a good neighbor by saving the man and having him nursed back to health. The Mosaic lawyer's question is thus turned on its head; rather than distinguishing neighbor, or friend, from foe, Jesus renders the commandment into a demand to prove oneself a "good neighbor" to any and all others, through compassion or mercy.

Mercy flows from love, and Jesus makes love (Greek: *agape*, Latin: *caritas*) central to his teaching. Divine love had of course been presented in the Hebrew Scriptures as ever manifested by God for his people. So in the famous psalm 136 – in which David sings of God's creation, the wonders he worked in liberating his people from Egypt, and in defeating Israel's enemies – every other line refrains: "for his steadfast loving mercy (*hesed*) endures forever." (This psalm is sung, moreover, as part of the Seder, the Passover Meal, which Mosaic law prescribed to commemorate the Israelites' liberation by God from slavery in Egypt, a liberation that entailed the destruction of vast numbers of Egyptians, including little children.) Nor is this celebration of divine love unique to this psalm. "Thy loving kindness," sings David in psalm 63, "is better than life." And the prophet Isaiah proclaims: "For the mountains may depart, and the hills be removed, but my steadfast love shall not depart from you ... says the Lord, who has compassion on you" (Isa. 54:10). Jesus fastens, as it were, on this steadfast, merciful, divine love, experienced most richly by David, as something to be emulated by *all* of his own followers, even singling it out as his "new commandment": "A new commandment I give to you, that you love one another; even as I have loved you, that you also love one another. By this all men will know that you are my disciples, if you have love for one another" (John 13:34). Love is now something *commanded*. "As the Father has loved me, so have I loved you; abide in my love" (John 15:9). Paul, after detailing the characteristics of love or of a truly loving soul, concludes by stating what came to be called the three chief Christian virtues and signals the priority of love over the other two: "faith, hope, love abide; but the greatest of these is love" (1 Cor. 13:13).

The tension between Jesus' teachings and those of the Pharisees – who had, since the Babylonian captivity, preserved and interpreted Mosaic law and the teachings of the subsequent prophets – is exacerbated by the large following that Jesus develops, owing in part to the miracles that he appears to be performing. Things finally come to a head when Jesus enters Jerusalem in a procession, to much acclaim. The chief priest, the Scribes, and the rabbis move to have the Roman authorities enforce their law against blasphemy. Following his own teaching concerning resistance to evil against oneself, and as an exemplar of it (1 Pet. 2:21–23), Jesus is eventually killed, "like a lamb led to the slaughter."

After a trial under the Roman governor Pontius Pilate, Jesus suffers a gruesome death on a cross just outside Jerusalem. This death comes to be understood as the redeeming, through atoning sacrifice of God's son-made-man, of all human beings from the sin and condign punishment initiated by Adam (Mark 10:45). Jesus is subsequently called the "last Adam" (1 Cor. 15:45) or the "new Adam." His death is not understood to be for the chosen people alone, but for all mankind: "Sin came into the world through one man and death through sin, and so death spread to all men because all men sinned," but "if many died, through one man's trespass, much more have the grace of God and the free gift in the grace of that one man Jesus Christ abounded for many" – "as one man's trespass led to condemnation for all men, so one man's act of righteousness leads to acquittal and life for all men" (Rom. 5:12–18).

Not only is Jesus' death to be understood as having redeemed all of humanity but, according to the Christian Scriptures, Jesus is *resurrected* to life on the third day following his death, appearing bodily to his disciples and explaining to them how he is the fulfillment of all that Moses and the other prophets had written. His resurrection is taken to be the evidence of the overcoming of death itself, evidence of the possibility of eternal life for all mankind (Rom. 6:5; 2 Cor. 4:10; Col. 2:12, 3:10).

According to the Gospels and the Acts of the Apostles, during his days on earth the resurrected Jesus also bids his disciples "receive the Holy Spirit," breathing on them (John 20:22) – as God had breathed on Adam to give him life – and thereby granting them an awesome privilege and responsibility with respect to humans' seeking of divine forgiveness: "Whoever's sins you forgive, they are forgiven them, and whoever's sins you hold bound, they are held bound" (John 20:22). Finally, Jesus instructs his disciples, before his ascent into heaven, to "go forth therefore and teach all nations, baptizing them in the name of the Father, the Son, and the Holy Spirit" (Matt. 28:19). These passages moved subsequent Christian theologians to declare that while God is one, he nonetheless has, mysteriously, three "persons": the Father, the Son (Jesus), and the Holy Spirit, the latter of whom bestows upon human beings certain sacred "gifts" that assist them in the path to heavenly salvation. The mission of the Jewish people is now understood by Jesus' followers to have reached its fulfillment and hence its conclusion in the revelations of God-Man; *all* nations are now to be included in the reception of the new revelation of the Trinitarian God.

Still, the disciples of Jesus for their part continue to adhere to the Mosaic law and to assume that Jesus came as a Messiah to the Jews. But how can this be, when Jesus has commanded them to go out and teach *all* nations – and non-Jews are prepared to accept Jesus as the Son of God, while many Jews are rejecting this claim? Must one be Jewish – accepting the covenants with Abraham and Moses – in order to be accepting of the Messiah and hence eligible for eternal life? At a subsequent council of the disciples held in Jerusalem, the question of baptizing Gentiles is debated and settled, and the requirements for Gentile converts to the new faith are spelled out (Acts 15:1–35). The crucial and momentous question of whether Gentiles need to be circumcised is answered in the negative: Even the sign of the everlasting covenant with Abraham is deemed no longer necessary. The members of the council communicate their decision by letter to the church of Antioch (Acts 15:22–35). Paul is then sent out on a mission to convert Gentiles in Greece and Asia Minor (Acts 15:36–20:38) Much of the Mosaic law comes therefore to be called by Christians the "old law," or the "ceremonial law," conceived as prescriptions that obtained only so long as the ceremonial worship of God in the temple lasted, but henceforth no longer in force.

The universalizing commandment to teach all nations is taken up especially by Paul, who calls himself "apostle to the Gentiles" (Gal. 1:16, 2:8). Paul was originally a persecutor of Christians; we first hear of him at the stoning of Steven (the first Christian martyr), which he looked upon with approval. But after what he describes as a personal revelation from Jesus, Paul becomes a zealous converter of others to Christianity (Acts 9:1–9). He more than anyone convinces the followers of Jesus that faith in Jesus *replaces* obedience to the Mosaic law. He is especially zealous in teaching the decision of the council of Jerusalem concerning the admission of noncircumcised people into the new faith. "The people of God," Paul explains, is no longer to be understood as a chosen nation or race, nor as followers of the divinely revealed Mosaic law. What characterizes its members, instead, is *faith* in the redemptive deeds of Jesus as the only Son of God, and following his teachings. Paul articulates this most forcefully in his letter to the Galatians, using a distinction Jesus had drawn between the spirit and the flesh to condemn Mosaic law itself as belonging to the flesh. "By works of the law," he says, "no one shall be justified."

Abraham, not Moses, becomes now for Christians the greatest figure in the Hebrew Scriptures, the exemplar of faith and therefore righteousness, or as he is called in the Catholic mass, "our father in faith." The laws of Moses were, Paul explains, a mere "custodian" of the people of God, until faith in Jesus Christ was revealed as the true way; now that this has been revealed, the law has been superseded. Salvation, eternal life through faith, is indiscriminate; it entails an amazing abolition of distinctions, not only between Jews and Gentiles but between slaves and free, and between women and men.

In the absence of Mosaic law, then, how are Christians to live? What are the economic, sexual, and political ramifications of the new Christian teaching?

Turning first to the economic realm, we find that the Christian Scriptures teach that one should be even *less* concerned with worldly welfare and gain than the Hebrew Scriptures had indicated. In an account given in all the Synoptic Gospels, a young man asks Jesus – this time not seeking to trip him up but in earnest: "What shall I do to inherit the kingdom of heaven?" Jesus replies with the standard answer: "Keep the commandments," and lists some of the most important of them. The young man responds that he has observed all of them. "If you would be perfect," Jesus replies, "go, sell what you possess and give to the poor, and you will have treasure in heaven; and come, follow me." The young man went away sorrowful, "for he had great possessions." Jesus then expounds on what has happened and, to the astonishment of his disciples, declares: "I tell you, it is easier for a camel to go through the eye of a needle than for a rich man to enter the kingdom of God" (Matt. 19:16–22; cf. Mark 10:17–31; Luke 18:18–26).

The unwillingness to part with one's many possessions is preceded, of course, by a desire to possess things in the first place, to acquire wealth, to be devoted to its increase. Paul addresses this desire, and the mistaken distrust toward providential divine care that lies behind it, in his First Letter to Timothy: "Those who desire to be rich fall into temptation, into a snare, into many senseless and hurtful desires that plunge men into ruin and destruction." For "the love of money is the root of all evils; it is through this craving that some have wandered away from the faith and pierced their hearts with many pangs." As for "the rich in this world, charge them not to be haughty, nor to set their hopes on uncertain riches, but on God who richly furnishes us with everything to enjoy" (1 Tim. 6:6–19).

On this crucial issue, of the bountifulness of the (created) world, Paul clearly follows the teaching of Jesus himself. Jesus draws a contrast between, on one hand, the desire for wealth – which he associates with the soul's desire to live a life of ease and pleasure, obscuring one's inevitable mortality and its unknowable hour – and, on the other hand, reliance on God's bountiful providence. Jesus implores his listeners to dispel their anxiety about the need for wealth by considering God's provident care for nonhuman life: "I tell you, do not be anxious about your

life, what you shall eat, nor about your body, what you shall put on." For
"life is more than food, and the body more than clothing." Consider
"the ravens: they neither sow nor reap, they have neither storehouse nor
barn, and yet God feeds them. Of how much more worth are you than
the birds!" Consider "the lilies, how they grow; they neither toil nor spin;
yet I tell you, even Solomon in all his glory was not arrayed like one of
these. But if God so clothes the grass which is alive in the field today and
tomorrow is thrown into the oven, how much more will he clothe you,
O men of little faith!" (Luke 12:13–30).

Private property, it almost goes without saying, is not presented as an
inherent "right" in the Christian Scriptures, and certainly not as a means
to a needed increase in the stock of goods available to humans. Instead,
the virtues of generosity, liberality, and piteous aid to the poor are commanded. The first Christians, awaiting the Second Coming as something
imminent, "were together, and had all things in common. And they sold
their possessions and goods, and distributed them all, as any had need";
"the company of those who believed were of one heart and soul, and no
one said that any of the things which he possessed was his own, but they
had everything in common" (Acts 2:44–45, 3:20, 4:32).

The Christian teaching on sexuality and the family is, similarly, a
combination of what is ordained in the Hebrew Scriptures and the new
commandments of Jesus. As we saw above, the Sermon on the Mount proclaims an even more severe stricture to maintain the monogamous family. And while there is in Genesis a clear subordination of women to men
as a consequence of the Fall, and an affirmation of this subordination
later (see, e.g., Esther 1:20–22), the subordination becomes emphatic
in the Christian Scriptures, especially in the Epistles, which reach back
to Genesis for justification of this subordination. In his First Letter, the
apostle Peter – who became the first bishop of Rome and hence the man
to whom all popes look as their first predecessor – after describing how
Jesus submitted to his suffering and death, calls for wives to submit in
a similar way to their husbands, to live reverently and chastely, to dress
modestly. Peter calls for husbands to show consideration to their wives as
"the weaker sex" (1 Pet. 3:1–8; see similarly Paul, in Col. 3:18–4:1; 1 Cor.
11:3–12; 1 Tim. 2:8–15).

As regards the *political* teaching of Christianity, things are still less
clear than they had been in the Hebrew Scriptures. Immediately after
the Sermon on the Mount, for example, Jesus is approached by a Roman
centurion, an officer of the imperial Roman army, who begs him to heal
his servant. The servant is at home, paralyzed, and the centurion says

that Jesus need not go there: "Speak but the word, and my servant will be healed." This is the only place in the Gospels, so far as we have observed, where Jesus is said to "marvel" at anything: He marvels at the centurion's faith, which goes beyond anything, he says, he has seen in Israel. He cures the servant instantly (Luke 7:10; cf. Matt. 8:5–13). Strikingly, Jesus does *not* tell the centurion to abandon his military office, nor upbraid him for holding it; he instead suggests to his disciples that men such as this, "from east and west," will sit at table in the kingdom of God with Abraham, Isaac, and Jacob. Likewise in Acts, Peter baptizes a Roman centurion (Cornelius), after having a vision in which he is told that animals unclean by Mosaic law may be eaten, since nothing that God has cleansed is unclean (Acts 10:10–48). The only question in this case appears, that is, to have been not whether a Roman *soldier* may be a good follower of Jesus, but whether the conversion of a *Gentile* was appropriate. It appears that the activity of "peacemaking" that Jesus had described in the Sermon on the Mount has to do with the disposition of one's soul rather than with one's office or occupation, even if it be in the service of the military activities of one's city or nation.

As to the question of devotion to one's city or nation and its regime, whatever it might be, there is little guidance offered. In one of the most oft-quoted passages of the Christian Scriptures, Jesus is asked by Pharisees, in yet another effort to trip him up, whether it is lawful to pay taxes to Rome. Obtaining a coin, Jesus then asks, "Whose image and inscription is this?" "Caesar's" is their reply. "Then render unto Caesar," says Jesus, "what is Caesar's, and unto God that which is God's" (Matt. 22:15–22; Mark 12:13–17; Luke 20:19–26). The reply entails a clear lowering of political life, dividing – as was never the case in the ancient city – the political from the higher divine.

Still, precisely because the ancient city was devoted to virtues of soul, including – as we have seen in Plato's *Apology* – the virtue of piety, Jesus' response invites more questions than it answers. What is Caesar's? What is God's? Should one obey the laws and commands of the non-Christian authorities? Should one honor the heroes of one's city or country, the exemplars of its virtues? Should one fight in its wars? What if they are unjust? Should one hold political office? As the clear teaching of the Sermon on the Mount is one of passive obedience and submission to evildoers, so the clear counsel of the disciples is that Christians should indeed obey their country's rulers and laws, wherever they happened to live. Concerning the Roman Empire in particular, Peter writes: "Be subject for the Lord's sake to every human institution, whether it be to the emperor as supreme, or to governors as sent by him to punish those who do wrong and to praise those who do right" (1 Pet. 2:13–17). Paul, similarly, counsels obedience to rulers: "Let every soul be subject to the ruling authorities." For "there is no authority except from God, and those that exist have been instituted by God." Therefore "he who resists the authorities resists what God has appointed, and those who resist will incur judgment" (Rom. 13: 1–3). The civil authorities, Paul points out, punish wrongdoers, and he advises his listeners to live in love, to avoid wrongdoing, to avoid retribution, and to honor those to whom honor is due. The full and problematic import of Paul's counsel of obedience becomes clear when we realize that it was written under Nero, one of the most tyrannical of the Roman emperors and one who was persecuting Christians. The central guiding thought of a Christian, it is clear, is that humans are mere pilgrims on this earth, living in a vale of tears and awaiting both a Second Coming of Jesus and an eternal life after death.

But since the Second Coming did not arrive immediately, as the earliest Christian had thought it would (consider Rom. 13:11–12), the question became acute: How is one to live in the meantime, especially when the world becomes Christian – when the old law has been abandoned and the new law is radically otherworldly in its direction? Should Christians be good citizens of Rome, or of any other city? Should they be good soldiers for Rome and its empire? What of the injunction to turn the other cheek? How is a redeemed Christian to live in an unredeemed world? It is to these questions that the Christian political theologians addressed themselves. We turn next to the most influential of these: St. Thomas Aquinas.

5

St. Thomas Aquinas's *Treatise on Law*

The great achievement of St. Thomas Aquinas (1225–1274) is to have brought together in a grand synthesis the teachings of the pagan rationalist philosophers, above all Aristotle, and the revelation taught in the Holy Scriptures. Thomas contends that reason or science, wisely understood, leads up to or points toward the truth of the Christian faith and, conversely, that faith-based truth, if properly understood, presupposes while completing rational philosophy and science. Thomas insists that the truly honest scientific mind – because it is keenly aware of its own limits – is the mind open to and welcoming of Christ's inspiration. By the same token, the thoughtful Christian welcomes, as a gift of God, Aristotle and his exemplary demonstration of all that the reasoning of man can and should discover and clarify on its own, as the basis for wisely accepting and interpreting revelation.

The Broad Historical Context

At the time Thomas began to write and teach, it was far from clear that this sort of outlook would prevail in Christendom. In the twelfth and thirteenth centuries, the works of Aristotle were reintroduced into the West, from the Muslim world. For five hundred years previously in Christian Europe, Greek thought, and especially Greek political philosophy, were poorly known. Meanwhile, in the Islamic world, the Greek texts became well known and had an enormous impact on thinkers in Judaism and Islam. The most fraught influence was through Platonic political philosophy. The major political philosophers – most notably al-Farabi and Avicenna and Averroes in Islam, and Maimonides in Jewry – contended that the Scriptures, as the revelation of an all-wise deity, must be understood to be written wisely: much like Plato wrote his books but with an even more "wily graciousness" (in the famous formula of Maimonides). God has deployed a subtle strategy of responsibly civic, educative rhetoric that teaches the unequal levels of humanity differently, through conveying many levels of meaning, the most serious and complex of which God has deliberately hidden from most readers. The surface message of the Bible or Koran, these Islamic and Jewish Platonists suggested, consists of edifying myths, or noble lies, which are good for and needed by the less thoughtful majority. Only when one reads the Bible or Koran after learning how to read from the books crafted by Plato and Aristotle does one find, under the surface and between the lines, a truer message. That message shows that much of what sub-philosophic pious people believe about God, the soul, and divine providence, is not really true. God is much less like a human being, especially in his emotions, than he seems to be on the surface of the Bible. God is much less involved in a drama with individual humans than he seems to be according to the surface message of the stories in the Bible. God is in truth much more removed, impersonal, without anger or love or other emotions – more purely mind and reason. Philosophers like Averroes and Maimonides went so far as to suggest that God does *not* really carry out retributive punishment; that God in his wisdom agrees with Socrates that all crime is a result of ignorance, that there is no sin, and no guilt; that the Bible only pretends that God becomes punitively angry at so-called sinners because that is the best way to get most people to behave better.

As awareness of this reading of Scripture spread in Islam, there were hostile reactions, especially among orthodox Muslim intellectual leaders. Led by the theologian Algazel (who for a time was tempted by the outlook of the philosophers, but then decided their outlook was deeply in error), thoughtfully pious Muslims decried the influence of philosophy, as corrupting the reading of the Koran and thus corrupting Islam. Philosophy became more and more seen as subversive and heretical. Philosophy had to go more deeply underground, and had to make more intense efforts to accommodate its writing to nonphilosophic religious thinking. But these efforts met with only mixed success.

In Christianity, the first reaction to the rediscovery of the moral and political writings of Aristotle, together with the Islamic philosophic commentaries, especially by Averroes, was also quite hostile. Aristotle, as interpreted by Averroes especially, seemed to deny many fundamental elements of Christian doctrine. There was a strong movement to suppress the study of Aristotle, to condemn and to prohibit teachings based on him.

St. Thomas led a counteroffensive – elaborating (with the assistance of the works of St. Augustine, whom Thomas quotes more than any other author) a new, alternative way of conceiving the partnership between reason and faith. Thomas contended that the Islamic and Judaic philosophers had gone too far in making the Scripture subordinate to Greek philosophy, but Thomas by no means condemned Greek philosophy. Thomas showed a way of making Greek philosophy subordinate to the Christian Bible. His new way of combining faith and reason, revelation and science, eventually won out in Christendom, and made Aristotle and Greek philosophy welcome ever since, especially in the Roman Catholic Church. The acute questions are whether Thomas did not distort Aristotle and whether Aristotle was not more accurately interpreted by "the great commentator," Averroes, and his teachers and colleagues. (There was a suspected minority within Christendom of "Latin Averroists," most notably Marsilius of Padua and Dante.)

The Distinctive Character of Thomas's Writings

Thomas's major works fall, roughly speaking, into two categories. On one hand are commentaries explaining Aristotle's major works and the Bible and the works of earlier theologians. On the other hand are two "Summas," or summations of Church teaching. The *Summa Contra Gentiles* ("Summation Against the Non-Christian Nations") combats key theses of Pagan, Jewish, and Islamic theologians, proving in debate the truth of the Catholic faith. The *Summa Theologiae* ("Summation of Theology")* is an enormous, unfinished work – Thomas died before completing it – intended as a compendium of Christian doctrine, elaborated "as briefly and clearly as the matter itself may allow," and "in such a way as befits the instruction of beginners" (in the words of the prologue). This work has a format that will strike today's readers as strange (but one that was at that time rather normal): It is entirely organized into what are called "disputed questions." The first strong impression the book gives, is the need to ask questions. But the questions are almost always answered,

---

* Cited in this chapter as ST; we recommend the translation by William P. Baumgarth and Richard J. Regan, *Saint Thomas Aquinas on Law, Morality, and Politics* (Cambridge, MA: Hackett, 1988). Translations are from this edition, with minor emendations. References in the text are to the *Summa Theologiae*, the specific question, and the specific part of the question. For example, "ST I-II, Q 79, art. 12 ad 1" refers to the *Summa Theologiae*, first part, question number 79, article 12, response to question 1."

authoritatively. Yet the ST is not like a catechism; the questions are not simply answered. Thomas presents what he understands to be the ortho-dox Christian answer to every question, while still preserving, as much as possible, provocation to critical thinking. He almost always begins with objections to his own answer, objections based on leading authorities. Then he explains his own answer. And then he usually provides specific responses to the objections. But sometimes it turns out that one or more of the objections are valid. Thus Thomas tries to keep his readers think-ing, or on their toes.

Our focus is on key elements in Thomas Aquinas's political teaching, as they appear in a few "disputed questions" of the ST, comprising a sec-tion that came to be known as the *Treatise on Law*. The key overall point is this: Even prior to, or without the benefit of, the supernatural reve-lation delivered in the Bible, humans have extensive *natural*, rational capacities for grasping a large measure (but by no means *all*) of the truth about good and bad, justice and injustice. This moral and political truth available to *un*assisted reason was elaborated by Aristotle, "*the* philoso-pher," as Thomas calls him. But Aristotle of course did not have access to the bigger picture. He lacked the revelation given in the Bible. So his teaching, while true, is incomplete, in a radical sense that Aristotle him-self could not have realized. Aristotle's insights thus have to be reformu-lated, in light of the broader and deeper truth available only by biblical revelation.

Natural Law

At the core of the moral and political truth that is knowable to unassisted reason is the concept of *natural law* – the code of the basic rules of life. Thomas sharply distinguishes *natural* law from what he calls "*divine* law." Divine law is the code of laws knowable only through revelation, given in the Bible at certain times in history – and including especially laws which reason by itself could never figure out. Natural law, by contrast, is the code of laws that all humans, in all times and places, whether they are Christians or not, can and do know, as part of what it means to be human. For example, by natural law all sane adult humans know that murder, as the killing of the innocent, is always wrong and must be prohibited and punished. By divine law, in contrast, we are commanded to make the *seventh* day of the week sacred – something reason or natural law does not tell us and that we could never figure out without revelation. Natural law retains complete authority and validity even for people who do not look to the Bible as their authority in politics or morals. Thus, the natural law doctrine could be and was a foundation for Martin Luther King and, through him, the American civil rights movement. Thomas's natural law doctrine is one important basis of the papacy's claim to speak out morally and politically on behalf not only of Catholics but of all humans everywhere and always.

How Is Natural Law Known?

A crucial preliminary question is, how is the natural law "natural" in the sense of being known naturally? The answer Thomas gives is: through the *conscience*, or, to use the more technical Latin term, *synderesis*, whose *action* is the conscience (ST part I, question 79, articles 12–13). The conscience expresses a natural "habit" in our reason, which holds available for deployment the basic principles of right and wrong – which are conceived as laws. Thomas takes issue with certain predecessors who had said that the conscience is "a power *higher* than reason" (ST I, Q 79, art. 12). He insists, on the contrary, that the conscience is part of natural, innate reason, and is indeed the basis of practical reason, or reason governing choice and action.

The conscience is a habit that is profoundly natural in the sense that it, and the awareness of laws that it contains, are innate, implanted in our nature, and awakened to use as we emerge from babyhood. Thomas speaks of the principles of natural law as parallel to the principles of logic, which govern and are presupposed in all our scientific or speculative thinking. We do not have to learn the principle of contradiction, or for that matter of causality: These principles are presupposed in all learning. Without somehow knowing these principles to begin with, we could learn nothing; we could not think or communicate. Similarly with the basic statutes of right and wrong: All or most societies, save in exceptional cases (under pressures that clearly distort ordinary human existence and awareness), share basic universal norms. Murder, theft, and adultery are everywhere punishable crimes; in all societies, children must honor their parents; the bodies of the dead must be treated with respect; war heroes must be honored; and so forth. To be sure, there will be disagreement among societies over specific applications of or derivations from the basic moral rules – over exactly what constitutes murder, and the degrees of murder, and of theft, and so on. Adultery will mean something different in a polygamous society from what it means in a monogamous society. In other words, the natural law does *not* dictate all the ordinances that humans need in order to regulate life. Natural law provides only the basic rules. The more detailed or specific one gets in application, the more scope there is for legitimate divergence, as humans in different societies apply the basic rules in vastly differing circumstances (ST I-II, Q 94, art. 4).

But of course humans are also morally very fallible. Precisely the fact that there are everywhere penal laws, defining crimes and punishments, shows that not everyone, all the time, retains clearly or follows strictly the first principles – even when they are well known in a society. People regularly violate what they know to be right and wrong, distorted by passions and deep perversity or sinfulness (ST I, Q 79, art. 13; I-II, Q 94, art. 6). Thomas makes it clear that abuse, as well as bad or unnatural habituation or customs, can distort or dim the strength of the moral principles. Yet he also indicates that there is here a deep puzzle, in that so many people – indeed everyone – can be observed to violate so often the basic moral rules. If the rules are natural, why are they so often violated? Of course, one could observe that people are very often also illogical in their thinking, violating the rules of logic. But we learn from revelation, and revealed divine law, a much bigger and deeper dimension of the puzzle of why people so often violate the basic moral statutes: the mystery of original sin, inherited from the Fall of Adam and Eve, which has contaminated all of us and has entailed a drastic weakening and clouding of our natural moral sense. The original sin of disobedience is something for which we are all being punished, and God's punishment includes making human psychology "destitute of original justice and vigor of reason," as "a punishment [*poenalis*] and consequence of divine law, depriving man of his proper dignity [*propria dignitate*]" (ST I-II, Q 91, art. 6). This truth is a key example of the moral and political implication of divine omnipotence and God's power to change nature, miraculously. While we do not know this truth by reason, it adds a crucial dimension to our understanding of a puzzle we see by reason.

When we violate natural law, we are by nature punished. For there could be no natural *law* if there were no natural punishments or sanctions for breaking the law. Humans who violate the natural law suffer as punishment the carking pangs of a bad or guilty conscience. In everyone, even criminals, there will always be visible some powerful remnant of the conscience, its universal principles, and its punitive sanctions.

The Contrast between Thomas and Aristotle

As we can now readily see, Thomas's teaching entails a striking change from Aristotle's. For Thomas, political theory is largely or primarily a theory of law, a legal theory. For Aristotle, we recall, law is a strictly derivative phenomenon; the law depends on the regime, meaning, on which type of humans, with what conception of the good life, rules. The law varies with the regime; there is no natural law, or universal law of reason. There is natural *right*, or natural justice, that is, rational knowledge of what is right or just in accordance with human nature and its needs, the true common good for humans as political animals. But how this good can be maximized varies from regime to regime and from situation to situation within each regime and its constantly variable communal life. Thomas is aware that Aristotle does not speak of fixed rules or laws that are valid in all times and places (ST I-II, Q 94, art. 4, obj. 2). In fact, as we saw in the last part of book three of the *Politics*, Aristotle has a searching criticism of the limitations of all law and rule of law. Recall, finally, the task of political science as Aristotle laid it out at the start of book four of the *Politics*: There is a standard – the best regime – that is discovered by imaginatively thinking through what would be the regime that would best fulfill human nature. But that thought experiment leads one to see that the best regime is practically impossible, and that even the best imaginable regime contains certain specific deep tensions or difficulties, since human nature and its needs is not harmonious, but tension ridden. In Thomas's thought, some of these considerations continue to be present, but modified in light of the contention that Aristotle failed to articulate clearly enough something that the Stoics and Augustine recognized better: That there is at the heart of natural right a natural law, a code of moral rules, discernible by reason, and valid everywhere, in all regimes and all times and places and circumstances – "entirely unchangeable [*omnino immutabilis*]" (ST I-II, Q 94, art. 5). And the Bible, through its depiction of the regime of Moses and the Mosaic law in Exodus through Deuteronomy, has given an authoritative account of the simply best regime, which has actually existed.

   Yet we must not overestimate the difference between Thomas and Aristotle. For Thomas, the first principle of the natural law, and of all human action, is "seek the good," which is "happiness"; for Thomas as for Aristotle, humans are fundamentally happiness-seeking creatures. But genuine human happiness is *not* individualistic; it is the happiness of individuals as conscientious parts of a larger community, the *civic* community, to which individuals ought to be devoted. Thomas repeats the basic Aristotelian contention that the political community is *the perfect* community, and that "humans are by nature political animals" (ST I-II, Q 90, art. 2). Like Aristotle, St. Thomas speaks very little of individual human rights; his focus is instead human duties, even self-sacrificial duties, to the political community (ST I-II, Q 100, art. 2). One can see the radical consequences that this outlook has had in American history in the twentieth century in Martin Luther King's "Letter from a Birmingham Jail" of April 16, 1963, where King, responding to criticism by a group of leading clergymen, declares that the basis for the civil disobedience to segregation laws is not so much individual rights as Thomas's doctrine of natural law: "to put it in the terms of St. Thomas Aquinas: An unjust law is a human law that is not rooted in Eternal and Natural Law. Any law that uplifts human personality is just. Any law that degrades human personality is unjust. All segregation statutes are unjust because segregation distorts the soul and damages the personality. It gives the segregator a false sense of superiority and the segregated a false sense of inferiority."

The Framework of Law

Thomas begins his treatise on law with a question in four parts, the answer to which gives Thomas's famous four-part definition of law: "From the four preceding articles, the definition of law may be gathered, and it is nothing else than a certain ordinance of reason, for the common good, made by him who has care of the community, and promulgated" (ST I-II, Q 90, art. 4). Now this definition provokes some questions or doubts – which Thomas has responded to in the preceding pages. Are all four aspects really necessary, or even appropriate? The last two of the four ingredients are hard to dispute. It is easy to grant that law must be made by someone who is ruling or taking care of the community; how else would the order be authoritative? It is easy to grant that law must be promulgated; how else would anyone know to obey it? But must law be rational? And must it be aimed at the common good? Are there not many irrational laws, and are not many laws aimed not at the common good, but instead at private interests of the ruling group, interests that entail the exploitation of part of those ruled? Thomas answers by making it clear that he means by his definition to indicate that many or most laws are in some degree defective or imperfect. His definition is normative, or includes an inherent standard for judging laws: "Every human law has just so much of the nature of law as it is derived from natural law," but "if at any point it deflects from natural law, it is no longer a law but a perversion of law" (ST I-II, Q 95, art. 2).

This is not merely an assertion on the part of Thomas; he has an argument or proof. Absolutely crucial to effective law, he observes (ST I-II, Q 90, art. 1), is that it "binds" us, in our hearts, to act in accord with it: The rule of law carries with it a deep sense of *moral obligation* to and *moral respect for* the law; otherwise there can be no rule of law. But humans can be morally obligated only by what they perceive to be right, just, or morally reasonable, in the sense of according with the principles of their conscience, which holds the natural law.

Having established his definition of what true law is or must be, Thomas goes on in the next question (91) to lay out the hierarchy of the basic kinds of law, and then in the subsequent questions he elaborates what is the meaning of each of the basic types of law in the hierarchy. First and overarching is the "Eternal Law" (ST I-II, Q 91, art. 1, and Q 93). This names the code of rules expressing the wisdom by which God with his providence governs his entire creation, in which every part is ordered to a common good of the whole – which is ultimately "God Himself" (ST I-II, Q 91, art. 1 and 3). As Thomas puts it (ST I-II, Q 93, art. 4), "all that is in things created by God, whether it be contingent or necessary, is subject to the Eternal Law." Humans know the Eternal Law only very partially.

Second is the natural law (ST I-II, Q 91, art. 2, and then ST I-II, Q 94), which comprises that part of the Eternal Law through which humans truly "participate, as *rational* beings," in the Eternal Law or in the divine providential plan. As rational beings, humans do not simply follow necessitated impulse, or instinct, but instead act after deliberating, judging, and on that basis making choices. Humans experience God's plan and direction as a set of commandments, which demand obedience and hence rational choice – with the possibility of disobedience. Thus, humans unlike other animals experience and participate in the Eternal Law as law, strictly speaking (ST I-II, Q 91, art. 2, reply obj. 3). Through natural law humans share with God responsibility, as subordinates; unlike other animals, humans are aware of themselves as stewards of nature.

Humans *apply* the natural law through *human* law, or the positive laws they make for themselves, which comprise the third level of moral law (ST I-II, Q 91, art. 3, and ST I-II, Q 95). Humans are not *simply* rational, but are rational *as* animals. We have within us also the subrational animal, which is not instinctually altogether ordered to follow reason, but whose drives we must master and subordinate to reason. When we humans fail to do so, those drives become a force ungoverned by reason, a kind of disconnected lawfulness or even a kind of sinful law – what Thomas calls a "law of concupiscence" fighting against the natural law of reason (ST I-II, Q 91, art. 6). This last is a fourth and the lowest level of law, and this manifests a distortion in us as a punishment for original sin.

God has intervened in the natural order to give to humans an additional law, higher than the natural law: a supernatural or *divine* law – which God has delivered as positive law in successive stages over human history. *Divine* law is thus not to be identified with the *Eternal* Law through which God governs his entire creation. God has given the supernatural, positive divine law for two basic reasons, one lower and one higher. The first and the lower reason is to give humans additional guidance in their making of the human laws that apply the natural law. In other words, divine law is given partly as a supplement to and clarification of the natural law. The laws of Moses in the Old Testament books of Exodus and Leviticus and Deuteronomy provide a clear model of *the* best regime and of *the* best legal code, in accordance with natural law. But second, and more importantly, God has revealed divine law in order to show humans that they have an even higher goal and fulfillment than their political fulfillment, and that they therefore have higher, more difficult duties – which ultimately prepare them for a higher and purer happiness, in the life to come after death.

Natural Law in Detail

With this overview of the conceptual framework, we can now narrow our focus to consider how (in question 94) Thomas lays out in more detail just what the basic provisions of the natural law are. We see here more clearly that the natural law is natural in a second basic sense. As we have already seen, natural law is natural in the sense that it is *known* naturally. But it is also natural inasmuch as its provisions are aimed at *fulfilling* human nature, at guiding us toward that happiness that is our deepest natural need. The provisions of natural law are arranged on three levels, corresponding to the three levels of what Thomas calls natural "inclination" (*inclinatio*) – that is, three basic levels of directness to, longing and yearning for, motion toward, the good or what we need for fulfillment, given our nature as political animals (ST I-II, Q 94, art. 2, with ST I-II, Q 90, art. 2 and ST I-II, Q 72, art. 4).

The first and most basic level of directedness, which we share with all other beings, is a strong inclination to seek preservation; yet we seek not mere preservation but preservation as humans, and that means not merely as individuals but as political animals, as members of our community. And from this we get basic natural law commandments such as: avoid endangering the life of yourself and others; never commit suicide; never commit murder; always seek and work to produce material sustenance for yourself, your family, your civil society; seek to keep safe and defend your civic society, even at the risk of your individual life. Second, and on a higher level shared in part with the animals, we are inclined or directed by nature to reproduce, in families, and from this we get higher basic laws such as: honor your parents; marry a spouse and remain faithful; care for and educate your children; never commit incest; never commit adultery. Third, at the highest level, we are inclined by nature to develop our rational faculties – to become self-governing, through moral and civic virtue, and to employ the intellect to acquire knowledge for its own sake, to develop theoretical or contemplative virtue, above all through inquiry into the first cause of the universe or divinity. From this we get imperatives to seek and to participate in a free and just civic government; to combat tyranny; to punish, even with death, guilty criminals; to risk our lives if necessary fighting and killing in just wars to defend our country and to punish unjust enemies; to respect and to protect private property and never to steal; to seek knowledge for its own sake – especially knowledge of God or of the divine as the source of the universe.

The implementation especially of the highest capacity of natural inclination and natural law entails the human law – the diverse and varying positive, man-made laws (ST I-II, Q 91, art. 3, and Q 95). *The* most important purpose and function of human law is to make men good, virtuous, doers of noble deeds, as Thomas says at length and repeatedly, echoing Aristotle (ST I-II, Q 92, art. 1; ST I-II, Q 95, art. 1). Human law should aim above all at the inculcation of virtue and the suppression of vice: "The intention of the lawgiver" first and foremost, "is to lead men to something by the precepts of the law, and this something is virtue" (ST I-II, Q 100, art. 9; cf. art. 2). Morals can and must be legislated, and that is the main task of human laws; government needs to use force and fear to make people virtuous (ST I-II, Q 95, art. 1 and art. 2). The primary reason is that most human beings need a good deal of discipline in order to learn how to control their passions and to bring them under the command of their reason. In order to become doers of noble deeds, humans need habituation, encouragement, shame and honor, models and inspiration, and the salutary fear of punishment. Moral virtue is mainly a matter of habituation – becoming virtuous is like learning to play a sport or a musical instrument: It takes much practice and exercise. But this spiritual exercise and practice of virtue is initially even more unpleasant than bodily exercise and practice. To get people to practice virtue, to exercise at virtue, you need to be able to coerce them. The need for coercion in moral education is *the* reason why morality must be legislated: "A private person cannot lead another to virtue efficaciously, for he can only advise, and if his advice be not taken, it has no coercive power, such as the law should have in order to prove an efficacious inducement to virtue, as the Philosopher [Aristotle] says" (ST I-II, Q 90, art. 3, reply obj. 2). "To advise is not a proper act of law, but may be within the competency even of a private person, who cannot make a law ... To reward may also pertain to anyone; but *to punish* pertains to none but the framer of the law, by whose authority *pain* is *inflicted.*" And "from becoming accustomed to avoid evil and fulfill what is good, through *fear* of *punishment*, one is sometimes led on to do so likewise with delight and of one's own accord; accordingly, law, by punishing, leads men on to being good" (ST I-II, Q 92, art. 2 and 2–4, our emphasis).

For a perfect model, in practice, of the best sort of positive legislation, Thomas looks to the moral dimension of the detailed ordinances of Moses, as elaborated in the biblical books of Exodus, Leviticus, Numbers, and Deuteronomy (ST I-II, Q 100). The divine law given through Moses in the Old Testament clarifies and elaborates on the natural law in ways that help us see more clearly what our conscience directs us to do. The last six or seven of the Ten Commandments are in large part simply restatements of the basic precepts of the natural law (ST I-II, Q 100) – not telling humans something we do not know by ourselves, in our consciences, but making clear these natural laws are *also* divine laws, reinforced by being also laid down through divine revelation. In addition, the more detailed moral legislation of Moses shows us a whole host of more specific moral statutes that necessarily follow from the most basic rules given in the Ten Commandments. These are also natural laws – but are not so clear to many who are not wise, or who have not reflected on the basis of much experience in life (ST I-II, Q 100, art. 1). Examples of such natural laws that a wise and good political community ought to enforce by law and punishment are: the honoring of all elderly people and all one's superiors (and not only one's parents); showing kindness to inferiors; prohibition of hate against a neighbor; prohibition of prostitution; prohibition of lying; prohibition of scandal mongering (ST I-II, Q 100, art. 11). The best regime as elaborated in the Old Testament shows that laws made by humans need to do such things as using the threat of punishment to coerce young people to get involved in public service, in the civil militia, and in law enforcement; to coerce habits of generosity and compassion by penalizing stinginess or hard-heartedness, and by honoring and rewarding charity. Human laws need to make people better family members by punishing adultery, by punishing and disgracing child abandonment or neglect, and by rewarding and honoring good parenthood. Human laws are needed to censor the arts, in order to make artists take the responsibility of encouraging good models of the fulfillment of natural law. Human laws are needed for compelling children to attend schools, where good morals and civic spirit are taught. Human "sumptuary" laws are needed to penalize luxury and conspicuous consumption while rewarding and honoring modesty.

There is another important consideration at work here, in which Thomas echoes what Socrates said in the beginning part of the gadfly section of the *Apology*. Obedience to lawful authority is in *itself* a very high moral virtue, a central aspect of good moral character (ST II-II, Q 104, arts. 1–6, especially art. 2). Becoming virtuous entails learning to obey lawful superiors, and the law itself, in civilian as well as military life. Closely linked (though not identical) to this is a consideration that goes beyond what we find in Aristotle: Aquinas contends that *the* greatest *moral* virtue is *religion*, or the habitual worship of and reflection on God (ST II-II, Q 104, art. 3). Human laws have as their highest function lending direct government support to religion and religious institutions, including religious instruction in public schools. This is a matter of natural law, prior to divine law. By natural law, Thomas argues, humans do know that there is a God, and that he is a legislative God, though they do not know all the rich details of his plan as revealed in the Bible; they certainly do not know about such mysteries as the Trinity or Christ's death and resurrection, and so forth. In a Christian society, to be sure, these should be part of legally enforced religious education. But even in a non-Christian society, the single most important business of human laws or of government is to habituate the citizens to be religious; to direct their minds and hearts to the ultimate issues and concerns of the human spirit; to promote and to require serious reflection on the nature of things, the universe, and the divinity who is the source and highest being in the universe. Theological reflection is the supreme fulfillment of human rationality, and its encouragement throughout the population is the highest purpose of government.

Natural Laws as Categorical Imperatives

In fostering the virtues dictated by natural law, human law thus completes and supplements or adds to the natural law. Natural law can therefore be changed – in the sense of being added to or supplemented, but human laws must never *subtract* from natural law, or legislate anything *contrary* to natural law (ST I-II, Q 94, art. 5). That is, human laws must not violate or fall below a basic minimum flooring of prohibitions that the natural law supplies.

To see more clearly what this means, we need to recognize that natural law has both a promoting or aspiring side, and a negative or prohibiting side. Natural law demands that we seek to achieve virtue and to avoid vice. Yet Thomas is keenly aware that human law is quite limited in how much it can insist on people behaving *truly* virtuously. Human law can direct and encourage people toward virtue, but it cannot succeed in making people fully virtuous – not by a long shot. The first problem (ST I-II, Q 96, art. 1) is that laws must be made for the whole community, and hence cannot attend to the individual differences in human capacity for virtue; laws can be made to deal with only the majority of cases. So the moral direction and discipline that can be given by human laws will always be somewhat crude and rough, not tailored to individual spiritual needs. The second problem (ST I-II, Q 96, art. 2) is that human law cannot prohibit all vices. It can prohibit only the vices that pertain to the way humans treat one another, and even then only to the external actions, not to the internal motivations or desires. Human law cannot discover what is in people's minds and hearts, and it can only very partially police what people do alone or in private. Something similar is true of promoting virtue: "Human law does not prescribe concerning all the acts of every virtue but only in regard to those that are ordained to the common good – either immediately, as when certain things are done directly for the common good, or mediately" (ST I-II, Q 96, art. 3). But Thomas adds that human law *does* command *every* virtue – because every virtue does have a public side, or a manifestation in how we treat others: "All the objects of virtues can be referred either to the private good of an individual or to the common good of the multitude," "but law, as stated above, is ordained to the common good; therefore, there is no virtue whose acts cannot be prescribed by law" (ST I-II, Q 96, art. 3).

On the negative side, human law must insist that people not slip below a basic minimum of decent behavior. It should implement certain absolute prohibitions that correspond roughly with what Thomas calls the "second table" of the Ten Commandments, that is, the prohibitions such as: do not murder (do not kill the innocent), do not commit adultery, do not steal, do not covet, do not bear false witness. Our conscience tells us already that these are among things that are always wrong, things that are never justified, and things that human law ought always to prohibit and punish. These imperatives, one can say, are *categorical*; they brook no exceptions: The moral aspects of the Ten Commandments "admit of no dispensation whatever" (ST I, Q 79, art. 12; I-II, Q 94, arts. 4–6, Q 95, arts. 2–3, Q 96, art. 4, Q 97, arts. 1 and 4, Q 99, art. 2 reply obj. 2, Q 100, arts. 1, 3, and 8; ST II-II, Q 66, arts. 5, 7–8).

The categorical character of natural law goes with the fact that Thomas does not simply identify natural law with utility. Utility or what is beneficial is only part of the concern of natural law. The natural law does indeed command us to promote the common good, and that usually means what promotes the welfare of the community. But the highest welfare is *spiritual* welfare, and for that higher part of the common good, it may be necessary to risk and sacrifice prosperity, health, even life itself. There are certain things that we are aware must never be done, even to promote otherwise great utility. One could also say that the harm we do to all our souls as members of the community in breaking the most basic prohibitions is so grave that it can never be justified by some other good. To put this another way, what St. Thomas calls "training" in virtue, discipline (ST I-II, Q 95, art. 1), or obedience to the law, obedience to the basic principles known in our conscience, is *in itself* a great spiritual good, central to virtue – even or precisely when we can see no other good reason to obey the natural law in a particular case, or where calculation of utility might suggest that there should be an exception. Our capacity to stick to the rules for their sake, to adhere to principle for the sake of the principle, even when it seems otherwise harmful, is a sublime part of our nature (see especially ST II-II, Q 104, "Of Obedience").

All of this highlights the fact that Thomas, just like Aristotle, does not recommend what we today know as a liberal, open, permissive society. He might grant that such a society is the best one can have in a rather decadent time and place (such as today in the West); a Thomist today would therefore try to find ways to introduce as much public concern for virtue and religion into liberal society as is possible without endangering the society and its liberal principles. But a genuine Thomist – like a genuine Aristotelian – would have to view ours as a mutilated society, whose members are to some extent alienated from their nature as political (and politically religious) animals.

Not the least challenging dimension of Thomas's natural law for us
today is Thomas's condemnation, in his elaboration of natural law, of
what we call "capitalism," and especially banking and investment – involving lending money at interest. "To take interest for money lent is unjust
in itself, because this is to sell what does not exist; and this evidently leads
to inequality, which is contrary to justice" (ST II-II, Q 78, art. 1); "among
other conditions requisite in a just man, it is stated [in Ezekiel 18:17]
that he 'has not taken interest'" (ST II-II, Q 78, art. 2).

Divine Law as Transcendence of Natural Law

The divine law does much more than supplement and clarify and complete the natural law. Divine law has a higher function, which includes
giving to humans a more sublime set of duties, involving more sublime conceptions of fulfillment beyond rationally knowable political
and intellectual fulfillment. The "old" divine law, revealed in the Old
Testament, teaches humanity a number of awesome theoretical and
practical truths – about God and his creation and his demanding love –
that extend far beyond what natural reason could ever by itself discover.
Divine law also responds to manifest signs within human experience,
prior to revelation, that the natural law, and the human law that imple-
ments it, is decisively incomplete. Human nature experiences itself and
its existence as longing and reaching out for a higher destiny and richer
fulfillment that is not evidently available in nature but is pointed to by
nature. *Immortality*, Thomas insists, is one of the "natural properties of
the soul [*proprietates naturales animae*]" (ST I-II, Q 94, art. 1, reply obj.
1), but nature gives no clue as to how immortality is possible. Our deep
natural need for immortality is the natural source of profound longing
and hope for – and our moral experience gives us a natural divination
that there must be – some realm beyond nature. In this way above all,
human nature and natural law, in its experienced incompleteness, prepares us for supernatural divine law, delivered through revelation given
by the Holy Spirit to the prophets and then by way of God himself as the
Christ (ST I-II, Q 91, arts. 4 and 5, and Q 98–105). The "new" divine law,
given in the New Testament, fully reveals the way to the immortality of
our individual souls – and discloses also the eternity of punishment and
reward that awaits us, depending on our obedience or disobedience to
natural and divine law. Both the old and the new divine law reveal cor-
respondingly higher, more difficult duties (many of which we can see
no reason for, beyond their being commanded). These higher duties

include especially duties of worship, adoration, love of God – that pre-pare us for a higher and purer happiness close to God, in another life. In the Old Testament, these duties comprise the vast array of laws of worship followed by observant Jews: what Thomas calls the "ceremonial" law. In the New Testament, these duties comprise new ceremonial worship (e.g., the Eucharist) and more universal brotherhood, universal charity or love – loving even one's enemies.

These higher dimensions of the divine law have profound political implications that take Thomistic political thought and life well beyond Aristotle. Divine law requires that, as much as possible, the chief purpose of human laws and political life should be the encouragement and fostering not *only* of the precepts of natural law and the civic and intellectual virtues knowable by reason but now also the precepts of the Christian divine law, and the higher virtues and more severe demands of the Mosaic law as transfigured by Christ's teaching centered on the Sermon on the Mount. This means that the Christian church and clergy, and Christian education, must be given a privileged place and support by the political community and human laws wherever possible.

Yet there are of course communities where Christianity does not prevail in the populace, or among the ruling portion of the populace. In such societies, Thomistic political theory would seem to dictate civic accommodation, to secular humanistic law, while trying as much as possible to keep reminding people of what is missing from public life (as did Martin Luther King, for example), and appealing to natural law, which underlies divine law and which is embedded in the consciences of all humans – something all can know and follow, whether they are Christian or not.

PART III

MODERN POLITICAL PHILOSOPHY

6

Machiavelli's *Discourses* and *Prince**

Niccolò Machiavelli (1469–1527) is the hinge of fate in the history of political philosophy. He is the first thinker to break fundamentally with both the biblical and the classical outlooks on political life. He thereby lays down the most basic moral and philosophic foundations of what came to be called "modernity." Subsequent "modern" philosophers profoundly modify, and often attack, his teachings. But they do so on grounds that he establishes.

In rejecting both classical philosophy and the Bible, Machiavelli does not by any means ignore them. He is constantly, if often only implicitly, arguing with these received authorities that he is rebelling against – to show how inadequate they are to explain the human phenomena. In order to understand Machiavelli, one must reflect constantly on his critical engagement with the tradition. But one must never lose sight of the proclamation of radical originality that he trumpets in the preface to the first part of his most capacious work: "I have decided to enter by a path, which, as yet not trodden by anyone, if it brings me trouble and difficulty, could also bring me reward through those who consider humanely the end of these labors of mine."

Machiavelli's Puzzling Initial Self-Presentation

To be sure, this extraordinary boast of originality is immediately followed by an apparent expression of modesty. Perhaps, Machiavelli adds, "poor

---

* *Discourses on the First Decade of Titus Livy* (*Discorsi sopra la prima Deca di Tito Livio*); we recommend the translation by Harvey C. Mansfield and Nathan Tarcov, *Discourses on Livy* (Chicago: University of Chicago, 1996). For *The Prince*, we recommend the translation by Harvey C. Mansfield, second edition (Chicago: University of Chicago, 1998). Our citations and quotations, by book and chapter and sometimes page number, are from these editions, with minor emendations. (All emphases found within quotations are our own.)

talent, little experience of present things, and weak awareness of ancient things" may make "this attempt of mine defective and not of much utility," but the attempt "will at least show the path to someone who with more virtue, more discourse and judgment, will be able to fulfill this intention of mine." On close inspection, we see that Machiavelli does not actually say that the problem is *his own* limitations; he may be referring to the limitations in his *audience*. He certainly makes it clear that the fulfillment of his intention depends on "virtue" as well as "discourse" and "judgment." But what does Machiavelli mean by "virtue" (*virtù*)? He says that in taking his new path he was "spurred by that natural desire" to "work" for "those things I believe will bring common benefit to each." Doesn't this suggest that Machiavelli's path is *not* new as regards the most important thing – "virtue" as devotion to the common good, to justice? Or will Machiavelli prove to have a radically new understanding even or above all of "the common benefit to each"?

An even bigger puzzle immediately confronts us. Machiavelli proceeds to give the impression that his proclaimed *new* path is after all merely a return to, and even a call to "imitation" (*imitazione*) of, *ancient* virtue – the virtue of pre-Christian Rome above all. This impression is given also by the title of the work. How can Machiavelli be radically original, if his enterprise is a renewal or imitation of ancient virtue?

The answer begins to appear in the next lines of the preface, where Machiavelli states the intention of his entire work. "In ordering republics, maintaining states, governing kingdoms, ordering the military and administering war, judging subjects, and increasing empire," Machiavelli laments, "neither prince nor republic may be found that has recourse to the examples of the ancients." Why not? "This arises, I believe, not so much from the weakness into which the present religion has led the world," as from the fact that the people who read the histories of "the most virtuous works" of the ancients do so merely for pleasure, "without thinking of imitating them, judging that imitation is not only difficult but *impossible* (*impossibile*) – as if heaven, sun, elements, men had varied in motion, order, and power from what they were in antiquity." It is out of a wish, Machiavelli says, "to turn men from *this error*," that he has written the entire *Discourses*. Now, since the purpose of the entire book is to remove this specific error, we must make sure we see exactly what the error is, in its momentous meaning.

The error consists in judging or believing that *something has happened*, in historical time, to change the very nature of all that exists – heaven, sun, elements, and humanity – so that existence no longer can be experienced or conceived in the way the pagan Greeks and Romans did. What is it that people think has happened in history to effect such a total transformation of existence? Machiavelli does not say in so many words. But he unmistakably gives the decisive clue, by his reference to "the present religion" in "Christian provinces and cities." The "weakness" into which this religion has led the world is only part of the problem. The heart of the problem, he implicitly indicates, is people believing that it is "impossible" to go back to living in accord with the virtues of the pagan Romans and Greeks because the biblical God has miraculously intervened in history, as Christ, to transfigure all of existence – including the nature of human virtue or excellence. *The* intention of Machiavelli's book is to turn men away from *this* erroneous belief. But we notice here something strange: Machiavelli does *not* say that his intention in this book is to *refute* this error; instead he says the intention is to "*turn men from* this error." He thus provokes one to wonder: *How* does he *know* that Christian belief is erroneous? What are the grounds of his fundamental stand? Could it be that he holds that his hoped for or expected success in *turning men from* Christianity is or would somehow be a substitute for *refuting* the truth claims of Christianity?

This much is clear: We are in a position to understand better how Machiavelli's return to, or call for imitation of, ancient Roman virtue can be an expression of radical originality. In attempting to effect the return, Machiavelli is seeking victory in a struggle that the ancients, even at their peak, never engaged in, against an enemy and delusion that they never knew. But this means that ancient virtue, and the return to it, is not simply the end, but is a means, a weapon, in a new kind of spiritual warfare. It then becomes doubtful whether ancient virtue is complete virtue. The Machiavellian return to ancient virtue begins to appear to be the path to a more complete virtue, one that comes into flower only on the grave of Christianity.

The Organization and Opening of the Discourses

Book one, Machiavelli indicates at the end of the first chapter, is devoted to the study, with the help of Livy, of politics "inside" Rome – with a focus on *publicly* expressed deliberations. Book two is devoted to external politics – again as expressed in public deliberations. Book three is devoted to "*private* counsel"; it explores what goes on in the hearts and minds of citizens and statesmen that cannot be expressed publicly. Accordingly, the longest chapter of book three (and of the entire work) is a treatise on conspiracy (3.6).

The order of Machiavelli's presentation within book one emerges as an alternating series of chapters that zigzag back and forth between sections focusing on the nature of the political elites (especially the elite of the elite, the founders and re-founders: chaps. 9–10, 16–18, 25–27, 33–45) and then on the nature of the masses, or "the people" (*il popolo*: chaps. 11–15, 19–24, 28–32, 46–59) – whose key characteristic is seen in their religiosity, or religion. But first, Machiavelli lays out arguments showing why the Roman republic, rather than the ancient Greek or modern republics, most deserves study, as the best.

At the outset, he shows his keen awareness that his elevation of the Roman republic is highly controversial, even or especially on classical grounds. The tradition of political philosophy, rooted in the works of Plato and Aristotle, has celebrated Sparta as the paragon. Sparta had a single, far-sighted lawgiver (Lycurgus) whose wisdom was displayed in a harmonious and balanced constitution, subordinating the docile populace to a lawful, leisured elite distinguished by an elaborate civic-moral education. The Spartan regime promoted stability and moderation by lawfully discouraging luxury and acquisitiveness on the part of both private individuals and the republic as a whole: no imperialism. Sparta maintained isolation from and exclusion of foreigners, who would have lowered or corrupted the civic education, and would have destroyed the society's homogeneity, so important to the fraternity of the elite and to the obedient subordination of the populace. The massive empirical proof of the excellence of the Spartan regime is that it lasted more or less unchanged for eight hundred years, "without any dangerous tumult" (1.2, 6).

Rome, in contrast, appears and is reputed to have succeeded by luck (fortune). The Roman constitution evolved through trial and error, under a series of imperfectly wise legislators responding to fundamental crises, caused by civil strife as well as grave foreign threats. The Roman republic became an imperialist juggernaut, acquisitive without limit and welcoming hoards of newcomers. It was constantly threatened from within by the competitive acquisitive ambition of its individual leaders as well as the populace. Worst of all, the Roman republic's political life was characterized by unending class struggle, sometimes erupting into open civil war but always rife with riotous tumults, tension, and suspicious distrust between patrician senators and plebeians.

Machiavelli seems at first overawed by the arguments he has marshaled against Rome. "I would well *believe*," he concedes, "that to make a republic that would last a long time, the mode would be to order it within like Sparta." But then Machiavelli turns from plausible words to harsh facts:

"Since all things of men are in motion and cannot stay steady, they must either rise or fall"; "when a republic that has been ordered so as to be capable of maintaining itself" *without* an expansionist ethos and policy sooner or later has to confront the "*necessity*" that "leads it to expand," this "would come to take away its foundations and make it come to ruin." While "on the other hand, if heaven were so kind that it did not have to make war, from that would arise the idleness to make it either effeminate, or divided; these two things together, or each by itself, would be the cause of its ruin" (1.6, 23). Machiavelli first reproduces the traditional, Aristotelian-type view – showing that he is altogether familiar with its apparent plausibility. He then trumps this view, with the observable, empirical "necessity" of foreign policy. It was not *Rome* that was lucky, but Sparta! Sparta appears more "reasonable" than Rome only so long as one thinks it is rational to ignore the "necessity" of (1) expanding, (2) undergoing being dominated or conquered, or (3) suffering internal decay. Sparta collapsed as soon as it was compelled to initiate an expansionist foreign policy, and the collapse was in large part because it had rotted within (see also 2.3).

Yet Machiavelli expresses the conclusion to this argument by repeatedly using the verb "I believe" (*credo*), as if he were stating a creed rather than a rigorous conclusion (1.6 end). He thus stirs us to see that he has conspicuously failed to confront and to dispose of some crucial considerations to which he knows thoughtful Aristotelians would appeal. In this same context Machiavelli highlights what appears to be a very big cost of the option for Rome: One must "tolerate the enmities that arise between people and Senate." An imperialist republic requires a large, armed, virile populace to man the military. Such restive plebs threaten a stable, harmonious, fraternal community governed by morally virtuous aristocrats – the sort of "best regime" promoted by the classics and Thomas Aquinas. Why, Machiavelli tacitly provokes his readers (born and bred in a Christian-Aristotelian world) to ask, ought one not and can one not run some risks with security in foreign policy, risks necessary, after all, for the sake of preserving the more important goal of a virtuous, fraternal, "quiet" or peaceful domestic life?

The New Conception of the Common Good

Looking back over Machiavelli's argument in the opening chapters, we see that his answer consists in the introduction of a new conception of the true common good, a conception that becomes more vivid and elaborate as book one subsequently unfolds. Machiavelli teaches that the classic view is mistaken not only, or even mainly, because it ignores the necessities of foreign security. The classic view is wrong above all because it misunderstands the truth about the virtue or excellence, and hence the common good, that suits and arises from human nature, as displayed in the individual and civic lives of the most flourishing and admirable human specimens in political history. Flourishing humans naturally seek vigorous independence, which entails being enabled and empowered to acquire riches and rule, thereby reaping the glory bestowed by other humans who witness with spontaneous, natural admiration the magnificent display of capacities deployed in the effective pursuit of prosperity and empire. As Machiavelli puts it near the beginning of *The Prince* (chap. 3), "truly it is a very natural and ordinary thing to desire to acquire; and always, when men do it who can, they will be praised or not blamed." The good that can be most truly common for a political society, and that therefore is and should be the goal of policy in healthy republics, is a collective freedom from being dominated, which becomes the basis for a glorious collective leadership or rule over other societies. It is the energized, armed and combative, poor masses who – precisely because they lack resources and leisure and education – are naturally less individually ambitious and more protective of freedom as shared in by all citizens; while it is the nobles, precisely because they are richer and more leisured and better educated, who are naturally more individually ambitious and more inclined to dominate fellow citizens. An aroused, armed, suspicious, and even somewhat rebellious populace benefits the city as a whole – even or especially the nobles. For one thing, the threat to the nobles from the restive and vigorous poor compels the nobles to be more unified as a class, or less inclined to fratricidal strife. For another, individual nobles are driven to become more capable leaders, on account of bracing competition from plebian leaders who rise from the ranks, as well as from fellow aristocrats vying to prove themselves better at enriching and glorifying the whole citizenry: In other words, the nobles are compelled by the watchful virility of the plebeians to seek glory and riches in ways that they share with the plebeians. What is more, in order to distract the plebeians from their discontents and suspicions, the nobles are induced to be much more aggressive and enterprising in foreign policy than they would be in a pure aristocracy (the Spartan model). The plebeians, for their part, are also made better – more prudent and moderate and public spirited, as well as vigorously courageous – by the burdens and responsibilities of pursuing and running an empire. Among other things, they are impelled to choose, or to consent to follow, more effective leaders, in a much wiser and more alert fashion than if there were no imperial burden upon the populace (see especially 1.5, 18, 28–30, 47–48, 50–51).

All these and other domestic benefits are foreshadowed in Machiavelli's initial argument made "contrary to the opinion of many." These "many" say that "Rome was a tumultuous republic and full of such confusion that if good fortune and military virtue had not made up for its defects, it would have been inferior to every other republic." These critics "are not aware," Machiavelli insists, "that where the military is good, there must be good order." Those "who damn the tumults between the nobles and the plebs blame those [very] things that were the first cause of keeping Rome free." They fail to understand "that in every republic are two divers humors, that of the people and that of the great (*grandi*), and that all the laws that are made in favor of freedom arise from their *disunion*, as can easily be seen to have occurred in Rome" (1.4). It is *not* the cultivation of fraternity, trust, harmony, and reverential deference to superiors, that in fact constitutes or promotes the true common good. The true common good depends on, and is produced only by, *competition* between mutually distrustful or suspicious, disharmonious classes, and among outstanding individuals, within each class and especially within the upper class. In fact, Machiavelli paradoxically contends, in the culmination of three chapters analyzing gratitude (1.28–30), Livy's history of Rome, wisely interpreted, shows that there is actually more trust, more gratitude, and more communal solidarity wherever the foundation of civic relations is continual competition, class conflict, and distrustful vigilance.

The Emerging Critique of the Roman Republic

In making this argument for Rome over Sparta, Machiavelli initially cultivates the impression that he learned from his authority, Livy, how perfectly the Roman republic developed into the best regime. But the more closely and inquisitively one looks, the more one sees that in fact Machiavelli is going beyond Rome, and even gradually disclosing to us what was wrong with Rome and why we must improve upon it. He initially enchants his reader with Rome, as a way of weaning the reader away from awe before – or intimidation or discouragement by – the authority of Christianity and the Bible, together with Aristotle and classical political philosophy. But a key to participating fully in the education Machiavelli intends his readers to undergo is noticing and then following the path of liberation from even the new authority of Rome, and of Livy.

At first Machiavelli has nothing but praise for the early Roman kings. Then, rather abruptly, he criticizes the Roman king Tullus (1.22). Soon after, he criticizes also the Roman people – for being too forgiving of good leaders who go wrong (1.24). But one first presumes that he means to indicate that the Roman people attained their excellence – becoming sufficiently virile, shrewd, demanding, and tough toward leaders – only after they had escaped from the rule of and tutelage to kings. Yet one is puzzled to notice that in this chapter (1.24) Machiavelli criticizes the Roman people as if they were already a *republican* populace. This starts to prepare us for what transpires eleven chapters later (1.35), where Machiavelli signals in the chapter title, and makes plainer in the subsequent opening sentences, that something very wrong came about as a result of popular elections in *republican* Rome: "The election of the ten citizens created by the Roman people to make the laws in Rome" led to those ten becoming "tyrants of Rome," who "without any hesitation seized its freedom." Machiavelli shows that the Roman people trusted their leaders with too much power and with terms of office that were too long. The people were too unsuspicious, especially of certain individual leaders, who were *apparently* of benevolent and popular character – in particular, Appius Claudius. Rome came within an ace of being subverted into a lasting tyranny under Appius and his minions. The Roman people learned their terrible mistake only by trial and error – a very dangerous error. But did they ever really learn their lesson? Two chapters later, we learn of an even graver and more enduring mistake of the Roman populace. It was not enough for the Roman plebeian class to secure itself against the nobles by the creation of the tribunes – "to which desire it was constrained by necessity," Machiavelli approvingly comments. For "having obtained that," the populace "began at once to engage in combat through ambition, and to wish to share honors and belongings with the nobility as the thing esteemed most by men." From this "arose the disease (*morbo*) that gave birth to contention over the Agrarian law, which in the end was the cause of the destruction of the republic" (1.37). Here we suddenly learn, to our surprise, that the Roman republic suffered from a progressively more and more virulent "disease" throughout its history. As the rest of this chapter indicates, the deeper problem was that Rome never really succeeded in controlling, or even becoming fully aware of, the dangerously greedy acquisitiveness in the populace but especially among the nobles – who set the example for the populace. After having criticized the populace, Machiavelli turns on the Roman senators, for their shortsightedness and lack of control over their greed, seen especially in their failure to share land sufficiently with the plebs.

Now at first Machiavelli tempts us to think that his critique of Rome entails a classical principle – that a healthy republic should have citizens whose good characters rise above, or stifle, greed. On closer inspection, we see that the basis of his criticism is almost exactly the opposite: The Romans, both populace and nobles, were mistaken in that they were *too trusting* in the possibility of individuals rising above or stifling greed. Two chapters later, Machiavelli surprises us still more by seemingly reversing, and certainly qualifying, what he has taught heretofore: He now shows that the Roman plebeians were excessively, or unreasonably, suspicious of their leaders when it came to the aggressive and expansionist foreign policy of the senate (1.39). Putting this together, we see that his message of criticism, and its teaching, is complex. The Romans were too trusting in moral virtue, in the capacity of men and especially leaders to transcend acquisitiveness; this trust allowed leading individuals to develop more extreme acquisitiveness; and this wound up arousing excessive suspicion of leaders on the part of the populace; and this provoked still greater, but more subtle, acquisitiveness in the leaders; and so on – in a sick cyclical dynamic. We are thus brought to see that the balance of suspicion and competition between the rich and poor was *not* perfected in the Roman republic. This failure was ultimately rooted not so much in poorly designed institutions as in a lack of self-understanding, a lack of understanding of human nature, which was a vice that marred especially many of Rome's nobles and leaders, who could have known better – and could have taught the populace better – if they themselves had been better taught.

A few chapters later, at the conclusion of his lengthy account of the terrible and revealing crisis caused by the Decemvirate led by Appius Claudius, Machiavelli presents a short and vivid chapter (1.42) that teaches that he, Machiavelli, sees more clearly than did the Romans how corruptible all "goodness" of human nature or of character is: "One also notes in the matter of the Decemvirate how easily men are corrupted and make themselves assume a *contrary nature*, however good and well brought up." "If this is well examined," Machiavelli stresses, "it will make legislators of republics and kingdoms more ready to check human appetites and to take away from them all hope of being able to err with impunity" (1.42). Most striking here is Machiavelli's employment of the key term "nature." He speaks of an individual's "nature" as something that can be *deliberately changed*; then he replaces the word "nature" with the word "custom." He thus indicates that what most people – even the Romans – take to be a person's "nature" is in fact largely a product of habits that are easily overthrown when even "a little ambition" conflicts with those habits. In other words, what people call "moral *character*" (especially self restraint of acquisitive ambition) is much more artificial, superficial, hence fragile and mutable, than traditionally supposed, even by shrewd and tough Romans.

Seven chapters later (1.49), Machiavelli gingerly raises the possibility for the first time that the great historian Livy himself, upon whose wisdom Machiavelli has hitherto seemed to be relying, "is defective" (*diffetivo*) because he failed to report a very important fact necessary to a proper understanding of Roman constitutional development. Then, in the title of the fifty-third chapter, Machiavelli delivers his most severe criticism yet of "the people": "Many Times the People Desires Its Own Ruin, Deceived by a False Appearance of Good; and That Great Hopes and Mighty Promises Easily Move It." As these words indicate, and as the body of the chapter makes clear, the massive problem in "the people" that Machiavelli focuses on here is a *permanent* problem, exhibited by the mass of mankind *everywhere*. "The people" are *always* moved, often in suicidal degree, by certain great and false hopes and promises. What does Machiavelli have in mind? He shows that in Rome (as everywhere) the plebeians – but not the nobles – had a deep longing for a life in another, better "site" or place. The mass of mankind has a profound escapist bent, if you will. This is perfectly understandable; the life of the mass is never satisfactory. They are poor and burdened with hard labor; even or precisely in the best sort of republic, their largely anonymous dignity depends on their having regularly to risk their own and their children's lives fighting wars. Above all, they never really come to the top; even in the best republic, they always see above them the more prosperous and glorious and commanding elite. Machiavelli indicates what is so dangerous about this by showing how the Roman plebeians were saved from the worst dangers of this escapist syndrome by two important advantages.

First, the Roman plebs did not yearn to live in a site that was *far away*; all that they yearned for was an improved version of life in or near, and like, Rome. What they yearned for was simply more of the worldly goods that they saw that the nobles had. They wanted to live in some place that would allow them and their families to be more prosperous and healthier, with more land and luxuries and peace and less inequality. The phenomenon of the Roman populace shows that when the masses are vigorous and free, they do not seek a radically different life or world, a *transcendence* of this worldly life and its goods; they are not strongly attracted to a *denial* of the goods of this world for the sake of fantastic heavenly goods. Still, Machiavelli lets us see that there was stirring in the masses, even or precisely of Rome, a longing that under less favorable circumstances can be magnified, redirected, corrupted, by religious leaders, into something much more fanatical and world-denying. There was visible, even in the Roman people, the latent germ of Christian or some alternative otherworldly, transcendent religiosity.

This brings us to the second, closely linked advantage the Roman masses had: Their religion was a *civil* religion, not least insofar as it was well managed by the nobles. As Machiavelli makes abundantly clear in his discussions of religion, starting back at chapter 12, little in mature Roman religion led the masses away from sound civic spirit. The religion of the Romans did not make them frightened or humble. It did not inhibit their ferocity and pride and military zeal. But it did instill in them a crucial reverence for civil and military leaders. In the next chapter (1.54), Machiavelli quietly indicates the unfavorable contrast on this score between the ancient Roman and his own time. The Roman Senate always had an ace up its sleeve that it could play in crises, so long as it didn't play the ace too often or in too obvious a manner: There were always older, apparently pious, senators in whom the people had "faith," and who could be trotted out to overawe the people enough to draw them away from their self-destructive proclivities. Elder secular leaders and military men were also priests, or were regarded as possessing religious authority equal to or greater than that of any priest. There was no powerful, rival, separate priesthood or church. "The great" could thus use the noble lie of religion to draw the masses back from irrational longings and excessive rebelliousness. "Today," in contrast (Machiavelli observes), statesmen and generals tend to be *excluded* from the priesthood; while priests are really respected for piety *only if* they are neither political nor military men. In order to have religious authority nowadays – in order to be the object of the faith of the masses – one has to be an unarmed priest such as Savonarola, who as such does not pride himself on military virtue. Christianity takes men away from, it induces men to think they can and should transcend, good soldiering and citizenship, especially in an aggressive imperialist republic. Christianity makes political leaders depend for their ultimate authority on distinct religious leaders who lack and who tend to undermine or even to denigrate vigorous political and military capacity. For Machiavelli, the separation of religious and secular authority, of church and state, is one of the worst or most debilitating features of political life under Christianity.

In thus spotlighting the universal escapist proclivity of the mass of mankind, and the need to have their religiosity managed by a superior elite, Machiavelli might at first seem to be moving back toward a more classically aristocratic perspective. That this impression is misleading Machiavelli now makes plain, as he approaches the end of book one (1.58). He delivers a criticism of Livy, not merely as an historian but as a political theorist – as an historian who expresses the consensus of *all* previous political philosophy. "That nothing is more vain and inconstant than the multitude," is what "our Titus Livy, like all other historians, affirms." Against this classic disparagement of the masses, Machiavelli strikes back: "I wish to defend a thing that, as I said, has been accused by *all the writers.*" Here Machiavelli lays down his gauntlet. He becomes the first political theorist in history to argue that the masses are *not* morally inferior to any elite, but on the contrary: The masses are morally superior to elites. Machiavelli here founds the modern philosophic attempt to bring about a solution to the problem of human existence by abandoning reliance on supposedly morally superior aristocrats, and building instead on the pedestrian moral spirit of the lowly mass of mankind.

But in precisely what does the moral superiority of the masses consist, for Machiavelli? He elaborates in the rest of 1.58, but he has from the beginning of the work been preparing the ground. To begin with, as we have seen, the masses are less inclined than the elites to be oppressive or to seek to dominate others. Sensing their own weakness and ignorance, their lack of education and of wide experience, plebeians are more defensive or passive in their fundamental disposition, wishing to be left alone. Second, the masses are more honest – more truthful or frank, less deceitful and guileful – than the elites, and they honor and respect truthfulness in leaders, while they abhor deceit; for they sense that the cleverer elites use deceit to exploit them. More generally, the masses are moral and moralistic, in opposition to unlimited pursuit of self-interest. The masses are, to be sure, hypocrites – but guilty hypocrites; though they often, or even regularly, act and think immorally, in pursuit of perceived self-interest, they soon feel guilty for doing so. Closely linked to this guilt is their belief in divine punishment. The masses associate religion with morality, and morality with religion; they believe that divinity sanctions moral behavior. This means that even though the masses are changeable or fickle, especially in moral judgments and actions, one can discern that at bottom they are more constant in their attachment to moral and religious opinion than are elites. Indeed, the changeability of the masses is largely explained by their underlying fidelity to morality and religion, interrupted by their succumbing to temptations of interest. This means that one can see consistency, even predictability, in their very mutability or fickleness.

The more negative meaning of this apparent praise of the masses over and against the nobles begins to emerge already in the second paragraph of chapter 58: "I say, thus, that all men particularly, and especially princes, can be accused of that defect of which the writers accuse the multitude; for everyone who is not regulated by laws would make the same errors as the unshackled multitude." This echoes what Machiavelli proclaimed near the beginning: "It is necessary to whoever disposes a republic and orders laws in it to presuppose that all men are bad (*cattivi*), and that they always have to use the malignity of their spirit whenever they have a free opportunity for it" (1.3). But in the interim we have learned about virtue or human excellence, which is encased in what Machiavelli at the start, speaking in a moralistic or even quasi-Christian vein, called "badness." Machiavelli's praise of the masses is the gentler, nicer-seeming side of his attack on the moral character of everybody, and especially of all elites – in the name ultimately of "virtue." The masses are attached to morality and religion because of their weakness; they sense deeply their need for protection, their need for rules (and gods) that will prevent the few who are gifted and privileged from exploiting them. The masses are more moral because they are weaker in spirit, compared with the elite – and especially compared with the *natural* elite, who may well start out as individuals scattered among the poor. The masses can be praised for "goodness" (*bontà*) – for *moral* virtue, linked to protective divine rewards and punishments. But in contrast to this "goodness," we find true virtue (*virtù*), human excellence, in the sense of the rare spiritual strength and insight that actualizes the capacity of a human being to be truly self-ruling and thus capable of ruling over others, in a flourishing that is amoral, even immoral, and essentially atheistic. Precisely because the true elite has this genuine virtue, it *cannot* have goodness and piety. In this light we can understand Machiavelli's initial claim that the masses are more prudent or intelligent than are princes and elites. The masses are intelligent if and when they have intelligent individual leaders competing for their allegiance; if their competing leaders induce the masses to exercise suspicious moral watchfulness over the leaders, then the masses can compel those leaders to exert their virtue in ways that benefit the populace as well as the leaders, instead of subverting the republic. The tension between the goodness or moralism of the masses and the very different, nonmoral but true virtue of competing leaders is a key to a free and glorious republic. Machiavelli's defense of the masses is thus seen to be quite ironic: The defense is a way of rhetorically veiling his offense – his teaching of a new conception of amoral human virtue or excellence constituting the true human elite.

Fuller implications of Machiavelli's break with classical political philosophy come to sight at the start of book two, where Machiavelli attacks Livy again, but now escalates the attack to include as target Plutarch, "a very serious writer" (*gravissimo scrittore*. Machiavelli never thus compliments Livy), as well as "many" others who have shared in a fundamental error. That error is to suppose "that the Roman people in acquiring the empire was favored more by fortune (luck) than by virtue." Machiavelli goes on to note that a *religious* version of this error was committed by the Roman people themselves, who "acknowledged" that "all its victories came from fortune, since it built more temples to Fortuna than to any other god" (2.1). Machiavelli leaves it unclear whether Livy shares this popular religious version of the error that ascribes so much power to luck or "*fortuna.*" Through this unclarity Machiavelli reproduces the ambiguity that pervades Livy: Precisely by leaving his own degree of pious awe for "*fortuna*" unclear, Livy, like the classical political theorists generally, tends to encourage such pious awe. Machiavelli signals a deep link between the pious outlook of the masses, including even the manly Roman plebs, and the political theorizing of the ancient political theorists – who all teach, in one way or another, that political life is dominated by fortune and misfortune. As we have seen, Plato and Aristotle indeed teach that the standards of virtue to which political life aspires are so high and pure that they can never be very fully realized in practice; therefore, the classical historians and philosophers try to induce in leaders a kind of resignation or patience based on a sense of the limits of what human action can achieve. This goes with the classical stress on the truly highest and most virtuous or excellent life being the trans-political philosophic life – as the pure life of the mind seeking truth and knowledge for its own sake. Machiavelli laments that all this has turned out to be a teaching that can be, and has been, taken over by the preaching of biblical religion, which has reduced humanity, including even some of the best specimens, to a state of inner weakness and of loss of confidence in human rationality. This Machiavelli shows most explicitly in the second chapter of book two: "Thinking then whence it can arise that in those ancient times peoples were more lovers of freedom than in these, I believe it arises from the same cause that makes men less strong now," which "I believe is the difference between our education and the ancient, founded on the difference between our religion and the ancient." Our Christian religion "makes us esteem less the honor of the world, whereas the pagans, esteeming it very much and having placed the highest good in it, were more ferocious in their actions." Ancient religion "did not beatify men if they were not full of worldly glory, as were captains of armies and princes of republics." Christianity "has glorified humble and contemplative, more than active, men." It has "placed the highest good in humility, abjectness, and contempt of things human." Classical pagan religion, by contrast, placed the highest good "in greatness of spirit, strength of body, and all other things capable of making men very strong." In short, Machiavelli concludes, the Christian "mode of life thus seems to have rendered the world weak and given it in prey to criminal men, who can manage it securely, seeing that the collectivity of men, so as to go to paradise, think more of enduring their beatings than of avenging them."

Machiavelli admits that Christianity does possess or inculcate a *kind* of spiritual strength – but it is the strength to endure suffering, rather than doing something mighty and aggressive to prevent or to stop suffering. Christianity teaches that for humans to take revenge is wrong; Christianity teaches that we must leave vengeance to God. (As the Bible says, "Vengeance is mine, sayeth the Lord.") True strength of mind, Machiavelli argues, demands that humans avenge themselves, and vindicate justice humanly, on this earth, in this life. Because Christianity teaches that people should leave retribution and vengeance to God, the disgusting outcome is that when Christianity prevails, petty criminals dominate political life – as Machiavelli sees all around him in his Italy. A deplorable keynote of Christian virtue, in Machiavelli's eyes, is finding perverted dignity or consolation in the status of being a victim, and labeling as wrong or sinful the naturally vigorous human impulse to avenge oneself and one's friends and to assert oneself in ferocious competition for rule and glory. In the not so long run, this situation of mass resignation corrupts the princes or elite – who become soft and self-indulgent and who then cannot protect the masses against outside aggression or internal subversion and civil strife. Christianity represents a greatly intensified version of an outlook that lurks as a potential in most people – and that has not been adequately countered, as it could and should be, by political philosophy. The result is the dreary classical cycle of regimes that Machiavelli describes at the outset of the whole book (1.2). Both masses and rulers will operate well – securing their own liberty, prosperity, rule, and dignity, as well as their safety – only by being taught much better.

Against the classical theorists, whose public teaching fundamentally adopted the moral outlook, Machiavelli in effect argues as follows. If we philosophers teach the political elites the harsh and ugly truth about moral virtue, then we will liberate the elites to develop, and in some measure to teach to the masses, a civic and personal virtue that is less of a noble lie, that is more in accord with the truth about human nature and the way things are, that is real in the sense of realizable, and that will enable leaders to strive successfully to achieve lower and less pure but more solid goals – goals that truly satisfy what humans by nature most want and need from political life. But if leaders follow the classics, and set their sights on the transcendent, self-sacrificing standard of moral virtue, they will never be able to do the ruthless things that must be done to create a life that can and will be in control of its own fate, to a degree undreamed of by the ancients.

The new meaning of virtue entails a moral flexibility, a capacity to embrace and to use what is morally blamed as well as what is praised, in a carefully managed combination or alteration. But this is to say that every truly virtuous leader is a potential tyrant, a man who seeks to acquire rule and glory without limit except the check and balance of other such men as rivals. A key illustration is Appius Claudius, who in his failure and imperfect virtue points to what true virtue would be like. Machiavelli passes judgment on him in the following remarkable words: "His astuteness in deceiving the plebes, pretending to be a man of the people, was well used"; "also well used was the audacity of creating himself against the opinion of the nobility." But "it was not at all well used," when "he had done this," to "change nature of a sudden, and from a friend of the plebs show himself an enemy; from humane, proud; from agreeable, difficult; and to do it so quickly that without any excuse every man had to know the falsity of his spirit" (1.41). We are astonished again by the way Machiavelli talks about moral nature or character: as something that one can change, in and by oneself, *so easily that one has to try not to make the change too fast and obvious!* But if virtue entails such extraordinary self-manipulation, we are impelled to wonder: Does virtue itself, the virtue beyond goodness or moral virtue, have a fixed character or center of its own?

In book three of the *Discourses*, where the inner, private or hidden, and even conspiratorial spirituality of individuals becomes a theme, Machiavelli makes it clear that there is a fixed, and magnificent, core that governs the virtuous character that possesses moral flexibility. Machiavelli tells of Cincinnatus, who was elevated from being a poor farmer-warrior to being dictator of Rome for a few weeks. He exhibited what "appears to be" an "impossible" switch of the "spirit": from humility, obedience, and reverence, to pride, love of honor, and authority – and then back again to the former, all within a few weeks. On what basis was this possible? Machiavelli answers by stressing that Cincinnatus *always* possessed "greatness of spirit" or "generosity," centered on personal, worldly honor – the proud determination to win recognition for manifest capacities to acquire and to maintain not so much private riches, as rule and freedom and thus glory for one's country, and thereby for oneself. "Here one sees two very notable things: one, poverty, and the fact that Cincinnatus and Marcus Regulus were content with it, and that it was enough to those citizens to get honor from war, and everything useful they left to the public." The "other, is to consider the generosity of spirit of those citizens whom, when put in charge of an army, the greatness of spirit lifted above every prince." They "did not esteem kings, or republics; nothing terrified or frightened them." And "when they later returned to private status, they became frugal, humble, careful of their small competencies, obedient to the magistrates, reverent to their superiors, so that it appears impossible that one and the same spirit underwent such a change" (3.25). The abiding core of virtue, of virtuous character, here appears as a love of shining forth as a leading exemplar of a people able to control its destiny without standing in fear or awe of anyone else.

Machiavelli does not mean, despite what he sometimes says in exaggeration, that fortune or luck can be completely mastered. Virtue needs opportunity, it needs virtuous comrades-in-arms, and it needs a political system that keeps ambition checked and balanced against itself (*or* the opportunity to overthrow the given political system in creating such a new and sound political system). Paradoxically, virtue as well as goodness needs harsh necessity – the challenge presented by danger and suffering and competition – to arouse in humans their best efforts. Here there is a qualified coincidence between Machiavelli's understanding and that of the ancient philosophers: "As it has been written by certain moral philosophers, the hands and the tongue of men – two very noble instruments for ennobling him – would not have worked perfectly nor led human works to the height they are seen to be led to, had they not been spurred by necessity." In this regard Machiavelli makes his highest use of Livy, who put into the mouth of a Roman general the following winged words, addressed to followers, that Machiavelli makes his own: "The armed oppose the armed; equal in virtue, you are superior in necessity, which is the last and greatest weapon!" (3.12, beg.; see also 1.3, 2.5, 12). It is through the welcoming of necessity that the truly virtuous are free of fortune, in the sense that they understand that the key to success and failure is virtue and necessity – that there is no need for any higher powers, any mystery, any false hope: "Among the other magnificent things that our historian makes Camillus say and do, so as to show how an excellent man ought to be made, he puts these words in his mouth: 'Neither did the dictatorship ever raise my spirits nor did exile take them away.'" Through these words, Machiavelli says, "one sees how great men are always the same in every fortune; and if it varies – now by exalting them, now by oppressing them – they do not vary, but always keep their spirit firm and joined with their mode of life so that one easily knows that for each, fortune does not have power over them" (3.31).

Machiavelli the Philosopher

The evocations in book three of these greatest figures and their virtue compel one to wonder what virtue means for Machiavelli himself, as a thinker. What becomes of intellectual-theoretical virtue, of philosophic virtue, of philosophy as a distinct, trans-political way of life, as the best life? This seems to us the most difficult question for our interpretation and understanding of Machiavelli, and we can only offer some thoughts that culminate in questions – which we hope may be at least heuristic. Roughly and provisionally speaking, we can glimpse three avenues along which the answer might lie.

One (the most obvious) is that for Machiavelli the knower can stand at the peak of life because or insofar as, through conveying and employing knowledge of "the things of the world," one may be able to change and to shape the world and thus become glorious as a founder, in far richer self-conscious awareness, and thus enjoyment and self-esteem, than those who rule or found but lack full knowledge. For Machiavelli, theoretical philosophy, the study that progresses to wisdom about nature and human nature, would be most valued as the way to the most supreme rule or dominion.

A second possibility is that Machiavelli embraces and deeply enjoys philosophizing, as the study of nature as a whole including human nature, and finds the steady progress in such knowledge the core of his own happiness and of the satisfaction of his own consciousness, *but* he does not think sustainable the classical claim that a life given over to such joy constitutes the entire peak fulfillment of human nature. The satisfactions of knowing for its own sake, great though they be, require the major, essential supplement of the satisfactions of actively employing knowledge to guide and to reform the world of practice. At the peak of the best life, the fulfilling joys of theory and of practice remain distinct but interwoven and complementary.

The third possibility is that the largely private theoretical understanding of nature and human nature remains for Machiavelli the whole heart of human nature's peak fulfillment – but that the way of life that this entails is reconceived, as needing much more political action and involvement as an essential *means* to, as an essential *defense* and *nurturing* of, the intellectual peak of life. And this gives to grand political ambition and action a higher, if still ministerial, status than it ever had in classical political thought.

We are impelled to entertain these three possibilities not so much by what Machiavelli says about himself, as by his presence, on every page, as a thinker and, what is more, as a writer exhibiting didactic skill of consummate subtlety, aimed at many levels of readers but not least at an elite of the most daringly and demandingly thoughtful. Taking proper note of this constant presence, we see that Machiavelli ceaselessly provokes the question: Where does he himself, as a knower, and above all as a writer who is a philosophic teacher, fit into his explicit scheme of things? For there is no obvious place that does justice to what we see him to be, on every page. Once we become engrossed in trying to grasp Machiavelli's self-understanding, we note that he speaks about himself most at the very outset, in the Dedicatory Letter – which is strikingly different from everything that follows. For in the letter Machiavelli speaks evocatively of intellectual friendship: of the close personal friendship he has with two gifted young men for whom the whole book is written, as a gift. He stresses that they are *not* rulers, though they deserve to rule because of their excellence. Dismissing, as contemptible flatterers, those who write books dedicated to *actual* princes, Machiavelli in contrast writes for friends from whom, he stresses, he cannot and does not expect riches or rule or public honors. In fact he does not value those external goods anywhere near so much as the private esteem of such knowers, of a very few friends (and, by implication, potential friends among future readers) who are truly his kin. Yet does not Machiavelli even here also imply that the most estimable kind of knowing is directed to knowing how to rule – and thus directed to engaging in practice, rather than in pure theory? Or could Machiavelli agree with Plato's Socrates and

Eleatic Stranger, in holding that an adequate theory of nature, and thus of human nature, and thereby of the good for man by nature, requires complete knowledge of and capacity for rule as essential to the wisdom that fully understands why one should not wish or seek to actually rule unless compelled to do so by unfortunate circumstances? But does this take adequate account of Machiavelli's attractive evocation of the enduring glory and satisfaction won by executing "religious" or quasi-religious writings that guide and reform active as well as theoretical life for masses of mankind in future generations?

It is again in book three, however, that Machiavelli stresses how little survives of Livy – the book Machiavelli makes his bible. He thus shows that he is keenly aware of how fleeting, from a philosophic point of view, is even the fame and influence that comes through enduring great books, not to speak of great and long-lasting regimes such as the Roman. This sobering reminder would accord with a hypothesis that Machiavelli's deepest motive in writing is not ambition for glorious literary-political transformation – that his deepest motive is rather the sharing of the bliss of the erotic contemplative life, enjoyed for its own sake, together with a few friends (actual and playfully future-imagined).

Yet Machiavelli does not ever celebrate the contemplative life. He mentions the contemplative life only once, as a leading theme of Christianity, coupled with humility and the refusal to try to avenge injustice and to rule decisively (2.2). He thus sharply reminds us that the contemplative life has been assimilated to Christian resignation and therefore (in Machiavelli's eyes) to contemptible weakness. But does this mean that Machiavelli abandons the autonomous contemplative life? Or only that he thinks that he cannot, in the Christian era, afford to praise it openly – since his praise would almost certainly be misunderstood and become grist for the mill of Christian propaganda?

The question of whether and why the engaged political life must be chosen over and against the private life, free of political ambition, Machiavelli does address in his remarkable discussion and unmatched praise of Junius Brutus, the founder of the Roman republic (3.2). The more closely one considers Machiavelli's specific praise of Brutus, the more perplexed and provoked to thought one becomes. For Machiavelli declares that Brutus's "operation" (*operazione*) of *pretending to be a stupid fool* "deserves" greater "esteem" for "wisdom" than any other work of any other human being: "There was *never anyone* so prudent, nor esteemed so wise for *any outstanding operation* [*egregia operazione*] of his, as Junius Brutus *deserves* to be [*merita d'esser*] *in his simulation of stupidity* [*stultizia*]."

Why in the world should successfully pretending to be stupid outrank in wisdom all other outstanding operations, in Machiavelli's eyes?

In a radical distortion of Livy (see the latter's book one, sec. 56), Machiavelli claims "that Titus Livy expresses none other but one cause [*non esprima altro che una cagione*] that induced Brutus to such simulation, which was to be able to live more securely and to maintain his patrimony." "Nonetheless," Machiavelli submits (stealing from Livy), when Brutus's "mode of proceeding is considered, it can be *believed* [*credere*] that he *also* simulated" the stupidity in order to be less observed so as to "have more occasion for crushing the kings and freeing his fatherland whenever opportunity would be given him." By radically altering Livy, by pretending to add on his own to the history of Brutus, Machiavelli creates or makes conspicuous a contradictory and thus puzzling duality in the motives of his "Brutus": For aiming at such extremely risky action as overthrowing one's powerful king seems essentially at odds with maintaining private security. How can such a contradictory pair of goals animate the wisest operation ever?

One possible answer is given when Machiavelli interprets, without warrant in Livy and even against his text, a piously worshipful action of Brutus as showing that the latter revolted against his human king buoyed up by the belief that there were "gods" who monitored and were favorable to his conspiratorial, public spirited, and risky thoughts or plans (*a' pensieri suoi*). The Roman gods as Machiavelli presents them, we are reminded, were believed to demand, and then to reward, deliberate risk or sacrifice of personal security for civic good.

Still, this hardly solves the puzzle of Machiavelli's bizarre, leading indication that what he regards as incomparably estimable for its wisdom is not Brutus's great political achievement – the founding of the best republic that has ever existed – but his simulation of stupidity. And the puzzle grows when Machiavelli proceeds to suggest that the mere simulation of stupidity cannot possibly be wise. For he next insists that the universal lesson to be drawn for "all those who are discontented with a prince" is that it is "impossible" for men "whose quality is notable" to remain in a private station under such a king: Such men must become politically active, either by "making war openly" on the king, or by "seeking with all industry to make themselves friends to him" through "following his pleasures and taking delight in all those things they see him delighting in."

Now to this general assertion there is an obvious but nevertheless profound objection, which Machiavelli introduces by way of refuting it: "Nor does it suffice to say: 'I do not care for anything; I do not desire either honors or useful things; I wish to live quietly and without quarrel!' For these excuses are heard and not accepted." Explaining what he means, Machiavelli makes explicit that he is now envisaging "men who have quality" who are "without any ambition": Such men *cannot* "choose to abstain, *even when they choose it truly and without any ambition*, because it is not believed of them; so if they wish to abstain, they are not allowed by others to abstain." "Therefore," Machiavelli amazingly concludes, on an intimate note to the reader, "one needs to play the madman [*pazzo*], like Brutus, and make oneself crazy [*matto*], praising, speaking, seeing, doing things *against your mind* [*contro allo animo tuo*] so as to please the prince." Imitating Livy's Brutus by simulating "stupidity" has expanded to include imitating Machiavelli's Brutus by playing "insanity," in the sense of successfully pleasing the prince through energetically sharing and *pretending* to praise and to embrace his political ambition (even while thinking such praise and embrace is madness), so as to get the opportunity, if possible, to overthrow the prince. In this light, Brutus's "operation" of "simulating stupidity," expanded by Machiavelli to include the "insanity" of pretended political ambition, can culminate in, rather than being distinct from, his work of revolutionary founding. Does not Machiavelli mean that it was only in simulating stupidity, including madness, in *this* grand way that his "Brutus" executed the "operation" unrivalled in wisdom? But the wisdom of such an extraordinary operation of pretending still remains puzzling. Machiavelli speaks as if a wise man of quality without political ambition has no choice but to play the madman by entering into political and even eventually revolutionary activity, pretending to have grand political ambition, since his wisdom about politics will inevitably be noticed and therefore he will be dragged into the arena as a victim if he does not succeed in dominating it. Now this seems, especially in this context, most dubious. Why could not a wise man retreat into Epicurean obscurity by rendering his "quality" not "notable": by successfully hiding his political wisdom and capacity, as Machiavelli points out Livy reports Brutus did, for many years – by faking stupidity, *about politics* (among other things: living "safe in contempt," *contemptuque tutus esse,* Livy 1.56)? Or could the prince Machiavelli is thinking of, above all, be a prince from whom it is believed impossible to hide, even in one's thoughts (*pensieri suoi*)? Could the prince whom Machiavelli has in mind, above all, be the biblical God? (Cf. 1.26: God is *the* example of the tyrant-prince.) Does Machiavelli in his Brutus present the avatar of a new human "prince" whose philosophic longing for security for his private life of thinking and friendship requires him to "play the madman" in eventually becoming (or inspiring) the essential overthrower of the threat posed by the apparent rule of the old purported prince who is believed to be the all-seeing biblical God? Is Machiavelli's political project motivated by the aim of securing the philosophic life, as the autonomous study of nature, through a massive political-empirical demonstration of the impotence and thus nonexistence of the purported biblical God – a demonstration to be achieved by founding a new civic culture, under a new, anti-biblical elite? Is Machiavelli's political project philosophically justified, at bottom, by what Machiavelli the philosopher sees to be the hitherto unmet need of the philosophers, as philosophers, to establish firm empirical grounding for their denial of revelation and miracles and for their assertion of a necessity-governed nature – to whose study in private they are in their hearts chiefly dedicated?

Explaining the Worldly Power of Christianity

But is not Machiavelli's whole practical enterprise, whatever its motivations, confronted by the terrible empirical problem of the worldly success of Christianity? If nature and the human condition are as Machiavelli claims, how could Christianity, which appears so contrary to human nature, ever have been so successful? Granted that once Christianity was established as the reigning outlook, its survival might be explained on the basis of its success in propagandistic education that "corrupts" the souls of the young, even or especially the elite. But how did Christianity ever become established as the reigning religious beliefs of even the elite, if humans or the best humans are by nature inclined to the virtue Machiavelli teaches? What happened to the Romans to make them become Christians, to make Rome become the home of the papacy? Is the fall of pagan Rome to Christianity not powerful empirical-historical evidence for miraculous, divine intervention or providence – and hence for the plausibility of the truth of the Christian faith?

Machiavelli's response emerges as he proceeds in book two to focus on Roman foreign policy and its ultimate effects on the world. We consider first what he indicates are the five pillars of a successful republican empire. First, one needs an armed populace of enormous size, as the backbone of heavy infantry. Population growth is made possible by what Machiavelli calls "loving" immigration policy (2.3), meaning an open door to healthy immigrants, combined with constant warfare against neighbors that makes life in surrounding cities intolerable for anyone with any spirit, driving them to emigrate with their families to Rome or to become Roman colonists in other places in the growing empire (see also 2.32, second paragraph). Second, one needs to maintain an enormous war chest – public money won by conquest, and not distributed to individuals except sparingly, hence not corrupting or softening. The key maxim for a successful republic is to keep individuals poor and the city rich (1.10; recall the Cincinnatus story). Third, one needs to make every war short and violent (aim to end every war in twenty days or less: 2.6); hence, avoid sieges, and do not rely on fortresses (2.24 and 2.32). Use what would later be called a Napoleonic strategy of dashing around heavily fortified places (*blitzkrieg*). Fourth, when a short war is won, but the enemy not yet crushed (especially if it was a republic), start immediately preparing for renewed war – especially by settling colonists on the borders (2.6, second paragraph – colonists are really hostages to the enemy). Members of the Roman leadership, being themselves republican, knew that an enemy republic, even or especially in defeat, will always be dangerous, a real competitor, until eventually it is completely crushed.

Yet in the fifth place, Rome had at the commencement of its growth, and for a long time – especially within Italy – a twofold policy against enemy republics. Those that the Romans could not demolish they made into "partners" (2.21, 2.24, 188). Rome claimed to create a "federation" of free cooperative republics. But this "partnership" turned out to be *the* big lie, *the* grand fraud, by which Rome deceived the world and truly succeeded. Machiavelli hints at the fraud first in the first chapter of book two, and then fully unveils the fraud in the thirteenth chapter: Rome could not have used "a greater deception in the beginning than taking the mode (discoursed of by us above) of making 'partners' (*compagni*), for under this name it made them servile, as were the Latins and other peoples round about" (2.13). When Rome's so-called partners finally woke up to the massive fraud, it was too late. The "partners" were by then surrounded by an empire beyond Italy, and overwhelmed by the enormous Roman metropolis and consequent massive legions.

With the grand fraud that underlay Rome's success in mind, we turn our attention to a major dimension of the analysis of Roman foreign policy in book two that we have thus far omitted. In a breathtaking pirouette, Machiavelli suddenly shows himself to be not a partisan of the Roman republic in its full growth but instead a sworn enemy of the republican empire's success! Now we learn that it was precisely the unchecked success of the Roman republic's imperial growth that destroyed all other republics and thus destroyed freedom everywhere in the known world. As we eventually learn, the unchecked Roman success was at the same time the cause of the Romans' own rotting from within (see especially 3.16, 255). As Machiavelli remarks almost in passing in his account of Cincinnatus (3.25), the times of Paulus Aemilius "were almost the last happy times of that republic" – that is, when Rome had *not yet* conquered Greece. The consequent worldwide spiritual abasement that was brought about by the Roman success is what explains the success of Christianity. It was the terrible and unchecked success of Rome that enslaved or instilled a slavish disposition in everyone and prepared the soil in men's hearts for their welcoming, as a desperate consolation, the slavish and weak Christian religion with its otherworldly hopes. This is the rationally intelligible cause of the apparently miraculous spread of Christianity. The Christian outlook fitted exactly the sick condition of humanity produced by the total success of the Roman republic (see especially 2.3). Rome was the first and only regime whose leadership figured out how to run correctly a foreign and military policy, based on the big lie; since no one else knew such policy, or knew it at best only in part – and failed to imitate Rome soon enough – imperial Rome eliminated all its competition and suffered the inevitably consequential rot (see esp. 2.4 and 2.19).

Machiavelli exposes and spreads the truth about the Roman Empire, and above all its fraud, in order to try to prevent such a fraud, and such a universal empire, from succeeding again. What he seeks, it turns out, is not another Rome, not another republic that monopolizes the truth about vigorous internal institutions and customs and a dynamic foreign policy, but *instead* a world with *many competing* Roman-type republics, or many competing civic elites, all or many of whom know the score, and thus constitute a civic world where no single republic can again demolish its competitors and with them all manly freedom. Machiavelli seeks a world where the pressure of competition among several imperialist republics will keep virtue always strong in some countries. Machiavelli seeks on the level of global politics what Rome created within its domestic politics.

But Machiavelli goes even further in his critique of the Roman republic. In a multipolar world with several imperialist republics checking and balancing one another, other possibilities become more viable. Machiavelli speaks near the beginning of book two, or in this same context, very favorably of the confederate system of the Etruscans that preceded and was destroyed and replaced by Rome (2.4). Machiavelli seems to recommend this non-Roman, genuinely federal alternative as a possible practical aspiration for the Tuscany of his own day. Key features of such a confederate alternative include a limit in size, and in capacity to expand; a dispersed authority, and hence more secure liberty; qualified independence in all members; a greater security than was available in a single republic such as Sparta, and hence less of a threat posed to neighboring republics.

Yet all this does mean that there will be less virtue within such confederacy, and less stimulus to virtue in neighbors; such confederacy is vulnerable to a Roman-type republic (though perhaps less so if the confederate republic's elite is imbued with Machiavelli's wisdom). In addition, money (avarice) and religion (the arts of peace) tend to be more influential in such a confederacy than they were in Rome, and this is another source of weakness or corruption – although the confederacy's armies can be rented out as mercenaries, like those of the ancient Tuscans and the modern Swiss, and maintain their tone by fighting foreign wars for pay.

There is of course another alternative, even more prevalent, especially in Machiavelli's own time: monarchy or principality. A monarchic imperialism, Machiavelli stresses, is less hard on subjects than a republican imperialism. For the prince is not so concerned with the common good of his own society and is suspicious of potential competitors from among his own people. This means that he is less repressive of alien, subject, or conquered peoples, and is more likely to choose his helpers from among them (2.2). This greater humanity toward foreigners that is characteristic of monarchies, in contrast to strong republics, helps us to understand how and why Machiavelli can maintain a kind of neutrality between republicanism and monarchy.

The other major reason why monarchies are in an important sense superior to republics is laid out near the beginning of book one, especially in chapters 9 and following. Successful founding or refounding, of an all-new regime, or all-new modes and orders, typically requires the concentration of power and authority of a single ruler or monarch or tyrant. This means that if Machiavelli's vision of a transformative change in the world, in his own time or in the foreseeable future, is to have success, he must become an advisor to modern princes, in the hope that he will inspire and guide one or another to undertake the kind of profound and broad revolution that would bring Christianity to an end as a dominant cultural power and set the world on the path to a new era of true virtue. This is the most obvious grand reason for Machiavelli's writing his other masterpiece, *The Prince*.

The Prince: *The Other Face of Machiavelli*

In turning to *The Prince,* we are reintroduced to Machiavelli, or forced by him to look upon human existence and politics from a different perspective. By presenting his teaching in two books, so different and yet so obviously meant to be read in conjunction, Machiavelli induces us to see that politics and human existence must be understood bifocally, as it were. Both books make virtue or excellence their theme. But while the *Discourses* focuses on how virtue operates within a sound republic, *The Prince* focuses on politics and life when it is lacking such a framework. *The Prince* focuses on what it takes to found or to create good order where it does not exist. We thus see delineated in *The Prince* more starkly the best and the worst of which human nature is capable. In particular, *The Prince* deals much more directly with the modern Christian world, the symptoms of whose sickness are more in the foreground – but as is, by the same token, the impetus to radical medicine, to a new founding, a cultural revolution, above all as regards religion.

This thematic focus on founding is linked to the fact that we are more directly confronted in *The Prince* with Machiavelli himself, in his relation to actual political rulers. The whole work is a kind of playful dialogue between Machiavelli as teacher and his prince as student – and the rest of us readers as the audience for whose enjoyable instruction the book is seriously written.

Machiavelli makes clear in the Epistle Dedicatory the basic respect in which he continues classical political philosophy. He declares that he possesses nothing that he cares for so much and esteems so greatly as his "knowledge, of the actions of great men." He further declares that he can conceive of no greater gift that he could give than this knowledge – which he has gained on the basis of "long experience with modern things" and "a *continuous reading* of *ancient* things". It is this knowledge, he says, that gives him the confidence "to dare to give rules for the government of princes." For Machiavelli as for the Socratics, knowledge is the supreme good.

But the break with the classical tradition also stares out at us. For Machiavelli begins to show that he has a dramatically new conception of the relation between theory and practice. *The Prince* is a new kind of writing in political philosophy, to an even more obvious degree than the *Discourses.* It is not a treatise like Aristotle's *Politics* or St. Thomas's *Treatise on Law,* and it is hardly a Socratic dialogue. What kind of writing is it? The overwhelming first impression is: It is a job application! In the dedicatory letter, Machiavelli puts in the foreground his practical, self-interested goal in writing this book. He makes it clear that he does not think and write in order to know and to teach only for its own sake.

But as soon as we begin to read the subsequent chapters, we are provoked to wonder where, when, and how Machiavelli ever gives his reigning prince of Florence any usable guidance as to how to deal with any specific problems in Florence. The book at once turns into a theoretical account of the various types of monarchic rule – rooted, to be sure, in a rich selection of examples from contemporary Italy (though few from Florence), as well as from classical history. We are compelled to add that there are notorious sections of the book that sound as though they belong in a handbook for gangsterism more than in a serious work of political theory. In this last regard, *The Prince* seems somewhat, or at least in part, repellent to the sort of readers to whom the *Discourses* is addressed. As we read on, we are more and more prompted to wonder: What is Machiavelli's true goal, and who are his most serious addressees?

The closing chapter (26) gives an answer, in terms very different from all that has gone before. Applying to "Italy at present" the theory he has previously elaborated, Machiavelli proclaims that he has a grand, public-spirited goal, involving "great justice" (with "thirst for revenge") and even "love": the liberation and unification of Italy, his native land. Machiavelli now suddenly presents himself as a passionately nationalistic patriot, with a project that will benefit the "entirety" (*università*) of Italy. He will become glorious, he implies, as the advisor to the Medici prince who "Seizes Italy and Frees Her from the Barbarians." Rome as the model shines forth in the passionate quotation (in Latin) from Livy, but Machiavelli at the same time invokes a curiously militant biblical piety: the hope for God's favor bestowed on wars that are just, because patriotically vengeful – wars of national liberation. Machiavelli goes further, playing the role of the enthusiast: He dares to compare himself to Moses, and as such to a reporter of miracles, sent from God, that he claims he knows have already occurred in Italy. He thus suggests, somewhat histrionically, that the Italian people may be conceived as the new chosen people, whose unification and liberation will inspire and guide other peoples and fatherlands all over the world.

The ending shows us that in *The Prince* we find a new kind of philosophic writing, which presents the permanent truth about human nature in a form aimed at grandly transformative political action, directed by a theorist reaching for political power and glory for himself and his people. We are in a very different world from that of classical political philosophy's understanding of its relation to political practice. We recall, especially from Plato's *Apology of Socrates*, that the classical philosophers fear that the direct injection of philosophy into politics, the popularizing of philosophy, is dangerous for at least two major reasons. First, the exposure of politics to philosophy's doubts and skepticism is likely to undermine the traditions, the faith, the trust, and the self-restraint, that are essential to a virtuous political life. Second, the classical philosopher does not want the burden of rule, direct or indirect. To accept it would compel him and his truest students to curtail and to distort their joyful and fulfilling theorizing. The classical philosopher's main concern as a political writer and speaker is to defend and to justify the detached philosophic life by showing that it can, while dedicating itself to the pure pursuit of knowledge for its own sake, also give modest and conservative, but crucial, illumination to political life, from the sidelines as it were.

Machiavelli's radically new conception of what the political philosopher seeks for himself and his truest students from politics, as well as his new notion of what makes for a healthy republic, has the momentous consequence that his writing is much less cautious, much more ambitious – and by example urges all other philosophers to be much less cautious and much more ambitious. Machiavelli is the first openly revolutionary political philosopher, the first to write in such a way that philosophy becomes the propagandistic source of inspiration, and even of plans, for dramatic improvements in political life. Machiavelli initiates the anticlassical understanding of the relation between theory and practice that produces distinctively modern works of political philosophy such as Bacon's *New Atlantis*, Hobbes's *Leviathan*, Locke's *Two Treatises of Government*, Rousseau's *Social Contract*, Marx's *Communist Manifesto*, and Nietzsche's *Thus Spoke Zarathustra*.

Nevertheless, to say that Machiavelli is far less cautious than the classics is not to say that he is without a distinct caution – a highly ambitious caution – of his own. Machiavelli's ambition to make rational theory rule or dominate future culture entails the need for a new kind of propagandistic rhetoric, by which the philosopher, with his radical plans for innovation, can gradually gain decisive influence over the hearts and minds of leading nonphilosophers, who begin by being psychologically attached to the traditions and beliefs of their times and places. The philosopher has to devise an escalator that will draw such readers up to his subversive truths, using as stairs his pretended agreement with certain contemporary respectable prejudices. Machiavelli's employment of a new kind of "noble lies" is most obvious in the most memorable part of the book, the part he knew would echo in the reader's memory – the famous last chapter, where Machiavelli appears to justify everything in the preceding chapters on the basis of patriotic justice and piety. He thus indicates what kind of reader he seeks primarily to attract and to arouse: the frustrated, virile, young patriots, dreaming of manly glory and chafing under Christian humility and its call for patient endurance of wrongdoing.

But precisely insofar as such readers are nobly moved, the last chapter impels the thoughtful among them to turn back to reread *The Prince*, in order to try to understand precisely how, and whether, its harsh and often shocking teaching is really explicable and justifiable as all in the service of divinely sanctioned and righteous patriotism. Their seduction by the wily Machiavelli begins.

Ascending Stages in the Teaching of **The Prince**

Machiavelli introduces himself as somebody rather traditional: a supplicant for royal favor, writing a salute and an offer of assistance to his prince. (But if we recall what Machiavelli said in the Epistle Dedicatory to the *Discourses*, ridiculing those who dedicate their books to those who happen to be the ruling princes, we are helped in discerning that the Epistle Dedicatory to *The Prince* is a subtle satire on this so-called magnificent Lorenzo, who was never a very impressive character, or thought to be deserving of such an epithet.)

When we proceed to the first chapter, we find that it continues to give a superficial impression of traditionalism, presenting what at first appears to be a dry, scholastic classification of regimes. The subversion consists in the way this classification compares with the traditional, Aristotelian classification (recall *Politics* 3.7). Machiavelli silently drops the most basic Aristotelian moral criterion for distinguishing among rulers: the difference between those that pursue chiefly the common good versus those that pursue chiefly their own good. As a consequence, Machiavelli's classification makes no distinction between kingship and tyranny; in fact, Machiavelli will never mention tyranny in this entire book. He coaxes the reader into forgetting the distinction between tyranny and monarchy. He thus begins to bring the reader toward the radical truth – that the very concept "tyranny" is naive; it depends on the untrue assumption that there can be princes whose rule is not chiefly aimed at their own interest. What takes the place of the Aristotelian criterion as the chief basis for Machiavelli's new classification is: How rule is *acquired*; acquisitiveness, in all its modes, is from the beginning Machiavelli's theme.

Chapter 2 begins with "I" (*Io*); Machiavelli steps forward, in his distinctiveness. He does so by saying that he will not "reason" about republics because he has done so "another time." But will Machiavelli really remain silent on republics in this book? Or is he only temporarily pretending that he will, so as to playfully hide his preference for republics? (He prudently refrains from disclosing to his prince that "another time" means in fact in another book, which praises republicanism and which begins by ridiculing books dedicated to princes.)

In the very next chapter, Machiavelli insists that *the* model for virtuous foreign and defense policy must be the Roman republic, whose strategies for conquest he lays out in some detail. So Machiavelli blatantly lied when he said he would not reason on republics. Still, *The Prince is* mainly about principalities. On the other hand, Machiavelli says in the Epistle Dedicatory that this book teaches "all" he knows. But how can that be, if this book does not provide his teaching about republics? Or is there a possibility that Machiavelli can teach all he knows by focusing either on principalities or on republics? But how could that be? *Unless* there is not such a fundamental difference between the two as most people think. Our study of the *Discourses* has prepared us to understand what Machiavelli means: the traditional distinction between republican and monarchic rule, between so-called virtuously free societies and so-called wicked tyrannies, is exaggerated. Every capable republican leader must be understood to be a potential "tyrant," such as Appius Claudius or Julius Caesar.

In the second chapter, Machiavelli's primary focus is on the *hereditary* monarch, whom he calls the "natural" prince, and who faces "much less difficulty"; it is "fitting" that the hereditary monarch be "more loved," because he does not need to offend anyone. Only "extraordinary and excessive" force can remove such a prince; only "extraordinary vices" can make him hated. This then would seem to be the best monarchic regime. Should we not focus on this situation – on conditions of peace, stability, and love, as a basis for building virtue and the arts and a rich domestic life, and perhaps also a "mixed regime" in which the king would begin to share some of the rule with his citizens, and move in a more republican direction, and thus become even more loved? This would be the traditional, respectable Aristotelian outlook. And from the title of the next chapter, this at first appears to be where Machiavelli too is going: The third chapter is on "Mixed Principalities."

But in this third chapter Machiavelli takes off the kid gloves and reveals that he is playing with us. A Machiavellian "mixed" regime means one made by "mixing" somebody else's country with your own and, thus, through conquest, acquiring a bigger and therefore better "new" country. The theme now becomes conquest, with the "new" prince becoming equivalent to the conquering prince.

Machiavelli focuses on the specific example of the conduct of Louis XII of France in his failed, recent – and therefore readily examined – attempt to conquer Italy. It was easy for Louis XII to overthrow the hereditary ruler of Milan, because "men willingly change their masters in the belief that they will fare better." So it turns out that in stressing in the previous chapter how "beloved" hereditary rulers are, Machiavelli was sardonically repeating the illusion by which traditional princes and their traditional subjects like to be comforted. In fact, foreign powers can always be invited or brought in by some of the discontented among the citizens. Once brought in, the foreigners will be welcomed, by still others – this, Machiavelli says, is "the order of things."

Machiavelli begins in this third chapter to arouse in the reader contempt for Renaissance princes, for what is going on in modern Italy; he expands the horizon and begins to appeal to the contrast with ancient republicanism. Here Machiavelli introduces "virtue" – not through some dry definition, but through a concrete, vivid, historical example: the Roman republicans. They, "seeing inconveniences from afar, always found remedies for them and never allowed them to continue so as to escape a war, because they knew that war may not be avoided but is deferred to the advantage of others." Virtue means primarily aggressive anticipation of war, based on understanding of the true, competitive nature of men and politics.

But the whole third chapter has a sinister side: It explains the strategy by which the French could and should succeed at conquering Italy, Machiavelli's native land. Machiavelli painstakingly explains the correctible errors that made Louis's attempt fail, and thus shows in detail how such an attempt could in the future succeed. How can such public treason be justified? Machiavelli is not, clearly, a simple patriot. He helps us to begin to understand the new spirit of Machiavellian patriotism – or of the patriotism Machiavelli seeks to cultivate. Three major justifications for Machiavelli's public treason emerge, if one considers the question in the light of the *Discourses* and of what follows in *The Prince*.

First, in order to prevent or to repel an enemy's conquest, one must see clearly the best possible enemy strategy, in order to then counter it.

To this, however, one could object: Yes, but why *publish* that best strategy? By now, the Machiavellian answer obvious: The whole Italian race has become so corrupt that it needs shock therapy.

Second, we recall the amazing attitude Machiavelli took toward Appius Claudius and his attempt to subvert the Roman republic. Machiavellian virtue teaches: May the best win! If Italy can't take care of itself, it does not deserve to be free. Perhaps Italy would be better off under a strong French ruler – who might provoke it to rebel and thus hone itself in a war of revolution (we note parenthetically that the eventual unification of Italy in the nineteenth century owed much to the Napoleonic conquest). Machiavellian patriotism is *not* love merely of one's own country; as true or rational patriotism, it is love of a virtuous country – preferably one's own, but if one's own is too corrupt, then a better country, maybe under a conquering virtuous people or prince.

Third, and most grimly: The so-called liberation and unification of Italy, even or precisely if it is by some Italian, really entails the conquest of Italy. We see now the meaning of the title of chapter 26: Italy must be "seized" (*capesso*) if it is to be "liberated."

After introducing virtue as exhibited by the ancient Roman republic, Machiavelli returns to the modern King Louis and his mistakes, spotlighting what makes Louis so inferior to the ancient Romans. Louis's biggest blunder was helping the pope, Alexander Borgia, take the Romagna (an area on the Adriatic, south of Venice), thus thwarting his own conquest of Italy by empowering a rival. Now why in the world did Louis do such a stupid thing? Machiavelli suddenly constructs a dialogue with those who defend Louis: They say, the king of France had to keep his promise to the pope, had to give the pope what the latter asked, because only the pope could dissolve Louis's marriage, and only the pope could allow Louis to get one of his own men appointed to a major ecclesiastical office in France. Machiavelli thus shows us what he meant when he said, just previously, that Louis made "the Church great by adding so much temporal greatness to *the spiritual one that gives it so much authority.*" The Church, the papacy, the modern priesthood, has a terrible *spiritual* power over the hearts of modern men, dominating even the biggest conquerors, such as Louis – something the Romans would have found grotesque.

Once we see that chapter 3 has culminated in identifying the papacy, in its spiritual power, as a key to the political ill health of modern politics, we are in a position to decipher the massive puzzle of the next or fourth chapter. For Machiavelli suddenly raises what seems a sort of merely historical question, and devotes a long time to it: Why did not the empire of

Alexander collapse immediately after his death? How were his generals able to hold it so well – even though it had just recently been conquered from Darius? Machiavelli says that in order to understand this, you have to realize that there are two sorts of empire or principality: one that is hard to take but easy to hold, and another that is easy to take but hard to hold. And Machiavelli explains in detail why each has the character that it does, and the different way in which one must take and hold each type. We are provoked to ask: What is the relevance of this discussion at this point? Why does Machiavelli suddenly cease to speak about Italy or anything contemporary? To decipher this mystery, it is necessary to consider these two clues: the name of the pope Machiavelli has just discussed is Alexander (as he stresses), and the Catholic Church must be like one of the two fundamental sorts of empire. Machiavelli in this chapter surreptitiously adumbrates the strategy for taking over the Catholic Church.

Chapter 5 returns to the biggest practical question that was left open in chapter 3: How does one hold a conquered territory that has been living in liberty under a republican government? This is obviously a very big problem in the "unification" of Italy. How do you master the republican cities? We now learn that there are just three methods, which Machiavelli illustrates by again appealing to the model Roman republic's strategy. First, you can ruin the conquered republic, breaking the spirit of its inhabitants. Second, you can go live there (but obviously that only works once). Third, you can establish an oligarchy dependent on you in the conquered republic. The leading ancient Greek powers (Sparta and Athens) tried the last and eventually failed, as did the Romans, initially – who drew from this failure the harsh truth: One must ruin republics, or expect sooner or later to be ruined by them. Machiavelli thus delivers a tribute, if a grim one, to the ineradicable ferocity of republics. But what is the silent implication for the fate of independent republican cities in the "unification" of Italy? In particular, what is the implication for Machiavelli's native city, Florence? How does Italian "patriotism" go with Florentine "patriotism?"

The Deepest Meaning of "the New Prince"

Having thus started to open his readers' eyes to the harsh grandeur of his teaching, in chapter 6 Machiavelli skyrockets to a perspectival viewpoint way above and beyond contemporary Italy, and even above and beyond the Roman republic. In his first sentence, Machiavelli predicts that the reader may well "marvel" at the supreme "greatness" of the "examples" he will discuss, the examples that show what he means by "new principalities that are acquired through one's own arms and virtue." The examples are Moses, Cyrus, Romulus, Theseus – "and the like." These founders are not just princes; Machiavelli calls them "prophets." They are the bringers of God or the gods; they are the founders of new religions at the same time as new political orders. These are the founders of the greatest known Western and Eastern civilizations – Judaism, Persia, Rome, and Athens. It is such figures who exemplify and clarify, in the fullest sense, what Machiavelli means by *virtue* (a word he uses twelve times in this chapter, while it has been mentioned only three times before). These, Machiavelli insists, are the models we must somehow imitate, even if only from afar or as a distant approximation.

What in the world does Machiavelli mean? How can we imitate prophets? Machiavelli's underlying thought may be expressed as follows. If we are to live on the basis of a true understanding of human nature, and of the truly fundamental human situation, we must think our way back behind the thick veils of convention and tradition that delude us into believing that the lawful, orderly civilizations or religions or cultures we see around us are given – by God or by nature. We must think our way back to the origins of lawfulness, of faith, of order, and of civilization, to see what *caused* men to become civilized. We must study old books, as Machiavelli has never ceased doing – but we must read them suspiciously, under his guidance. We must use our imaginations to discover the truth buried in the books – above all, in the Bible, in the story of Moses.

And what then do we find? At first, Machiavelli says that "one should not reason about Moses, as he was a mere executor of things that had been ordered for him by God." But then Machiavelli adds: "Let us consider Cyrus and the others who have acquired or founded kingdoms"; "if their particular actions and orders are considered, they will appear *no different* from those of Moses." Cyrus and the others we can reason about, following historians and philosophers who proceed only on the basis of empirical evidence. If we study their analyses, and then go back and read the Bible skeptically, we can see that Moses was in truth no different. *All* the "prophets" *created* their gods; they all *created* their orders. They did not get them from on high; they used their circumstances, and especially their peoples, like clay, or "the matter, enabling them to introduce any form they pleased."

This is Machiavelli's fundamental thesis or hypothesis about the human condition. All civilization, all order and law, all religion and culture, are creations of great, imaginative, intelligent, and – above all – courageously coercive, fear-inspiring individuals. This is the deepest meaning of "the new prince."

It is crucial to see that Machiavelli is rejecting the traditional Aristotelian doctrine that men are by nature political, or are inclined by their nature to evolve peacefully over time toward communal civic life. Machiavelli teaches that the evidence shows instead that humans must be compelled and intimidated, against their inclinations, to become political or civilized. At the root of political order is violent compulsion and terror – combined with the big lie of successful propaganda. "It is however necessary, if one wants to discuss this aspect well, to examine whether these innovators stand by themselves or depend on others; that is, whether to carry out their deed they must beg or indeed can use force." In the first case, "they always come to ill and never accomplish anything; but when they depend on their own and are able to use force, then it is that they are rarely in peril." From this it arises that "all armed prophets conquered and the unarmed ones were ruined." Things "must be ordered in such a mode that when people no longer believe, one can make them believe by force."

But big questions emerge when we focus on the armed prophets themselves, as Machiavelli urges us to do. First, what is it that motivates these virtuous individuals? Are not at least these rare geniuses by nature political and public-spirited? Second, and related: What specifically were their deeds? Just what kind of force and fear does it take to mold chaotic and scattered or oppressed people into a new and vigorous civilization? Third, and perhaps most fundamentally, what is the evidence for this claim of Machiavelli's, this hypothesis about the origins of civilization? In other words, the chapter whets our appetites to learn more about these prophet-founders – by studying them or the records we have of them, in the old books, under Machiavelli's tutelage.

In the next chapters, however, Machiavelli seems to disappoint this thirst he has stimulated; he ceases for a while to talk of or to discuss the greatest figures. He descends to lesser figures. This descent begins already at the end of chapter 6 – and in a revealing way. "To such high examples," Machiavelli says, "I want to add a lesser example" (the ancient tyrant Hiero of Syracuse) – which "will have some *proportion* with the others, and I want it to suffice for *all* other *similar* cases." Machiavelli here gives us the decisive clue as to how he will proceed. He will descend to lesser cases, of better-known and extensively studied historical examples, that give us the empirical evidence that allows us to estimate, in proportion – if we do some thinking for ourselves – the character of the legendary armed prophets. At the same time, he will thus provide us more readily imitable models for our own action here and now (in contemporary Italy, but also in other places), since we, or most of even his best readers, are probably of lesser natural abilities or virtue than the armed prophets.

The next or seventh chapter is the most famous in *The Prince*. It presents us with the portrait of Cesare Borgia, who superficially seems the hero of the work – the contemporary whom Machiavelli seems most to admire. We note from the start, however, what a qualification this implies. Cesare appears as the best of *contemporary* leaders; he is the best of a corrupt period. He is far from being one of "the greatest examples"; he is certainly not an armed prophet. More precisely, Cesare did not found "new modes and orders" but merely "renewed old orders with new modes." By "orders" Machiavelli seems to mean institutions, systems of belief, and ways of organizing authority that form a whole way of life. By "modes," he seems to mean ways of behaving or operating *within* "orders." Cesare was someone who tried to work within the existing system. From the title of the chapter, we see that Cesare is an example of someone who rose to power not through virtue, but through *Fortuna* or luck, and not through his own arms, but through the arms of others. Machiavelli contrasts Cesare with Francesco Sforza, who did rely on virtue and his own arms. The closer one looks, the more ambiguous the example of Cesare appears. What is Machiavelli up to?

The massive impression Machiavelli gives is that Cesare did the best anyone could, given that he acquired his rule by luck and the arms of others. Machiavelli does spotlight at the outset that Cesare wound up a total failure. But Machiavelli attributes this to "extraordinary" bad luck. More precisely, Machiavelli stresses that all Cesare's *deeds* were admirable. Near the end of the chapter, he repeats the praise of Cesare's *actions*; then, at the very end, he suddenly says that Cesare made a terrible mistake in the choice of the new pope (after Pope Alexander VI, who was his father, died), and that was the cause of his ruin. Cesare's bad choice turns out to be no incidental misstep. It grew out of and expressed a profound error concerning human nature: "Whoever believes that among great personages new benefits will make old injuries be forgotten deceives himself. So the duke erred in this choice and it was the cause of his ultimate ruin." What is going on here? Why does Machiavelli first suggest, quoting what Cesare himself said to Machiavelli (32), that the only problem was the unexpected brevity of Cesare's father's life and especially Cesare's own sickness, at the time of his father's death – and then say at the very end

(33) that the cause of Cesare's ruin was his profound misunderstanding of human nature? What is the link between the brevity of Cesare's father's life and Cesare's big mistake? Why did Cesare make so big a goof after his father died, and why did Cesare think the only problem was his own sickness? Cesare did not even see that he was messing up! He never understood his own gross ignorance that was the cause of his failure. Does Machiavelli not quietly let us see that Cesare desperately needed his father to help him see what to do?

In fact, Machiavelli reveals the full truth in chapter 11 ("Of Ecclesiastical Principalities"): "then Alexander VI arose; of all the pontiffs there have ever been he showed how far a pope could prevail with money and forces. With Duke Valentino [the popular title of Cesare Borgia] as his *instrument* and with the invasion of the French as the opportunity, *he did all the things* I discussed above in the actions of the duke". And "after his death, the duke being eliminated, the Church fell heir to his labors." Cesare was really only the tool of a much greater man, his father, the shameless Pope Alexander VI, who was the one pope who tried to transform the Christian order from within – who tried to use the power of the papacy to create a new military, hereditary monarchy, led by his son, and on that basis to unite Italy. But the project failed. Both the attempt and the failure reveal the essential limits on any such effort to reform Christianity under the papacy. This is the deeper meaning of Machiavelli's saying that Cesare tried to "renew old orders through new modes." The failure shows that we need not only new modes but new orders, a transformation of the institutions as well as the spirit of the Church.

What, then, is the key institutional problem with the papacy, the problem revealed when we put chapter 7 together with chapter 11 – the problem revealed by the fact that only Alexander was able to show what might be done? We see more clearly from chapter 11: The popes are almost always old men, who as celibate priests lack sons. Alexander is the exception that proves or shows the rule: He could be so politically dynamic *only* because he was the unique pope who had a vigorous young son. This is the tragedy of Italian politics. The papacy is just strong enough to prevent anyone else from uniting Italy, but never strong enough to do the job itself.

But as Machiavelli goes on to show in the chapters before and after chapter 11, this problem in the papacy reflects, at a deeper level, the sick nature of Christianity. The character of Christian belief leads the Church to honor old men, who lack political ambition, in part because they are not fathers (except in a strange, priestly and otherworldly, sense). Love of, and ambition for, the Church and its imagined, otherworldly God, replaces or takes complete priority over love and ambition for any earthly fatherland or family. The Church is infected with, and spreads the infection of, the sick belief that its authority does not depend on human virtue or excellence or strength: ecclesiastical principalities, Machiavelli says in chapter 11, "alone have states, and do not defend them; they have subjects, and do not govern them; and the states, though undefended, are not taken from them; the subjects, though ungoverned, do not care, and they neither think of becoming estranged from such princes nor can they." Thus, Machiavelli concludes with bitter irony, "only these principalities are secure and happy."

But there is of course a positive and hopeful dimension of Machiavelli's presentation of Cesare: his *deeds*, such as "should be done by a prudent and virtuous man" (27), which Machiavelli asks us to admire and imitate. What are these key deeds?

First, we see here the other side of the promise Louis made that destroyed him: Alexander secured the Romagna as the power base for his son Cesare by manipulating Louis's respect for religion. A successful revolutionary must, Machiavelli thus suggests, manipulate and thus take advantage of the existing religious beliefs of opponents – and in modern times, this means their Christian beliefs.

Second, Cesare acquired new friends and an army of his own *from his enemies*! How? By practicing strict meritocracy and rewarding the true qualities of those turncoats who joined him, Cesare made his erstwhile enemies deeply grateful, dependent, and reliable. A new prince can outbid and undercut his established opponents, who will tend to practice favoritism rather than reward in accordance with merit.

But of course the most powerful enemy faction in Rome, the Orsini, finally caught on to what Cesare was doing and gave him big trouble; Cesare disposed of them by his third grand move. He bestowed enormous gifts on one of their trusted number (a Signor Paulo), and thus seduced him into agreeing to invite everyone to a peace banquet – where Cesare murdered all of them. One must use deceitful generosity and apparent longing for peace on a grand scale to lull one's opponents to their mass murder.

But the single most important lesson is the fourth. "This point," Machiavelli says, "is deserving of notice." Once "the duke had taken over Romagna, he found it had been commanded by impotent lords who had been readier to despoil their subjects than to correct them." So, "he put there Messer Remirro de Orco, a cruel and ready man, to whom he gave the fullest power," and "in a short time Remirro reduced it to peace and unity, with the very greatest reputation for himself." Now because Cesare "knew that past rigors had generated some hatred for Remirro, to purge the spirits of that people and to gain them entirely to himself, he wished to show that if any cruelty had been committed, this had not come from him but from the harsh nature of his minister." He had Remirro "placed one morning in the piazza at Cesena in two pieces, with a piece of wood and a bloody knife beside him. The ferocity of this spectacle left the people at once satisfied and stupefied." One needs to practice cruelty, with terrifying police work, to make people obedient, especially when they have been ruled by petty criminals and warlords. This reign of police terror will of course cause hatred as well as fear, but one can "purge" the hatred by turning on one's police chief, venting resentment but leaving fear and awe mixed with gratitude. One must use punitive justice – spectacular punishments – to gratify the people's lust for revenge. One must exploit the passion for justice or moral indignation. So it turns out that for Machiavelli one aspect of justice is very important: the natural lust for vengeance. The wise man does not let himself be blinded by this stupidity, but he does use its strength in others to manipulate them, for their good as well as his own.

As a result of his action against Remirro, Cesare was both loved and feared by the people: These two can go very well together. And this combination is deeply gratifying for the ruler, a terrific reward for political success. We see here one chief constituent of the motivation of virtue. We see here a supreme goal of the most virtuous, even or especially the armed prophets. They reap the spiritual pleasure of being loved and feared by the people. Is this not a clue to the true meaning of the biblical God? Love does, then, have a place in Machiavelli's understanding of the virtue of men such as Cesare. It is natural to want to be loved, and on a vast scale. But to desire in an intelligent way to be loved, one must realize that one should desire simultaneously to be feared. This is what Christians deny – in human relations, but not simply. For the Bible, shrewdly read, teaches precisely this. The greatest human love, human love of God, goes together with the greatest fear. ("He has mercy on those who fear him, in every generation," as Mary says in her Magnificat expressing her love of God.) Part of what Machiavelli sees as sick about the biblical teaching is that it would take away from humans, and invest in this grotesque imaginary being, the virtue and gratification that is and should be available to humans.

Chapters 8 and 9 clarify further the motivations of virtuous men – although these chapters come as a surprise. For at the start of chapter 8, Machiavelli suddenly adds two additional and previously unmentioned categories to his classification of the types of new prince. The first is "when one ascends to a principality by some criminal and nefarious path," and the second is "when a private citizen becomes prince of his fatherland by the support of his fellow citizens." There was no hint of these two types in the classification of principalities back in chapter 1; at the beginning of chapter 2, Machiavelli implied that he would discuss the types of regimes he had laid out in chapter 1 – and until now he has indeed followed that plan. Why does Machiavelli now transcend that plan to discuss acquisition of power through crime? How is this a necessary next step in the reader's education?

A fairly obvious answer suggests itself. As the reader has learned that what Machiavelli means by "virtue" is acting like Cesare Borgia, the reader naturally wonders with alarm whether "virtue" is anything other than successful criminality. Machiavelli now at first reassures the reader that the answer is no: Criminality, as a path to rule, is treated in a separate chapter, as distinct from virtue. Criminality is paired with another category, also distinct from virtue, which is in effect the capacity to destroy a republic, by the consent of the people, so as to become tyrant in it.

The example of a criminal new prince is Agathocles of Sicily: "He *always* kept to a life of crime at *every* rank of his career." Nonetheless, Machiavelli states, "his crimes were accompanied" with "virtue of spirit and of body." Agathocles used his spiritual and physical virtue to protect his people from foreign domination, after having destroyed the oligarchs who had dominated and failed to defend the republic. Yet "it cannot be *called* virtue," Machiavelli says, "to kill one's citizens, betray one's friends, to be without faith, without mercy, without religion; these modes can enable one to acquire empire, but not glory" (our emphasis). Machiavelli seems at first here to be laying down the following decisive criterion that distinguishes virtue from virtuous criminality: Virtue is what wins lasting *glory* for oneself, rather than infamy. Virtue would then be distinguished from virtuous criminality by its success in attaining popular admiration. Being loved by the people – as was Cesare Borgia – is then *not* the most important thing. Being admired by the people, in future ages, is more important. Agathocles is not so admired.

Yet this would seem to mean that virtue, to be fulfilled, depends ultimately on popular approval in later ages. And we know from the

Discourses as well as from later chapters of *The Prince* that the people tend, according to Machiavelli, to be stupidly moralistic as well as pious. The people do not understand what virtue is. How then can a truly wise or prudently virtuous man be very gratified or impressed by *popular* fame? No wonder Machiavelli goes on to question or indeed seemingly to contradict what he has just said about Agathocles: "If one considers the virtue of Agathocles in entering into and escaping from dangers, and the greatness of his spirit in enduring and overcoming adversities, one does not see why he has to be *judged* inferior to *any* most excellent captain". Then Machiavelli reaffirms that "his savage cruelty and inhumanity, together with his infinite crimes, do not *permit* him to be *celebrated* among the most excellent men". Agathocles *did* have complete virtue, the same virtue as that of the most excellent captains, in the judgment of the few wise – who, like Machiavelli, still admire him centuries after his death; however, given popular illusions, his virtue cannot be "called" virtue. It cannot be "celebrated" as such. "Glory," insofar as it means future *popular* judgment, is not then the final word on what the love of and satisfaction from glory means for the truly virtuous. Popular fame is at most a kind of means or vehicle for gaining the attention and then the admiration of the truly wise, the few who understand the harsh truth about the world and its iron necessities. True virtue does *not* necessarily need to be "celebrated" as virtue.

At the end of chapter 8, Machiavelli returns to Agathocles and praises him still further, saying that in fact Agathocles remedied to some extent his standing, with God, as well as with men. For Agathocles was not simply cruel; his cruelty was "well used." In fact, his example teaches the way cruelty should be used, or the difference between cruelty "well used" and cruelty "badly used." Cruelties can be called "well used" that are done "at a stroke, out of the necessity to secure oneself, and then are not persisted in, but are turned to as much utility for the subjects as one can." Cruelties are "badly used which, though few in the beginning, rather grow with time than are eliminated."

Next, as Machiavelli suggested in the first sentence of chapter 8, in chapter 9 he provides a thumbnail sketch of his analysis of republics – from the point of view of how to take them over or subvert them – that is, from the point of view of monarchists who wish to destroy a republic. This chapter reveals more than any other part of *The Prince* just how Machiavelli understands the nature of republican politics. It is a condensation of the central political teaching of the *Discourses*.

Religion's Effect on Modern Military Power

With chapter 9 Machiavelli has completed his analysis of the different types of principality; accordingly he turns in chapter 10 to discussing the military force that "all principalities" need. Yet the chapter treats the theme of military power in a very strange way: While Machiavelli says that the only sound military is one that can go on the attack, and does not rely on fortresses, he discusses mainly how to manage best if you have to rely on fortresses. This reliance on fortresses, Machiavelli says, is a sign that you cannot really defend yourself but must rely on someone else. He provides only a modern example – the cities of Germany. He claims to give a good strategy for holding out behind fortified walls. But when we read the chapter carefully, we see that he quietly shows the perfect way to defeat the so-called good defensive strategy. Why then focus only on the weaker, defensive type of military, and why give only modern examples?

We get a big surprise, which indicates the answer, in the next or eleventh chapter, when Machiavelli examines another type of principality that was not mentioned in the original plan – ecclesiastical principality (i.e., the papacy). Here, as we have seen, Machiavelli gives the key to deciphering the real meaning of chapter 7 on Cesare Borgia. And here Machiavelli shows the problem that is the key to deciphering the mystery in chapter 10. The power of the papacy, or the clergy, over men's minds is the answer to why moderns rely on defensive military organizations.

In chapter 12 Machiavelli begins the discussion of military matters all over again – having forced us to wonder about why moderns are so defensive minded, and then having forced us to think about the papacy and its spiritual influence. Chapter 12 is the first of three chapters devoted to the topic of "arms," thus constituting the second main part of the work. Machiavelli commences with one of his characteristically brutal formulations of his anticlassical outlook: "Because there cannot be good laws where there are not good arms, and where there are good arms there must be good laws, I shall leave out the reasoning on laws and shall speak of arms." For Machiavelli, arms are not only a necessary condition for good laws – the ancients would have agreed that they are – but are also a *sufficient* condition for good political life and good laws. Machiavelli agrees with Aristotle that law is a derivative phenomenon, but he disagrees over what law is derived from. For Aristotle, it is the regime's success in cultivating the virtues of peaceful leisure as well as military virtue. For Machiavelli, the fiercely competitive nature of mankind renders peaceful leisure an illusion. This illusion breeds and is strengthened by the Christian outlook, which in the rest of chapter 12. Machiavelli shows to be the cause of the reliance on mercenaries, and hence the ruin, of modern Italy.

In chapter 13 Machiavelli ascends from the unqualified evil of mercenary troops to the dubious reliance on allies, or auxiliary troops. The only fully worthwhile arms are those that are faithful to you and to you alone. And this is what Machiavelli means by "one's own arms." Machiavelli returns to the example of Cesare Borgia, whose *actions*, he says again with some irony, are a model. But while Machiavelli says that he wishes to stick with contemporary examples, he shows himself to be drawn, like a magnet, to ever more ancient and grander examples. Chapters 13 and 14 ascend from the Roman republic to Hiero of Syracuse, and then to King David of the Bible, and then finally, in chapter 14, to Cyrus – one of the four armed prophets presented in chapter 6. But this time Machiavelli spotlights Cyrus as written and taught about by Xenophon, the student of Socrates.

Machiavelli now makes explicit that his theme is education. He stresses the reading of old books – but in the right way, with a Machiavellian eye and suspicion and alertness. In retelling the story of David and Goliath in chapter 13, he gives us another example of how he reads the Bible critically. But Machiavelli now makes it clear that the single greatest book of the past in his eyes, the book that allows one to begin to understand the Bible because it tells the truth, or much of the truth, about armed prophets, is Xenophon's *Education of Cyrus* – which was the guide for the Roman republican leader Scipio. "Whoever reads the life of Cyrus written by Xenophon will then recognize in the life of Scipio how much glory that imitation brought him, how much in chastity, affability, humanity, and liberality Scipio conformed to what had been written of Cyrus by Xenophon." This has a very strange implication: At this point, Machiavelli almost seems to be saying that he really is not necessarily in fundamental disagreement with at least one of the Socratic thinkers, Xenophon. He implies that everything he has said up until now does not yet constitute a complete break with what Socrates or at least his wisest student taught. But it turns out that Machiavelli is once again setting us up to be startled. For on the very next page, in chapter 15, Machiavelli announces his break with all his predecessors.

The New Meaning of the Traditional Virtues

The first sentence of chapter 15 launches a third section of the work and a new topic, for which we have not been prepared; it commences a series of nine chapters, constituting a third of the book, devoted to the discussion of domestic policy, or the internal rule of the virtuous prince, in his relations "with subjects and with friends." The overall, four-part plan of *The Prince* is now becoming clearer; the plan is signaled by the words Machiavelli uses to start the beginning chapters of the second section (chapters 12 and 14) and now the third section.

By announcing his break with all past thinkers in chapter 15, immediately after having acknowledged his indebtedness to and agreement with a Socratic philosopher at the end of chapter 14 Machiavelli shows that the deepest issue between him and the classics is not so much the founding, or foreign policy; it is domestic policy – how one ought to rule after the founding, and when you are not having to fight for survival. The classics, or at least Xenophon, Machiavelli suggests, were aware of the harsh measures that might well be required to defend oneself in foreign policy, and even of the harsh things required to found civilized order. The classics did not, however, focus on these ugly truths, and did not teach that one ought to take one's bearings from these extreme situations. The classics were concerned with investigating and clarifying the highest aspirations of civic life, as those might be realized in peace and leisure, within a society already founded, possessed of a stable tradition, and largely freed from the harsh necessity of fighting brutally for survival. The classics imaginatively constructed envisioned "best" regimes, meant not as practical proposals or plans for actualization, but as polestars guiding from afar the modest efforts at reform practicable in actual political life, and, above all, as thought experiments revealing the full, perplexing meaning of all that humans seek and love in their passionate concern for justice and nobility. It is precisely this "utopian" focus of classical philosophy that Machiavelli attacks head-on in chapter 15: "Many have imagined republics and principalities that have never been seen or known to exist in truth," but Machiavelli has found it "more fitting to go directly to the effectual truth of the thing than to the imagination of it"; for "it is so far from how one lives to how one should live that he who lets go of what is done for what should be done learns his ruin rather than his preservation."

Here then is the keynote of Machiavelli's break with the classics: Whatever the classics really thought, what they *taught* – or the influence they have had by their books – has made people aim too high. The "goodness" the classics teach leaves one exposed to being exploited and taken advantage of, since human beings are not good. What is more, humans do not truly respect or admire "goodness" – even though they often claim that they do. As he shows concretely in the chapters that now follow, Machiavelli teaches that we must take our bearings from what truly brings admiration in the world. People come to be misled by taking too seriously what people say, rather than what they actually do. People say, and sometimes even believe, that they admire one quality, such as keeping faith or not lying, but in fact they truly admire achievements that require and presuppose the willingness to tell big lies. In a deep sense, people want to be deceived; they do not want to face the truth about themselves or about human nature or the human situation. Because of this, human life is pervaded by deep hypocrisy – and to succeed, one must self-consciously join and use that hypocrisy, but one must not be taken in by it.

Machiavelli is also arguing that the people who try to be good, or who believe in the myth of goodness, mistakenly praise, in absolute terms, what should be praised only conditionally. They mistake what it is best to do mostly, or in what one might call "normal" circumstances, for what it is best to do always. But the so-called normal times are made possible by the extraordinary or extreme occasions, which are the real test of whether one is virtuous and wise, or merely good and stupid. The people who try to be good or moral fail to see the deeper causes of the ability to be good; they do not see that in order to be what they call good, one must first, and from time to time, be what they call bad.

The focus in the subsequent chapters now becomes the following: What is the "effectual truth" of the various specific "qualities that bring praise or blame" – what qualities does one need to become famous and admired? Machiavelli focuses on rulers, since they are the peak, the greatest or hardest cases. But he stresses in the title and body of chapter 15 that he wants the lesson to be applied in *all* walks of life, private as well as public, in the family or in business as well as in politics; he is speaking not only of political virtue or excellence but of all *human* virtue and excellence.

Space does not permit us to follow the fascinating path of Machiavelli's analysis of the specific virtues; we must leave that as a challenge to the student.

Humanity's Power over Its Fate

The Prince ends with a three-chapter, fourth and final, section that addresses the question of how Machiavelli's teaching may be applied here and now to his native land. In chapter 24, Machiavelli berates his contemporaries, exhorting them to stop "accusing fortune" as the source of their political disasters, and to start recognizing their own "indolence" as the cause – to rely on themselves and their virtue. But this prompts the profound question that Machiavelli addresses in the central chapter of this section, chapter 25: How much are human affairs capable of coming under human control, and how much must they remain under the sway of fate or fortune?

The chapter title sounds a note of defiant "opposition to Fortune." But Machiavelli opens by acknowledging, and at first apparently accepting, the outlook of "many" who hold "that worldly things are so governed by fortune and by God, that men cannot correct them with their prudence." These words evoke or remind of the biblical outlook of guilt-ridden and humble acceptance ("God's will be done"). By the end of his first sentence, however, Machiavelli has dropped God and changed fortune to "chance" (*sorte*). He thus tacitly prompts the question: May it not be that there is no discernible intelligence behind the forces that environ and frighten us?

But Machiavelli returns to speaking of fortune, and, sounding a bit like an ancient Roman, personifies her as a female goddess, Fortuna. "In order that our free will [*libero arbitrio*] not be eliminated," he judges that it might be that Fortuna "leaves half, or close to it, of our actions for us to govern." Machiavelli shows by example how easy it is to begin to think of fate or destiny as a divine personality whom we must worship and hold in respect or awe, but that personality need *not* be like the biblical God. Machiavelli playfully sketches here the outline of a religious outlook that would give more encouragement to human virtue and independence. But Machiavelli immediately adds a twist: The world we live in is such that the divinity behind it is to be conceived to be very dangerous to humanity; he likens the goddess "to one of these violent rivers which, when they become enraged, flood the plains, ruin the trees and the buildings, lift earth from this part, drop in another; each person flees before them, everyone yields to their impetus without being able to hinder them in any regard." But is this last kind of fearfully helpless human reaction necessarily justified? Machiavelli insists that it is not. Even as dikes can drastically reduce the power of floods and tame rivers, so virtue, when it is present, tames Fortuna's sway over humanity's political destinies. In other words, what men are tempted to conceive of as an alien, divine, superior power that puts their fate beyond their control is nothing but the way life becomes (chaotic and disastrous) when men lack virtue. Machiavelli suddenly advances the belief, the amazingly hopeful belief, that human virtue can conquer chance and destiny.

What does Machiavelli mean by this extraordinary claim? Can virtue eliminate bad luck? Machiavelli says at the start of the second paragraph that he will say no more about "opposing" fortune in general but will turn to concrete and specific examples. He focuses on the problem of leaders failing to control their distinct individual natures. Princes prosper but then come to ruin – as the times change and they do not change their particular natures. Different natures, different capacities and proclivities, belong to different human types and suit different circumstances. In general, there are two basic human types: the cautious and the bold (or the patient and the impatient, the artful and the violent). Each type succeeds or fails depending on whether circumstances call for his type's behavior or not.

Is this then not a fundamental limit on human success? Is our capacity for success or failure not predetermined by the sort of nature each of us is endowed with, and the times in which we have to operate? At first, this is what Machiavelli seems to be teaching. To illustrate this power of nature over us, he gives a single clear example – that of Pope Julius, who succeeded well because his impetuosity fit the times but who would have failed at other times. By now we have learned how suspicious we must be when Machiavelli gives only one modern example, especially when it is a pope. We may recall what Machiavelli taught in the *Discourses* about the flexibility of what men think is fixed human nature. When we look more closely, we see that Machiavelli suggests that men are *not* necessarily determined by nature – not, at least, if they are among the few who have enough prudent virtue to discover and to work upon the flexibility of their own "nature." The problem is that a man may not "be found so *prudent* as to *know how* to accommodate himself to this, whether because he cannot deviate from what nature inclines him to or also because, when one has always flourished by walking on one path, he cannot be *persuaded* to depart from it". And so, "the cautious man, when it is time to come to impetuosity, does not know how to do it, hence comes to ruin: for *if he would change his nature* with the times and with affairs, *his fortune would not change*". Machiavelli concludes that when fortune varies and men remain "obstinate [*ostinati*] in their modes," men are happy while they fit the times and unhappy when they don't. Yet he qualifies this conclusion: "I judge this indeed, that it is better to be impetuous than cautious, because fortune is a woman," and "it is necessary, if one wants to hold her down, to beat her and strike her down." And "one sees that

she lets herself be won more by the impetuous than by those who proceed coldly." And "so always, like a woman, she is the friend of the young,
because they are less cautious, more ferocious, and command her with
more audacity."

   To understand the most serious point of this playfully shocking metaphor, we need to follow the hint of the opening sentence of chapter 25,
and contrast this teaching on human nature with the classical and biblical teachings. Both the Bible and the classics teach that our humanity
is constituted above all by our soul's high destined end or fulfillment.
The exercise of the moral, and especially of the intellectual, virtues constitutes in itself the supreme goal or end of existence, the core of truly
human happiness – in a higher kind of life on earth, or in a life after
death. We must not distort or abuse the highest in us by making it mainly
a means to, a tool of, our lower needs and desires. We must not give in
to the temptation to make virtue serve the acquisition of wealth, security, power, or even honor and glory. Machiavelli teaches that such an
outlook contradicts the facts of human life and experience, which show
that human nature, or humanity, is not directed to such a natural end
or supernatural fulfillment. When humans try to live in terms of these
imaginary goals, they are baffled by the fact that they cannot do so – by
the fact that their lives seem drastically incomplete, as they are ever slip-
ping down and away from what they believe they ought to do and to be.
Humans are hence led to believe that they are under the rule of hidden,
mysterious beings – God, gods, angels, devils, spirits of all sorts (summed
up in "Fortuna") – whose help, purifying or energizing, they need and
whose enmity they must assuage or oppose. But once we see all this, once
we see what most people's true natures and natural needs are, we are
in a position to recognize that there is no good reason why we should
not use our "higher" faculties as tools to get what they really want and
need. Here in chapter 25, Machiavelli states most explicitly what it is
that men seek: "glories and riches" (second paragraph). To secure these
ends, men can and should reinterpret virtue as the qualities that lead
toward success in securing them. Men should see that they can and must
employ the so-called moral vices as well as the so-called moral virtues.
They should learn to be flexible about their own souls and their souls'
moral habits. If we make the goals of humanity lower – less pure, more
selfish, more worldly – human life will be lived more in accord with the
truth of nature. Humans will live in pursuit of goals that are attainable,
and that make human existence and human psychology both understandable and manageable without any mystery or mumbo jumbo.

In this way, humans will be much less inclined to feel and believe that we are in need of or in the grip of mysterious forces or gods or goddesses. We may then begin to solve not only the practical problem of what politics is all about but the deepest theoretical problem that has bedeviled all philosophers since Socrates: the question of whether or not there exists something divine that surpasses scientific or rational explanation. For Machiavelli expects or hopes that the apparent evidence in human experience for such a higher presence will gradually but steadily disappear from social existence, as that existence delivers the solid goods that the mass of mankind truly wants and needs.

In the century after Machiavelli's works were published posthumously, the influence of his revolution on the conception of human existence, of god and of nature, was immense. But there was always, from the beginning – and as Machiavelli had himself predicted in chapter 18 of *The Prince* – an enormous obstacle to the acceptance of his teachings: His teachings are all too obviously irreligious and immoral as well as warlike. Machiavelli does teach and even preach virtue, but what he means by "virtue" is courage and wisdom, rather than justice, charity, or even moderation. The modern political philosophers who follow in Machiavelli's wake – and let us never forget that there have been great thinkers who have remained unconvinced by his critique of the classics and the Bible – hold that Machiavelli was correct in many fundamental ways but incorrect or impractical in his neglect or abandonment of justice and charity and in his stress on the virtues of war as opposed to the virtues of peace. Machiavelli's successors formulate new teachings about the nature of justice and charity and peace, doctrines that take as their basis Machiavelli's rejection of the high goals or conceptions of humanity that are found in the classics and the Bible, and that are based instead on a much more individualistic and materialistic or this-worldly conception of human nature. In the next chapters we will examine the most influential and perhaps most profound of these distinctively modern philosophic heirs of Machiavelli. Through their transformations of Machiavelli's teaching, they laid down key principles underlying our modern technological, liberal-constitutional, and capitalist orders.

7

Bacon's *New Atlantis*

Francis Bacon (1561–1626) is best known as the chief original articulator of the modern scientific method. His most important writings in this regard are *The Advancement of Learning* (1605) and *The New Organon* (1620). But Bacon was also a highly successful statesman under Queen Elizabeth and James the First, and – more momentously, for our purposes – an outspoken admirer of Machiavelli, as well as the employer and older friend of Thomas Hobbes. Inspiration from Bacon was gratefully acknowledged by subsequent early modern political philosophers such as Spinoza (another open admirer of Machiavelli) and Locke. Thomas Jefferson, arguably the most theoretically inclined of the American founders, counted Bacon (along with Newton and Locke) as one of "the three greatest men that have ever lived, without any exception, and as having laid the foundation of those superstructures which have been raised in the Physical *and Moral* sciences" (Letter to Richard Price, January 8, 1789, our emphasis).

Bacon's Machiavellian Scientific Method

We can best begin to understand the relation between the scientific and the political strands in Bacon's thought if we start from his expressed indebtedness to Machiavelli. In *The Advancement of Learning*, Bacon cites Machiavelli a full ten times, almost always favorably – and this at a time when such a display of favor to Machiavelli entailed considerable daring. Bacon similarly cites Machiavelli with approval in his *Essays*. Why Bacon does so, not only in his political but *especially* in his scientific works is not immediately apparent. We can identify, however, three key ideas in Machiavelli's reflection on human nature that became roots of Bacon's new method for the science of nature in general.

The first idea is most visible in Machiavelli's description, in chapter 6 of *The Prince*, of the four greatest founders. Those "armed prophets," we recall, were afforded opportunities that "gave them the *matter*, enabling them to introduce any *form* they pleased." Machiavelli thus suggests that human nature can be regarded as essentially unformed or malleable material that strong, visionary leaders can shape like clay. The second idea is manifest in chapter 25 of *The Prince*. Machiavelli there introduces the possibility of, and the need for, *conquering* fortune, likening fortune to a river against whose flooding provident men can build dams and dikes. The nature that surrounds us as well as the nature within us, he thus suggests, far from being ordained by a just and loving God, is in itself hostile to humanity. Nature is not to be respected or accepted with resignation or humble prayer; instead, nature is to be subdued, by audacious and intelligent human beings, to whatever ends they wish or need. The third idea appears most vividly when we bear in mind that Aristotle had presented proud greatness of soul (magnanimity) as the virtue opposed to what he considered to be the vice of humility or meekness; especially in chapter 15 of *The Prince*, Machiavelli substitutes for magnanimity the virtue of "humanity" – meaning the virtue by which superior men generously and confidently attend to the this-worldly needs of all human beings irrespective of city or country. Let us see how Bacon employs these three ideas as crucial strands in his weaving of his new scientific method.

The Critique of Aristotle

The first part of Bacon's *New Organon* criticizes ancient and primarily Aristotelian science as regards its aims, its method, and its starting point. The Aristotelian starting point, which is our prescientific awareness of the division of the world into commonsense kinds or classes or forms of things (the different sorts of animals, plants, heavenly bodies, etc.), Bacon repudiates. Concentration on these primarily evident classes or forms obscures, he argues, our potential access to a more fundamental or underlying realm, one of *homogeneous* matter pervaded by qualities such as heat or light or sound or the pull of gravity. These "simple natures," as Bacon christens them, can be conceived to operate according to general relational and causal principles that Bacon calls (and was the first to call) "*laws* of nature." These are "laws" that neither have nor presuppose any lawgiver other than science itself; the "laws of nature" are emphatically not "first principles" in the sense of *ultimate* causes (which, according to Bacon, we cannot know). They are instead hypothesized explanatory rules. They are posited by the scientists and then tested or verified by the extent to which they allow scientists to predict and to manipulate, even to transform, the observable world. The laws emerge in the scientist's mind when nature is put to "tests," or "bound and tortured," "under the vexations of art": that is, with controlled experiments. The new end, a theoretical activity of a new kind, thus requires a whole new *approach* to inquiry, entailing armies of experimenters and researchers. Their work is to be conducted in accordance with eliminative induction, through precise experiments, with the help of ever-improving assistance from new scientific instruments.

The aim of science, therefore, ceases to be the sort of understanding sought by Aristotle – the careful articulation and contemplation of the various kinds of beings or "natures" as they naturally manifest themselves to us. The aim of science becomes instead a new sort of theory interwoven with practice, aimed at the *conquest* of nature, or a progressive "lordship over the universe" by human beings, all of whom stand to benefit from the vast increase in human *power* that the new science makes possible.

Problems begin to loom, however, when we consider the application of the new scientific method to us humans, to human nature. The new science calls into question, as "unscientific," as merely preliminary or even primitive, the apparent insight afforded by our prescientific experience of our human nature in its distinct, fixed character and needs. The questions then arise: What is the human character, and what are the human needs that our new science ought to serve, given that our human character and its needs are understood to be, like all of nature, changeable or alterable by our new science? Where do we get our standards for judging which manipulations of human nature are good and which bad? How can Bacon's whole project have an end or purpose that is knowable as *the* good for humans? Once we see that there lurks within the new manipulative science a lack of clear limits or guides as regards its goals, must we not begin to question whether the vast increase in manipulative power made possible by the new science is something that will be good for us? Is the answer that the new science gives us more truth? But why should we, precisely as seekers of truth, be focused on a humanly constructed, hypothetical realm of "laws of nature" conceived as underlying the commonsense world of different classes of beings – when it is the latter (the primary, common-sense, world) that is the only world for which we actually care, the only world in which we actually live, and the only world of which we have direct experience, to which all hypothetical modeling must ultimately refer back, for the test of its validity? In the final analysis, can Baconian science, in its perspective on reality, claim greater truth than the perspective of common sense? As we have seen in previous chapters, the ancient Socratic philosophers were not unaware that embedded in our commonsense perception of the world are enormously powerful mental distortions: illusions created both by universal human cravings and by the diverse longings and beliefs instilled by the upbringing of the young in the various specific cultures (or "caves") of particular times and places. Yet the Socratic philosophers did not take the path taken by Bacon (and anticipated in some measure by ancient atomist-materialists such as Democritus and Epicurus); the Socratics did not call into radical question the reality of what is perceived by common sense. On the contrary, the Socratics objected that to take such a step would lead to an obscuring of our only access to reality. The Socratics even insisted that reality or being was best understood as *constituted* by the interrelated forms of beings given in our commonsense experience – even though that experience no doubt needed severe purification by critical, conversational self-scrutiny. What is it that convinces Bacon that this insistence is untenable? What is it that in Bacon's view the ancients failed to account for or to overcome, thereby dooming to failure their attempt to make progress in knowledge of reality?

In *New Organon*'s aphorisms #45–52, and especially 48, Bacon traces the errors of previous thinking to certain influences and prejudices that he calls types of "idols." The first of these, "the idols of the tribe," is the most crucial, since in articulating it Bacon indicates what prevented the ancient philosophers from even approaching the scientific method that he is proposing. The reason why mankind at large, seconded by the ancient philosophers and especially Aristotle, are so resistant to knowledge of general principles of the sort Bacon proposes ("laws of nature") is that human beings deeply long to find *instead* principles that can be referred to "final causes," disclosing *purpose* and purposefulness in all that exists. Bacon associates this longing with a desire for a beneficent, divine ruling power. The ancient philosophers, he charges, were moved fundamentally *not* by a desire for knowledge but instead by a "shallow" desire to find in the world a kind of rescue from the world. Bacon's new scientific method, in contrast, unmasks this and all other "idols of the mind." The new Baconian method posits laws of nature that do not and are not intended to disclose final causes or purposes. These laws will instead enable scientists to bring to a *haphazardly* ordered nature a new, *imposed* order that is conducive to the satisfaction of human desires and purposes.

Still, while the new scientific method is directed explicitly against teleo-theological thinking, the new method cannot by itself settle the great issue of whether the world is in truth ultimately governed by divine purpose and meaning, or by blind forces of grim necessity. And given the wide prevalence, everywhere in human history past and present, of many humans beings testifying to their vivid personal experience of the presence and influence of mysterious divinity that places severe moral limitations, backed up by terrible punishments, on what science ought to do, the new science of nature stands in serious need of some means of disposing of the doubt as to whether or not reality is at bottom governed by such divinity. Bacon's answer to this need would seem to lie in his hopes for and from the vastness of the practical success and popular impact of the new science.

The old science was "barren," Bacon charges. That is, it was constitutionally resistant to humans undertaking the transformation of the given world so as to impose on it the fulfillment of human purposes, above all that of vastly improving mankind's physical condition – a condition that is, prior to transformation by scientific inventions, impoverished and miserable. Through what has come to be called "technology," the new science will correct nature's stingy accommodation of human needs. As mankind progresses steadily away from its naturally vulnerable situation, the consequence will be that "slowly and by degrees scarce perceptible," all of humanity will be increasingly ready to admit that our natural situation is not purposefully ordered but is instead appalling. People will feel less and less inclination to deny humanity's original, natural misery, and will be less and less prone to hope for a divine purpose in, and a possible divine redemption from, that misery. The mastery over nature, "for the relief of man's estate," will lead eventually to the extinction of the debilitating, misdirected hopes and longings to see the world as intrinsically ordered by a beneficent but mysterious divinity. It is in the *New Atlantis* that Bacon paints most vividly this vision of a future, of a scientifically and technologically satisfied humanity that is ready to accept the truth about its condition.

The Narrator's Opening

The *New Atlantis** presents itself as a tale narrated by an unnamed officer on an English ship that has survived serious trouble. He has brought back to Europe the hitherto secret workings of "Salomon's House": a vast scientific laboratory of experimentation that crowns a new way of life in a previously unknown island nation. At the story's outset, we hear of the dire straits in which the narrator and his crew found themselves after a terrible storm: on board a ship in the Pacific, blown off course, without food, in "the greatest wilderness of waters in the world," and facing death. Their reaction to their situation is to pray to God for deliverance; the captain attributes their desperate condition to their sinfulness, and orders his men to seek divine forgiveness. The opening thus contrasts strikingly, both in its gripping peril and in the sailors' understanding of the peril's cause, with the tale's happy conclusion, which depends on the activities of Salomon's House.

As if in response to their prayers, an island appears on the horizon, and a delegation of people comes out in a boat, forbidding them to land and then reading to them an official scroll: The message is that 'you have 16 days to leave, but in the meantime, tell us your wants.' There is, significantly, a cross on the scroll, which to the English sailors is a "presage of good." Three hours later a "Reverend" appears, and the sailors are asked explicitly if they are Christians. The narrator, having seen the cross, is not afraid to respond affirmatively. The attendant to the Reverend then explains the earlier behavior of the lord who had read the decree to them. That lord had refrained from boarding the ship *not* through pride, the attendant explains, but because he had been warned of the danger of contagion. For the island's city has an authoritative "Conservator of Health," who gives advice or warnings to the rulers. Bodily health is the first or primary national concern of which we learn (38–40).

The sailors are brought to "Strangers House," and are asked to stay there (quarantined) for three days. They reply with expressions of heartfelt and respectful gratitude, and with the declaration that "God surely is manifested in this land." They are given food and drink better than those found in Europe, and the sick are given both oranges and white pills to hasten their recovery (41–43).

---

* We have used the text found in *New Atlantis and the Great Instauration*, ed. Jerry Weinberger (Wheeling, IL: Harlan Davidson, 1989). Page references are to this edition.

The following day, our narrator addresses to the whole crew a deeply pious exhortation. Beginning with an emphatic reference to the biblical Jonah, and the seafaring miracles in which that prophet was involved, he reminds the men of the continuing threat of death that hung over them, and hence of the need to reform their ways so that God will continue to reward them with protection; their suffering may well have been a divine punishment. Certainly their preservation has been miraculous, and they will need another miracle to survive and to return to Europe. Their fate is in the hands of the just and merciful God. But he notes that it is also in the hands of a people "full of piety and humanity," who will likewise show them grace in accord with their comportment. The narrator initially understands their situation according to biblical theology. Even the rapid healing of their sick over the next few days is understood in this manner: The sick think themselves cast "in some divine pool of healing." All of this, however, is about to begin to change (43–44).

The narrator recounts next the first of four conversations that he had with people of the island. The conversation is with the Governor of the House of Strangers, who is also a Christian priest. The men fear that he will be issuing a sentence of life or death upon them, and they submissively bow to him. He wishes to speak to only a few of them, however. He comes chiefly as a priest, but has been given permission to tell them some welcome things in his official office: The state has determined that they may stay six weeks, and perhaps even longer if he intervenes for them. Their own cargo will be well cared for or else paid for in gold or silver. And he bids them make any request that they wish. He asks only that they stay within a 1.5-mile radius

The hitherto very apprehensive men reply to this generous offer by expressions of overwhelming gratitude. It seemed "that we had before us a picture of our salvation in heaven; for we that were awhile since in the jaws of death, were now brought into a place where we found nothing but consolations." As "for the commandment laid upon us, we would not fail to obey it, though it was impossible but our hearts should be inflamed to tread further upon this happy and holy ground." Instead of the terrifying prospect of death, with hope of salvation only from God, the unexpected and therefore gratefully embraced prospect of salvation in this "happy and holy ground," now starts to captivate the men. Their hopes are still in something "holy," but they have taken a significant turn toward seeing their salvation as in the hands of human beings – to what extent becomes clear when they add "that our tongues should first cleave to the roofs of our mouths, ere we should forget either his reverend person or this whole nation in our prayers" (45–46). This addendum echoes the famous words of psalm 137, mournfully sung during the Israelites' Babylonian captivity: "If I forget thee, O Jerusalem ... Let my tongue cleave to the roof of my mouth; If I prefer not Jerusalem above my chief joy." The psalmist, held captive in a strange land and asked to sing for the entertainment of his Babylonian captors, expressed fierce and defiant devotion to God's holy city, which had been razed by the Babylonians. The narrator's echo of that psalm stands in shocking contrast. Not a violent and humiliating destruction and captivity of God's people, but a healing and comforting accommodation of their every wish, in a strange land, is moving the men to remember *not* Jerusalem but their human saviors. The men view their new alien location as "a land of angels, which did appear to us daily and anticipate us with comforts." The contrast becomes more pronounced as we soon hear that the name of the island is "Bensalem," the "Son of Salem," or the *New* Jerusalem.

A New Christian Revelation

The narrator and nine others learn more about the island from one of its governors, and the question of whether their devotion is to the old or to the new Jerusalem becomes explicit. The Governor explains that the people of Bensalem know well most of the habitable earth, but are themselves unknown. For by law they travel in secrecy, and their remote location keeps their home hidden. But this secrecy is about to change; the Governor invites the newcomers to ask anything they wish about the island. The Europeans respond by inquiring first about how the island became Christian. In response, the Governor relates a remarkable tale of the divine revelation that led to the island's conversion to Christianity. The revelation came, according to the Governor, twenty years after the ascension of Christ – so around AD 53 – to members of a remote small village on the island named Renfusa (or "Sheepnatured"). The inhabitants saw a pillar of light a mile out to sea, with a bright cross on the top, and went out in boats to investigate the marvelous sight. They were held back from the pillar of light by a kind of force field, and so sat "as in a theater" around it. But not all the viewers were from the remote village; by some strange coincidence, in one of the boats there happened to be a "wise man" from "Salomon's House," which the Governor calls a college that is "the very eye of this kingdom." And this man uttered a remarkable "prayer" certifying that what everyone saw was indeed a miracle – and beginning to disclose the awesome powers of "Salomon's House":

> Lord God of heaven and earth, thou hast vouchsafed of thy grace to those
> of our order, to know thy works of creation, and the secrets of them, and to
> discern (as far as appertaineth to the generations of men) between divine
> miracles, works of nature, works of art, and impostures and illusions of all
> sorts. I do here acknowledge and testify before this people, that the thing
> which we now see before our eyes is thy Finger and a true Miracle; and for-
> asmuch as we learn in our books that thou never workest miracles but to a
> divine and excellent end, (for the laws of nature are thine own laws, and
> thou exceedest them not but upon great cause) we most humbly beseech
> thee to prosper this great sign, and to give us the interpretation and use
> of it in mercy; which thou dost in some part secretly promise by sending it
> unto us. (48)

The "wise man's" boat was at this point suddenly released from the force
field, and he rowed toward the pillar of light, which then burst (like
fireworks) into many stars; the wise man found at the foot of the pillar a cedar ark containing all the canonical books of the Old and New
Testaments, including at least one that had not yet been written. A note
in the ark explained that the apostle Bartholomew received the ark from
an angel, with instructions to commit it to the sea, and that the people of
the land where God ordained it to land should receive salvation, peace,
and goodwill "from the Father, and from the Lord Jesus."

A number of things about this tale must strike us as very odd. In the
first place, the sage from "Salomon's House" utters a prayer – allegedly
before anyone on the island had any knowledge of the Bible – to a single
"God of heaven and earth," who has created the world, and who works
miracles and signs, to divine ends; this God shows grace or favor to certain men, and can be beseeched in "humility" to act mercifully. The sage
even uses the biblical term "thy Finger" to describe the miracle. How
could the wise man from Salomon's House have known all of this about
God *before* he received the biblical revelation? On the other hand, and
in the second place, the sage distinguishes "divine miracles" from "works
of nature" and then speaks of nature as governed by "laws of nature"
(Bacon's own, original term). These "laws of nature" are described as not
being manifest to everyone; they are available only to those who know
"the secrets" of the works of creation, who pry into those secrets with, as
it seems, the blessing of God. But the wise man then describes these "laws
of nature" as God's "own laws," which He contravenes or "exceeds" when
working a miracle, for some "great end." The laws are, then, not permanent necessities that bind even God, but laws that God has, as it were, put

in place to govern normal relations of natural bodies, and that He contravenes when He wishes to disclose something great. But this indicates something problematic in the wise man's certification of the miraculous character of the revelation. For a full, complete, final knowledge of such "laws of nature" would be needed in order truly to distinguish miracles from natural events – to confirm with any certainty, that is, that a given wonder is indeed a miracle, rather than either a rare phenomenon intelligible on the basis of the more fully grasped laws of nature, or a work of human artifice and magical deception achieved through knowledge of the laws of nature. These difficulties show the ambiguous character of the prayer that was uttered by the wise man for his listeners

Founding the New Order

The Governor's account of the original revelation is cut short just after he compares the arrival of the Bible in the ark to the salvation of the human race through Noah and his ark – thereby suggesting the momentous significance of Bensalem for the future salvation of the human race (49).The next day, however, the Governor returns and again invites the visitors to ask any question they wish. The men reply by speaking of "our former life" as something far less desirable than their present time with the Governor, and ask – hesitatingly and with reluctance and begging to presume upon his "humanity" – a question that shows that the wondrous tale of the previous day, along with the island's secrecy, has raised some bewilderment if not suspicion: How is it that you people know so much about us, while we Europeans have had no inkling of you? Being hidden and unseen to others while having those others open and in light seems, they say, to be "a condition and property of divine powers and beings." The Governor replies that rules of secrecy will require him to omit many things, but that his answer should nonetheless satisfy them (49–51).

The island, the Governor explains, was once well known through its nautical trade – some three thousand years earlier, when navigation was, hard as it seems to believe, more expansive than now. The island had most of its commerce with the peoples of the Americas, including members of "the great Atlantis," the imperial city of North America. The Governor knows that that name will ring a bell with his listeners because of the tales told in Plato's *Timaeus* and *Critias* about a city in the far western seas whose attack on Mediterranean countries in the distant past was allegedly repulsed by the ancient Athenians. Atlantis was, he claims, one of three "mighty and proud kingdoms in arms, shipping, and riches" in the Americas – along with Peru ("Coya") and Mexico ("Tyrambel"). Coya made a major expedition against the island of Bensalem. But Bensalem's king, Altabin (or "Twice Lofty") "a wise man and a great warrior," defeated Coya easily, through "knowing well both his own strength and that of his enemies." Unlike the Athenians, who seem to have had the "glory" of killing all the invading Atlantians, King Altabin mercifully permitted all the invading Coyans safe conduct back home after they swore an oath that they would not again bear arms "against him." What, then, happened to Bensalem? How did it become unknown, and does it still have proud and merciful kings? For this is the first we hear of any political or military life on the island (51–53).

Everything was changed, according to the Governor, by "the Divine Revenge," which "overtook, not long after, those proud enterprises." As he goes on to explain, some 100 years later a "particular deluge" destroyed Atlantis, flooding all of America and driving its remaining inhabitants into the hills, where they reverted to primitive life, reduced to taking pride in wearing the feathers of birds that fled with them to the highlands. The island's commerce with the peoples of these other empires was lost "by this main accident of time," while navigation in the rest of the world decayed, so the island of Bensalem became isolated (54–55)

The Governor's explanation of the flood that destroyed Atlantis – that it was caused by Divine Revenge upon Atlantis for its proud, imperial ambitions – explicitly echoes the biblical account of the earlier universal flood, with the suggestion that sinful pride brought about divine vengeance in both cases. Yet the Governor's conclusion, which seems to attribute the flood to an "*accident* of time," and which similarly attributes the worldwide decay in navigation to either "wars" or "a *natural* revolution of time," would seem to point in an altogether different direction: to a mere accident of nature, rather than God, as the source of the destruction. The Governor's account includes, then, an explanation that tends *away* from any "Divine Revenge" as the source of the catastrophe and toward an explanation in terms of an accident with a natural cause. Now, which was it? And how did the monarchs who succeeded Altabin, which was spared destruction – its navigation is still "as great as ever" – understand the destruction of Atlantis, and so take measures to prevent it from happening to them? What caused the people of the island to "sit at home" rather than to continue with their former worldwide commerce and activities? And how did they avoid the decay in navigation experienced by everyone else?

The answers come in the Governor's description of a refounding of
the island that soon occurred, under one King Solamona, who ruled,
according to the Governor, around 288 BC. The people of the island
still adore this king as a mortal, a "divine instrument," and still esteem
him as "the lawgiver of our nation." King Solamona's disposition appears
to have been quite different from that of his proud warrior predecessor, Altabin (who sounds like a kind of Machiavellian glorious prince).
With echoes of biblical passages that describe Solamona's namesake
(King Solomon), the Governor attributes to Solamona neither pride
nor mercifulness to enemies nor martial prowess – Solamona was not
intent upon glory through conquest either offensive or defensive – but
was instead "wholly bent on making his kingdom and people happy."
Solamona's observation of the new isolation of the island and its natural
fertility moved him, in conjunction with his "memory" of how it might
be "altered for the worse," to a policy of isolationism. With the fate of
Atlantis in mind, Solamona first turned his nation's powerful fleet into a
mere local fishing fleet and merchant marine, and he laid down laws to
protect his happy people from the "novelties, and commixture of manners" that strangers might introduce (56–57). But which of the two contrary interpretations of the fate of Atlantis moved this re-founder of the
island so dramatically to pull in his nation's sails in this way?

Solamona's laws appear directed in general by an awareness of the
need for him and for his people to avoid the imperial pride and search for
glory through conquest that incurred "Divine Revenge." But this appearance proves to be only partially true. For it turns out that Solamona had
in mind an *alternative* to humble devotion to divine law as a means of
escaping any devastating flood. That alternative depends on understanding events such as the flood as accidental natural cataclysms. Our first
indication of this is that the Governor describes Solamona's intentions
as "noble and heroic" rather than humble or meek (56). They differ not
in their ultimate aim, we could say, from those Machiavellian motives of
the former leaders of Atlantis, but only in the means chosen to achieve
the ultimate aim. Second, we recall that the narrator had spoken of the
"piety and humanity" manifest in the Bensalemites' treatment of its
strangers. The Governor, in contrast, speaks (thrice) only of Solamona's
"humanity" in making the provision for relief of distressed strangers; he
makes no mention of Solamona's piety. He adds that an attempt "to join
policy and humanity together" is what informed Solamona's decision to
permit strangers either to stay on the island at the state's expense or to
return home. Solamona's "humanity" is a virtue that continues the pride

and clemency of Altabin but without either his martial valor or his disposition to rely on oaths. It is *not* linked to any piety.

Moreover, as the sequel makes clear, the "policy" that Solamona combined with the practice of humanity consisted of buying off all strangers
who were permitted to land on the island, by offering those strangers
state pensions for life if they stayed or safe passage home if they wished
to return. Not a single ship, says the Governor proudly, has ever returned
home, and only thirteen individuals ever chose to be returned – and
their accounts of the island to their countrymen can safely be assumed to
have been dismissed as the product of a dream (57). (In the sequel, we
learn that once word got out among the rank-and-file English sailors of
the possibility of staying on the island with a lifetime pension, it became
extremely difficult for the narrator and the other leaders to keep the
men from begging the Governor for this alternative.)

What makes the Governor so sure that life on this isolated island is
indeed the best life for human beings? On what grounds can he claim
that the island's people are not being kept in the dark about the best –
the happiest – human life but instead are simply being guarded against a
"corruption" of that best life through the adoption of customs and manners that would lead away from it?

Those grounds, and the enormously ambitious end that King
Solamona actually had in view with his refounding, become clear when
the Governor describes a significant *exception* to Solamona's prohibition
against travel abroad, an exception that finally explains how the people
of the island know so much about others while remaining unknown to
others. Certain members of "Salomon's House" are, in recurring twelve-
year missions, constantly engaged in scientific and technological espi-
onage around the world. This policy shows that King Solamona feared
not any and all outside influences upon the life of the people of the
island; he was not closed to any improvements for his people that could
be made through the incorporation of the science and inventions found
in other nations. The Governor clearly wishes to ensure that his listeners
will grasp the deep significance of this exception to the general proscrip-
tion on travel. Before telling of it, he makes an explicit digression, to
provide his listeners with a fuller account of the activities of the members
of Salomon's House. The house is "dedicated to the study of the Works
and Creatures of God," through "the finding out of the true nature of
all things (whereby God might have the more glory in the workmanship
of them, and men the more fruit in the use of them)." Salomon's House
is a scientific think tank that looks into "the true nature of all things,"

for the production of fruitful goods from their inquiries (58). Those of its members who spy on the rest of the world in their missions, dolling out oodles of gold, bring back knowledge, inventions, and instruments that assist in this endeavor. Still, this whole enterprise is presented as an innocent, indeed as biblically sanctioned activity: God has the glory in the workmanship, while men have the fruits of the inquiry into it. What, then, does this tell us about the understanding of the best life by which King Solamona directed his people? Where does his understanding come down on the great issue of whether God and his justice are behind events like the destruction of Atlantis, or whether, instead, it was an accident of nature?

The Truth about Salomon's House

To answer this question, we must look ahead, to the third description of the activities of Salomon's House. There we find a "Father" of that house disclosing to the narrator in a private, frank conference held before the latter leaves the island: "The End of our Foundation is the knowledge of Causes, and secret motions of things; and the enlarging of the bounds of Human Empire, to the effecting of all things possible" (71). In this third, final, true statement of the purpose of Salomon's House, *nothing* is said of God or his purposes or his glory or his work. Instead, the narrator hears a frank disclosure of the most ambitious, imperial human endeavor imaginable: "the effecting of all things possible" – a statement that is followed by a description of scientific experiments and inventions that discloses a staggeringly ambitious endeavor to utterly transform or to remake the natural world. The account ends with the following statement: "Lastly, we have circuits or visits of divers principal cities of the kingdom: where, as it cometh to pass, we do publish such new profitable inventions as we think good." And "we do also declare natural divinations of diseases, plagues, swarms of hurtful creatures, scarcity, tempests, earthquakes, great inundations, comets, temperatures of the year, and divers other things; and we give counsel thereupon what the people shall do for the prevention and remedy of them" (83). What King Solamona envisioned for the future of the island and the happiness of its people entails predicting and controlling, and thereby overcoming, by scientifically informed human action, the destructive effects of events such as the flood that overcame Atlantis. This was the heart of Solamona's confidence that his would become a self-sufficient, enlightened, confident, and wise nation.

Nor is the new science practiced in Salomon's House limited to defending human beings against the catastrophes that had hitherto been taken to be part of God's mighty quiver of punishment. The experiments that go on in Salomon's House yield instruments, inventions, and machines touching every part of human life, and eliminating from it want, sickness, drudgery, physical suffering, and even, perhaps, death itself. Many of these are listed in the second of four sections of the final disclosure that the Father of Salomon's House gives to the narrator: the scientists' "preparations and instruments" (71–80). Not the least notable are gardens dedicated to testing varieties of soil and to experiments of grafting and cross-breeding; artificial alteration of seasonal production of fruit and flowering; and artificially altered speed of fruit production. "We make them also," says the Father of Salomon's House, "by art greater much than their nature" (74). One plant can be made to "turn into another" (74). In parks and pools, animals are raised not to be looked upon, or for their rarity, but rather for dissection and experimentation – for "trials," upon beasts, birds, and fish as subjects of poisons, surgeries, and medicines, of things potentially useful or harmful to humans, *including the resuscitation of things apparently dead.* "By art likewise, we make them greater or taller than their kind is; and contrariwise dwarf them, and stay their growth; we make them more fruitful and bearing than their kind is; and contrariwise barren and not generative." Through cross-breeding, there have been produced "many new kinds, and them not barren" (74–75). Species, in other words, have been manipulated as neither permanent, nor respected as belonging to a purposed order. Kinds or species are remade, in accordance with perceived human need and the quest for genuine knowledge of nature as manipulative power over nature.

In their kitchens the scientists produce new food and drink with "special effects," dried fruits and condensed juices that can last many years, vitamin drinks and foods that allow people to "live very long," that cut down on the need to eat, and that build muscle. Medicine shops produce a great variety of drugs (75–76).

Their mechanical arts make synthetic papers, linens, silks, and dyes. Enormous furnaces of widely different degrees of *heat* allow for its study as a homogeneous force, and certain furnaces even imitate the heat of the sun, to produce "admirable effects" (77).

In houses of optical instruments, light and colors are studied, not as they "naturally" appear, but separated out; far-traveling and nondispersing artificially produced lights (lasers) are made, and "delusions and deceits of the sight, in figures, magnitudes, motions, colors." They have many telescopes and microscopes that "make feigned distances," with which to observe far-off bodies and minute bodies in urine and blood. Natural and artificial minerals, metals, glasses, and magnets of prodigious power are studied, produced, and transformed. Sound is likewise studied, and artificially produced in amplifications and modulations, with woofers and tweeters; hearing aids are invented (77–79).

Very important are the houses that make "engines and instruments for all sorts of motions," including guns and cannons and basilisks "exceeding your greatest," gunpowder, unquenchable fires, fireworks, airplanes, and submarines (79–80). The island is clearly in a position to defend itself from an imperial attack.

Looking back over the way in which the technological activity of Salomon's House has been presented, we see that Bacon has conducted the reader through three steps or phases in the gradual disclosure of the ends of the new science. In step one, there is a co-optation, through reinterpretation, of Christianity, as compatible with and even vouched for by the activities of science. Nature's laws are presented as God's laws, and their uncovering as divinely sanctioned. The second step is the implementation of the transformational findings of science among a Christian people, satisfying their needs and making them happy. Third, and finally, is the private but authorized disclosure of the vast and even in a sense limitless transformative power of science as a means of a purely earthly salvation.

The Father's long description of the "Preparations and Instruments" concludes, significantly, with an account of the "houses of deceits of the senses," where the scientists reproduce, among other things, "false apparitions, impostures, and illusions; and their fallacies." They could, says the Father, if they wished, deceive the senses and work to make particulars "seem more miraculous," but "we" have severely forbidden impostures and lies to the fellows (80). But is this last credible? Who, after all, will hold the chief scientists to account if and when they decide that a deception of the populace is needed? We recall in this light that in the Governor's account of the revelation of the Bible, a member of Salomon's House was said to have been coincidentally present, and able immediately – without any of the kind of careful investigation that goes on in Salomon's House – to proclaim the apparent revelation to be an authentic miracle, distinguishing genuine miracles not only from "works of nature" but also "works of art" and "impostures and illusions of all sorts" (48). And we are now in a position to see that all the wondrous elements of that tale of revelation are mentioned as *replicable* by the members of Salomon's House: lasers, fireworks, the impediment of locomotion, and, most significantly, "impostures." (Salomon's House was founded by King Solamona, who lived "about 1,900 years ago," that is, about 288 BC. It would then have been in existence, according to the tale, for 338 years *before* the alleged revelation took place.) Putting two and two together, we are able to see that the alleged revelation of the Old and New Testaments was indeed a giant hoax, its perpetration permitted by both the haze of time past and the knowledge of the control of nature that had been acquired by the men of Salomon's House. But far more importantly, we are provided, through the full description of the activity of Salomon's House, with the principle through which alleged miracles of the past are soon to be refuted: Knowledge of the laws of nature affords human beings the ability to replicate what *seem* to have been wondrous events, and thereby to remove their miraculous quality. Manifest human accomplishment removes the human need to resort to the divine for an understanding of purposeful causes. Only ignorance of the laws of nature and of the enormous capacity of human beings to reproduce extraordinary effects, in other words, leads to the credulity that characterizes "young," un-technological peoples.

Yet if the true, deep, practical goal of Salomon's House is an eventual disclosure to the world of human power, replacing divine power, why does the Governor, and at times even the Father of Salomon's House, disguise this in the pious garb of a version of the Christian religion? Why do the elite present this thoroughgoing atheistic effort, at least for the time being, as a pious endeavor, sanctioned by religious faith and by the Christian faith in particular?

Bacon, it seems clear, has found in Christianity and its emphasis on meekness and charity not simply a present obstacle but also a potential ally for his endeavor. On one hand, meekness or humility and the hope that by supplicating and practicing devotion to a powerful God there is to be found redemption from human suffering are grave mistakes, which impede the proud human activity of conquering nature through art. But on the other hand, the Christian commandment to charity, to love of one's fellow human beings, can be transformed into a new virtue, the virtue of "humanity" – by means of which the activities of Salomon's House, that is, of Baconian science, can win popular support for the transformation of the world through science. To put this another way: In practical agreement with the biblical understanding, Bacon finds the Machiavellian love of honor or glory achieved through proud martial conquest of other human beings to be fundamentally mistaken, and in need of significant redirection. But the redirection cannot come from Christianity as it is currently understood. The Christian virtue of charity must be "secularized." Christianity and its moral teaching must be gradually reinterpreted, so as to be enlisted in the progressive scientific project that will lead to the withering away of at least traditional Christianity, if not Christianity altogether.

The Father of Salomon's House makes it clear, finally, that the leaders of that institution hold the real authority on the island: Whether the inventions will be disclosed or withheld is up to the scientists. And while the Governor's tale spoke emphatically of the deeds of King Altabin, and the founding achieved by the scientist-king Solamona, we hear nothing of the deeds of any other kings. The present king of the island (whoever he is) seems to sign official state papers, nothing more. The most regal public ceremony is reserved for the Father of Salomon's House, when he comes to visit the narrator and to disclose to him the truth. (While the Governor had not permitted the men to kiss his tippet in reverence, this Father of Salomon's House does so; he accepts reverence.) And the greatest scientists and inventors of Salomon's House are given vast monetary prizes and statues erected in their honor; there are no statues to any political or martial leaders. Life on the island appears to have been significantly depoliticized, the monarch and his governors reduced to mere figureheads of state. It also seems utterly pacified; the people stand at attention to greet the Father of Salomon's House like ranks in an army, but this underscores the absence of any actual army or police in Bensalem. Two additional parts of the narrator's tale – the description of the Feast of the Family and the account of the narrator's conversation with Joabin the Jew – permit us to grasp this depoliticization in all its amazing complexity and thoroughness. They show us that both the moral and religious education of the island's inhabitants have been privatized and disclose the understanding of erotic longing that informs this privatization.

The New Moral Ethos

Between the Governor's account of King Solamona's founding and the disclosure of the workings of Salomon's House to the narrator, nineteen days have elapsed. During that time the visitors' transformation has proceeded apace. "We took ourselves," says the narrator, "now for free men, seeing there was no danger of our utter perdition; and lived most joyfully, going abroad and seeing what was to be seen in the city and places adjacent." Does the narrator refer here to the "utter perdition" of their bodies only, or also of their souls? Have he and the others perhaps lost their fear of hell – of the perdition of their souls? The narrator certainly speaks, strikingly, no longer of the piety but only of the "humanity" of the inhabitants of Bensalem, whose free desire to take in strangers "was enough to make us forget all that was dear to us in our own countries" (60) Does this forgetting not entail, again, the "forgetting" of Jerusalem – of God's holy city and all that it promises? He and his fellows met, he tells us, "many men, not of the meanest quality," but the only conversation he reports is with Joabin, a Jew (64–69). Are Jews as worthy, then, in this city as Christians? Has faith in Jesus as the Messiah become fundamentally unimportant? The narrator and his men observed many things "worthy of relation," but the one of which we learn is "the Feast of the Family," a state-sanctioned celebration of a private event, to which two of the men were invited.

As the narrator explains, the state pays for this feast, which honors any man who has lived to see thirty of his bodily descendants above the age of three. The narrator calls it "a most *natural*, pious, and reverend custom," but one of its purposes seems to be to encourage procreation as the highest honorable activity, outside Salomon's House, for the men of the island. Two days before the feast gets under way, three friends of the fecund man's own choosing, along with the local governor, assist him in settling by appeasement any and all discords within his family. Impoverished members of the family are also offered material relief, and those "subject to vice" are "reproved and censured." Direction is also given at these meetings to family members who are considering marriage and various careers. The only role played by the state is for the local governor "to put in execution by his public authority the decrees and order of the Tirsan [the father], if they should be disobeyed; though that seldom needeth; such reverence and obedience they give to the order of nature" (60–61). This arrangement seems, and to a truly remarkably extent is, "bottom-up," with the state executing the decrees of a merely private individual over members of his family. But what is meant here by the term "the order of nature?" Does this refer to the authority of the father as father? Or the inducements to obedience supplied by the monetary largesse of the father, inducements made possible by the state? Are the members of the Tirsan's family not in a sense bought off, as are the strangers, by monetary rewards?

The feast in any event clearly honors and rewards *fecundity*, not only by honoring a man with thirty living descendants but also with appeals to biblical characters who exemplify this trait. We hear of Adam and

Abraham and Noah, but nothing of Enoch or Isaac or David. There is, however, one significant exception to the honoring of male fecundity: Any member of the family who belongs to Salomon's House, male or female, sits at the head table with the Tirsan (63). Salomon's House and what it represents stands, then, as the alternative to the patriarchal ordering of human relations represented by the Feast of the Family.

The Feast's next part is a "divine service" attended solely by the father, followed by a procession into the dining hall, with boys in front of the father and girls behind him. The mother "sitteth but is not seen." Her position is strikingly similar to the Bensalemites with respect to the rest of the world (seeing but not seen). She, not the "Tirsan," we may say, is the image of Bensalem. She quietly makes possible a taming of the male desire for glory, a redirection of it toward fruitful human procreation. The ruling characteristic of Bensalem is then fundamentally "feminine." In accord with this, the distinction by sex ends among all the others once they enter the dining hall – except that the *men*, not the women, serve the Tirsan as he eats dinner; the women stand around, leaning on a wall. The men are reduced to servants of a man whose highest goal in life is to have many descendants over whom he can rule as familial father. The Herald reads the king's charter, which reflects the number and dignity of the family. When the charter is handed to the Tirsan, all present utter the fully secular proclamation: "Happy are the people of Bensalem." The Tirsan then receives as badge of honor a golden vine of grapes, which the "son of the vine," the son whom the Tirsan has chosen to live with him henceforth, subsequently displays before the Tirsan whenever the Tirsan goes in public. The image of a fruitful vine steadily growing and extending itself into the future is *the* image captivating the Bensalemite men, *the* symbol of their highest ambition, the highest public honor of anyone outside Salomon's House – to have many children (63).

There is a short dinner, and a hymn sung to Adam, Noah, Abraham – the august progenitors of the Old Testament – and to the *nativity* of Jesus (*not* to his death or resurrection). The Tirsan then withdraws for private prayers. And then he gives a blessing, in the order that pleases him, though it is usually by age. The Christian blessing is to both daughters and sons: "Make the days of thy pilgrimage good and many." This is a very strange blessing, since pilgrimages are usually difficult, and one would wish them speedily fulfilled; the blessing encourages a longing for strictly earthly satisfaction and longevity. Nor is anything said in this blessing about virtue or moral goodness. There is, moreover, a second blessing given to at most two sons "of eminent merit and virtue." These do not have to kneel, and they are given a pious but still strange blessing: "Persevere to the end" (64). This blessing is the only indication in the *New Atlantis* of any need for endurance of an unrelieved hardship on the part of anyone on the island. The feast concludes with music and dancing.

The picture that emerges from the feast is of a society, ruled over by fathers with the aid of state largesse, that (in addition to science) esteems nothing above propagation, longevity, and health; there is an honoring of virtue, but it is not given the highest honor.

The New Religious Toleration and Pluralism

The second major part of the depoliticization of the island becomes clear in the narrator's account of his conversation with Joabin. The name "Joabin" that Bacon bestows upon this character, whom the narrator calls "a wise man, and learned, and of great policy" (65) comes from the name in the Bible of a very significant advisor to King David; Joabin's biblical namesake helps us to understand what he represents in Bacon's narrative. In the Bible, Joab is the head of King David's army. It is he who eliminates Abner, Saul's son and David's rival, and later convinces David of the need to eliminate his own rebellious son Absalom, as well as Amasa. The pious David is ever denouncing Joab, but it is Joab who appears to keep David on the throne – as one sees, for example, in his strenuous protest against David's weeping over Absalom. Joab accuses David of loving those who hate him and hating those who love him, and points out that his weeping over his rebellious son's death must stop, or he will lose the faithful soldiers who put that rebellion down (2 Sam. 19:7). Joab is keenly attentive – as David is not – to the distinction between friend and foe, and what that distinction means to the men who are devoted to David and who suffer on his behalf. The final deathbed order of David to his son and future king, Solomon, is to kill Joab, because, according to David, Joab does not follow the "ways of the Lord" but instead "policy." The *new* Joab, Bensalem's "Joabin," represents indeed "policy," but a new policy that bids to overturn the distinction between friend and foe. Not Solomon, but Salomon's House, gets rid of the *old* (biblical) Joab.

When Joabin is first introduced, as a merchant and a circumcised Jew, the issue of religious strife is raised: "They have some few stirps of Jews yet remaining among them," the narrator says, "whom they leave to their own religion." This "they may the better do, because" the Jews of Bensalem "are of a far differing disposition" from "the Jews in other

parts." For whereas Jews elsewhere "hate the name of Christ, and have a
secret inbred rancour against the people amongst whom they live," the
Jews of Bensalem "give unto our Saviour many high attributes, and love
the nation of Bensalem exceedingly" (65). The rancor of Jews to which
the narrator refers has of course a deep cause in the Christians among
whom they live, since the latter have rancor against the Jews for refusing
to accept Jesus as their Savior. The solution suggested by Bacon to the
rancorous standoff is, in a word, assimilation – a solution with which
we today are of course very familiar. The Christians of Bensalem do not
require the Jews to convert, and in return the Jews, rather than cursing
Jesus as a false Messiah and contemning Christians as fools, pay their
respects to Jesus: Joabin, the narrator tells us, "would ever acknowledge
that Christ was born of a Virgin, and that he was more than a man; and
he would tell how God made him ruler of the Seraphims which guard
his throne"; the Jews of Bensalem, the narrator further says, call Jesus
"also the Milken Way, and the Eliah of the Messiah; and many other high
names; which though they be inferior to his divine Majesty, yet they are far
from the language of other Jews" (65). Now to many devout Christians –
and not only in Bacon's day – there is something not only dissatisfying
but a bit ridiculous about this characterization of Jesus. Pretending that
he was some kind of superior human or angel avoids confronting the
issue of his divinity. But the Christians of Bensalem don't mind such
patronizing statements: They are as lax in their disposition toward religious doctrine as are the island's Jews.

  Joabin is also a lover of the nation of Bensalem. How, then, can he
square this with his devotion to "Jerusalem" – to the Jewish nation and
its God? It turns out that Joabin along with the other Jewish residents
wish "to have it believed that" all the Bensalemites "were of the generations of Abraham, by another son, whom they call Nachoran; and
that Moses by a secret cabala ordained the laws of Bensalem which they
now use; and that when the Messiah should come, and sit in his throne
at Hierusalem, the king of Bensalem should sit at his feet, whereas the
other kings should keep a great distance" (65). The narrator dismisses
these as "Jewish dreams," but Joabin's claims are of course no less plausible than the Governor's claim about the lost scientific writings of King
Solomon, which the narrator had easily accepted. Instead of abandoning
their Judaism or abandoning their devotion to Bensalem and its laws,
Joabin and his fellow Jews have reinterpreted their theological tradition,
making it conform to what is attractive in the present and turning it even
into the hidden source of what is deemed good in the present.

Bensalem has so succeeded in making its people happy that its minority religious community has been drawn to reinterpret their tradition so as to make it compatible with the majority religious community. The Jews have been seduced away from orthodoxy and the hard path it would require them to follow. At least for the time being, the deep human desire for reassurance, which religious faith had previously answered, does not yet permit a full abandonment of the Jewish faith. It does permit, however, a radical reinterpretation of that faith – a reinterpretation that overcomes fundamental and previously antagonistic religious differences. Human life is able *thereby* to become tolerant. For in the absence of state-enforced religious orthodoxy, human beings become fundamentally indifferent to the differences that had formerly animated and divided religious peoples. Members of religious sects reinterpret their former enemies to accord with the new virtue of humanity, and with the material, earthly satisfaction that has begun to change their felt needs. In the face of increasing material security and satisfaction, the importance of divergent religious doctrines becomes a thing of the past, accepted and perpetuated only by the "fanatics" who existed in former dark ages. The advance of scientific civilization eventually causes serious religious devotion, and strife, to be outlived.

We thus see by the work's end that we have been given a kind of allegorical tale showing what it will mean in the long run to follow Bacon's dramatic turn to a scientific culture. The tale's heroes, besides Joabin and the scientist-king Solamona, are the other nameless scientists, inventors, and pioneers who inhabit the Salomon's House. The tale points to no villains; it points only to benighted human beings who, to their misfortune, have been for ages intimidated into a fundamentally mistaken understanding of the world. That mistaken understanding, Bacon teaches, will soon become not only a thing of the past but a thing visibly and emphatically belonging to the primitive age of human consciousness. Thanks to the new science, progress can finally replace return – repentance – as the guiding disposition, the lodestar, of human life.

This vision of the possibility of a human existence finally set right by science is taken up and given a much fuller and more satisfying political and legal elaboration by Thomas Hobbes, Bacon's younger friend and student.

8

Hobbes's *Leviathan*

Thomas Hobbes (1588–1679), more clearly than anyone else, elaborated the conceptual framework that has predominated in all distinctively modern political thought ever since: government conceived as a "social contract" among radically independent individuals intending to protect their personal, pre-political liberties or "rights." Hobbes laid out this framework and provided its philosophic justification, in several successive treatises, but his acknowledged masterpiece is *Leviathan*.*

The Broad Historical Context

In the century and a half immediately prior to Hobbes, there had been two momentous reshapings of the intellectual landscape: first, the Protestant Reformation, which split Christianity forever into competing and, for a long time, warring sects; second, the emergence of modern, materialistic-mathematical physics – and the new, Baconian project of technology that we studied in the previous chapter. Hobbes's political thought is deeply shaped by both these transformations.

Hobbes was transfixed by the sight of the horrible religious wars convulsing Europe, and he detected as their chief cause the fight among sects over clashing interpretations of what the Bible teaches government ought to implement in order to foster the "highest good" – the piety and the justice that maximize virtue as the source of the health or salvation of the soul. Hobbes reacted by leading the way to the implementation of a

---

* We recommend Edwin Curley's edition (Cambridge, MA: Hackett, 1994), which indicates the changes Hobbes made in his Latin translation of the work and affords a very helpful index of Hobbes's scriptural references; our quotations are from this edition, by Hobbes's chapters and by the paragraphs as numbered by Curley.

new, drastically lowered, conception of the goals of government. Hobbes was the first to propose a conception of civic justice and the common good that removed from civic purview the whole question of the good life, in the sense of spiritual fulfillment.

Hobbes found in the new mathematical-materialistic modern science a wonderfully helpful tool and method for understanding civic life and human existence in these lower, despiritualized terms. He is the first thinker to carry out in a thoroughgoing way the application of the modern scientific method to the understanding of justice and morality. As a friend or interlocutor of Galileo, Bacon, Descartes, Gassendi, and other giants of early modern materialist science, Hobbes was himself a leading philosopher of modern science. His thought propels what came to be called "the Enlightenment" – a vast cultural revolution against the previous two-thousand-year-old tradition rooted in Socrates and Aristotle and the Bible. The word "enlightenment" has its root in Hobbes as much as in Bacon; Hobbes labeled all previous culture, and the whole cultural world in which he grew up and against which he rebelled, "The Kingdom of Darkness." He proclaimed himself the first true bringer of light to the world of politics.

The Attack on Aristotle and Aquinas

The most vivid expression of Hobbes's rebellion against the classical tradition is found in *Leviathan*'s penultimate chapter, 46 – titled "Of Darkness from Vain Philosophy and Fabulous Traditions." But if we are to appreciate Hobbes's subtlety, we must take note of one important way in which Hobbes does not entirely break with the ancients. After he finishes a withering critique of Aristotle's metaphysical teaching – about the existence of spiritual beings, beyond the simply bodily or material beings that Hobbes insists are the only things that truly exist – Hobbes suddenly says (46.18) that maybe Aristotle did not really believe any of it but put it all forward in public out of fear of religious persecution and as a way of *pretending* to conform, in some measure, to religious belief: "[T]his shall suffice for an example of the errors, which are brought into the Church, from the *entities* and *essences* of Aristotle (which it may be he knew to be false philosophy, but writ it as a thing consonant to, and corroborative of, their religion – and fearing the fate of Socrates)." Hobbes thereby makes it clear that he is aware of the classics' rhetorical strategy of pretending to conform to religious views while subtly questioning and indicating skepticism. We are thus prepared to recognize

that Hobbes forges for his own teaching a new, though more transparent, religious veil for what is an essentially irreligious and atheistic
teaching. While Hobbes trumpets his break with the whole tradition
of political theology, rooted in Thomas Aquinas's use of Aristotle, he
pretends to treat the Bible itself, and Christianity as based on the Bible,
with deep respect. He elaborates a radical new Christian theology, and
scriptural exegesis, which he claims or pretends is the first exegesis that
accurately captures the true political message of the Bible – which turns
out to teach, as God's supernatural lesson, exactly the political theory
of Hobbes! His is the first political theory, Hobbes claims, that is based
on the true meaning of the divine revelation, after centuries of misin-
terpretation of the Bible by Catholics, and then by their opponents,
the recent Protestants. Hobbes devotes the entire second half of his
Leviathan to his detailed exegesis of the Bible, both the Old and the
New Testaments, claiming to prove that the Scriptures, properly interpreted, teach exactly the political philosophy elaborated in the first part
of *Leviathan.*

In the sixth paragraph of chapter 46, Hobbes sketches a history of
all previous philosophy, spotlighting the most obvious sign of the failure of philosophy hitherto: endless and disgraceful disagreement, over
the very nature of reality, among various sects or schools – Platonists,
Aristotelians, Epicureans, Stoics, Cynics, Skeptics, and so on. Each sect
has its own different and conflicting physics and metaphysics. This ceaseless disagreement is proof that none of the different schools can actually
prove anything. For if any of them could provide genuine *proofs* of their
doctrines, the rest would have to either agree or else show themselves
manifest fools. The only branch of traditional science in which one finds
real proofs, and thus knowledge, and hence universal agreement, is
geometry. But none of the ancients, with the notable exception of Plato,
realized that therefore geometry or mathematics could and should be
the key to truth, as regards nature as a whole. And even Plato made the
mistake of thinking that mathematics could not be joined with materialism. Hobbes is sure that such a combination – mathematically governed and interpreted materialism – is *the* way to genuine knowledge of
nature.

What exactly is it that makes geometry consist of proofs, and hence
indisputable knowledge? All the complex figures and relationships that
exist in a plane or in a solid are fully and truly understood because we
can show and compare how they can all be generated or constructed,
by us, from a small number of very simple elements (the point, the line,

the plane), manipulated and combined according to clear and distinct rules (axioms and postulates). Geometry does not *assume* that squares or triangles or circles or any other more complex plane figures exist. It does not *assume* that any of the properties of plane figures exist. Geometry *proves* that they all *must* exist, if or once you make a few basic and largely self-evident assumptions and then proceed with strict logic. Geometry starts from what no one can sensibly deny and then discovers how, from this, you can prove the *necessary* existence and properties of the complex figures and relationships in space. Geometry shows us that we genuinely know something complicated only when we can see how to make it, to generate or to construct it, from its simplest elements, combined and manipulated according to transparent rules. Hobbes begins chapter 46 by summing up these characteristics as the criteria by which one defines truly scientific philosophy, or a philosophy that leads to certainty and thus genuine knowledge: "By PHILOSOPHY is understood *the knowledge acquired by reasoning from the manner of the generation of anything to the properties, or from the properties to some possible way of generation of the same, to the end to be able to produce, as far as matter and human force permit, such effects as human life requireth.*"

Hobbes soon claims that the same problem that is obvious in traditional physics also blights all traditional moral and political philosophy (46.11): disgraceful disagreement obtains, signifying the absence of proofs and hence of any real knowledge. All previous moral and political philosophy, Hobbes concludes, is nothing more than the philosophers asserting their competing "tastes," as he puts it. Each philosopher claims, without proof, that the way of life that he – and people like him, or people who agree with him – prefer, constitutes "the good" life, for all humans. But these claims fly in the face of the obvious fact that most humans disagree – that there is a "diversity of tastes." Different people have different preferences, and conflicting conceptions of the good life. And no one has any proof that what is the good life for him is the good life for all humans.

The worst practical consequence of this traditional moral and political "philosophy," especially that shaped by Aristotle, is that it has influenced people, especially the young and restless, to think that the good life requires political regimes that honor and enable extensive political participation, in small self-governing communities. This leads to people being terribly discontent with their actual existing regimes, since, if the regimes are sound and stable, they tend to be centralized monarchies, with very little political participation. The influence of classical and especially Aristotelian political philosophy thus subverts healthy political authority (46.32 and 35). Hobbes makes it clear that one major goal of his political thought is to combat the influence of Aristotle and the classics that makes people morally contemptuous of strong, stable, and secure monarchies (see also 21.8–9).

That contempt Hobbes sees as feeding into and fomenting the religious wars that have convulsed Europe. The classical philosophers teach people that they should be concerned, in politics, above all with their souls, their spiritual welfare; the classics teach people to feel deeply dissatisfied with the mere physical security and prosperity – the essential but mundane blessings – that stable government can truly bestow. The classics thus feed and fuel a politics obsessed with religious teachings, coming from the Bible, that tell of another life to come that is far more important than anything in this life and that demands all sorts of sacrifices of peace and welfare and security in this life, so as to deserve salvation in that other life. But we lack scientific knowledge, and hence a solid basis of agreement, concerning that other life and its demands. There are only mysterious revelations that conflict, or have conflicting interpretations, and thus generate irresolvable, sharp disagreements that have led to vicious and endless religious wars.

The New Foundation in the Passions

What is desperately needed is a whole new approach, one that does not begin from, or even make important, the achievement of spiritual purity and fulfillment. What is needed is a normative political science, a science of justice, of right and wrong, modeled on mathematical science – which means, starting from basic elements of human motivation and action and concern that are obviously and indisputably powerful in everyone. Everyone feels pleasure and pain, fear and hope, love and hate, anger and pity; everyone is moved by these passions to reason about how to satisfy them. But while the same *passions* are obviously at work in everyone, when it comes to the *goals* of these passions, people vary, often in conflicting ways, and usually without being self-aware or honest, even with themselves. As Hobbes puts it at the outset of *Leviathan* (intro., para. 3): "Whosoever looketh into himself and considereth what he doth, when he does *think, opine, reason, hope, fear,* &c. and upon what grounds, he shall thereby read and know, what are the thoughts and passions of all other men upon the like occasions. I say the similitude of *passions,*" which "are the same in all men, *desire, fear, hope,* &c," but "not the similitude of the *objects* of the passions," which "are the things *desired, feared, hoped,* &c: for these the constitution individual and particular education do so vary," and "they are so easy to be kept from our knowledge" that "the characters of man's heart, blotted and confounded as they are with dissembling, lying, counterfeiting, and erroneous doctrines, are legible only to him that searcheth hearts." Hobbes stresses how necessary it is to get beneath the self-deluding and flattering interpretations that people tend to put on their own actions and aims. Partly on account of the distorting influence of centuries of classical philosophy and theology, people want to believe that they are nobler, purer, or more spiritual, less easily reduced to universal and simple psychological passions, than they really are. People want to believe that their existence is directed to high fixed goals, which are or constitute *the* good, and are not merely matters of subjective and mutable or temporary taste. To get at the truth about human psychology requires a searing and ruthless, painfully honest, introspection or self-analysis that most people are likely to eschew or even to hate.

In the first five chapters, Hobbes lays out his science of how we know things. All knowledge begins from memories in the brain that are decaying imprints of sense perceptions, which are always of particular, individual events. These the mind, serving its passions, puts together into classifications and class relationships; people cooperate in this construction by means of the most basic of all human constructions, language.

But this implies that the one aspect of reality that we are immediately in touch with is our passions, which we can see are shared by all other humans. In chapter 6, Hobbes lays out his science of the passions. In effect, he gives us the results of his own ruthlessly honest self-analysis, applied to a vigilant observation of the behavior and self-expressions of others. His account of the passions expresses a bracing frankness, a transparent clarity, an utter lack of sentimentality, and a rich if somewhat cynical experience of the world. He analyzes the emotions as the expression of complex physical or material processes; he speaks as a scientific materialist. He begins from a distinction between two sorts of inner motions. The first he calls the "vital motions," or those biological processes over which we have little conscious control (hunger, digestion, breathing, etc.). The second are what he calls the "animal," or the voluntary and conscious motions. These are of two basic sorts: *desire*, or motion toward what pleases us, which we call "good," and *aversion*, or motion away from what pains us, which we call "evil." And here Hobbes presents his classic statement of the relativity of good and evil: "[W]hatsoever is the object of any man's appetite or desire, that is it which he, for his part, calleth *good*; and the object of his hate and aversion, evil; and of his contempt, *vile* and *inconsiderable*. For these words," of "good, evil, and contemptible are ever used with relation to the person that useth them, there being nothing simply and absolutely so," nor any "common rule of good and evil, to be taken from the nature of the objects themselves," but "from the person of the man (where there is no commonwealth), or (in a commonwealth) from the person that representeth it, or from an arbitrator or judge whom men disagreeing shall by consent set up, and make his sentence the rule thereof" (6.7).

Each individual is the standard of what is good, for himself – *unless* a number of persons "consent" that some other will "represent" them all, despite or because they cannot otherwise agree among themselves. And here we get the first clue as to what lies at the end of the educational voyage on which Hobbes is going to take us. Hobbes is *the* philosopher of *representation* and of *representative* government, established by a mutual contract among men who cannot agree on what is good – and who, realizing that they cannot agree on the good, see that they must agree to disagree on that and make their basis of agreement something that is more important than "the good" (than their conflicting primary goals). But what can that be?

The next step is to see what happiness or felicity must really mean: "*Continual success* in obtaining those things which a man from time to time desireth, that is to say, continual prospering, is that men call FELICITY; I mean the felicity of this life." For "there is no such thing as perpetual tranquility of mind, while we live here; because life itself is but motion, and can never be without desire, nor without fear, no more than without sense" (6.58). Here we see an important consequence of the relativity of the good: Life is in constant motion or change, as people's passions propel them from one taste, and its object, to another – the gaining of one leading only to yet another. The subjectivity or relativity of the good is radical, in the sense that even within the same person there is no fixity. It is not merely that the good is relative to each person; the good is relative to each person *at a particular time* in his or her life. It does not remain the same even for a single person. Hence what *is* true of everyone is a profound restlessness, an absence of tranquility, an endless dissatisfaction and quest for more and different satisfactions. As for the happiness promised by Christianity, in another life, that is simply unintelligible, Hobbes dares to say, and thus can give no guidance to us in this life: "What kind of felicity God hath ordained to them that devoutly honour Him, a man shall no sooner know, than enjoy; being joys, that now are as incomprehensible, as the word of school-men *beatifical vision* is unintelligible" (6.58).

Hobbes reduces the beautiful or noble to the good, and the good to pleasure (6.11). He is a hedonist; all human life is aimed at pleasure experienced by oneself. "Beauty" he defines as simply what *promises even-tual* pleasure for oneself. The classics, and the biblical tradition, would of course protest: Does not the noble and the beautiful call us to transcend or even to sacrifice pleasure – and to endure pain? Hobbes denies the validity of any such call. His whole analysis is rooted in a distrust and dis-missal of the noble opinions that serious statesmen and citizens express in public life about what is motivating them. What *is* universally evident is that the good, as that which humans truly seek, is one or another of the following, and nothing more: either a *present* physical pleasure or the diminishing of a *present* physical pain; or else something *useful* for getting such pleasure or relieving such pain, in the *future*; or else something that *promises* such pleasure in the future, and hence is called "beautiful"; or else a pleasure of the *mind*, which consists of *understanding* the pleasant or painful consequences of things. Here, for a moment, we glimpse that Hobbes does admit the distinctive pleasure of philosophy. But Hobbes says little about this pleasure of the mind. He leaves it rather enigmati-cally in the background and focuses on the more physical manifestations of the good or pleasant.

Hobbes proceeds to show how all the different complex human pas-sions can be understood as built up out of the simple motions toward pleasure and away from pain, combined with different opinions or esti-mations of the costs and benefits of acting in one way or another to maxi-mize pleasure and to minimize pain – always bearing in mind that what is pleasing and what is painful varies and changes (6.14–22). On this basis, things traditionally called virtues and spoken of as self-transcending are shown to be not so. Courage, for example, appears as merely a complex of passion and opinion – fear, combined with the opinion that one can triumph over the source of fear, by resistance. (*Heroic* courage, in the sense of self-sacrifice, does not really exist.)

A crucial consequence of Hobbes's account of the passions is that there is no free will: In defiance of the teaching of Thomas Aquinas, Hobbes presents the will not as a faculty but merely as the outcome of a struggle among the passions; the passion that wins out people call, in their delusive self-flattery, "the will." Humans are not free to rise above their passions (6.53). Noteworthy too is Hobbes's account in chapter 6 of piety or faith: Piety is simply fear, of invisible powers (6.36). Hobbes ignores the possibility that piety grows out of or expresses adoration, or self-overcoming, or gratitude.

Yet Hobbes's account of the passions shows that from the start he understands humans as intensely *social* animals – involved with one another, needing one another, with passionate concerns for one another. He recognizes that humans do or can take pleasure or pain in what is done to others. Humans are not *simply* selfish. Hobbes contends, however, that the enjoyment of another's enjoyment, or compassion for another's suffering, is fully explained by the pleasure or pain, for oneself, that one gets from seeing what happens to others, or from helping them. Hence we do not help others if it does not please us – or if a hope for another, greater, pleasure is in competition.

Above all, we see that the delight in prestige or glory plays an enormous role in Hobbes's account of the human passions. Humans are deeply social – in an intensely competitive way – in that they seek respect, prestige, and recognized superiority in relation to others. Humans hence are constantly comparing themselves, and competing, with others. The joy that humans feel from seeing their own superiority over others is what Hobbes defines as "glorying." But Hobbes stresses the detrimental way in which this pleasure tends to carry people away to an exaggerated, false estimation of their own power – which he calls "vainglory," something to which humans are highly susceptible (6.39).

Hobbes links the delight in glory with something else: the delight in the thought of one's own *power*. Indeed, the concern for power pervades Hobbes's explanation of the passions. Thus, laughter and weeping are interpreted as sudden strong reactions to our sense of our comparative power or powerlessness. All joke telling is a way of triumphing over others and enjoying our own power (6.42).

In chapter 8, Hobbes carries his thought a big step further by contending (8.16–20) that insanity is revealing, in its extremeness, of what is moving all humans. Insanity discloses in an exaggerated way what is present in more controlled form in all of us. Madness, Hobbes argues, is best understood as caused either by an exaggerated belief in one's power (manic vainglory) or by an exaggerated belief in one's powerlessness (severe depression). In other words, it becomes clearer and clearer that Hobbes is arguing that humans are animals deeply preoccupied with, even obsessed with, *power* – either the possession or the lack of it – in *comparison* with *others*.

The Centrality of Power

Chapter 10 marks the first thematic treatment in human history of power, power simply, power without qualification. Hobbes is *the* philosopher of power, of the drive for power, as the key to human nature. Hobbes taught the world to think in terms of power, by which he does not mean only, or even primarily, political power or rule (which is what Machiavelli means when he uses the term "power"). Hobbes means something more amorphous, more general, less narrowly focused on politics. He is the first to say that the competitive quest for power pervades every human relationship, from that between a newborn baby and its mother to that between two philosophers talking. Power pervades even all relations between humans and the nonhuman world: The primary reason humans want to understand the world is not for the pure joy of knowing but in order to have power over the world. After Hobbes, people talk casually all the time of the quest for power, power trips, power-hungry people, power relations between the sexes, the need for power. Hobbes taught the world to speak a new language, one that carries with it a massive assumption about human nature, about ourselves and what makes us tick. Prior to Hobbes, no one – not even Machiavelli – spoke this way; reflection on the first sentence of the tenth chapter, in which Hobbes defines power, helps us to understand what is so new: "The power *of a man* (to take it universally) is his present means to obtain some future apparent good" (10.1).

Since power is for some future apparent good, previous thinkers focused their inquiries on the question: What are those goods? They contended that only *after* one has answered the question of what one is seeking, as a goal, can one inquire as to what would be the best means to, the "power" needed for, that goal. Prior to Hobbes, people would be puzzled by talk of power in itself. They would ask, as Aristotle or an Aristotelian would: "Do you not have to specify first what the power is a power *for*? Is not power to rule quite different from power to win heavenly salvation, which is quite different from power to understand the nature of things, which is quite different from power to win the love of another person – and so forth?" Hobbes is the first to argue, to the contrary, that power is best conceived of and sought as the force that will allow you to achieve *all sorts* of *yet unspecified* ends. A leading example of power so understood is money – because money enables its possessor to acquire vastly different and changing things that one may from time to time wish for. If what is good and bad, noble and base, is subjective and relative and constantly changing, even for each person, then the question of the "right" *ends* is eclipsed by the question of the right way to attain *means* to *whatever* ends one may come to seek.

Hobbes's central thought about human nature is summed up at the start of chapter 11, which is about "manners," or those moral qualities that we must build on to create healthy and just society: "[T]here is no such *Finis ultimus* (utmost aim) nor *Summum Bonum* (greatest good) as is spoken of in the books of the old moral philosophers"; happiness "is a continual progress of the desire, from one object to another, the attaining of the former, being still but the way to the latter." The cause of this is "that the object of man's desire is not to enjoy once only, and for one instant of time, but to assure for ever the way of his future desire" (11.1). Here again is Hobbes's basic premise as to the relativity and changeability of every pleasure for which people have a taste. But now Hobbes stresses that as a consequence, because and as people come to realize this about life – because and as they experience the fact that no satisfaction is lasting, that nothing remains their enduring purpose, that their pleasures and hence purposes are always changing – they cease to be so attached to any one or another of their shifting pleasures and purposes. They instead switch their concern more and more to getting that which will empower them to get whatever it might be that they might want in the future. And this – the *means* that will allow us to get the largest variety of *whatever* it is we might someday want – is the new meaning of power. Hobbes draws his momentous conclusion: "I put for a general inclination of all mankind, a perpetual and restless desire of power after power, that ceaseth only in death." And "the cause of this is not always that a man hopes for a more intensive delight, than he has already attained to, or that he cannot be content with a moderate power, but because he cannot assure the power and means to live well which he hath present, without the acquisition of more" (11.2). In these last words, Hobbes adds a further dimension: Power is something that is itself not stable or enduring. In order to keep and to assure the power that you have now, you need to be increasing your power.

In chapter 10 Hobbes proceeds to give a careful analysis of exactly what affords power, in this new sense. "Natural" powers are one's own individual capacities. But these natural powers become very strong only inasmuch as they are used to accumulate another much greater sort of power that Hobbes calls "instrumental" (10.2). Of the latter type, riches and reputation head the list, followed by friends. Strong power is something *social*. Strong power is whatever makes *other people* do what you want them to do – to help you or to refrain from hindering you. And that depends on what others *think* of you. You get others to do your bidding when they think they will get something from you, or avoid some hurt from you. So, for example, Hobbes goes on to say that money is power only if you are thought to be willing to give it to others. Otherwise, it is a negative, because it arouses envy and makes people prey on you. It follows that the measure of your power is what other people will do for you, or will give to you, in order to get you to favor and to help them.

Human worth or dignity is to be understood in these terms. It is completely social, and strictly relative to others, established by public opinion: "The *value* or WORTH of a man is, as of all other things, his price, that is to say, so much as would be given for the use of his power; and therefore is not absolute, but a thing dependent on the need and judgment of another" (10.16). Not only the ends we pursue but our very dignity or worth are strictly relative, and determined according to an aggregate of anonymous others – constituting the "market," as we say, with all its shifting values determined by supply and demand.

But what is the sign or indication that one actually has superior power, dignity, worth? How do you know your "worth" on the market of power? How do people signal to one another how much they value one another? "The manifestation of the value we set on one another is that which is commonly called honouring and dishonouring." To "value a man at a high rate is to *honour* him; at a low rate, is to *dishonour* him" (10.17). In the rest of chapter 10 Hobbes gives a series of wonderfully vivid lessons, teaching how one reads this signaling (10.19ff.). He also introduces another key thought: To be honored is not only a sign of power; it itself constitutes more power – even as dishonor constitutes a loss of power. Those who honor you, and those who witness them honor you, intensify the public opinion of your importance, of your capacity to do others ill or well, and hence of everyone's need to accommodate you. Hence, as Hobbes had said earlier, "reputation of power is power" (10.5).

We may summarize what has been disclosed in Hobbes's train of analysis of the human condition as follows. If or since for humans the good (the objects that please) is relative and subjective, then power necessarily becomes a human being's chief concern. And if the mark and key constituent of power is honor – meaning reputation or prestige – then it follows that human life naturally tends to become obsessed with seeking repute, prestige, even glory.

The next step is to see that prestige, honor, glory, and the power they signal are essentially scarce and intensely competitive: things that one can have *only* by becoming superior to others, by putting others beneath you in rank, by dominating others. Only a few can have vast honor, prestige, and hence power – the distribution of which is always pyramidal. Thus in the next or eleventh chapter, after the classic statement on life being an endless quest for power that we have previously quoted, Hobbes momentously adds the following: "Competition of riches, honour, command, or other power, inclineth to contention, enmity, and war: because the way of one competitor to the attaining of his desire is to kill, subdue, supplant, or repel the other" (11.3). The necessary outcome of a relativistic conception of the ends of life is that life is by nature an endless power struggle for prestige and wealth. And the power struggle naturally tends to become a life-and-death struggle. For the most effective way to dominate other people is to seriously intimidate them, to make them think their very life depends on you; this cannot be achieved without showing from time to time that you can exterminate opponents. In doing this, you teach all others, who witness this, a lesson in fearing and obeying you. So the natural tendency of human relations is to drift steadily toward fights to the death over power and its mark, prestige. The condition that is the *natural* outcome of the human passions, centered on power and prestige, is *a war of all against all*. But precisely as people begin to experience and to recognize this terrible truth about themselves, about human nature, Hobbes will go on to argue, they react by learning something else, that turns out to be *the most* important truth about themselves, about human nature. Humans learn that to suffer violent death at the hands of another human is absolutely, and not relatively, *the greatest* evil. Hobbes's next step, in chapter 13, is to teach his readers this decisive truth by taking them vicariously through the description of the human condition that is "natural" in the sense that it is the necessary outcome of the nature of the human passions, when the passions are allowed to follow their spontaneous course, and are not repressed.

Opposing the Biblical Conception

But first Hobbes pauses, in chapter 12, to confront a massive obstacle or alternative to his whole outlook: the religious or biblical conception of the human condition. The Bible teaches that the original or fundamental state of humans is life in the garden of Eden – a state of blissful peace and love, from which we fell on account of our own blamable sin. The problem of human existence, according to the Bible, is not human *nature* and its *necessary* tendencies, as Hobbes teaches, but human *sin*. The only true solution is not rationally trying to figure out how to control human nature but instead confession of guilt, atonement, praying to God for forgiveness, and hoping for redemption through miraculous divine grace.

In chapter 12 Hobbes shows how religion, as passion, can be explained in scientific terms, on the basis of the psychology he has now laid out. He gives a purely naturalistic, psychological history of the development of religion as of a desperately erroneous misconception men have invented, in order to try to avoid the terrible truth about the situation into which their nature necessarily leads them. Most ignorant people, Hobbes suggests, have actually believed the myths they have imagined. But there have always been a few others, a clever few, who have perpetrated religious frauds as a way to advance their own power, using the "seeds of religion" in the passions to secure for themselves the fearful obedience and awe of their fellows. Hobbes's purpose in chapter 12 is most obviously to deconstruct, to ridicule, to debunk the claims of all religion (which, we recall, he defined back in chapter 6 as "fear of powers invisible"). But at the same time Hobbes prods us to see that the doctrine of human nature that he has been putting forward is a doctrine directly opposed to serious religion in all its forms. He prepares us to recognize that his whole account of the state of nature is directly opposed to everything taught in the Bible. On this basis, Hobbes turns in chapter 13 to lay out the culmination of his purely naturalistic account of the human condition – his famous "state of nature."

The State of Nature

Hobbes's state of nature is, as he puts it (13.9), an "inference, made from the passions." The state of nature is what we might today call a scientific model, which reveals where human relations necessarily tend if or insofar as humans are allowed to surrender to the spontaneous drift or pull of their passions. Hobbes stresses (13.11) that he is not insisting that all mankind was ever necessarily in this condition. But he speculates that it is probable that humans were originally in a condition close to this imagined model, and he suggests that much of uncivilized mankind is still in something close to this condition. He submits that one can see empirical evidence for this, by observing how civilized humans behave toward one another when artificial law and order breaks down – most usually in war and civil war. For then people are unleashed to act on their strongest desires and impulses. But from this one also learns something else of the utmost importance. One sees that *the* purpose of government and law is to *repress* and to *control* human nature in its passions.

In other words, all civilized society can best be understood as humans continually trying to effect some kind of repression of their natural inclinations, through their artificial and conventional arrangements; one can see those repressed natural inclinations break out when the conventions break down. Hobbes is in effect claiming to clarify – by thinking through fully for the first time – what has always been dimly and gropingly at work in humanity's creation of lawful societies. Always before, humans have in various ways hidden from themselves the grim truth about themselves and their nature – through all sorts of religious myths and vainglorious philosophies, by which they have convinced themselves to believe flattering, or desperately hopeful, falsehoods. These have gummed up humanity's efforts to follow what reason can tell it should be done. Hobbes is the first to make all this clear, and to publish it for everyone to share. By thinking our way through the human condition – as one of beings naturally competing for power and prestige – we can think our way back to the founding of civilized life, to the original situation, that is recapitulated in every breakdown of law and order, or in every extreme situation, when humans are free to act out their passions. Above all, we can discover that the human species is by its nature *the* dangerous species – above all for itself. The human species is the most self-destructive, the most antisocial in its very sociability, the most mutually murderous, of any species.

But to see this is to undergo a deep emotional reaction, one that compels insight into the true and solid foundation of morality or justice. Fear – the fear of violent death in the natural war of all against all, to which human nature tends – is a passionate reaction that makes sense, Hobbes argues. The love of glory won through risking one's life in war for prestige does *not* make sense, unless the risk is necessary in order to maximize our chances of becoming safer from violent death. In other words, the thirst for honor or prestige too easily loses sight of the crude but essential fact that, once you are dead or dying, your power drops to zero; you cannot enjoy glory or its fruits after you are dead. Machiavellian pursuers of glory are deluded by *vain* glory – by the focus on honor or prestige that forgets that, while it is true that there is no greatest good, there is indeed a greatest evil. That evil is not merely death, which after all comes to everyone and may come painlessly, at the end of a long life, or at least peacefully and by nonhuman agents. What is truly horrible is to die prematurely and violently. The greatest evil is violent death at the hands of another human. For such death is horribly painful, brutally premature, and a humiliating manifestation of someone else's domination over you, depriving you totally of all your comparative power.

It turns out, then, that there is after all one absolute – of a kind – that emerges from nature: a negative absolute, an absolute evil. And this gives us, or can give us, our absolute guidance. Relativism, when thought through and lived through, emotionally, turns into a negative absolutism. Once we see how utterly devastating it is to be violently killed by a competitor, we realize that we seek above all else to avoid this single worst evil – to put the biggest distance between ourselves and the possibility of being so brutally and totally dominated. Once we have grasped this fundamental truth, we realize that the pursuit of glory or prestige, if or when it is won through undergoing violent death, no longer makes sense. We realize that we must limit and regulate our pursuit of power and honor by this absolute negative standard. The cardinal rule of life becomes: Never pursue power and honor into the valley of violent death if or insofar as it can be avoided. And when ordinary fearful folks get together in large numbers to organize themselves and to pool their defenses and military resources, they can become much stronger than the minority of crazies who forget or lose sight of this basic, absolute truth. Collective action and mutual assistance rooted in selfish fear and the quest for security is the foundation of a new notion of commonwealth and justice.

Yet there remains, Hobbes stresses, a terrible human tendency to become blinded – drunk, as it were – by the passion for glory or prestige. Vainglory or pride turns out to be the worst thing about humans, because it so easily blinds them to their deeper, truer, more rational passion – which is for avoiding violent death and thus seeking peace. And this vainglorious passion is, as we saw in chapter 12 fueled by religion. People want to believe and can be deluded by religion into believing, that they somehow live on after death – and hence can still have their glory and power, *if* they subordinate it to the glory and power of an imagined god. Insofar as humans fall into this delusion, they become much more dangerous. Here we see why religious belief is *the* enemy of human well-being, for Hobbes.

Hobbes begins his elaboration of the new, rational, true teaching about justice that will lead us out of danger by laying down the proposition that all humans are by nature equal. Hobbes is the first political philosopher to ground his teaching on justice in the assertion of the equality of all human beings by nature. But the basis on which all humans are equal by nature is not terribly flattering. We are all by nature equally dangerous *murderers*; any human can kill any other, and thereby inflict the absolute evil on another (11.1–2). It is true that in physical strength humans as individuals are somewhat unequal, and thus somewhat unequally dangerous. But Hobbes insists this is not as important as it first seems. For every weak human can gang up with others to overpower even the strongest individual. In other words, from the outset, Hobbes makes it clear that the state of nature is not a state of simply independent or isolated individuals – it is a gangland.

From this rough equality of strength, humans by nature have equal *hope* of getting what they seek, and, since all want power and honor, they start competing for these, and then fighting, and then fighting to the death: "And from hence it comes to pass that, where an invader hath no more to fear, than another man's single power, if one plant, sow, build, or possess a convenient seat, others may probably be expected to come prepared with forces united, to dispossess, and deprive him, not only of the fruit of his labour, but also of his life, or liberty." And "the invader again is in the like danger of another" (13.3). The threat is from "others" (plural), "with forces united" – that is to say, gangs. But the gangs are rather small, shifting, unstable, insecure. Every gang has to anticipate being attacked by other gangs – and thus has to try to attack first. Factions develop within the gangs. But what really keeps the pot boiling is the fact that even if some, or most, people sooner or later want to remain on the defensive, and minimize the risk of violent death, there are always a substantial few people who are intoxicated by the love of their own power beyond what security requires – the Machiavellian glory-lovers, the war-lovers, the risk-takers. What is more, their activity affects the relations of all men, in a grimly compelling fashion: "Because there be some that, taking pleasure in contemplating their own power in the acts of conquest, which they pursue farther than their security requires, if others (that otherwise would be glad to be at ease within modest bounds) should not by invasion increase their power, they would not be able, long time, by standing only on their defence, to subsist" (13.4; cf. 18.11). In the natural condition, *everyone has* to go on the offensive, whether one wishes to or not, in order to prevent, by preemptive strikes, attacks and dominion by anyone stronger in the neighborhood – since that person is all too likely to be or to become one of those drunk with vainglory.

The Natural Basis of Justice

This necessity of preemptive offensiveness has, however, a potentially moral dimension that turns out to be of the greatest moment: What one is compelled to do, as a rational being, one cannot reasonably be *blamed* for doing. And, at the start of the fourteenth chapter, Hobbes takes a further giant step: One has to be granted the *right* to do whatever one is compelled, as a rational being, to do. In the state of nature, one has a *right*, a *natural* right, to increase one's power without limit, in order to preserve oneself; one has a *right* to all things.

But everyone else has also a right to all things; you have a right to your body and life, but everyone else also has a right to take your body and life – even as you have a right to take their bodies and lives. There is no exclusive right of property, even in oneself or in one's own life (14.4). Hobbes states the matter with some exaggeration near the end of chapter 13: "To this war of every man against every man, this also is consequent: that nothing can be unjust." The "notions of right and wrong, justice and injustice have there no place. Where there is no common power, there is no law; where no law, no injustice. Force and fraud are in war the two cardinal virtues" (13.13). Yet as we learn at the start of chapter 14, the absence of justice is not total, but arises from the presence of the universal *right* – and the inevitable mortal conflict among the possessors of this right. Force and fraud may be expressions of the prosecution of one's natural right to do whatever is needed to increase one's security in a terribly insecure environment. Justice is not simply absent in the natural condition but is, so to speak, naturally self-impeding. And this points or goads to the possibility and necessity for human reason to figure out a way of preventing justice, as the natural right of each, from being self-impeding.

Hobbes's last words in chapter 13 refer to passions that incline to peace and to the moral "laws of nature": "The passions that incline men to peace are fear of death, desire of such things as are necessary to commodious living, and a hope by their industry to obtain them." And "reason suggesteth convenient articles of peace, upon which men may be drawn to agreement. These articles are they which otherwise are called the Laws of Nature: whereof I shall speak more particularly, in the two following chapters" (13.14).

The strongest natural passion is fear of violent death, seconded by a desire to remove oneself as far as possible from violent death, through securing a comfortable and peacefully respectable life, attained by calculation and industrious labor. This set of passions is frustrated and horrified by the natural outcome of these very passions, above all inasmuch as they tend to become perverted by the vainglorious lust for power. But this frustration and horror can summon reason, which is *the* tool of the passions, to figure out an artificial way to overcome the state of nature, to repress and to control human nature's spontaneous drift or tendency. Reason, working for fear, electrified by the desperate need for security from violent death, figures out how to construct a whole code of artificial rules of behavior, devised in order to overcome the natural condition, to bring about as much peacefulness and hence security as possible among humans – ultimately through a grand treaty or compact or contract.

Hobbes calls these rationally constructed rules of behavior the "laws of nature" – usurping the traditional terminology and radically transforming it from the sense in which Thomas Aquinas and the whole previous philosophic tradition used it. Precisely because there is *no* natural law, *no* natural right or natural justice, in the *traditional* sense – precisely because humans have *no* natural conscience, no (or very minimal) natural sense of obligation to others, no political nature or strong natural communal sense, no reliable innate impulses to love and to help and to sacrifice for one another – humans must, in order to survive in security, use reason to devise an artificial substitute. The artificial laws reason constructs are "natural" in the paradoxical sense that they are what our nature needs as an artificial crutch to make up for the fact that we are naturally so morally crippled.

Hobbes stresses what an enormous break this represents with all previous notions of "natural right." Always before, "natural right" meant not the "*liberty* each man has to use his own power, as he will himself, for the preservation of his own nature," but rather chiefly the *obligation*, the *duty*, each had to the community beyond oneself and beyond one's own individual good – a duty that entailed some substantial risk or sacrifice of personal liberty and security. Hobbes is the first philosopher to say that pristine natural right means simply self-serving liberty. As we shall see, the purpose of government becomes limited to securing for the individual as much of this individual right as possible. The purpose of government is no longer any higher, allegedly greatest good, or virtue, or spiritual fulfillment. Government henceforth will be a permissive kind of government, in the sense that its function is no more and no less than to protect us in our fundamental self-seeking liberty. In Hobbes there emerges for the first time the idea of government as the powerful "state" that is "liberal," or dedicated to liberty, in the preceding sense. Government that is thus "liberal" uses its awesome power to secure, but leaves otherwise unregulated, the web of voluntary competitive relations among individuals that came to be called "society," "the economy," and "culture."

Specifying the New Moral "Laws of Nature"

From the recognition of the liberty that is "natural right," there follows with logical necessity the concept of a general rational and thus (in the new sense) "natural" law or commandment or rule of life: *Never do anything that threatens your own security, and never omit to do anything that promotes your own security* (14.2). Reason, formulated as "natural law," forbids you from doing whatever you please. Reason as natural law proclaims that you need and ought to be prudent, to regulate your behavior and to restrain your passions out of a concern for long-range security from violent death. Natural law declares that any Machiavellian glory-seeker is in violation of natural law inasmuch as he seeks glory at the risk of violent death.

Now, initially, this first and fundamental law of nature appears still purely self-regarding. But we must never forget that humans do not live alone; humans by nature live with other humans in an antisocial war of all against all – that is the overwhelming source of insecurity. From this it follows that the fundamental thing each human must do in order to achieve any improvement in security for himself is to seek to end the war, to *seek peace* – which necessarily means peace and security also for others, for one's neighbors as well as oneself (14.4). The first and fundamental specific "law of nature" is to seek peace if and when one can – and to carry on war only so long as one cannot get peace (and, hopefully, as a means to getting peace, perhaps by exterminating Machiavellians in the vicinity).

The *second* law of reason or nature commands what we need to do in order to get a secure peace: "from this fundamental law of nature, by which men are commanded to endeavour peace, is derived this second law: *that a man be willing, when others are so too, as far-forth as for peace and defence of himself he shall think it necessary, to lay down this right to all things, and be contented with so much liberty against other men, as he would allow other men against himself.*" Though Hobbes has not made any place whatsoever for religion in his account of humanity's natural condition, he now boldly asserts that all he has been saying is not so different from the teaching of Christ. This is that law of the Gospel: "Whatsoever you require that others should do to you, that do ye to them. And the law of all men," he states, is to *not* do unto others what one would *not* have done unto oneself (14.5). The second law of nature dictates that a social contract or compact must be struck, by which each party agrees with every other party to give up that portion of his or her liberty, of his or her natural right, that must be given up by all parties, in order to establish secure peace among the contractors (who *together*, as a group, remain in a state of nature or war with all the *rest* of humanity).

In the rest of chapter 14 Hobbes defines and explains in detail what is involved in all sorts of contracts or promissory agreements. He does so in order to clarify exactly what is required for a valid social compact that establishes peace, ends war, among the members. The special kind of contract that stable and secure society requires Hobbes calls a "covenant." Whereas a contract may be very short term, or even just an immediate exchange, a covenant is a mutual promise to perform what is promised not simply in the present but in the future and even the distant future or indeed forever.

But this and every promise would be absurd, or would make no sense, unless the promise implied that each party felt *obliged* to *keep* whatever promises each makes. At first, this might seem to go without saying or to be in need of no emphasis or distinct iteration as a separate law. But it is this dimension of the making of a covenant that is transformative of the lives and characters of the people involved. Hobbes spotlights the importance of this moment in the elaboration of his natural law doctrine by making it into a separate third law of nature, set off by being introduced at the beginning of the next chapter (15): "From that law of nature, by which we are obliged to transfer to another, such rights as, being retained, hinder the peace of mankind, there followeth a third, which is this": that "*men perform their covenants made*" (15.1). This third law of nature, that one must *keep* one's contractual promises, is "the fountain of justice," or indeed is "justice" simply, Hobbes says. Justice comes fully into being, justice becomes a defining quality of human existence, when the *keeping* of the covenant, and thus the constant maintenance of one's obligation to and thus concern for *others*, becomes central to one's life, for the rest of one's life. While we have no spontaneously natural, reliable care for others, we can, out of fear for our own security, compel ourselves, artificially, to have such care, by making and *keeping* a solemn commitment, a solemn promise. Our frightened or fear-impelled reason tells us that unless we all discipline ourselves, and encourage one another, so as to make manifest our shared reliability in keeping our promises, the war of all against all will recur. Or perhaps something even worse will happen to us: Others will form a compact, and we will be distrusted, and excluded, targeted as a menace. So it is very much in the long-term interest of each of us to establish with others the reputation of being someone who keeps promises, even or especially when it is costly or painful to do so in the short term. For in the long run, each of us will be much safer with a reputation as a firm promise keeper. This is the core of Hobbes's argument refuting "the fool," who "hath said in his heart: 'there is no such thing as justice'" (15.4). Since following this third natural law is a matter of instilling in ourselves a habitual character, which guides us through life, and that we display to one another in order to reassure one another, this deserves to be called the *virtue* of justice or righteousness (15.10). A righteous person, a person of just character, is someone who forces himself, against much of his natural inclination, to habitually live manifesting himself to others as keeping his contractual promises, even or especially when they are costly or painful in the short run.

Following upon righteousness, so understood, is a rather long train of moral qualities, habits, and practices that reason dictates each of us ought to strive to instill in ourselves and to practice constantly, and to teach and to encourage in others. The rest of chapter 15 lays out sixteen additional laws of nature describing those traits of character and modes of behavior that should be inculcated and encouraged in order to make humans good contractual partners, and peaceful, as well as accommodating and helpful competitors. This moral code is a directive for private persons in their own lives and in the education of their children, but also a lesson to governments, to guide rulers and all public education.

Hobbes launches here what came to be called the "bourgeois" ethic. It entails a new kind of self-restraint, and cooperativeness, in peaceful competition, that does not come from Protestantism, except in the sense that Protestantism was corrupted and taken over by Hobbes and those he influenced. Nothing in Hobbes's code suggests that humans are sinful in the Christian sense, or that they need atonement and redemption by divine grace. The new moral code lays down the new limited virtues of anxious, security-seeking, prosperity- and prestige-loving, selfish and competitive individuals who see that their self-interests can be secured and advanced only if they promote peace and civility, and who realize that human nature, their own nature, is very dangerous and must be kept repressed.

One sees vividly the spirit of the new ethic in the *fourth* law of nature (15.16), which requires that one always show gratitude, by returning favors; this is to be done, Hobbes explains, not because it is intrinsically noble, or because gratitude is spiritually enhancing, but because in this way other people will be encouraged to help one another by seeing that it *profits* them. The *fifth* law of nature requires what Hobbes calls "complaisance" (15.17) – what today is called "civility." Then come natural

laws requiring mutual forgiveness or pardon and strictly prohibiting retribution; only rehabilitation and deterrence should animate penal law
(15.18–19). For the only legitimate point of punishment is to prevent
future harm, not to exact revenge, which is irrational vain-glorying or
triumphing over others, and provocative of further hatred and strife,
threatening to bring back the natural state of war. At the psychological
basis of the outlawing of retribution is the assumption that there is no
such thing as guilt in the sense of willful sin, needing atonement, as is
taught by the Bible. Each person, whether acting lawfully or criminally, is
simply doing what he is determined to, by his calculation or miscalcula-
tion of the pleasant and painful consequences. The only reasonable goal
of punishment is to restructure the criminals' calculation so that they
will recognize the greater benefit to be had from obeying the law.

One of the most revealing natural laws is the *ninth*, "against PRIDE" –
which is branded a grave vice, *the* crime against equality and equal
respect, *the* stimulus to strife and dangerously vainglorious competition.
Even if or inasmuch as humans are unequal with regard to the highest excellences, such as wisdom, natural law commands us, for the sake
of promoting security, to treat others as equals. Here Hobbes attacks
Aristotle by name: "I know that *Aristotle* (in the first book of his *Politics*,
for a foundation of his doctrine) maketh men by nature, some more
worthy to command (meaning the wiser sort, such as he thought himself to be for his philosophy), others to serve (meaning those that had
strong bodies, but were not philosophers as he), as if master and servant
were not introduced by consent of men, but by difference of wit; which
is not only against reason, but also against experience." There are "very
few so foolish that had not rather govern themselves than be governed
by others"; nor "when the wise in their own conceit contend by force
with them who distrust their own wisdom, do they always, or often, or
almost at any time, get the victory." If "nature therefore have made men
equal, that equality is to be acknowledged; or if nature have made men
unequal, yet because men that think themselves equal will not enter into
conditions of peace but upon equal terms, such equality must be admit-
ted." And "therefore for the ninth law of nature, I put this *that every man
acknowledge another for his equal by nature*. The breach of this precept is
pride" (15.21). Hobbes is the original philosophic source of the notion
that "elitism" is a grave vice. Because the consent of others is crucial
to establishing peace, people who proclaim that they believe in politically relevant human excellence, and in consequent civic ranking among
humans, are troublemakers; they are not expressing and promoting the

equality of dignity necessary to maintain the social contract. They are stirring up dangerously proud ambitions in the young.

The whole code is summed up in Hobbes's repetition of a negative version of the golden rule (15.35): "Do *not* that to another which you would *not* have done to yourself." One's deepest obligation is not to love others but to leave them alone. These nineteen laws of nature, Hobbes insists, "are immutable and eternal" (15.38), and he lays out in a nutshell how they follow necessarily from the premise of the relativity of all goods (15.40). The amazing fact is that relativism concerning the good, as pleasure, when thought through, leads necessarily to a new and unprecedentedly strict absolutism regarding what is right. Following these nineteen laws constitutes the only true, rational "moral virtues" (15.40).

But of course the foundation and purpose of these moral virtues and of this commitment to keep promises means that one has these duties only insofar as they conduce to one's long-term security: Prudential reason does not dictate unbreakable rules, categorical imperatives – not even a categorical imperative to keep contracts. Hobbes reminds us at the start of chapter 15 that promises therefore become *really* always worth keeping only when peace has been established because the fundamental promise that is the social compact has been forged. For only then is it clearly in each person's interest to continue keeping other commitments.

The question now becomes: What conditions especially must the social compact meet in order to be truly binding on rational, self-interested individuals? Hobbes elaborates the answer fully in the second part of *Leviathan*.

The Social Compact

Each of us as parties to the contract must promise to give up forever our natural right to threaten other contractors with violent death or any lesser physical harm. We must each instead "authorize" a specified one or few among us to retain and to monopolize that right, allowing this one or few to act as the "sovereign representative" of each and all of us – and endowed with the authority to draft us into assisting whenever needed. Hobbes is the first theorist of unqualified "representative" government and unqualified "sovereign" government. What do these two terms mean exactly?

Government must be "representative" in the sense that the state is to be understood as nothing more and nothing less than the agent of each and all of the citizens or subjects, doing what they have authorized it to do – no more and no less: namely, to repress the natural human condition, to secure the peace, and to promote nonthreatening, competitive pursuit of prosperity and prestige in accordance with the "laws of nature" (30.1–3). Hobbes is the first philosopher to teach that all legitimate governmental authority comes solely from the unanimous consent of the governed, and that government is severely limited in the ends that that consent has authorized it to pursue. Government has no legitimate authority to try to bring about human fulfillment, or happiness, or virtue as excellence, or spiritual purity – except to the degree that government must educate and impel and compel people to act and to think in accord with the "laws of nature" that promote security. The classics and political theorists before Hobbes, in contrast, had argued that government or the rulers ought to derive their legitimate authority in part, and above all, from their superior virtue or wisdom, together with superior strength or force. Consent mattered, but only as a part of what makes authority legitimate – and as secondary. Consent was understood to be the necessary acknowledgment, by those being ruled, of the virtue of those leading the whole society toward a better life. And because those ruled have something to contribute in the way of wisdom and virtue, Aristotle argued, we recall, that even a democracy bases its valid claim to rule, the claim of the majority, on the majority's superior wisdom and virtue. Hobbes rejects the idea of superior virtue and wisdom that is politically relevant in Aristotle's sense. All humans are equal, because, in the first place, they are equally dangerous killers, and, in the second place, they are equally capable of being rational enough to see how to alleviate the danger – by authorizing a government that has no higher legitimate purpose than collective security. For Hobbes, and all modern politics after him, the aim of politics is vastly simplified and lowered.

"Sovereignty" of government means that, in order to achieve its radically lowered and simplified goal, government must wield a coercive power that is absolutely supreme, both morally and physically. Government must be both overawing and frightening: It must be the "Mighty Leviathan" – that will, by absorbing all legitimate authority and by the terror of an efficient police force and judiciary, inflicting capital punishment as well as lesser punishments, make it in everyone's clear interest as well as duty to keep the compact and all implementations of it. The number of people who enter into the compact must not be few, but enormous: enough to frighten any and all neighboring groups. Hence a large state, even a very large state, is good; Hobbes no longer sees any valid grounds for preferring smaller, more participatory republics. Political participation is not seen as a noble end that fulfills people. It is instead seen as an onerous policing and administrative job that someone has to do – and get paid for, in money and honor, so that most people can go about their private pursuit of economic prosperity and peaceful acquisition of prestige and power. The covenant must be understood to be entered into in perpetuity, without anyone having the reserved right to opt out. For if everyone could reserve the right to opt out, no one could ever be sure another might not suddenly assert his natural right to kill and to steal and to lie. The sovereign must represent the entire populace with one unified will and voice; the government must not be divided within itself when it comes to its final decisions and decisive actions. For that would start the pot boiling, with intensifying violent competition between parties or factions that will tend, given human nature, to spiral toward civil war and the recurrence of the state of nature.

Above all, government established by the contract is the highest *religious* authority on earth (23.6, 26.41). No one – no priest, no theologian, no prophet – has any valid religious basis for claiming any authority higher than that of the government created by contract. The only religious preaching or teaching that is just and morally or religiously justified is that which is licensed and thus established by the government – for the sake of peace. For as Hobbes insists, God and the Bible, rightly interpreted, completely endorse the Hobbesian principles. The government is literally the voice of God on earth, the one and only voice authorized by God in the Bible. Speech and publications are all allowed or disallowed according to what the sovereign decides is best for peace. Every contracting subject lays down his or her natural right to free speech and freedom of religion. The sovereign may well be best advised to decide to allow considerable freedom of speech and of religion. In fact, at the time Hobbes published the English version of *Leviathan*, he notes in the Latin version's appendix (appendix 3.1), there was no censorship law whatsoever being enforced under Cromwell – and Hobbes approved of this policy.

But why is it rational and rationally necessary for everyone to consent to such an all-powerful government? Why does Hobbes, who with his doctrine of individual rights and of representative government founds fundamental principles of liberal regimes, insist that such unified and total power be vested in the "sovereign?" Hobbes makes it clear (18.20) that he knows that it is his doctrine of the rights of the sovereign – the almost total power he insists must be given to government, and the taxation that accompanies it – that his readers will find hardest to swallow. But he insists that human nature is so dangerous – because it tends so easily to be dominated by shortsighted, vainglorious passion – that the only real alternative to centralized and almost unlimited governmental power is the endless threat of civil strife and a return of the state of nature.

Organizing and Administering Government

What form of government is best – and what are the options? The first stage of the compact is of course unanimous (though it may be tacit or by "inference" – 14.14, 18.5): Anyone who does not join is not a member (and remains in a state of war, legitimately subject to elimination as a mortal enemy by the others). But it is utterly impractical to make any decisions, after the initial one, depend on unanimity, especially since the society should be enormous in numbers. Hence part of the initial agreement or covenant is a promise to abide by the *majority's* decision as to who is to be invested with the sovereign power and as to how to handle succession to that power. Sovereignty may remain vested in the majority (democracy) or it may be placed in a minority (oligarchy) or in the hands of one (monarchy). The form of the government is not dictated by natural law or reason: What is dictated by natural law is, rather, that whichever form of government is decided upon, the government must be "sovereign," all-powerful.

Yet Hobbes argues that in most times and places, the most stable and effective form of government is hereditary, absolute monarchy. He gives four principal reasons why hereditary monarchy is usually best – or superior to republican government – in his account of the advantages and disadvantages of the three forms of government, in chapter 19. In the first place, all men must be assumed to be selfish; in monarchy, there is a much closer link between the ruler's self-interest and the public prosperity than in any republic. The monarch sees the whole country as his own and so is less likely to favor one part over another. In republics, one has the dominance of private, competing, and potentially destructive interest groups. In the second place, kings get better advice, because they can call on anyone, and in secret, whereas in republics, discussion is more under the glare of publicity, and as a result everybody lies constantly, whipping up indignation with appeals to justice in order to advance private or group interests and prestige. Third, monarchies are more unified, and better capable than republics of acting with energy, secrecy, and steadfastness; monarchies are thus especially superior in foreign and defense policy. Finally, the succession is clearer and less contested if the monarchy is hereditary; elections are always a time of dangerous instability and rife with the potential for the outbreak of civil war.

Hobbes relies on the popularization of his philosophy to teach sovereigns that their interest lies in promoting the peace and material prosperity and security of their subjects, and to teach subjects that their interest lies in not trusting themselves or one another with political power. As he stresses in chapter 30 (see also 18.16), one of the most important duties of a government is public education, especially in political theory and political philosophy – the true, Hobbesian political philosophy. No political theorist prior to Hobbes ever stressed anywhere nearly as much as he does the crucial importance of popular mass education in political theory (19.9, 23.6, "Review and Conclusion," 4). In marked contradiction to what Socrates and Aristotle taught, for Hobbes, the philosopher is no longer supposed to bow to religious and poetic tradition – as in Socrates' gadfly section of the *Apology*. Instead, it becomes the business of the philosopher to replace classical civic and biblical religious traditions with a new theoretical basis for life and a new interpretation of the Bible.

"Inalienable" Individual Rights

Hobbes's doctrine of sovereignty is qualified to some degree by his teaching that "not all rights are alienable" (14.8). There are some rights that no one can be presumed to have ever contracted away. First and foremost, no one can ever be presumed to have agreed to sacrifice his own life, or to have authorized anyone else to violently threaten his life (14.29). Hence, Hobbes explains, when police come to arrest you, even if you have committed a crime, you have an absolute right to resist arrest. The sovereign's police forces, which likewise have the right to arrest you, must expect resistance and come with overwhelming force. Moreover, once you have been convicted of a crime, you have a perfect natural right to try to escape prison or to elude punishment; again, the state should know this, and be prepared to guard you with overwhelming force and intimidation (21.11–21). By the same token, no one can be asked to testify against himself – or against his close family. Hobbes is the philosophic source of the Fifth Amendment provision against self-incrimination enshrined in the American Bill of Rights. Furthermore, no *ex post facto* law is ever legitimate – Hobbes is the philosophic source of this prohibition in the American Constitution and other documents of liberal regimes. Again, no evidence that comes from torture is admissible in court (14.30). Hobbes is likewise the first political philosopher to strongly urge the need for trial by juries, which ought to have the final say as to law as well as fact, and over whose selection the indicted criminal or the individual parties in a civil suit ought to have a veto (23.8–9, 26.27). Nor can anyone be obliged to risk his life in battle (21.16); the sovereign must use military police to make sure that the threat of violent death from them is so much more certain than from the enemy that self-preservation dictates facing the latter. And Hobbes never ceases to stress that government should keep in mind its very limited objectives – protecting public and private physical security.

Sovereignty by Acquisition

Hobbes of course admits that there is no guarantee the government will keep to its limited legitimate objectives. The problem becomes more acute when Hobbes adds an additional big twist to his doctrine of the social compact. It turns out that there is another way in which the sovereign is established by consent or compact – a way quite different from the compact that Hobbes first focuses on but a way that is in fact much more usual or common in actual historical practice. There is sovereignty not only by "institution" – which we have described – but also by "acquisition," or "despotic" conquest (chapter 20, "Of Dominion Paternal and Despotic"). When a conqueror takes over a country and demands from the inhabitants a promise of eternal obedience, and offers in return permanent security, this is another valid covenantal origin of legitimate civil society.

In fact, Hobbes goes on to admit, this is the actual historical basis for most real regimes. If one looks into the history of almost every country, one will find some form of conquest at the origin – not a compact among the future subjects but instead a "compact" between the ruler of an already existing society and new subjects whom he conquers, at the point of a sword. But how exactly is such a covenant between conquerors and conquered justified under natural law? What are its distinctive principles once it comes into being? All covenants, Hobbes argues, are after all made out of fear. The only difference in the case of sovereignty by acquisition or dominion (conquest) is that one enters the compact out of fear of the conqueror, as well as of one another, whereas in case of sovereignty by institution, it is out of fear of one another. In both cases fear is the compelling motive; in both cases the purpose and the basis of governmental authority is the same. Government exists to bring about collective security, sought by rationally terrified individuals. And, Hobbes stresses, the rights and duties of sovereign and subjects are exactly the same in the two types of sovereignty.

Indeed, Hobbes later argues, this kind of sovereignty by acquisition or conquest is the basis of God's legitimate authority, first over the Hebrews and then through Christ. This is how Hobbes interprets the biblical covenant, first between God and Abraham, then with the Hebrews under Moses, and then between Jesus and mankind. We obey God because he is our conqueror, who threatens us with violent death, or worse, unless we agree to obey Him in everything – in which case he agrees to protect our life and liberty. Hobbes interprets the Bible as a perfect model of sovereignty by acquisition.

Moreover, this kind of sovereignty is, Hobbes argues, the basis of the human family. There is no family by nature, but only by the artifice of contract (the marriage contract, most obviously). The basis of the marriage contract is insecurity, fear: Parents have authority over their children because they terrify the children into promising to obey in return for security. First the mother does this, and then the father, or some man who by agreement is called honorifically the father – who, in nature, terrorizes the mother into obeying him. Civil society regulates the contract by preventing the father from threatening the wife with death or physical harm. No male has any authority over any female or her children except by consent of the woman, rooted in her anxiety or insecurity – which by nature the husband can of course obtain by conquest as well as by persuasion. Only in artificial civil society is the marriage contract made in a way that excludes the implicit threat of death to the female from the stronger male. Hobbes is the first great outspoken philosophic opponent of patriarchy, or of any conception of natural hierarchy between men and women or within the family.

It is especially the authoritarian character of Hobbes's solution, his conception of the kind of government that should be understood to be set up by the social compact, that his great follower John Locke disputes. Locke accepts with some qualifications the moral foundation that Hobbes teaches, but he has grave criticisms of the doctrine of the state – the government – that Hobbes built on those foundations. In the next chapter we will consider Locke's effective elaboration of, and major revisions to, Hobbes's teaching.

9

Locke's *Second Treatise of Government**

In moving from Hobbes to John Locke (1632–1704), we follow a key
development within modern political philosophy, entailing the qualified
acceptance of the fundamental principles of human nature as articulated by Hobbes, but accompanied by a severe criticism, and rejection,
of the way Hobbes implemented those principles in his prescriptions for
government. Locke argues that Hobbes has not adequately recognized
how easily government itself can become a threat to security and peace –
a threat far graver than the threats from groups and individuals in the
state of nature. For government has at its disposal more terrible power
than is possessed by any individual or group in the state of nature. That
terrible power can be abused by the humans who wield it, unless the
"mighty Leviathan" (sec. 98) is itself restrained, from within, by some system of checks and balances. Locke took Hobbes's basic theoretical foundation (the new conception of human nature as extremely dangerous)
and argued for building on that foundation a different and safer governmental structure. Locke thus set the agenda for the modern tradition of
liberal constitutionalism, constitution framing, and constitutional law.
(At the same time, we must not forget that the purer Hobbesian tradition, or what one might call the statist, or authoritarian, rights tradition,
has always continued to have deep influence and leading exemplars –
such as Napoleon in France; Bismarck in Germany; Atatürk in Turkey;
and Putin in Russia.)

---

* We recommend and use Peter Laslett's critical edition: *The Two Treatises of Government*
(Cambridge: Cambridge University Press, 1991). This is not only an accurate and well-an-
notated edition but, unlike most, it preserves the original italicization and capitalization
that Locke indicated was of importance to him. Our references will be by Locke's section
numbers, with our few references to the *First Treatise* indicated by the abbreviation "1T."

276

Locke's Rhetorical Genius

With this bird's-eye view of how Locke departs most obviously from Hobbes, we are *almost* prepared to turn to Locke's *Second Treatise*. But if we are going to understand Locke's writing – whose true message is more difficult of access than is Hobbes's – we have to begin by focusing in on an important disagreement Locke has with Hobbes concerning human nature. According to Hobbes, fear – anxiety about security – is *the* passion that is to be counted upon and built upon. Fear is the passion that can become reasonable, that can link up with and be guided by reason, and can therefore form the basis for a minimal but solid justice. Locke finds this insufficient. Hobbes stresses, on the other hand, that *the* dangerous passion is pride, or the desire for prestige – and Hobbes insists that the great purpose of the state and its education is to dampen and to repress human pride (see especially *Leviathan* 28.27). Here Locke again partly agrees: "The Natural Vanity and Ambition of Men" is but "too apt of it self to grow and increase" (1T sec. 10); however, Locke adds a major critical question and qualification. Can and must not reason also *make use of pride* – as a passionate concern for good repute and dignity, properly educated and molded – in order to give the necessary *spirited* strength to people's attachment to the rational rules, the so-called natural laws, that maintain peace and security? Does not Hobbes himself appeal to, and rely on, such a concern for reputation and prestige – the pride of being known as a person of honor and reason, a person who keeps his word, who can be trusted to keep the compact, and to abide by the natural laws? The trouble is, Hobbes does not take enough account of this (see especially *Leviathan* 15.10). In fact, Hobbes's whole teaching insults or affronts human pride, or humanity's sense of dignity. It does so by advocating a political system that is too authoritarian, by creating a political system that treats people too much like children, under a terrifying father. What is more, Hobbes does not take sufficient account of how deeply a sense of dignity is tied up with people's attachment to tradition and to traditional ways of thinking – especially patriotism, traditional religion, and (most immediately in Christian England) the Thomist natural law tradition. And here Locke, who belonged to the generation after Hobbes, could look around and see what the impact of Hobbes and his writings had been. In the generation after Hobbes published *Leviathan*, the book and Hobbes's name became, as Locke put it, "justly decried," as expressing atheism and enmity to human freedom as republicanism.

Locke strikes from the very outset a keynote of nationalistic pride and manly republican courage. The preface to his *Two Treatises of Government* states their purpose as being "to justifie to the World, the People of England, whose love of their Just and Natural Rights, with their Resolution to preserve them, saved the Nation when it was on the very brink of Slavery and Ruine" (referring to the Glorious Revolution of 1688). The first sentence of the introduction reads: "Slavery is so vile and miserable an Estate of Man, and so directly opposite to the generous Temper and Courage of our Nation; that 'tis hardly to be conceived, that an *Englishman*, much less a *Gentleman*, should plead for't."

Locke saw that Hobbes had failed to grasp the correct way to advocate an innovative and shocking teaching. He discerned that if the enlightenment Hobbes sought was going to advance – if the mass of humanity, starting with the educated opinion leaders, was to be won over to the novel, lowered, but true view of human nature – then that new view would have to be presented in a much more attractive way. Readers must be beguiled into thinking that the new view is merely a different version of the old and familiar – the traditional Christian and Aristotelian outlook. Readers need to be lulled into accepting a modified Hobbesian view of humanity, supposing that they are merely supplementing – not breaking with – the high view of the Bible and of the Greeks. In Locke's own words, "like a wary Physician, when he would have his Patient swallow some harsh or *Corrosive Liquor*, he mingles it with a large quantity of that, which may dilute it; that the scatter'd Parts may go down with less feeling, and cause less Aversion" (1T sec. 7).

What Locke achieved rhetorically reminds one a bit of Socrates and the Socratic rhetoric that pervades classical philosophic writing. Locke certainly rediscovered the need of philosophy to hide its radicalism under a veil of apparently conservative rhetoric. But there is an enormous difference in purpose, and thus in nature, between Lockean and Socratic rhetoric. Socratic rhetoric hides the radicalism of philosophy in order to keep philosophy and politics separate, to avoid entangling them. Socratic rhetoric is concerned that healthy politics will become corrupted if philosophy becomes very influential in society. Socratic rhetoric is even more worried that philosophy will become corrupted, or lose the purity of its independence of mind and freedom of questioning, if it takes over from religion the guidance and spiritual rule of society. Locke, following Hobbes, casts aside these twin concerns; Locke, following Hobbes, aims to make philosophy *the* source of guidance for a new, rationalized civil society and civil theology. Locke uses rhetorical veiling not to keep philosophy apart from politics but instead to make philosophy the shaping force behind politics. And Locke was, rhetorically and historically, extraordinarily successful. He was the one who really made the doctrines originated by Hobbes catch on, first with the literate and influential public, and very soon with the public at large – not only in the English-speaking world but also in continental Europe. Locke found a way to present the ideas of the state of nature, of natural rights, of acquisitive individualism, in such a way as to make those ideas no longer shocking to moralism and Christian piety. This was Locke's greatest original accomplishment. He became much more influential than Hobbes, partly because of genuine improvements he made in the substance of Hobbes's teaching, but mainly because of his extraordinary skill as a rhetorician.

Locke wished for a few future leaders, such as his close friends the Lords Shaftesbury, to catch on to his genuinely revolutionary, post-Hobbesian game plan. But he wanted most of his contemporary readers to be lulled into thinking that he was merely giving them a new and better way to be good Christians – only adding to, while liberalizing and making more effective, the traditional Thomist-Aristotelian political theory. Accordingly, Locke regularly cites and claims to be following venerable authorities – especially the Bible, and Richard Hooker, the theologian whose great work, *Laws of Ecclesiastical Polity*, rewrote the political theory of Thomist Aristotelianism to make it fit the Church of England. On the other hand, Locke never once refers to Hobbes. Locke makes it very easy for his contemporary readers to get the impression that he opposes Hobbes. But Locke never actually says a single word in criticism of or opposition to Hobbes; he simply never mentions him – even and precisely while adopting Hobbes's basic framework: the state of nature, the social compact, the priority of the individual and of individual rights, and the identification of natural law not with any innate, *a priori* moral principles or conscience but instead with reason and its *a posteriori* deductions.

Instead of attacking Hobbes, Locke presents his political philosophy as a polemic against another, much more obscure political theorist – Sir Robert Filmer, "and his followers" (see the full title of the *Two Treatises*: *Two TREATISES of Government: In the Former, The False Principles and Foundation of Sir Robert Filmer, And His Followers, Are Detected and Overthrown. The Latter is an ESSAY Concerning The True Original, Extent, and End of Civil-Government*). A generation before Locke and at the time of Hobbes, Filmer wrote vociferous defenses of biblical patriarchy as the basis of the divine right of kings. What makes Filmer so special (there were other more famous and influential theorists of the divine right of kings and biblical patriarchy, such as King James I, whom Locke also eventually quotes) is that Filmer published the very first traditionalist assault on Hobbes's *Leviathan*, right after that work was published. Filmer assailed *Leviathan* because he saw, correctly, that Hobbes totally rejected the biblical-divine right of kings and the whole traditional idea of biblical patriarchy as the foundation of the family and society. Filmer set out to refute the radical new foundation that Hobbes gave to monarchy and to the family and to all society – natural individual rights, and a new kind of natural law, based on the idea of the "state of nature."

So: while never mentioning Hobbes – except when referring to Filmer's work, entitled "Observations on Hobbs" – Locke devotes the first of his two treatises to refuting the arguments by which Hobbes's primary traditionalist critic tried to refute the new Hobbesian outlook. Locke thus tacitly *defends the soundness of Hobbes's underlying principles*. But the refutation of Filmer is at the same time an attack on *all* absolute monarchy. In the course of refuting Hobbes's refuter, Locke *shows that the foundations of Hobbes are irrefutable*. Locke rejects Hobbes's political solution, but on the basis of Hobbes's own underlying principles. To cover his trail, Locke appeals in the *Second Treatise* (but *not* in the *First*) to the authority of the leading Anglican Thomist Aristotelian, Richard Hooker; Locke duplicitously claims to be merely following Hooker.

The State of Nature

After summarizing in section one of the *Second Treatise* his previous refutation of Filmer, Locke announces in section two the theme he will now pursue: explaining the true meaning of "political *power*." In phrases that echo somewhat distantly the opening of Aristotle's *Politics*, Locke declares that one must distinguish the power of a political magistrate from that of a father, of a master, and of a husband. After this traditional-sounding start, in section three Locke gives a summary of his own understanding: "*Political Power*, then, I take to be a *Right* of making Laws with Penalties of Death, and consequently all less Penalties, for the Regulating and Preserving of Property, and of employing the force of the Community, in the Execution of such Laws, and in the defence of the Common-wealth from Foreign Injury; and all this only for the Publick Good." A little reflection discloses two highly significant departures from Aristotle and Aquinas. First, Locke speaks the language of "power" – the new language of Hobbes. Second, and more massively, Locke asserts that the purpose of domestic politics is limited to "regulating and preserving property."

Locke says nothing about virtue, or about making citizens the doers of noble deeds. Nor will Locke ever speak of the purpose of political life being virtue (*the* purpose of political life according to Aristotle, Aquinas, and Hooker).

In the second chapter, Locke suddenly introduces the state of nature – as a radically anarchic state: "To understand Political Power right, and derive it from its Original," he asserts, "we must consider what State all Men are naturally in"; and that is "a *State of perfect Freedom* to order their Actions, and dispose of their Possessions, and Persons as they think fit, within the bounds of the Law of Nature; without asking leave, or depending upon the Will of any other Man." A state also of "*Equality*, wherein all the Power and Jurisdiction is reciprocal, no one having more than another" (sec. 4). We recall that Aristotle in the second chapter of the *Politics* had also turned to the pre-political origins of the city. But Aristotle did so in order to argue that the human is by nature a political animal, and that the natural human condition is that of political rulers and ruled in cities. Locke argues the complete contrary. He follows Hobbes in contending that in their natural state all humans are absolutely free and equal, without any political order or rule of any kind.

But just as the reader might begin to ask whether this isn't Hobbesian doctrine, Locke rushes in with the rhetorical fire hose. All this, Locke insists, comes from good old Richard Hooker (5): "This *equality* of Men by Nature, the Judicious *Hooker* looks upon as so evident in it self, and beyond all question, that he makes it the Foundation of that Obligation to mutual Love amongst Men, on which he Builds the Duties they owe one another, and from whence he derives the great Maxims *of Justice and Charity*. His words are" – and Locke gives a long quotation from Hooker's *Laws of Ecclesiastical Polity*.

Now many of Locke's contemporary readers will glide along, content to see that Locke is quoting good old Hooker. But the alert readers see that in appealing to and quoting Hooker, Locke introduces a radically opposite way of conceiving human nature, and especially human equality. Hooker, as a good Anglican Thomist, speaks of an equality entailing *obligation* to mutual *love*, and "*Duty*," including above all *charity*. In the actual quotation that Locke gives, moreover, Hooker refers to the care of the *soul* and to the desire to *be loved* – as all fundamental to the Christian conception of human nature. Locke himself, when he is not quoting Hooker, when he is speaking with his own words, even here, does not employ any of these traditional terms or conceptions. Locke will almost never refer to mutual love, charity, or duties owed on such a basis (cf.

sec. 94 and 1T sec. 42). Conversely, Hooker for his part never once, in the hundreds of pages of his writing, mentions the "state of nature" and never says human beings are free by nature. Hooker teaches equality, but *not* on the basis of individual liberty. Locke, however, goes merrily on as if Hooker had in fact mentioned a "state of liberty": "[T]hough this be a *State of Liberty*" (Locke writes), "yet it is *not a State of Licence*: though Man in that State have an uncontroleable Liberty, etc." (sec. 6).

We have then, right at the start, a beautiful illustration of how Locke writes. He uses grand religious authorities in such a way as to pull the wool over the eyes of, and win agreement from, the majority of his contemporary, pious readers. Meanwhile, he grounds his doctrine on the conceptual framework of Hobbes: the state of nature, as a way of conceiving humans to be by nature totally independent individuals, without any political order. Locke exploits the revered Hooker, who never employed the Hobbesian categories at all, to make the Hobbesian categories and terminology appear respectable and even traditional. At the same time, Locke shows revolutionary readers how profound (and how outrageous, though also comic) a break he is making with the traditional biblical-Aristotelian authorities.

Locke next defines the difference between liberty and license: Though every human has by nature an "uncontroleable" liberty, "yet he has not Liberty to destroy himself, or so much as any Creature in his Possession, but where some nobler use than its bare Preservation calls for it" (sec. 6). So the first and fundamental limit on liberty, which distinguishes liberty from license, is exactly as in Hobbes: No one has a liberty to destroy himself. Self-preservation would appear to be the basic "law of nature." But there is a second dimension to this, in which a certain difference from Hobbes does appear. Locke speaks at once of *possessing* other creatures, as one's own private property, and the limitation on liberty is extended to a prohibition on destroying one's own property. And we see that the primary meaning of property in Locke is the private possession of other *living* creatures, whom one can *kill* or "destroy" – but only for a "nobler use" than *their* own preservation. Locke leaves us momentarily wondering what such a "nobler use" might be.

Locke elaborates further on the "Law of Nature" that defines the difference between liberty and license: "Reason, which is that Law, teaches all Mankind, who will but consult it, that, being all *equal* and *independent*, no one ought to harm another in his Life, Health, Liberty, or Possessions" (sec. 6). The law of nature Locke identifies with reason, not with the conscience, and unlike the conscience in Thomist theory, for

Locke reason is operative only if and when it is "consulted": Contrary to Aquinas and Hooker, Locke in his *Essay Concerning Human Understanding* (bk. 1, chaps. 3–4) explicitly and unqualifiedly denies the existence of any innate moral ideas. Even more striking is the fact that Locke's natural law, like that of Hobbes, is negative. The law of reason tells us *not* to harm others, to *avoid* what is bad. It does not tell us to *seek* the *good*, or to *help* one another. There is no hierarchy of natural inclinations as in Thomas Aquinas or Richard Hooker; instead, as in Hobbes, there is only the lowest basic level of natural inclination to self-preservation – which has been transmogrified from a positive duty of mutual love into a negative avoiding of harm to one another.

But just as the pious contemporary reader might again think that this is sounding a lot like Hobbes, Locke gives yet another, different, reason and basis for the natural law: "Men being all the Workmanship of one Omnipotent, and infinitely wise Maker; All the Servants of one Sovereign Master, sent into the World by his order and about his business, they are his Property, whose Workmanship they are, made to last during his, not one anothers Pleasure" (sec. 6). At first sight, it is easy to assume that Locke is talking about the biblical God and expressing some version of a Christian religious outlook. But if one looks at this reference to the "Maker" and "Master" (Locke does not speak of "God," let alone of Christ) more closely, one sees that this omnipotent being is very different from the Christian or biblical God. Locke does not say humans are "created in the image of God." Locke here uses no biblical language. He does not characterize the "Master" as good, or as just, or as loving. The "Master" whom reason can see in nature is simply an all-powerful and wise owner: What he is concerned with is *his* business, for which he uses us as his chattel slaves. We are left wondering: What is this "business" that we are supposed to be doing for this Master who owns us? Locke does not say, and he will never say. What he does go on to say is that we *are free to destroy* all the inferior ranks of creatures, for our own use – thus taking back, or drastically qualifying, what he had first said, when he wrote that we were not allowed to destroy the other animals except for a nobler use than their preservation. That nobler use turns out to be anything we happen to need – such as breakfast or shoe leather.

Locke gives a third argument why humans ought not to hurt one another, and this is a perfectly Hobbesian argument, though rendered in noble-sounding phraseology: "Every one as he is *bound to preserve himself*, and not to quit his Station willfully; so by the like reason when his own Preservation comes not in competition, ought he, as much as he can, *to preserve the rest of Mankind*, and may not unless it be to do Justice on an Offender, take away, or impair the life, or what tends to the Preservation of Life, Liberty, Health, Limb, or Goods of another" (sec. 6). For the "*like* reason" that you preserve yourself, you should seek peace and preservation for everyone else – *so long as your own preservation comes not in competition*. By this Lockean natural law, it is always a violation of natural law, always a crime or sin, to sacrifice one's life for anyone, or anything.

The next big question Locke addresses is: How is this minimalist law of nature enforced? "[T]he *Execution* of the Law of Nature" is "put into every Mans hands, whereby every one has a right to punish the transgressors of that Law to such a Degree, as may hinder its Violation" (sec. 7). Our "Omnipotent ... Master" in no way enforces the law or protects the innocent; unlike Aquinas, Locke makes no reference to the pangs of a guilty conscience as the natural punishment that enforces the natural law – even though Locke now mentions the conscience, together with reason, as the sole restraint on human individuals' execution of retributive punishment as singular vigilantes. Under Lockean natural law, every single person has a perfect right to execute any other person or persons anywhere in the world whom he thinks may pose a threat to anyone else's property (sec. 8): "[E]very man" may "restrain, or where it is necessary, destroy things noxious to them, and so may bring such evil on any one, who hath transgressed that Law, as may make him repent the doing of it, and thereby deter him, and by his Example, others, from doing the like mischief." Locke immediately admits that this will seem "to some" a "very strange Doctrine" (sec. 9); then, repeating, he soon agrees that in fact this *is* a "strange Doctrine" (sec. 13). No one in human history, not even Hobbes, had ever argued for such an extreme right before – a natural right in every person to kill any- and everyone else, anywhere, as a retributive executioner. (Hobbes had spoken only of a right to kill in self-defense, not in executing retribution for threats to a third party.) A little later Locke makes even more explicit that everyone has a natural right to execute anyone whom he judges a threat, not only to himself but to anyone else anywhere on earth (sec. 16). But Locke rushes in with his cover, this time apparent biblical authority (sec. 11): "[U]pon this" (he claims) "is grounded the great Law of Nature, *Who so sheddeth Mans Blood, by Man shall his Blood be shed. And Cain* was so fully convinced, that every one had a Right to destroy such a Criminal, that after the Murther of his Brother, he cries out, *Every one that findeth me, shall slay me*, so plain" (Locke claims) "was it writ in the Hearts of all Mankind." When we examine the actual biblical passages that Locke brings in and refers us to here (Gen. 9:6 and 4:14) we see that in fact the Bible directly contradicts Locke. In the Scripture, when Cain says everyone will kill him, God immediately says that that is wrong, that no one will do so. And the divine *positive* law, which lays it down that capital punishment is the penalty for murder, is instituted only *many centuries* later, after the flood. Locke jams together two quite different biblical passages, referring to epochs eons apart in the biblical narrative. While pretending to reproduce the biblical teaching, he reminds the careful reader that of course in the Bible there is no state of nature at all; there is a state of paradise, which men lost because of their sin, followed by a state that lasted a long time, before the flood, when there was no meat eating allowed (no killing of animals for food), and there was no capital punishment. Only after God intervened with the flood, many generations after the Fall, does God finally allow humans to eat meat, and, at the same time, also imposes on humans the divine *positive* law of capital punishment for murder. While pretending, then, to show how biblical his concept of natural law is, Locke quietly helps us to see how "very strange" it is – how *totally un*biblical it is.

Locke's "strange Doctrine," of everyone having by natural right the executive power to kill anyone else deemed a threat to anyone anywhere, implies that the state of nature is as dangerously antagonistic as Hobbes taught, or maybe even more so – although for reasons somewhat different from the ones Hobbes gave. Here we see a slight but significant difference in the two thinkers' conceptions of what makes humans so terribly dangerous by nature. This difference comes out in section 13, where Locke suddenly conjures up someone disagreeing with him and questioning him and his "strange Doctrine" of the executive power in the state of nature. The questioner argues that Locke's doctrine implies that the state of nature is a condition of terrible war and anarchy; surely this cannot be right. Surely God has given us government? In response to this questioner, Locke readily concedes that what he has been saying means that the state of nature would be a condition, as Locke says, "not to be endured." For while everyone has the right to impose capital punishment, "it is unreasonable for Men to be Judges in their own Cases," and "Self-love will make Men partial to themselves and their Friends"; on the other side, "Ill Nature, Passion and Revenge will carry them too far in punishing others"; and "hence nothing but Confusion and Disorder will follow" (sec. 13). Locke agrees that this is the case. But he does not agree with the objector's suggested solution. There is no God-appointed government; God gives no solution to the "Evils" of our natural condition. The only remedy available is a man-made, artificial remedy: "civil government" – whose basis is a "social compact," among humans, in which God plays no part, as Locke specifies in the next section (sec. 14). The God discernible in nature has left men to fend for themselves, to invent government as their remedy for their unendurable God-given condition. But Locke also indicates his political disagreement with Hobbes. The best solution is *not* absolute monarchy. In fact, Locke here says, absolute monarchy is worse than the state of nature.

At the end of the second chapter, Locke anticipates someone making the objection that there never was such a state of nature, without government. Echoing Hobbes, Locke answers: International relations *always* are such a state of nature. Locke adds – again echoing Hobbes – that individuals are in such a state, in relation to one another *wherever* there does not obtain between them the social compact. But then, to soften the argument, Locke in conclusion (sec. 15) appeals once more to Hooker, covering his trail to marvelous effect while again indicating his radical break with Hooker.

By the end of the second chapter we may well be wondering whether in fact Locke has not implied that the state of nature is simply a state of war. In the third chapter Locke turns explicitly to this question, or to the precise relation between the state of nature and the state of war. He loudly insists that the state of war is different from the state of nature. He thus seems to highlight a big difference between himself and Hobbes. But *how big* is the difference between the state of nature and the state of war, and thus between Hobbes and Locke on this matter?

Locke begins to answer this question by elaborating even more clearly than before that every person has a perfect natural right, whenever anyone has been threatened, to treat the one who has posed the threat like a vicious animal who has launched a state of war. At first Locke speaks as if only very unambiguous forms of life-threatening aggression constitute the beginning of war. But then in section 17 he argues that whenever anyone tries to get another man under his absolute power, this also constitutes a life threat. For freedom, Locke says here, is the "Fence" to "my Preservation."

Then, in section 18, Locke argues that all this implies that even theft, carried out by force, even without any actual bodily hurt, or any clear indication of intention to do bodily injury, constitutes a deprivation of liberty, and thereby a life threat that justifies killing the thief or attempted thief. Locke here makes it clear that private property and its protection are intimately bound up with the true meaning of liberty, which is valued as the fence to preservation. His implicit reasoning here is as follows. We must survive, and in order to secure survival, we must remain at liberty – that is, we must retain a liberty that meaningfully protects our security. Such liberty must include the liberty to acquire and to keep and to protect material possessions, so that we won't starve. Therefore, anyone who threatens our property may rightfully be killed as a vicious animal.

All this, Locke says next, shows the plain difference between the state of nature and the state of war. But his formulation is very ambiguous: "[H]ere we have the plain *difference between the State of Nature and the State of War*, which however [much] some Men have confounded, are as far distant, as a State of Peace, Good Will, Mutual Assistance and Preservation, and a State of Enmity, Malice, Violence and Mutual Destruction, are one from another" (sec. 19, beg.). But how far is that, in nature? In section 21, Locke observes that in the state of nature "every the least difference is apt to end" in war. This is "one great reason of Men's putting themselves into Society, and quitting the State of Nature." The difference with Hobbes shrinks the closer one examines Locke's account of the state of nature and its constant tendency to rapidly degenerate into a state of war. In fact, when he revisits the state of nature teaching in chapter 9, Locke makes this plainer: "If Man in the State of Nature be so free, as has been said; If he be absolute Lord of his own Person and Possessions, equal to the greatest, and subject to no Body, why will he part with his Freedom?" Why will he "subject himself to the Dominion and Controul of any other Power?" "To which," Locke declares, "'tis obvious to Answer," that "though in the state of Nature he hath such a right, yet the Enjoyment of it is very uncertain, and constantly exposed to the Invasion of others." For "all being Kings as much as he, every Man his Equal, and the greater part no strict Observers of Equity and Justice, the enjoyment of the property he has in this state is very unsafe, very unsecure." This "makes him willing to quit this Condition, which however free, is full of fears and continual dangers" (sec. 123).

But we must not overlook the significant difference that remains between Locke and Hobbes on this point. Locke never says, as does Hobbes (near the end of chapter 13 of *Leviathan*), that the notion of justice has no place in the state of nature. Locke speaks as if humans have by nature a readier ability to think morally – to regard their lives, liberty, and property as theirs by right. But this very fact, which at first seems to soften as well as to elevate somewhat the state of nature, and the conception of human nature, makes human nature in a major sense *more* violent, more dangerous, than Hobbes had said. For as Locke stresses,

the fact that humans so readily conceive of their self-preservation as a
right, or in moral terms, means that humans are by nature very inclined
to be punitive and retributive. To put the contrast another way: Whereas
Hobbes sees pride, or the proclivity to vainglorious lust for domination,
as the chief threat, Locke speaks less of simple pride or vain glory and
instead highlights the dangerous expression of human pride taking a
moralistic form – as a retributive reaction, or payback, in the name of
a self-righteous assertion of essentially defensive rights. Still, this means
that for Locke, what naturally drives men to kill one another has more of
a basis in a passionate sense of justice – something that can, if it is made
reasonable, be a basis for stable peace through law and order.

In chapter 4, Locke deepens his account of human nature, or the natural state, by discussing thematically the nature of human liberty. But
he does so in a strange way: He focuses on the negation of liberty – slavery. Here Locke indicates in yet another way his important secondary
disagreement with Hobbes. Locke insists that however chaotic and dangerous it is to live as a free individual in the state of nature, there is something even worse, and that is to be a slave to some other human. And
as Locke will later stress, some governments reduce subjects to slaves.
Locke stresses more than does Hobbes the importance of liberty – as "so
necessary to, and closely joyned with a Man's Preservation, that he cannot part with it, but by what forfeits his Preservation and Life together"
(sec. 23). Liberty is not here presented by Locke as something good in
itself; liberty is to be valued as an *essential means*, to preservation. In this
respect there is no difference from Hobbes. Where Locke differs from
Hobbes is in his understanding of what is the most important expression
of liberty: He stresses much more than did Hobbes the importance of
economic liberty – of freedom to protect and to preserve one's material
property.

Property

This becomes vividly clear in the next chapter – the fifth and most
important chapter in the work – where Locke lays down the moral foundations of what came to be called capitalism. Locke is the first philosopher in history to give a moral argument claiming that justice, or the
common good – of all humanity – requires society to devote itself chiefly
to encouraging every individual to pursue the limitless, self-interested
acquisition of ever more and more private material possessions and economic buying power (money), so long as each person respects the right

of every other person to do likewise. In other words, Locke is the first to argue that peacefully competitive acquisitiveness is the core of justice and civic morality.

To understand the full significance of what Locke is doing in chapter 5, we must remind ourselves again of the historical context – of what the moral culture was *before* the enormous influence of this chapter changed everything. We need to recall what Aristotle taught about moneymaking in book one of the *Politics*, and what Thomas Aquinas taught, following Aristotle and the Bible. We have to stop taking for granted the decency of capitalism, and see how questionable capitalism looked in the light of the religious and moral views that reigned before Locke. Only then will we appreciate and follow what Locke is going to argue – and how artfully his rhetoric proceeds, in weaning people away from the biblical and Aristotelian outlook.

As we have seen, the Christian-Aristotelian traditions, like the Judaic and Islamic Aristotelian traditions of political philosophy – all rooted in Socrates, and what he said in the gadfly section of the *Apology* – sternly condemn material acquisitiveness. They all view the love of money as a degrading and addictive corruption of the higher, spiritual purposes of politics: the cultivation of virtue, civic and intellectual, conceived either as the core of human happiness, or as the worldly preparation for happiness in a life after death. The concern with material property is supposed to be strictly subordinated to being the "equipment" (as Aristotle calls it) needed for a virtuous life, including above all the virtue of charity or generosity, which is expressed in the wise and noble giving away of one's property. Aristotle in book one of the *Politics* discourages, while Aquinas prohibits as sinful, the use of one's surplus property to make more money by getting interest from investing it. Furthermore, the property that one does keep, as privately owned, is to be understood – in the classical and Christian framework – as belonging, fundamentally, not to oneself but to the community, for which the legal owner should be understood to be acting as temporary steward.

In Hobbes, as we have seen, the basis of this whole outlook is overthrown. Virtue is drastically reinterpreted to mean not spiritual fulfillment or fellowship, but simply those artificially cultivated habits and dispositions that conduce to peaceful coexistence of humans, understood as by nature essentially competitive and mutually endangering individuals. And Hobbes makes it clear that it is economic competition, and the quest for material prosperity in a market of free buyers and sellers, that is the safest and most reasonable form of competition for power and prestige. Hobbes thus takes the first big steps toward the moral outlook that undergirds what came to be called capitalism or the free market. But Hobbes still does not make productive labor, and acquisitive entrepreneurship, key moral virtues; Locke does. Hobbes does not entirely break free from the view that economic competition is a zero-sum game, with the winners essentially making things worse for the losers; Locke is the first thinker to make this break. Hobbes does not clearly make economic security the most important form of security; Locke does. Hobbes does not identify the most basic natural right – to self-preservation – with the natural right to exclusive, private material property; Locke does. Hobbes does not make the chief purpose of government the protection of property; Locke does. Hobbes does not teach that any of the laws of nature strictly limit the government's power to tax, or to take away material possessions; Locke makes precisely such a natural law limitation *the* most important limitation on government. "No taxation without representation" is the rallying cry of Lockean political theory (sec. 142).

In presenting his teaching on property, just as in presenting his teaching on human nature, Locke allows and even encourages most of his contemporary pious readers – whom Locke knows will be less than careful and thoughtful readers – to suppose that they can adopt his new understanding while still holding on to the traditional Christian understanding. At the same time, by drawing attention to that traditional view, Locke prods his thoughtful readers to see how decisively he is breaking with it.

Locke begins chapter 5 (sec. 25) in his usual traditional-sounding way. We can be guided, he says, either by natural reason or by supernatural revelation, since they both teach the same. He thus sounds again like a version of Aquinas or Hooker. But when one looks more closely, one sees that according to Locke, reason and revelation do not in fact teach the same. Reason teaches the *natural* right to self-preservation, and *hence* the right to *meat* and other things. Therefore, or on this basis, we can conclude that the God *visible in nature* has given the earth to mankind in common. In contrast, revelation or the Bible teaches that God is the owner of all, and, as owner, gave specific, *very limited* grants to mankind, and that it is only on the basis of these positive divine permissions, not on the basis of natural right, that mankind owns the earth in common. Locke quietly indicates that the right to self-preservation plays little or no role in the Bible. (In fact, such a right is never mentioned anywhere in the Bible.) And Locke reminds readers that in the Bible, what God gives to mankind is a very limited grant, with very strict dietary restrictions – above all, for most of human existence, until after the flood, no *meat* eating was allowed – no hunting of the other animals for food (cf. 1T sec. 39).

Locke then specifies the big puzzle, or what appears, as he puts it, "to some to be a very great difficulty": How, from original *common* ownership, does there derive the moral right individuals have to *exclusive private* property, especially in land, without any need to get the agreement of the rest of humanity, who are previously fellow owners (sec. 25)?

The first step in Locke's answer (sec. 26) is the observation that God, who gave the world to men in common, also gave them reason, which tells them to "use" the world for their "advantage" and "convenience" and "comfort": *Reason* tells humans to be utilitarian in their attitude toward nature. Locke does not say a word to the effect that reason tells us to contemplate the world with admiration, or to be stewards of nature as intrinsically good. Locke speaks only of the direction given by God *through reason*; he ceases to speak of the direction given by biblical revelation.

The second step (still in sec. 26) is the proposition that if humans are to "use" the earth and all therein, then they must be able as individuals to "*appropriate*" from the common property, so "that another can no longer have any right to" that originally common property. Locke's leading example is the deer that must be *killed* so as to be then eaten as *venison* by a Native American. From the outset, the right of private property is conceived as a right to *consume*, even or especially by *killing* and eating. As Locke put it in the *First Treatise* (sec. 92): "Property, whose Original is from the Right a Man has to use any of the Inferior Creatures, for the Subsistence and Comfort of his Life, is for the benefit and sole Advantage of the Proprietor, so that he may even destroy the thing, that he has Property in by his use of it, where need requires." How exactly does a person acquire so total a right over what began as common property?

In a third step (sec. 27), Locke argues that humans have exclusive property in their own persons. Locke rather glaringly contradicts, or drops, his opening claim (back in sec. 6) that each of us is the property of God. That claim plays no part in Locke's thematic discussion of the truth about property. He next adds a major corollary: Whatever *labor* any person does *with* his or her body or person *also* belongs *exclusively* to the laboring person.

Locke then takes a momentous further step. Whatever anyone changes or alters from its natural condition through one's labor – by killing, or destroying, such as the deer slain by the native American – becomes *entirely* the property of the *individual* person who so labors and destroys. Locke is silent about any duty to try to make the property, so "appropriated" through labor, benefit others, who were originally co-owners. Locke makes no reference whatsoever to any duties of stewardship or charity. He thus provokes the thoughtful reader to ask: What justifies this exclusively selfish and destructive attitude toward appropriation and use? Locke does add one large limitation on the right of appropriation: One may take what one wishes from the common stock "at least where there is enough, and as good left in common for others" (sec. 27 end).

Locke moves in the next section (sec. 28) to give two very different answers to the question of why there is no need to get any fellow owner's consent to consume what begins as common property. His first answer is that people would starve to death if each had to get *all* the rest of mankind's express consent whenever each took something from the common property for his own private benefit. Yet to this there is an obvious Thomistic objection: Why should not reason or natural law dictate that at least *neighboring* fellow owners in the vicinity should be consulted, for their consent, and why should not each of us by natural law have some duty of charity dictating that we offer some share of the benefit to those neighboring fellow owners? Locke silences all such objections by immediately giving a second answer: there is *natural abundance*. Material goods are like the water flowing in a fountain (sec. 29), or like the fish in the ocean (sec. 30). Locke repeatedly speaks here of nature as "our common Mother," as if there is a benevolent nature that flows with milk for us all as "her children." There is no need to consult or to worry at all about the welfare of fellow owners, because there is abundance for all.

Now to this Locke himself raises a major objection (sec. 31), which he anticipates some thoughtful reader making. What has been said so far implies that anyone may acquire *without limit*. Locke answers by taking another step. *Reason* severely limits how much anyone can appropriate. How so? Any goods acquired by labor, if accumulated beyond a very modest amount, *spoil*, before their owner can use, consume, or enjoy them. In original nature there was therefore little or no competition, for these two reasons: First, because there was plenty for everyone, and, second, because the *rational* limit on taking, spoilage, kept everyone's private property very bounded.

But then Locke suddenly jumps (sec. 32) from the original natural condition to the contemporary economy "now," in England – when property is mainly not in deer and fruits, but rather in the land, "the *Earth it self*," as "that which takes in and carries with it all the rest." But the land is "now" all appropriated and divided up! In the contemporary developed economy – as Locke has indicated in passing (at sec. 28, line 22), with his striking reference to an employer *owning the labor done by his hired* "Servant." The majority have to sell their labor power, for wages, to the minority who own all the land and raw materials. How is this enormous inequality justified? Locke quietly prompts us to see that the moral puzzle he is posing is even bigger than first seemed.

Locke takes the first step in resolving this bigger puzzle by beginning to show quietly that the account thus far has deliberately exaggerated the plenty and abundance of nature. Locke has been imitating what the Bible and Aristotle claim – that mankind is situated in a natural order that is fundamentally good for, or adequate to, human needs, and that it is only human sin or vice that makes nature seem scarce, or that makes us think that we are under some natural necessity driving us to accumulate without limit. Locke has reproduced this traditional outlook in order to let his pious contemporary readers think he agrees with it, while prodding his thoughtful readers to see that he is challenging it.

Locke begins to shift to his true premises when he says for the first time that when God gave the land in common, he "commanded Man also to labour, and *the penury of his Condition required it of him*" (sec. 32, our emphasis). Human labor is not just God's command, as given to Adam in a plentiful Garden of Eden. Hard labor is a *natural necessity*. By nature, there is *not* abundance but "penury," *poverty*. Locke goes a step further (still in sec. 32): Mankind must not only labor; mankind must "subdue" the earth – the earth is like an enemy.

But then Locke takes a step back, and repeats in the next section (sec. 33) his insistence that in the beginning there was always "enough, and as good left" for others. By again repeating the analogy of water from a fountain – as if nature plentifully produces, by itself, without our labor, all that we need, our philosophic teacher makes it clear that he wants us to confront the puzzle. In the next sections, Locke intensifies the puzzle. In section 35, he points out how dramatically different from the conditions of original nature are the conditions in a developed country such as England, where the land is all enclosed, and where "there is Plenty of People under Government, who have Money and Commerce." There has, then, been a vast increase in population and in accumulation of wealth, through trade, which has accompanied the removal of all land from the common ownership of humanity. Still, how is all this justified, or even sensible, given the spoilage limitation, and given the fact that it entails the freezing out of later generations from access to any common, unowned land?

Locke next introduces (sec. 36) *the* key point that will solve the riddle that he has so posed. He observes that in places where there is still uncultivated or unclaimed land, as in parts of Spain, the people are *grateful* for anyone who goes out and clears it, fences it in, makes it private, and thus makes it productive. For prior to that, it is "neglected, and consequently waste Land." In other words, Locke begins to point out that when land is uncultivated, left in common, it is wasted, because unproductive.

Locke then turns (sec. 37) to explain why or how the spoilage limitation ceases to have any effect. He notes that humans invented *money* – as something that does *not spoil*, and that can be *amassed*, therefore, *without any limit under natural law or reason.* Money was invented first in the form of gold as well as other metals or stones that are scarce and pretty but not subject to spoilage, and there was a tacit agreement to let these things be exchangeable always for a given amount of each of the other truly useful things. This artificial invention revolutionized human existence. It allowed industrious persons to amass wealth or buying power without any limit, and to use their amassed wealth to hire others to work for them on more and more land that they fenced in. The invention of money drove the process that leads to the commercial nations of today, in which there is no more free land. Money allows the growth of an extreme inequality in property, based on enclosure of all the land. Government was created to regulate and to secure this unequal distribution of property, together with the hierarchy of owners and wage laborers that accompanies it.

In sections 35–39, Locke speaks at some length, but ambiguously, about this whole process – referring in section 38 emphatically to the biblical depiction of early economic conditions. He seems, on one hand, to condemn the discovery of gold and the invention of money – as if it overturned a pastoral simplicity and purity and equality that was truly good for humans – a kind of Golden Age. This outlook, he makes clear, harmonizes with the Bible, which implies that mankind is intended to live a simple pastoral existence, like Abel or later Abraham.

Yet at the same time that he invokes and reminds us of this traditional outlook, Locke continues to point out that prior to cultivation, the land was such as to be waste. And then suddenly Locke gives us the solution to the puzzle, the answer to the big question of why it is morally justified to enclose and privatize land. He argues that since land left to itself is waste, and since there is in fact terrible *scarcity* by nature, it follows that he who takes land out of the common and fences it in, and converts it to private property, in fact *does the greatest service to mankind.* Far from taking away anything of value from anyone, such a person is creating desperately needed value for all: "[H]e who appropriates land to himself by his labour, does not lessen but increase the common stock of mankind." For "the provisions serving to the support of humane life, produced by one acre of inclosed and cultivated land, are (to speak much within compasse) ten times more, than those, which are yielded by an acre of Land, of an equal richnesse, lyeing wast in common." And "therefor he, that incloses land, and has a greater plenty of the conveniencys of life from ten acres, than he could have from an hundred left to Nature, may truly be said, to give ninety acres to Mankind." Nay, Locke continues, "I have here rated the improved land very low in making its product but as ten to one, when it is much nearer an hundred to one." For "I aske," Locke expostulates, "whether in the wild woods and uncultivated wast of *America* left to Nature, without any improvement, tillage, or husbandry, a thousand acres will yield the needy and wretched inhabitants as many conveniencies of life as ten acres of equally fertile land doe in *Devonshire*, where they are well cultivated?" (sec. 37). The example of the Native Americans shows that prior to enclosure and cultivation, humans live "needy and wretched" lives. Greed, which motivates honest labor, and limitless accumulation, are not exploitative but beneficial for all mankind.

This also gives us the moral justification for the invention and use of money, which liberates the human thirst to acquire property without limit (sec. 48): "As different degrees of Industry were apt to give Men Possessions in different Proportions, so this *Invention of Money* gave them the opportunity to continue and enlarge them." For "[w]here there is not something both lasting and scarce, and so valuable to be hoarded up, there Men will not be apt to enlarge their *Possessions of Land*, were it never so rich, never so free for them to take." "[I]n the beginning," Locke declares (quietly echoing, while defying, the Bible), "all the World was *America*, and more so than that is now; for no such thing as *Money* was any where known." But "[f]ind out something that hath the *Use and Value of Money* amongst his Neighbours, you shall see the same Man will begin presently to enlarge his Possessions" (sec. 49). Locke returns time and again to the Native Americans for his empirical proof: "There cannot be a clearer demonstration of any thing," he submits, "than several Nations of the *Americans* are of this, who are rich in Land, and poor in all the Comforts of Life; whom Nature having furnished as liberally as any other people, with the materials of Plenty, *i.e.* a fruitful Soil, apt to produce in abundance what might serve for food, rayment, and delight; yet, for *want of improving it by labour*, have not one hundredth part of the

Conveniencies we enjoy" (sec. 41). The truth about the human condition emerges if we turn away from the Bible, or Aristotle, and look at America and the Native Americans. Then we see that not sin but horrible natural scarcity is the human problem. Humans are not wrong to want to transform nature, because nature left to itself is "waste"-land for humans. And the love of money, if it is a love of money made through honest labor, and investment in hiring such labor, to transform the earth by cultivation, is not at all sinful – to the contrary! The few who own the land and hire people to work on it are not exploiting anyone but instead making everyone's lives better. Again Locke appeals to the empirical example of Native Americans. Look at how they live, he says, in comparison with the poorest classes in England; what do you find? "[A] King of a large fruitful Territory" in America "feeds, lodges, and is clad worse than a day Labourer in *England*" (sec. 41, end).

This is crucial. The lowest of the low in the working class, a day laborer, in a country where the land is all fenced in, is better off than the highest of the highest class among the Native Americans, where there is no money, the spoilage limit remains, and hence the land is left in common. The vast inequalities that result from acquisitiveness are justified because they vastly elevate the material condition of even the lowest rung of society, if they are workers. Human labor does not, then, really "appropriate" value from nature, in the sense of accepting it as one drinks water from a fountain; that is a totally mistaken, traditional view. The truth is that human labor *creates* value, out of an intrinsically almost worthless nature: It is "*Labour* then which *puts the greatest part of Value upon Land*, without which it would scarcely be worth any thing." "Nature and the Earth furnished only the almost worthless Materials" (sec. 43).

This gradually disclosed truth about our natural condition has enormous political implications for what ought to be the goal of wise policy, and what is the true meaning of "protecting" property. A rational public policy, aimed at justice as the common good, must not merely protect possessions, especially of land, but must stimulate more and more productive work on land – and not only on land but on all other raw materials – in such a way as to produce more food and goods that will allow more people to survive in greater and greater physical well-being. Those who devise machines and techniques for using the land and resources that they own to make them more and more productive, and who then invest the money they thus make to hire others to work under them to create more and more money, generate more and more wealth and hence physical comfort for everyone. The new civil society will indeed, then, be devoted chiefly to the protection and regulation of private property, but private property understood in a specific new spirit, which later came to be called the "spirit of capitalism." The point is to encourage everyone to labor, to work productively, both mentally and physically. For almost everything of value, everything humans need in order to survive in security, has to be created by human labor. And the only reliable incentive to hard mental and physical labor is, on the positive side, guaranteeing to people that in return for working they will accumulate more and more property, more and more economic buying power of their own – without limit. The negative side of the incentive is ensuring that those who do not work productively in this sense suffer deep insecurity, by dint of their lack of money. Locke interrupts his account of the origins of private property rights in land to speak of what is implied for wise governance as follows: "This shews, how much numbers of men are to be preferred to largeness of dominions, and that the increase of lands and the right employing of them is the great art of government," and "that Prince who shall be so wise and godlike as by established laws of liberty to secure protection and incouragement to the honest industry of Mankind against the oppression of power and narrownesse of Party will quickly be too hard for his neighbours" (sec. 42).

The preeminent practical challenge for wise government is not, then, as the Bible and Aristotle claim, how to share or to divide up, to distribute wealth, or how to use it nobly, in charity and generosity. The challenge is instead how to *generate* wealth by human labor – since there is nothing but poverty and "worthless materials" by nature. Locke implicitly argues that the basic teaching of both the Bible and Aristotle is unjust, immoral – because based on a destructive falsehood that intensifies rather than alleviates natural *poverty* and perpetuates the enslavement of some humans by others in order to escape that poverty.

This is the justification for Locke's assertion about the end or purpose of government as being simply "the protection of property," as Locke said from the start (sec. 3) and repeats again emphatically in the chapter on the ends of government (sec. 124). But this notion of protection of property is accompanied by or involves also the "regulation" of property, as Locke says repeatedly (secs. 3, 50, and 120). Locke is *not* advocating that government merely maintain whatever happens to be the given distribution of property, especially in land. We must not suppose that he is saying that all or even most ownership in a developed society arises from labor on the land or on property owned. Labor is only the original, natural title to land and to other property. In a *developed* commercial society, most actual ownership results from purchase or inheritance. What people acquire through their labor is not the finished products that they make but instead money – for which they have sold their labor power and its fruits. Money gives to the workers buying power, which they use to acquire things they never worked on, or which they invest buying interest-bearing securities, or which they leave to their heirs. What Locke calls "the great art of government" (sec. 42) is the art of *regulating* property, and the market, and inheritance, and taxation, so as to prevent the accumulation of power and property in a few *idle* hands, and to promote accumulation in the hands of those who work the hardest and most intelligently or productively. Locke is all for redistributing land and wealth away from the idle rich to the hardworking rich and ambitious or upward-mobile poor. Government should strive to enhance incentives for the working rich and poor – to make everyone see that they can hope by hard work to become more and more prosperous. Accordingly, while the frame of government that Locke elaborates as a model in the later chapters is very much rooted in the example of the English system emerging after the Glorious Revolution, Locke has little if anything good to say about the landed aristocracy of the England of his time; the House of Lords, or any distinct political power for a hereditary landed nobility, has no place in Locke's recommendations for government.

But Locke himself does not develop the "great art of government" or what came to be called "political economy." He leaves its elaboration to his successors, the theorists who brought into being the modern science of economics – thinkers such as Montesquieu, David Hume, Adam Smith, David Ricardo, and Alexander Hamilton. What Locke provides is the fundamental moral justification, and the basic goals and structure of the kind of government that is to protect and to promote economic rationality. In the rest of the *Second Treatise* he elaborates the consequences for the family and for politics.

The Family

In chapters 6 through 8, Locke explains the moral bonds that should constitute a rational conception of the family. He rejects the traditional notions of the patriarchal family and all notions of the family as an institution conceived as having a clear *natural* structure that legal conventions need only reinforce. Following Hobbes, but working out the implications with more subtlety, Locke insists that the human family is *not* natural but is instead an *artificial* human contrivance based on *contract* between two free and equal human beings. He admits that parents do have some natural affection for their children – as extensions of or "a part of" themselves (see especially 1T sec. 97). But he never concedes that children naturally have any love or affection for their parents. And he tries to show that the family will operate with much *less* exploitation of women and children by fathers or males, and will become a much *more* productive economic unit – one that will make all members harder working and hence better off – if the family is conceived to be united less by love and trust and natural rank or authority, and much more by economic interest and the stimulating impetus of mutual independence and competition among the members.

Locke quietly makes some suggestions about the family (secs. 81ff.) with radical implications. He argues that there is no reason why marriage should not be temporary, like other contractual arrangements, and what is more, that there is no reason why the same person could not have different sorts of marriage with different people at the same time (a sexual contract with one, a shared parenting contract with another, etc.). Above all, Locke repeatedly stresses that by nature and reason fathers have no natural right to rule their children except insofar as they gain a right, through caring for the child economically, and thereby gain a legitimate expectation of some return on their investment.

The key political implication of Locke's treatment of the family is the rejection of paternalism in politics. Political rulers are not rightly in the position of being the parents of their subjects, as if subjects were like children. It is in this regard that Locke is most clearly critical of Hobbes – although on essentially Hobbesian premises. One should not conclude, as Hobbes does, that legitimate government can be modeled on the relation fathers have to children, in the state of nature, or on a right established by conquest, followed by a contract between conqueror and conquered that gives the conqueror unchecked governmental power. A social contract forming a government should be understood as made only among the people, who create the government as their servant and agent, which needs to be kept checked and limited by internal balances and competition. Locke goes so far as to declare that "*Absolute Monarchy*, which by some Men is counted the only Government in the World, is indeed *inconsistent with Civil Society*, and so can be no Form of Civil Government at all" (sec. 90).

The Civic Spirit of a Lockean Commonwealth

Yet Locke entirely agrees with Hobbes that the essence of government is terror, "the Magistrates Sword being for a *Terror to Evil Doers*, and by that Terror to inforce Men to observe the positive Laws of the Society, made conformable to the Laws of Nature" (1T sec. 92). The question then becomes how to create a "mighty Leviathan," as Locke calls it (sec. 98), that is somehow itself checked or intimidated. How to have a government that is terrifying but also itself terrified of becoming oppressive?

At the basis of Locke's constitutional teachings is the idea that the individuals who make or enter into the compact ought to retain, to a greater extent than in Hobbes's doctrine, responsibility to be vigilant about the government overstepping its legitimate bounds. The new stress on protection of property rights as the end of government, with property understood as self-reliant industry and its fruits, entails a conception of a more active and enterprising citizenry. But it is a citizenry whose action, and hence pride, or sense of independence, is much less dangerous than Hobbes feared. For pride is channeled into the peaceful and constructive quest for economic power and economically based prestige. Political power or control is seen as only a means to protection of private property and economic power. The new ideal of citizenry is of a people mainly preoccupied with economic advancement – but, for that reason, out of economic anxiety, attentive to and watchful of the tiny minority among them who are delegated as "representatives" to manage the government, which is supposed to protect the free enterprise economy.

A key sign of Locke's disagreement with Hobbes concerning the spirit of citizenship is that Locke insists much more than does Hobbes that every full citizen must actually and explicitly enter into the compact on reaching adulthood. What Hobbes called "tacit" or merely presumed consent is not enough to make one a full citizen (secs. 121–122). The social compact itself is, in its *first* stage, very much like what Hobbes described as sovereignty by institution. The original compact is a unanimous agreement to surrender to the majority much of one's natural rights and property, and above all one's natural authority to wreak capital punishment. Then, in a *second* stage, those rights are surrendered to whomever the majority designates as its representatives (secs. 95–99). Thus as in Hobbes the majority selects the form of government (chap. 10). But contrary to Hobbes, Locke argues that the majority does not then give away forever its authority. The majority may set a term of office for the government, or the majority may and should insist that to some degree or under certain fixed rules, the government representatives must be periodically reelected by the majority (sec. 132).

Unlike in Hobbes, then, the majority remains the ultimate voice of what Locke calls "the commonwealth," and the commonwealth is not the same as the government. The government can be dissolved and the commonwealth remain, for at least a short time. Authority can revert to the people, understood as the majority. This becomes the basis of the right of revolution, which marks a dramatic difference between Locke and Hobbes, and which played so big a role in justifying the American and also the French Revolutions. When the majority becomes convinced that government has betrayed its trust and is becoming despotic or absolute, and if there is no other recourse available, then as a last resort the majority can rise up or be aroused and led to rise up in violent rebellion – without simply collapsing back into a state of anarchic nature and disconnectedness. This legitimate threat and possibility of just revolution becomes the ultimate sanction intimidating and keeping government in check.

Constitutionalism

But this right of revolution is of course a kind of ultimate weapon that should never have to be used if government is well designed. What then are the principles of the good design of government? First and foremost, the supreme power in government should be conceived as a legislative power, or as a body that must govern through making laws that apply to everyone in the same way. And all positive laws passed by the legislature must be seen to be in conformity with natural law. That is, all positive laws must be reasonable deductions from the need to protect the life, liberty, and property of all, to the greatest extent possible. Locke states in brief compass the four basic principles of natural law or reason, once civil society is in existence. "These are the *Bounds* which the trust that is put in them by the Society, and the Law of God and Nature, have *set to the Legislative* Power of every Commonwealth, in all Forms of Government": "First, They are to govern by *promulgated establish'd Laws*, not to be varied in particular Cases, but to have one Rule for Riche and Poor, for the Favourite at Court, and the Country Man at Plough." Then "[s]econdly, These *Laws* also ought to be designed *for* no other end ultimately but *the good of the People*." Then "thirdly, they must *not raise Taxes* on the *Property of the People, without the Consent of the People*, given by themselves, or their Deputies." And "[f]ourthly, The *Legislative* neither must *nor can transfer the Power of making Laws* to any Body else, or place it any where but where the People have" (sec. 142).

Yet Locke makes it clear that it is reasonable to suppose that the majority have consented to impose some qualifications for voters, so as to ensure that those who do the voting for representatives are not under the control of others and are capable of independent judgment. This is the basis for denying the vote to children, and also to women – so long as women are not economically independent. This is the chief reason for having a property qualification: enough to ensure that voters can truly vote their own minds. Yet there is a deep current in Locke's thought that points toward expanding the franchise, if and when more and more people attain economic independence.

Almost as important as the rule of laws made by elected representatives is the separation of powers, elaborated in chapter 12. The persons who administer and execute the laws must be different from the persons who make the laws. In this way the lawmakers will realize that they will not get to apply and to interpret the laws that they make but will be subject to other people's administration and interpretation of the laws. This will induce the lawmakers to draw up the laws much more carefully, narrowly, and fairly, or in a way less subject to abusive interpretation. On the other hand, those who administer, apply, and interpret the laws are hemmed in by the knowledge that they cannot themselves make the rules that they apply and interpret.

Partly in order to facilitate this separation of powers, but also in order to create further internal competition in government, Locke is much more favorable than was Hobbes to a mixed regime, where there are elements of monarchy, oligarchy, and democracy all present. With this end in view, the design of the legislature may well give disproportionate weight to representation of the propertied.

At first glance, Locke's constitutionalism reminds of Aristotle's mixed regime. But the basic principle is radically different. Aristotle sought in polity a regime that would bring out the distinctive virtues of each of the classes, and especially of the middle class, as a farming class rooted in patriotic military service in a civil militia. Locke's principle here is that one should rely as little as possible on the virtue of the citizens or the rulers, and instead try to forge institutional mechanisms that will set groups in competition with one another, and thereby keep them acting in ways good for the public even if they are selfish or not virtuous. Accordingly, Locke's favored middle class is a commercial class, not a farming or patriotic militia class.

Locke's fundamental principle of relying on selfish competition within government has been subsequently worked out in many directions and variations by modern constitutionalism. There are two major aspects of subsequent constitutionalism that are missing or not at all prominent in Locke. The first is a powerful judiciary, entering into the separation and checking and balance. The judiciary in Locke is subsumed under the executive; there is no hint of a supreme court with the power of what we know as judicial review. The second is competing political parties, which have become especially important under the parliamentary system as we know it, and also quickly developed in America under the presidential system. More or less permanent political parties would seem to embody a very subdued, lawful version of the regime struggle Aristotle saw at the heart of politics.

As a further element of good government design, Locke points out that the two basic powers, executive and legislative, need to be structured very differently in order to do well the different tasks assigned to each. The executive, especially when – as is natural – it has chief jurisdiction over foreign policy and national defense, needs to be constantly in operation, and needs to act with energy and speed and often secrecy (especially as regards war and foreign policy). It is not essential that the executive be elective, and if it is, the elections need not occur very often. The executive may be a king, chosen by heredity or elected for life, or appointed by the legislature. Locke does acknowledge that the person or persons who hold the executive power need "Prudence and Wisdom" (secs. 147, 154, 156, 165–166; recall 42), and here Locke comes closest to Aristotle, or seems to have to admit that indeed there is a need for rare excellence and superiority in statesmen. Yet Locke, following Machiavelli, does not say anything about a need for special justice or moderation or charity in the executive. The chief executive needs to have practical prudence, intelligence, shrewdness; his moral qualifications are much less significant.

The legislature, in contrast to the executive, need not be always in session. Once it makes the laws and reviews what the executive has done in administering the laws, the legislators can go home. But it is important that the legislature be reelected regularly, and fairly apportioned among the citizenry. It is one of the most important duties of the executive to police this re-apportionment, and to insist on re-apportionment regularly, even if or especially when the legislature refuses. And here we have the leading example of how the executive must be invested with what Locke calls a "prerogative" to *defy* the legislature sometimes – and to do so perhaps by defying even their laws, or at least by acting outside and even against the letter of the law.

In chapter 14 Locke elaborates on this prerogative, and comes closer than has previously appeared to Hobbes, in some ways, and to Aristotle's critique of law in others. While the rule of law is crucial, and the supreme power should be a lawmaking power, Locke is aware that (as Aristotle taught) there are profound limitations on the rationality of all laws or rules – limitations so profound as to make it irrational to try to have a society live by strict laws and rules. All sorts of emergencies arise that are not covered by any law, or that even demand the suspension or violation of existing laws. In addition, it may be that the legislature, as in the question of reapportionment, is passing laws that are deeply and manifestly contrary to the good of the people, and need to be corrected. Hence something like a temporary version of Hobbes's sovereign, something like temporary dictatorial reserve powers, are a legitimate authority of the government – usually and mainly (but not exclusively) on the part of the chief executive.

As a consequence, in chapter 14 it becomes less clear that the legislature is simply supreme; the executive must have a reserve power to trump, at least temporarily, the legislature. And a deep tension appears to exist necessarily at the heart of a well-balanced government. The reserve authority of "prerogative" in the executive only intensifies the need for unusual wisdom in the persons who hold the executive power. Yet Locke paradoxically but characteristically warns of a deep danger precisely in the times of "wise" princes or rulers: "[H]e, that will look into the *History of England*, will find, that *Prerogative* was always *largest* in the hands of our wisest and best Princes: because the People observing the whole tendency of their Actions to be the publick good, contested not what was done without Law to that end"; the "People therefore finding reason to be satisfied with these Princes, whenever they acted without or contrary to the Letter of the Law, acquiesced in what they did, and, without the least complaint, let them inlarge their *Prerogative* as they pleased." But "[u]pon this is founded that saying, That the Reigns of good Princes have been always most dangerous to the Liberties of their People" (secs. 165–166). Here we find an agonizing conundrum at the heart of Lockean constitutional government.

Locke concludes the chapter on prerogative by stressing that the ultimate limit on government is the authority and capacity of the people, the majority, to rise up in war against their rulers. Popular distrust and watchfulness of government, and a willingness or readiness finally to rebel, are crucial to a healthy society. In this key respect, Locke is furthest from Hobbes; Locke thinks the threat of violence on the part of an armed and infuriated populace is essential, and that occasional revolution or civil war is not necessarily a simply bad thing. In making this argument, Locke once again confronts an imagined objector, who Locke has say that this right of revolution is too dangerous. Locke answers, in a famous and influential passage, that inspired Jefferson's Declaration of Independence: "[S]uch *Revolutions happen* not upon every little mismanagement in publick affairs. *Great mistakes* in the ruling part, many wrong and inconvenient Laws, and all the slips of humane frailty will be *born by the People,* without mutiny or murmur." But "if a long train of Abuses, Prevarications, and Artifices, all tending the same way, make the design visible to the People, and they cannot but feel, what they lie under, and see, whither they are going; 'tis not to be wonder'd," that "they should then rouze themselves, and endeavor to put the rule into such hands, which may secure to them the ends for which Government was at first erected" (secs. 223 and 225).

Locke then adds something paradoxical: Promoting this doctrine of revolution is likely to make revolutions *less* likely – because it instills a salutary fear in the government. *"[T]his Doctrine* of a Power in the People of providing for their safety a-new by a new Legislative, when their Legislators have acted contrary to their trust, by invading their Property, is *the best fence against Rebellion,* and the probablest means to hinder it." For "Rebellion being an Opposition, not to Persons, but Authority, which is founded only in the Constitutions and Laws of the Government; those, whoever they be, who by force break through, and by force justifie their violation of them, are truly and properly *Rebels.*" It is those "who set up force again in opposition to the Laws," who "*Rebellare,* that is, bring back again the state of War, and are properly Rebels" (sec. 226).

Locke does not limit this right of revolution to the majority. He declares that every individual citizen retains a right to resist by force governmental acts that threaten his basic rights, but Locke observes that the individual is unlikely to exercise this right, or, if he does, is unlikely to be considered as sane by the majority (sec. 208). It is only mass revolt – majoritarian uprisings – that have a realistic chance of success. Yet Locke hints (sec. 209) that it may make sense for individuals or small groups to try to arouse the majority to an awareness of the dangers to all that are implicit in the oppression of a few: "If the Mischief and Oppression has light only on some few, but in such Cases, as the Precedent, and Consequences seem to threaten all, and they are perswaded in their

Consciences, that their Laws, and with them their Estates, Liberties, and
Lives are in danger, and perhaps their Religion too, how they will be hin-
dered from resisting illegal force, used against them, I cannot tell." This
is "an *Inconvenience*, I confess, that *attends all Governments* whatsoever,
when the Governours have brought it to this pass, to be generally suspected of their People; the most dangerous state which they can possibly
put themselves in" (sec. 209; cf. 210). But Locke here stresses also that it
is easy for government to avoid this danger, if government recognizes it.
Once again we see that the right of revolution is something like nuclear
deterrence – it is a threat that one can hope will very rarely ever have to
be carried out, but that is all the more salutary as a frightening threat.
The right of revolution provides a foundation that gives those in power a
strong incentive to support the rule of law and constitutional checks and
balances – which are the usual and ongoing basis for a system that protects economic liberty. And the leading question for all the debates in the
subsequent Lockean tradition becomes: What institutional designs best
maximize the rule of law along with checks and balances? The extremely
influential proponent of a more complex, tripartite institutional design,
such as could be discerned at least as a potentiality of the British constitution, is Montesquieu – to whose thought we turn next.

10

Montesquieu's *Spirit of the Laws*

The vast masterpiece of the Baron de Montesquieu (1689–1755) became extraordinarily influential almost overnight. Its most famous contributions were: a new theory of participatory democracy (which inspired Rousseau among others); a new theory of "despotism" (*l'état despotique*: the term first became current through Montesquieu); a new theory of federalism; a new theory of the decisive influence of climate, geography, and history in shaping human existence; a new theory of the separation of powers (legislative, executive, and judicial); and a new, reformist theory of civil and criminal law to provide greater security for the accused and more reasonable procedures for parties in lawsuits. It was the last two that made Montesquieu *the* authority for the framers of the American Constitution, and for Blackstone's reform of English law in his *Commentaries on the Laws of England* (1776). In addition, *The Spirit of the Laws** is the single most important philosophic inspiration for the eventually successful movement, initiated by English disciples of Montesquieu, to abolish racial slavery of Africans (relying especially on bks. 15–17, and above all the mordantly ironic 15.5). Last but not least, *The Spirit of the Laws* is the work that made authoritative the idea that the peaceful common good of all mankind can be best advanced through the worldwide spread and intensification of globalized commercialism.

---

* The best available translation is that of Anne M. Cohler, Basia Carolyn Miller, and Harold Samuel Stone (Cambridge: Cambridge University Press, 1989). Translations in what follows are our own, from the second volume of *Œuvres complètes de Montesquieu*, ed. Roger Caillois (Paris: Pléiade, 1949–1951). Numbers refer to the books and chapters of *The Spirit of the Laws*. We will focus on books one through eight, ten through twelve, and nineteen through twenty.

The Norms of Nature

Montesquieu begins with an account of the causal matrix governing the entire universe. The first originating cause is god: not the biblical God, but the god of nature, the god discernible by human science. This true god is identified with "a primordial reason" (*une raison primitive*) generating the rest of the universe in accordance with unvarying "laws" that are "the necessary relations that derive from the nature of things"; "thus the creation, which would appear to be an arbitrary act, presupposes rules as invariable as the fatality of the atheists" (1.1). By implication, there are no miracles, and in particular no miracles of revelation. The miraculous, and revealed teachings play no role in Montesquieu's account of human reality.

In the second chapter, we learn that the "necessary" laws or principles that primarily define human nature are to be found by considering humans in a "state of nature" that is "prior to the establishment of societies." This state has nothing to do with anything in the Bible. Humans in their natural state have no knowledge of divinity at all, Montesquieu stresses. We see at once that we are within the framework established by Hobbes. Yet Montesquieu indicates that he differs in important ways from Hobbes in the characterization of the natural state. One clear sign of this is that Montesquieu does *not* – as did Hobbes – look to international relations as an expression of the natural condition. Montesquieu insists that Hobbes failed to think through consistently his insight into the historically constructed character of human society. That insight becomes fully illuminating only when we conceive what is natural, in the sense of innate and original in humans to be much more minimal than Hobbes realized. We must imagine what humans would have been like in a truly presocial condition. Then we need to speculate, imaginatively but rigorously, on what would have been the basic stages by which humans developed into the social and political beings we see around us. Only in this way will we avoid the grave mistake that Hobbes made, of "attributing to humans, before the establishment of societies, that which could not happen to them except after that establishment." Most importantly, "the desire that Hobbes gives at the start to humans, to subjugate one another, is not reasonable." If society is not natural, then the very notion of, and concern with, "empire and domination," with prestige, rank, and honor, would have been absent by nature, and would have developed only after humans were used to living together in (artificial) societies.

As Montesquieu begins to make clearer in chapter 3 – and spends much of the rest of *The Spirit of the Laws* elaborating – the failure to think through the full implications of the idea of the state of nature has led Hobbes and his successors to make two sorts of mistake. On one hand, they have not recognized sufficiently the hopeful possibilities implied by the degree to which humans are mutable, malleable, and moldable by their environment and their reactions to it; they have not appreciated the degree to which humans may be able to reshape human societies, and themselves, as more congenial social beings, on a more rational basis. But on the other hand, Hobbes and his successors have also failed to see the daunting or discouraging implication: That humans as we find them *today* have *already* been deeply shaped and molded, into highly diverse sorts of beings by their varying national or ethnic histories.

There is a need, therefore, to appreciate better how profoundly diversified humans have become in different nations, as products of distinct and contrasting historical-national cultures. There is a need to recognize how deeply resistant humans are to any social change, even rational reform, on account of humans' cultural second nature, as it were. We must realize how much attempts at reform must *adapt* universal normative principles of reason, based on the underlying, elemental natural needs of humans, to the variety of very different national or cultural circumstances by which humans have been spiritually molded. The standard of nature – nature or natural right as norm – thus becomes much more ambiguous and subtle in Montesquieu: "It is better to say that the government most in conformity with nature is the one whose particular arrangement best relates to the disposition of the people for whom it is established" (1.3).

Accordingly, Montesquieu does not place nearly as much stress as did Hobbes (and Locke after him) on universal, rational, or natural moral laws and rights. He does take his basic normative orientation from the ultimate universal goal, preservation, as dictated by what he calls "the law of Nature" (e.g., in 10.3). And he does agree with Hobbes, and other predecessors, that "the political and civil laws of each nation should be only the particular cases to which human reason is applied." But, he immediately adds, "laws should be so appropriate for the people for which they are made that it is very unlikely that the laws of one nation can suit another" (1.3). Political philosophy as Montesquieu understands it should focus less on deducing universal moral rules or laws from human nature and more on elaborating a scientific explanation, based partly (but only partly) on the universal principles of human nature, of why and how the laws and customs, and hence the very characters, of people socialized into one or another particular set of laws and customs are so enormously different in the diverse nations. Montesquieu calls this differing character of the laws and customs in different cultures "the spirit of the laws." On the basis of knowledge of the differing national characters, and the resulting "spirit of the laws" in its variety, political philosophy should show how, in each of the different nations, rational improvements that promote the one true universal need and principle of human nature, security, can be brought about. In different nations, this will take place in very different ways and degrees, through very different norms and laws, which will be adapted to and therefore not overly destructive of the often fragile existing conventional orders, and the basis for security that those historical conventions already provide.

In Montesquieu's political theory, the state of nature therefore plays a smaller normative role than it does in Hobbes or Locke. Still, he regards it as crucial that we start from a clear conception of the original state of nature and the key steps in the development out of it, so that we can see what is and what is not the minimal natural core of needs of the human being. Montesquieu's brief picture of the original state of nature, in chapter 2 of book one, portrays the natural human experience as one of isolation, fearful anxiety, and desperate, hungry concern for self-preservation. Montesquieu argues that from this it follows that, contrary to Hobbes, the primordial natural law or relation to others is *peace* – caused by humans' anxious *avoidance* of one another.

Yet this mutual avoidance would "soon" embolden humans to approach one another, Montesquieu immediately adds, especially since humans do share with other species an animal pleasure in such approach, as well as a natural attraction to the opposite sex. Humans would not then have been by nature *totally* asocial, but very timidly and anxiously and tentatively social (a bit like orangutans, we might say). The original natural state began to be transformed only when "eventually," humans came to have "knowledge" (*des connaissances*) that went beyond the "feeling" (*le sentiment*) that they shared with other animals. This development of knowledge would give humans "a bond other animals lack" and "a new motive to unite." What Montesquieu seems to mean is that slowly, over eons of time, scattered humans, coming together more and more in loose association and temporary cooperation, would eventually have acquired enough knowledge to gain better and better capacity to calculate how to benefit themselves through enduring cooperation.

The second chapter concludes by declaring that "the *desire* to live in society" is "*therefore*" a "law of human nature." To understand this, we must stress the "therefore." Montesquieu is saying that permanent or stable human society gets its impetus chiefly from self-interested calculation. Humans, living originally as disconnected individuals, slowly came to *desire* more permanent connections, in order to advance their self-interests better. Especially in conditions of competitive scarcity, selfish calculation is much stronger than the feelings of fellowship or sympathy. All this becomes vivid with the rather shocking opening of the next or third chapter. "As soon as humans are in society," Montesquieu says, "the state of war begins." Each particular society "comes to feel its strength, producing a state of war among nations." The individuals "within each society begin to feel their strength; they seek to turn to their favor the principal advantages of the society, which brings about a state of war among them." It is "these two sorts of states of war" that "bring about the establishment of laws among men" (1.3).

So Montesquieu's outlook is not *as* different from that of Hobbes as he at first makes it seem. And we must keep in mind the key historical fact, noted in the previous chapter on Locke, concerning Hobbes's reputation after he published. Hobbes was decried for his shocking frankness about human nature; it was shameful, it was unacceptable, to be a Hobbesian. To gain a respectable hearing for any book that entertained the idea of the state of nature, one needed to give the rhetorical appearance of distancing one's thought from Hobbes – especially if one's thought was, like Montesquieu's, deeply rooted in Hobbes's.

Montesquieu agrees with Hobbes that all positive laws and governments are established in order to end the war of all against all – which, Montesquieu agrees, is the inevitable tendency of human nature, once its calculative reason awakens, in society. What all human societies are most striving to achieve at bottom, and most basically, is the same, and is rooted in the core nature that we all do share. All humans, all societies, are seeking individual *security*, relief from anxiety about pain, and especially about painful death. Montesquieu further agrees with Hobbes that the war of all against all and the concomitant hunger for security can be seen in international relations. But Montesquieu contends that all this comes to pass not in the original natural condition but as a result of humans developing *out of* that condition.

Having declared that entry into societies causes a state of war to develop among humans, Montesquieu does not go on (as do Hobbes and Locke) to elaborate a doctrine of the social contract or a code of natural rights or laws – universally valid normative rules that reason can devise to minimize insecurity and maximize security. Instead, he resuscitates the idea of a positive or conventional, if unwritten, "right or law of nations" (*droit des gens*) that develops in and through the historical evolutions of peoples. Montesquieu emphatically does not characterize this law of nations as timeless or universal; he points to the wide difference among different nations' conceptions of it. At the same time, he makes it clear that he is not a relativist: "All nations have a law of nations; and even the Iroquois, who eat their prisoners, have one"; "the evil is" that "this law of nations is not founded on the true principles." As the treatise unfolds, Montesquieu will show that he discerns, and seeks to advance, enormous *progress* in the law of nations, in modern times. A new and more rational consensus has been developing, among European nations influenced by the new Hobbesian outlook. When Montesquieu most fully lays out the new law of nations involving norms of just and unjust war, in the opening chapters of book ten, he writes: "Here homage must be paid to our modern times, to contemporary reasoning, to the religion of the present day, to our philosophy, to our mores" (10.3). What are the "true principles" revealed in the modern law of nations? The modern law of nations is "by *nature* founded on the principle that the various nations should do to one another in times of peace the most good possible," and "in times of war the least ill possible, *without harming their true interests*" (our emphasis). The "object of war is victory; of victory, conquest; of conquest, preservation." All "the laws that form the right or law of nations should derive from" these two principles. On inspection, we see that these two principles are reminiscent of what Hobbes called natural right and law, not least because they cut out or ignore the higher dimensions of natural law and the law of nations that we saw taught by Thomas Aquinas. The law of nations as Montesquieu understands it is not aimed at humanity's spiritual fulfillment or happiness. By the same token, this law of nations does not point or lead toward the divine law of the Bible. The law of nations dictates no duty ever to risk one's own security or national security.

In order to promote intelligently throughout the world this historically emergent, more rational (more in accord with nature) law of nations, Montesquieu thought, we need to understand the history of Europe and its most influential shared national traditions, in contrast with the very different national traditions of non-Europeans. Hence Montesquieu does not proceed, after the third chapter of book one, to explain the more rational law of nations that he sees emerging in his time. He postpones doing so, for hundreds of pages (and we have leaped ahead to book ten in order to see his eventual destination). He first takes us, in books two through eight (or in the rest of part one), through a detailed study of the different kinds of political society that have emerged historically in Europe and in Asia. Only on the basis of such a study can we understand the vastly differing social situations or conditions within which, and adapting to which, reason can and should discover rules and institutions and practices that implement in varying degrees and ways the underlying normative principles of nature.

Montesquieu discovers in previous history three or four "forms of government": republics (democratic and aristocratic), monarchies, and despotisms. Each of these is defined by its own peculiar "nature" – meaning the way it structures the "sovereign" power that puts an end to the state of war. Each form's structure or "nature" is animated by what Montesquieu calls a distinct "principle": a specific "modification" of human psychology, a peculiar configuration of the passions, that is the necessary "spring" providing the necessary, peculiar human fuel that energizes the functioning of each structure (3.1). In explaining these "natures" and "principles," Montesquieu makes clear how severely normative his political science is.

Despotism

The key to Montesquieu's standards and goal is the negative pole that is provided by "despotism" – the simplest, most primitive, and unfortunately the nigh-ubiquitous solution that humans have devised to the problem of the state of war of all against all. In despotism the unchecked, willful, and capricious rule of a single "prince" terminates the state of war and thus provides a kind of "security" and "protection" for the mass of subjects. The "horrible" price of this system is its principle, which is routinized terror, wringing abject obedience from all, and especially from the leading subjects (3.9). Despotism crushes the spirit of anyone possessing honor, proud ambition, or a courageous sense of self-worth. Montesquieu strongly disagrees with Hobbes that pride and a strong sense of dignity are as dangerous as the latter claims. Montesquieu insists that humans need to have also their pride and sense of dignity protected, as a key part of what they mean and experience as genuine security. Despotism is thus so imperfect a response to the basic, natural human need – for personal security – that Montesquieu terms despotism a "monstrous" government (3.9), in which, he says, "human nature is insulted" (8.8, 8.21), and reason is stifled or crippled (5.14, 6.13, 8.10, 12.17). Yet despotism is the most prevalent form of government, because it is the simplest, the easiest to figure out and to construct. One could say that this is the stage at which most political inventiveness gets stuck. It is also the stage to which society tends to revert when the more complex and rational systems break down. Despotism is, so to speak, the default political order.

There is another crucial dimension to Montesquieu's analysis of the nature and principle of despotism, a dimension to which our attention is directed by the striking account of the true God with which Montesquieu opened *The Spirit of the Laws.* In despotism, revealed religion or religious law, Montesquieu teaches, is the one force that can check the terrible, lawless power of the despot – especially when the religious belief is in a higher, all-powerful, superhuman despot whose sway extends to an afterlife with punishments. The fear of a superterrestrial despot can frighten and thus check the human despot. Equally or more importantly, it can make the human despot's subordinates afraid to carry out his orders whenever the orders violate religious law. A religion that teaches obedient fear of an all-powerful legislative god, who is radically mysterious or beyond reason – who issues his commands through revelations that come only to privileged prophets, and who commands obedient love of that god, and of other humans, based on the fear – is in *accord* with the principle of despotism and functions to limit that principle *from within.* It is "a fear added to the fear," as Montesquieu puts it (2.4, 3.10, 5.14, 8.21; see also 12.29, 17.6, 19.16–21, 25.8).

As one reads carefully this dimension of Montesquieu's analysis of despotism, one sees that he is quietly presenting a very impious or blasphemous attack on all biblical religion – on Christianity, Judaism, and Islam. He in effect suggests that these religions are all human inventions, instituted by Eastern, Asiatic people who have desperately imagined some power in existence that would give them some protection from their despotic human rulers. Biblical religion is to be explained as a somewhat rational response by terrified humans trying to mitigate their fearful life under despotism. The presence of such religion in European nondespotic societies is therefore to be explained as some kind of result or relic of the intrusion into Europe of despotism and despotic psychology or the despotic principle.

Monarchy and Republicanism

It is almost only in European history, Montesquieu contends, that we can see two other, much more rational – much more truly secure and nonoppressive – forms of government that humans have figured out. Montesquieu admits or indeed stresses that climate and geography may make some form of despotism the "best" that can be expected or hoped for in vast regions of Asia. He focuses especially on China as a place where this may be the case (6.20, 7.6–7, 8.21). In other words, Montesquieu is very judgmental, but his negative judgment goes together with a deep appreciation of the limits that may be imposed on human possibilities by climate, geography, and previous history.

The sharpest contrast with despotism is seen in monarchy, a system that emerged out of the peculiar European history of savage barbarian invasions giving way to the feudal system. The "nature" of monarchy is "constituted" by its subordinate, intermediate powers – above all the hereditary warrior nobility, but also powerful independent cities with their urban merchant or bourgeois class, and also a separate church establishment. These intermediate powers, each with its own independent power base and source of legitimacy, stand between the sovereign and his subjects, compelling him to rule by "fixed laws" (2.1, 2.4). The animating psychological principle that energizes monarchy is "honor," or the selfishly proud demand for personal distinction, primarily as a courageous individual in battle and combat. The principle of monarchy is thus at the opposite pole from the principle of despotism (fear). Honor, says Montesquieu, is "dangerous" in a despotic regime. "Honor," he says, "has its laws and rules, and does not know yielding" (3.6–8, 4.2, 5.12). Unlike Hobbes, Montesquieu teaches that under the right historical circumstances, what Hobbes condemns as "vainglory" can play a very constructive role in achieving liberation from despotism, and hence more security in dignity for all. But Montesquieu also makes it clear that he regards monarchic honor as involving considerable irrational "prejudice," and as entailing some real dangers to security (3.8, 3.10, 4.2n, 5.19).

The third historical alternative, which has also arisen only in rare and lucky (mainly European) circumstances, is participatory republicanism. The finest examples of republics are found in classical antiquity, but republics have also flourished in medieval northern Italy and parts of medieval Germany. In Montesquieu's time, republicanism is vigorous in Switzerland and the Netherlands, and to a lesser extent in Venice. Montesquieu also notes that at the time he is writing, republicanism is being tried out in British North America; he mentions in particular William Penn's Quaker settlement in Pennsylvania (4.6). Republicanism comes in two variants – democracy and aristocracy. The first puts the sovereign power in the hands of most of the free male population, which can assemble, debate, and come to decisions by majority vote. The second puts sovereign power in the hands of a minority of wealthy families (2.2–3).

The strongest and most secure republics, Montesquieu argues, are democracies, when they are wisely tempered or qualified (as was republican Rome). In such democracies, the people are led by magistrates who are chosen according to some combination of special qualifications, elections, and lot. The government is administered, on a daily basis, not by the assembly (which leads to mob rule) but instead by elected officials who have short terms of office and must report back to the assembly to justify their actions – at occasional meetings. A democratic republic has a government that is directly responsible to the people, but that is not a government of the assembled people. It is a government in which many people would nonetheless, from time to time, have an important role, ruling and being ruled in turn (2.2, 5.5).

Especially important to a democratic republic is the civil militia, which is not only the backbone of military defense but a key to civic spirit. A democratic republic has as its principle what Montesquieu calls "virtue," by which he means a passionate, patriotic, communal, egalitarian, civic ethic. A democratic republic requires of each individual that he "continually prefers the public interest to his own," out of a "love of the fatherland" (4.5). This passionate identification of the individual's chief goal with the good of the whole citizenry presupposes a lawfully enforced equality, rooted in lawfully enforced frugality and austerity. Virtue, as the animating principle of a democratic republic, needs laws forbidding luxury and all sorts of conspicuous consumption. Democracy needs to inculcate a strong sense of fraternity and solidarity and must repress individualism, self-interest, inequality, and diversity (3.3–5, 4.4–8, 5.2–7, 6.8, 8.3). Virtue requires a cultural and religious homogeneity, rooted in strong customs of conformity to a shared moral ethos. There needs to be a single, established, shared religion whose tenets strongly support civic virtue and in no way divide the allegiances of the citizenry, never leading them to question and to doubt their wholehearted commitment to the community and to active, passionately committed citizenship (5.7, 8.13, 19.4). Separation of church and state is terrible for a democratic republic. Separation of church and state belongs instead to monarchy – which is not animated by virtue.

Furthermore, the egalitarianism of a strong democracy requires a discouragement or suppression of individual excellence or superiority and ambition: "Ambition is dangerous in a republic" (3.7). "The good sense and the happiness of the individuals consists very much in the mediocrity of their talents and their fortunes" (5.2–3). The democratic republic is characterized by the institution of ostracism, whereby any individual who does begin to seem superior, especially in politics, is sent into exile either for years or permanently (26.17, 29.7). The republican principle of virtue is thus opposed to the monarchic principle of honor, which is essentially ambitious: "Ambition gives this government [monarchy] its life"; honor characterizes and animates a proud society of "pre-eminences and ranks" (3.7).

The other version of republics, aristocracy, if it is to be successful, must be animated by a "lesser virtue," which Montesquieu calls "moderation" (3.4). It is not the people, the majority, who need this "lesser virtue," but rather the rulers, the aristocrats. They must not be animated by the spirit or principle of monarchic aristocrats – honor and its passion for distinction. That spells doom for an aristocratic republic. Republican aristocrats must instead be animated by a prudent self-control that makes them repress their ambition and assimilate themselves as much as possible to the people, so that the people feel as little dominated and inferior as possible. But this is a fragile situation, and Montesquieu sees an aristocratic republic as much more vulnerable to external and internal upset. He argues that the closer an aristocratic republic moves toward democracy, the more secure it becomes (2.3, 3.2, 3.4, 5.8, 8.5, 12.13).

The Philosopher's Critical Perspective

Montesquieu's initial typology of the three or four basic forms of government give the initial impression that Montesquieu is showing that the simply best form of government is democratic republicanism, especially as it was perfected in Greco-Roman antiquity. He certainly looks back to the Greeks and Romans with enormous admiration: "When that virtue was in full force, things were done in those governments that we no longer see, and that astonish our small souls" (4.4–6). But this praise stands at a deep tension with what Montesquieu indicated at the start, in book one: the idea that everything political is not natural but artificial and constructed, that humans are by nature radically individualistic and self-concerned, self-interested, anxious beings seeking personal security. If we bear this in mind, we can understand better why, as the whole *Spirit of the Laws* unfolds, the initial picture slowly but dramatically changes. Indeed, the closer we look as we reconsider part one in the light of the rest of the work, the more we can discern foreshadowing of the change. We begin to recognize that Montesquieu is reinterpreting classical republicanism, in a profoundly unclassical spirit and framework – on a modern, more or less Hobbesian, basis. He is *not* looking at republican life in the way a republican citizen would (or as Plato or Aristotle do). He looks at republics from a kind of height, or detachment, based on the modern conception of human nature he outlined in book one.

From that perspective, republics appear as one of several types of government, all of which are understood to be artificial constructs, whose deep purpose or function is to achieve *security*, the basic natural need. In pursuit of this end, each form of government has to reshape human nature, so as to turn humans into something they are *not*, naturally. The republic persuades its citizens to see virtue as all-important. Montesquieu, in contrast, evaluates and judges virtue, and the whole democratic system, not as the end, or the purpose, but rather as a means, whose rational and natural purpose is ultimately to achieve individual security for members. But democracy, in order to obtain that security, must deceive its citizens into thinking virtue is more important than security: Democratic collective security requires that the citizens subordinate and even sacrifice their individual security for the community. Democracy can function well only if the fundamental truth about human nature is not seen clearly by the citizens. This is perhaps the deepest reason why Montesquieu says that democracy needs a citizenry that is of mediocre intelligence.

As part one unfolds, Montesquieu takes his readers through a kind of educational process, by which he first enchants them with the grandeur as well as the security achieved by democratic republics, and then gradually reveals the democratic regime's limitations or grave problems, from the perspective of the deepest need of human nature – security for individuals. He slowly allows the thoughtful reader to see that the virtue on which depends the "happiness" exhibited in democratic republics is a "modification" of human psychology that entails a *repression* of the citizens' naturally self-regarding passions: their natural desire for increasing their economic prosperity and personal comfort, their natural preference for their own families and their private family life over the good of the larger community, their natural competition, caused by vanity or the desire for preeminence of all kinds.

Eventually (in book eight) Montesquieu brings to the fore the fact that democratic republics are constantly threatened by "corruption." Citizens regularly fail to live up to their communal responsibilities. This "corruption" reveals that even in the good citizen the natural aim of the passions is not virtue but individual security, liberty, comfort, power, prestige, and wealth. As Montesquieu eventually says: In order to avoid becoming corrupt, "a republic must be in dread of something" – usually, of some foreign enemy. "What a strange thing! The more these states have security, the more, like water that is too quiet, they are subject to self-corruption" (8.5). Republican virtue, in Montesquieu's words, is "a sacrifice of one's dearest interests," and is thus "always a very painful thing" (3.5 and 4.5).

At the same time, by presenting classical democracy always in juxtaposition with *monarchy*, Montesquieu leads us to see certain great competing advantages of monarchic honor. Honor is a principle much more in accord with the naturally individualistic bent of the human spirit than is democratic virtue. Essential to republican virtue are censorship and mutual surveillance, the confinement of women, the prohibition of luxuries. But in monarchy, these repressive features are all unnecessary, and even contrary to "that spirit of liberty," as he says, that characterizes a monarchic court (7.9). "In monarchies," Montesquieu observes, "politics accomplishes great things, with the least possible virtue"; "each pursues the common good, believing that he pursues his personal interests" (3.5–7). In other words, monarchy is animated by a principle through which the true common good, the security of everyone, is advanced by having *no one* caring much about the community. The checks and balances of monarchy arise from the expression of competitive self-interest or even selfishness, not from their repression.

Yet the monarchic principle of honor is not free of deep contradictions with the basic needs and desires of human nature. Honor is rooted in knighthood and chivalry and remains closely linked to a warrior spirit that endangers everyone's security. Honor makes people disdain gainful employment, productive work, acquisitive business, commerce, and trade. The principle of honor tends therefore to undercut the kinds of ambition that are most economically productive, most needed to produce prosperity and thus material security. Honor, and the system it animates, leaves the vast majority of inhabitants suffering in degradation and even insecurity or poverty. By the end of book eight, Montesquieu is prodding his readers to ask, "Is there not a better alternative?"

The Superiority of Moderns to Ancients

By focusing in books nine and ten on international relations, Montesquieu intensifies, and prepares the answer to, this question. For he not only presents us with a sharp, sobering reminder of our most natural, basic, universal, human concern – with security, but also stresses the progress that has been made, in modernity, toward its achievement. In the second chapter of book ten, Montesquieu makes explicit that precisely because defense is what defines a war as just, it follows that preemptive (aggressive) war *is* justified, and obligatory, even against a neighbor that has done and at present intends to do no harm, but whose sheer growth in power poses a future, serious, and likely threat: "Hence small societies more frequently have the right to wage wars than large ones, because they are more frequently in a position to fear being destroyed."

For "the right of war," he reminds us, "derives from *necessity and strict justice*." Montesquieu follows Hobbes in the insistence that justice must be reconceived so as not to contradict, so as to be rooted in, the natural "necessity" or the "law of nature" that impels humans to seek their own security as their overriding goal. As becomes clear from the immediate sequel, this implies that for Montesquieu as for Hobbes, the love of glory, national honor, recrimination, punishment, answering an insult, or delight in the contemplation of one's power are *not* compelling or at any rate justifying necessities.

Initially Montesquieu seems in this chapter (10.3) to be saying that conquest is justified only when it is necessary for military defense, and that therefore a conquered people should be kept subjected only for as long as needed for the conqueror's military security. But as Montesquieu proceeds, it becomes clearer that a certain kind of humanitarian conquest is allowed. This becomes still more explicit in the next chapter (10.4), whose title is "Some Advantages for the Conquered People." Montesquieu stresses how much it is to the conqueror's own advantage and interest, understood as security, to leave the conquered people alive, free, and able to pursue economic prosperity and thereby able to contribute to the prosperity of the conquerors. Montesquieu goes beyond this, however, to indicate that human nature dictates a certain humanity, a secondary but important unselfish and compassionate species concern for others. This becomes explicit at the end of chapter 5, when Montesquieu defines the norms of conquest: "It is for the conqueror to make amends for part of the evils he has done. I define the right of conquest thus: a necessary, legitimate, and unfortunate right, which always leaves an immense debt to be discharged if human nature is to be repaid" (10.5). Then Montesquieu takes a further massive step; he opens the door to benevolent imperialism. This is justified if and when it truly advances prosperity and security for *both* conqueror and conquered. He indicates that the Spanish *could* have carried out such a conquest of the Americas, especially because they *could* have, through imperialism, brought about the removal of what Montesquieu calls "harmful prejudices" – by which he shows he has in mind especially religious prejudices, the barbarous human sacrifices practiced by the natives. The Spanish did so very imperfectly, he implies, inasmuch as they brought with them the harmful prejudices of Roman Catholicism. But there is no bar to justified imperial aggression *if* it really benefits both populaces, the conquering and the conquered – especially by liberating the latter from harmful superstitions. This becomes still clearer as book ten culminates, in chapter 14, with high praise for Alexander the Great as a conqueror, whose conquests brought to numerous peoples ground down by Asiatic despotism a more secure and prosperous and powerful existence – not least through encouraging and protecting trade and commerce, but also by inducing tolerance among the existing religious and familial customs and traditions of the peoples he conquered. "There were few nations," Montesquieu admiringly expostulates, "at whose altars he did not sacrifice." Alexander thus set and in effect legislated a magnificent example of an imperialism that spread religious tolerance along with commercial prosperity.

The Apotheosis of the English Constitution

In the wake of this reminder of our concern with security, of this recognition of progress toward its achievement, and of the intriguing suggestion of the possibility of furthering progress through humane imperialism, Montesquieu turns in book eleven to a new modern form of government that is different from anything in previous history. He has fully prepared us to welcome the introduction of what he calls the "one nation in the world that has for the direct object of its constitution political liberty" (11.5). In England we find a monarchy – but of a new kind. England is a nation, Montesquieu had declared in book five (chap. 19), "where the republic hides itself under the form of the monarchy." England is a republic – but again, of a new kind. England is not animated by "the principle" of traditional democracy, or traditional aristocracy, or traditional monarchy. While there is some sense of honor left among the English nobles, they are becoming more and more involved in commerce and business. Still less is England animated by the democratic principle of virtue. The English tried to set up a virtuous republic under Cromwell, and failed – because, Montesquieu affirms, there was "no virtue at all" in the populace (3.3)! What animates England is a more natural, far less virtuous meaning of "liberty." The English system allows and encourages everyone to be a competitive individual, who competes not so much over honor, through dueling, and loving war (as in traditional monarchy), but instead over economic and political power sought for the sake of material security. England is a *commercial* society. And precisely because the English form of government does *not* rely at all on virtue, England possesses much stronger guarantees of individual liberty and security.

The English constitution, we now learn, is constructed like a kind of very efficient machine that, to a degree, maintains its balance automatically. England's complex constitutional system keeps government from becoming despotic through checks and balances within and among the institutions of government – above all by the separation of powers, which was almost totally unknown to classical or participatory republicanism. The most democratic part of the English constitution is an independent judicial branch rooted in popular juries – which are the only way the people directly participate in government. The juries in the English system have a radically different animating spirit from the juries in classical democracies. The English juries adjudicate a criminal and civil legal code that is keenly attentive to the rights of individuals, and these are rights, not to be virtuous, not to participate in ruling, in the old democratic spirit, but rather rights to live and do as one pleases with one's property, so long as one does not infringe upon anyone else's congruent rights. In other words, liberty in the new English republican monarchy (or monarchic republic) means something very different from what liberty means in a classical democracy.

The other republican aspect of England is the House of Commons, where a tiny minority of commoners, elected by the rest, make the laws – and which is checked and balanced by a second house of the legislature, the House of Lords, where nobles have their say, competing with the commoners. Both of these legislative houses are in turn competing with the king, who holds the executive power. The king cannot make laws, but he manages the power that carries them out, and through his veto he can block legislation. The whole system is a constant tense political battleground, where each power center in the government is jealously guarded and hence checked and balanced by the others, preventing despotism. In these principles of the English constitution, Montesquieu declares, "liberty appears as in a mirror" (11.5). We see for the first time the best form of government that can be devised, by reason working through history, to secure the kind of liberty (individual security) that our nature most profoundly needs.

But it turns out that Montesquieu's presentation of England and its way of life has a strange order or arrangement. He splits the presentation up, placing it in two parts separated by hundreds of pages. In part two, book eleven, he gives the constitutional and legal order of England. But not until the end of book nineteen, which closes the third part, does he present, in the longest chapter in the whole book, his elaborate account of the way of life of the new English individualistic and competitive commercial society – the way of life that he says is promoted and protected by the constitutional system. Why arrange things this way? What goes on in the hundreds of pages of part three (books thirteen through eighteen) sandwiched between the two parts?

The Allure of Globalized Commercialism

What Montesquieu shows in part three is that the model English institutions can only rarely and with enormous modifications be transported to other nations, even in Europe, and still less in Asia. Montesquieu lays out in staggering detail his famous teaching on the way in which differing climates and physical geographies of the world, and then the complex social systems humans have developed over the ages in response to the differing geographies, diversify mankind ethnically, into the many nations, each with its own unique "general spirit." But Montesquieu presents this in the light of his teaching on the best possible solution to the human need for freedom – namely, the construction of a liberal republican monarchy like that of England. In other words, he forces us into agonizing over the question: How might the liberties that England enjoys ever be spread to the rest of the world, if the English political system is rarely if ever well suited to the natural geography and the human traditions that have shaped social existence in the rest of the world?

Most of part three at first leaves us depressed, by the evidence of how deeply rooted in most of the world is slavery – not only political slavery, or despotism, but also chattel slavery, humans treated as animals to be bought and sold, and domestic slavery, women treated as property within and outside the home. Yet in these books Montesquieu also repeatedly insists that it is the task of the wise lawgiver to work within each nation to oppose the enslaving vices or proclivities of climate and tradition (14.3–8, 16.12) – and he gradually provides indications as to how this might be done, with the appropriate gingerly caution. As we reach the end of part three, and then in the dramatic beginning of part four, we begin to appreciate the hints he has given as to the liberating power of commerce or the commercial spirit (especially 13.10–11, 19). For it turns out that what England has to offer the world is not only her marvelous legal and constitutional system but something else embedded in her way of life, the way of life to which her legal system has given unprecedented freedom, scope, and encouragement: the love of material gain and economic power, achieved through the liberation and protection of commerce and commercialism. This commercial spirit, Montesquieu contends, while it is promoted by the English constitution, is by no means simply dependent upon that constitution. The spirit of commerce is transportable in part because the nature of commerce is adaptable and flexible, as Montesquieu shows in book twenty-one by a detailed study of the history of commerce.

The effects of commerce and commercialism are both material and spiritual. And the latter – that is, the effects on the opinions and the hearts of mankind, the way people think and feel – are the more important. Montesquieu's key statement is at the start of book twenty on commerce: "Commerce cures destructive prejudices; and it is an almost general rule, that everywhere that there are gentle mores, there is commerce, and that everywhere that there is commerce, there are gentle mores." It follows, he says, that "one should not be surprised if our mores are less fierce than they were formerly." Commerce "has spread knowledge of the mores of all nations everywhere; they have been compared to each other, and good things have resulted from this" (20.1). But then Montesquieu shows the underbelly: "The laws of commerce perfect mores for the same reason that these same laws ruin mores." Commerce "corrupts pure mores, and this was the subject of Plato's complaints; commerce polishes and softens barbarous mores, as we see every day" (20.1).

First and foremost, then, commerce makes people everywhere aware of their cultural diversity – and thereby aware of what all people have in common. It shows humans in different cultures that their own ways are not necessarily the only, or the true, the natural ways. At the same time, commerce helps people to see what the truly universal, natural needs and attractions are. Commerce makes people aware of their shared most basic needs and desires – for security, achieved through peaceful material prosperity; for the comforts and pleasures such prosperity brings; and, in addition, for the prestige or gratification of vanity that can be thus peacefully achieved through acquiring conspicuous luxuries. People who become commercial are "softened" in their ways in the sense that they become less and less inclined to be willing to sacrifice or to risk their security and prosperity. The softening effect of commerce is thus a "ruining," as Montesquieu says, of traditional mores that demand individual sacrifice. Commerce "corrupts" people everywhere in the sense that the commercial spirit goes against and undermines the demands of the classical republic, that is, of participatory democratic virtue.

Commerce also tends – though to a lesser extent – against monarchic honor and its demands, insofar as honor exalts war, and instills contempt for business and material gain. Commercialism corrupts honor into more meretricious and effeminate competition (19.8). Commerce thus creates a very different sort of republican and a very different sort of monarchic spirit – a commercial republican spirit and a commercial monarchic spirit. This spirit has its own kind of virtues, but not of a sacrificial or heroic kind. As Montesquieu said in a remark that loomed as a puzzle back in an early chapter, "the spirit of commerce brings in its train frugality, economy, moderation, work, wisdom, tranquility, order and rule" (5.6). This can change even despotism, as the despot and his minions realize more and more that they need commerce in order to gain wealth, and that they can have commerce only if they set up a legal system that protects private property and thereby gives the inhabitants more and more protection for their security. In other words, commercialism can gradually make despotisms more lawful systems. Commerce can't bring an English system, but it can bring some of the protections that the English enjoy.

To understand the deepest reasons why Montesquieu embraced and favored the commercialization of the world, we must not overlook what he indicates is the effect of commercialization on *religious* life and religious conflict. Commercialization causes people to become less serious about the truth of their own religion by causing them to be become less concerned with the next life. Prosperity, Montesquieu contends, saps the roots, the felt need, for religious consolation and hence worship, because prosperity makes people satisfied with earthly life: A "sure way to attack religion is by favor, by the commodities of life, by the hope of wealth; not by what reminds one of [religion], but by what makes one forget it; not by what brings indignation, but by what makes men lukewarm, when the other passions act on our souls, and those which religion inspires fall silent" (25.2). Montesquieu strongly suggests that the longing for immortality is not nearly as strong by nature as the biblical religions spawned under despotisms would seem to indicate. The apparent strength of the longing for immortality or for a life after this one is caused, Montesquieu suggests, by how materially and physically miserable people are or have been in this life.

We are now in a position to understand the full, if veiled, significance of Montesquieu's very high praise of Alexander the Great as a conqueror. This praise represents a qualified and muffled approval of a benevolent European empire that would "corrupt" Asian mores by bringing them closer to European, commercial and commercial-religious, mores. Such an imperialism would advance the cause of world peace and security. For as nations become more and more commercial, they see more and more the need for peaceful competition, and hence for international cooperation and mutual security, to keep the markets open and trade flowing. Nations that engage in trade can easily see that war disrupts trade, that war is bad for most business (20.8). Nations that trade with one another become mutually and peacefully dependent: "The natural effect of commerce is to lead to peace. Two nations that trade with each other become reciprocally dependent" (20.2). Furthermore, Montesquieu points to the dependence of trading nations on international monetary agreements, and stock exchanges, which limit governmental acts of arbitrary authority (22.13). As nations focus less on wealth in land and more on *movable* and liquid wealth, represented by paper money and stocks and bonds, the world manifests itself more and more as a single world society (21.21, 26.1), whose members' fluid property is more secure from the clutches of despots (20.23).

Yet Montesquieu is keenly aware of the moral cost – the inhumanity – that is the other side of the coin of commerce. He recognizes that there is among individuals within each commercial society a diminished generosity. Commerce, he does not fail to note, brings more petty disputes over money: "If the spirit of commerce unites nations, it does not unite individuals." In commercial countries, "there is traffic in all human activities and all moral virtues; the smallest things, those required by humanity, are done for money." The spirit of commerce "produces in men a certain feeling for exact justice – opposed, on one hand, to banditry, and on the other, to those moral virtues that make it so that one does not always discuss solely one's own interests and so that one can neglect them for those of others" (20.2).

In addition, Montesquieu is not unqualifiedly sanguine about the effects of global commercialization on the prospects for world peace. He admits that there is still the potential for an outbreak of wars caused by commercial competition, among rivals armed with unprecedented weaponry and mobilization made possible by commerce and its fruits. On the whole, however, Montesquieu is more hopeful than he is uneasy about commercialism's potential for spreading peace. Subsequent philosophers and statesmen were not so sure. Perhaps growing commercialization and globalization through commerce can lead to world federation, or even world government. But perhaps a global coalition of commercialized societies is an illusion, one that overlooks some deep lessons taught by the ancients – lessons about the character and the strength of the noble civic and erotic longings of the human soul. These questions become the great subjects of debate after Montesquieu, above all through Rousseau, who raises thoroughgoing doubts about the whole direction of Montesquieuian commercial republicanism, in the name of a return to the classical participatory democracy that Montesquieu so eloquently portrayed in part one.

PART IV

MODERNITY IN QUESTION

11

Rousseau's *First* and *Second Discourses**

Jean-Jacques Rousseau (1712–1778) launched the first modern philosophic rebellion against the Enlightenment – that vast cultural revolution whose philosophic foundations we have studied in Machiavelli, Bacon, Hobbes, Locke, and Montesquieu. As we have seen, the Enlightenment entails a lowered conception of humanity's moral nature. This new, lowered view of humanity is to be popularized, spread to the mass of mankind, by the philosophers and their followers writing as educational propagandists. Philosophers aim to reshape Christianity into a religion of (modern) reason, and to make scientific philosophy, rather than pious traditions, the source of mankind's conceptions of "nature's God." This constitutes a dramatic break with the classical view of the proper relation between rationalist philosophy or science and healthy political society. The ancients, starting with Socrates, had taught that philosophy or science should keep muted or hidden its critical questioning, because healthy republican society, centered on self-transcending moral and civic virtue, needs to live in a medium of tradition and opinion that is endangered by philosophic skepticism.

Rousseau returns to something like the Socratic view of the relation between philosophy and healthy civil society. But he does not do so on the basis of Socratic or classical political philosophy. He contends that we can and must appreciate the practical wisdom and virtue of classical political life on a modern or even ultramodern philosophic and scientific basis. Otherwise stated, Rousseau effects a kind of synthesis between

* The best translation of the *First* and *Second Discourses* is by Roger D. Masters and Judith R. Masters: *The First and Second Discourses* (New York: St. Martin's, 1964). Our citations are to page numbers of this translation. The translation has sometimes been slightly emended.

ancient practice and modern theory, or between classical republicanism and the modern philosophic and scientific conception of nature and of human nature. It is a synthesis that subordinates the ancient ingredient to the modern. But Rousseau argues that his modern predecessors have failed to grasp the full, radical, and problematic meaning and implications of their own discoveries about human nature.

The Historical Context of the First Discourse

In his *Confessions*, Rousseau tells us in some detail how he was provoked and inspired to write his explosive first major work. In 1750, a prominent scientific club or "academy" in the city of Dijon announced an essay contest on a curious topic: "Has the Restoration of the Sciences and the Arts Tended to Purify Morals?" The topic indicated that some in that academy were morally troubled by the cultural revolution that was the Enlightenment – and wanted to stimulate some critical discussion. Rousseau had been living in Paris, as an intimate friend and collaborator of some of the foremost figures in the French Enlightenment, but he had also for years been studying the works of the ancients, especially Plato – and thinking long and hard. When he read in a newspaper the announcement of the essay contest, he was walking to visit in prison a friend, the famous Diderot, who was the editor and leader of the great multivolume work called *The Encyclopedia* (which was in a sense the Bible of the Enlightenment). Diderot had been imprisoned by the censorship authorities for published writings of his deemed impious. This alerts us to something that we must never forget about the historical context in which Rousseau was writing. The threat of persecution – imprisonment and book burning – on grounds of impiety, was still very real, just as it had been for Socrates in Athens. In order safely to publish anything that involved questioning of orthodox Christian teachings, one had to adopt some version of rhetorical accommodation, hiding, writing between the lines. But the partisans of the Enlightenment, led by Diderot, were struggling to change the world so as to make this no longer so necessary; they were constantly pushing the envelope, and sometimes getting punished as a consequence.

One might think that this situation – Rousseau visiting a close friend imprisoned for promoting free thought and speech – might have intensified Rousseau's attachment to the Enlightenment. Instead, something like the opposite happened. As he read the announcement of the topic for the essay contest, there was provoked in him a kind of awesome inner revelation. He suddenly realized that this question spoke to the profound doubts he himself had been developing about all that was going on around him culturally. He was inspired to bring together and to begin articulating a complex new conception of human nature and of the human condition that had been gestating deep in his mind.

The essay Rousseau wrote won the prize, but much more came as a result of it. Almost overnight he became the most famous, and the most hated, man in Europe. For he had dared to attack – with staggering rhetorical power and subtlety of thought – everything that was thought to be the triumphant wave of the future. He did so while at the same time making clear that he was no reactionary, that he was as opposed to traditional Christianity and monarchy as anyone. From the beginning, he was met with a bewildered mixture of admiration and revulsion. He came to be shunned, for the rest of his life, by many of his previous closest friends. He was labeled a lunatic, and was persecuted and driven from places in which he tried to live – sometimes by governments, sometimes by stone-throwing popular mobs. His books were publicly burned in various cities, most notably in his native Geneva.

But those books had an amazingly wide and deep popular as well as intellectual influence. In the first place, Rousseau had a profound influence on the French Revolution, and especially on its radical left wing, under Robespierre and St. Just. But Rousseau was also, in the second place, the chief inspiration of the greatest antipolitical artistic movement in human history – Romanticism. He wrote an enormously popular romantic novel (*Julie or the New Heloise*), as well as a novel on education (*Emile*). All the great novelists and playwrights and artists of the rest of the eighteenth and the early nineteenth century were deeply inspired by his example and thought (e.g., Lessing and Goethe and Schiller and Hölderlin in Germany, Austen and Thackeray in England, Stendhal in France, Tolstoy in Russia, Hawthorne in America). In the third place, through his philosophic student, Immanuel Kant, Rousseau gave the decisive impetus to the philosophic movement known as German idealism, with its "philosophy of history," reaching through Hegel and Fichte and Schelling and culminating in Marx. In the fourth place, Rousseau was the most influential theologian of the eighteenth and nineteenth centuries. Especially in his "Confession of Faith of the Savoyard Vicar" (in *Emile*) he laid the foundations for modern liberal Protestantism, as a religion centered on compassion, humanism, and nature, without the ideas of sin and hell and the need for miraculous redemption. He was the chief source of the image of Jesus as not God but instead a suffering, compassionate, marvelous human paragon of natural virtues.

The amazing diversity of these influences reflects the baffling complexity and tension-ridden, apparently contradictory, character of Rousseau's thinking. Each of his influential followers seized on one or another major parts of his teaching and felt compelled to reject other parts as incompatible. But Rousseau himself insisted that there was a consistent, integrating basis for all the apparently contradictory or conflicting aspects of his thought – and that no one, at least in his lifetime, had ever grasped the unifying core of his thought. He insisted that the bewildering complexity and apparent contradictions in his writing were an accurate reflection of the truth about our human being, which is rife with tensions and contradictions. Rousseau also suggested that it was in his first short discourse – despite or because of its immaturity – that he had brought everything synoptically together, more than in any of his longer and more elaborate later works, each of which develops more thoroughly a part of his multi-faceted outlook.

The New Meaning of "Virtue"

In the "Preface" to the *First Discourse* (33) Rousseau announces his intention to attack all that is most respectable in his time, knowing that he will as a consequence become "universally" hated and misunderstood, by all except "a few wise men." But he proclaims that he is one of those few who are not "destined to be subjugated by the opinions of their century, their country, their society," and that he plans to have an influence far into the future.

He commences the body of the discourse (34) by associating himself with the famous paradoxical formula of Socrates, in Plato's *Apology*: He will speak as "an honorable man who knows nothing and yet does not think any the less of himself." He speaks as if he were on trial, before judges who will not easily understand his complex outlook: "It will be difficult, I feel, to adapt what I have to say to the tribunal before which I appear. How can one dare blame the sciences before one of Europe's most learned Societies," and "reconcile contempt for study with respect for the truly learned? I have seen these contradictions, and they have not rebuffed me."

He begins to show immediately what it is in the name of which he will "blame the sciences": "I am not abusing science, I told myself; I am defending *virtue*" (emphasis added). Rousseau's first theme or task is to explain what he means by virtue. He identifies virtue as "integrity," truthfulness – linked to the upholding of "a just cause" (34b). He then turns to indicate what he does *not* mean by virtue. Here he speaks indirectly, for this is a dangerous topic: "That part of the world which is today so enlightened lived, a few centuries ago, in a condition worse than ignorance. A nondescript scientific jargon, even more despicable than ignorance, had usurped the name of knowledge" (35m). These words implicitly deprecate Thomas Aquinas and the whole tradition of Christian theology; however, Rousseau will never be so imprudent as to say so explicitly.

He proceeds (36–38) to elaborate what he means by virtue and the virtuous man. Virtue is "the strength and vigor of the soul" that disdains all "ornamentation." The virtuous man "dares to appear as he is." Virtue is the opposite of "base and deceptive uniformity"; virtue is the proud and joyous display of oneself in one's "difference" or uniqueness. Among the virtuous, "differences of conduct announce at first glance differences of character." The virtuous person loves competition – but not over money and power. Virtue loves competition that tests and displays the genuine, distinct or individual, talents and capacities of each competitor while inviting and inspiring others, one's competitors, to do the same: "The good man is an athlete who likes to compete in the nude." Virtue means living among others in a society of spiritual *transparency*, "seeing through each other" – which is the necessary basis for "real esteem," "well-based confidence," and "sincere friendships." In all the preceding aspects, virtue is the expression of "human *nature*," of the "natural" in the sense of "that original liberty for which men seem to have been born" – liberty that is covered, repressed, stifled, enchained by the iron conventionalities of our social existence.

The newly emerging, supposedly "enlightened" form of society shapes people more and more to live a conformist life of hypocrisy, of deep dishonesty about themselves and even to themselves. People more and more pretend to be, and pretend to feel, what they are not and do not really feel. People are not competitively expressing their true and unique selves, but instead live a life dominated by vanity, or the constant struggle to appear before others in ways that will impress and make each *seem* superior in conventional ways, while *pretending* to respect and to care for one another.

Rousseau here launches his critique of what he later will christen the *bourgeois* character of modern society and its moral outlook (*Social Contract* 1.6 note; *Emile*, bk. 1 beg.). He attacks what we saw to be at the heart of Hobbes's "laws of nature" – the new moral outlook that Hobbes and Locke promote. According to that outlook, secure civilization rests on and requires the artificial subduing and repressing of a murderously dangerous and ugly, self-centered human nature. Rousseau contends that this is a terrible misunderstanding and degradation of human nature, which is fundamentally *not* dangerous and ugly in its true, *natural* self-centeredness. Humans are not naturally murderous; they do not naturally seek for power after power, over and against one another; they do not naturally seek for prestigious display and domination. They *can* and do become *distorted* into such monstrous beings, but that happens on account of unhealthy social and political conditions. And the new kind of society being brought into existence under the guidance of the liberal capitalist individualism is peculiarly sick.

Rousseau is the philosophic founder of the conception of virtue as sincerity, authenticity, daring to uncover and to be true to one's inner, unique self – and on this basis, for the sake of this, determining one's own life, as independently as possible, in a fraternal community with others whom one truly knows and respects. All this he designates as true freedom, which is practically identifiable with virtue as he is characterizing it.

We can now begin to see the complex way in which Rousseau both resembles and differs from the ancients. Like the ancients, he sees nature and the natural as a positive standard, as the source of health and of virtue as strength of soul. But to a greater extent than the ancients, Rousseau sees our human nature as something easily lost, something that has to be recovered, rescued from society's attempts to repress and to cover it over with artificial, conformist, pseudo-virtues. Rousseau's stress on individuality shows from the start that he agrees with Hobbes and Locke, against Aristotle and the classics, that humans are by nature *not* political or social animals but instead independent equals. Against Hobbes and Locke, however, Rousseau insists that as independent equals, we are by nature *not* anxiously power-hungry, acquisitive, prestige-obsessed animals. It is true that *all society* has a terrible tendency to *corrupt* us in this direction – and this shows that we have a terrible natural weakness or susceptibility to such corruption. But Hobbes and Locke, and their political philosophies, mistake that corrupt state for our natural state; they propose as a cure a new form of social existence that exacerbates our alienation from our deeper, truer, healthy nature.

Rousseau is sure that humans feel this corruption in themselves, without understanding it. He is convinced that the whole vast modern cultural revolution that is the Enlightenment is bound to fail, because of the ultimately intolerable degree to which it forces humans into unnatural forms of self-expression. Rousseau means to offer a way out, at least in the sense of a way to understand what we truly are and, on that basis, to begin to take a deep inner distance from the artificial spiritual cage into which modern society tries to lock us. But Rousseau also wants to preserve what he regards as the most important achievement of modernity: its liberation of humanity from traditional, medieval Christianity, which in another way takes humans far away from their natural wholeness.

The Least Unhealthy Political Order

The big question Rousseau's opening account of virtue provokes is: How can *any* political society ever accord with human nature and natural virtue? Rousseau characterizes *all* society as imposing "iron chains with which men are burdened" (36t; see also the opening of the first chapter of *The Social Contract*). But Rousseau insists that civil societies can nevertheless be ranked as *more or less* unnatural; he insists that different kinds of polity differ enormously in the *degree* to which they distort and enslave human nature.

To show this, Rousseau proceeds (40–47) to give a historical sketch of a variety of examples of societies. He first gives examples of historical societies that have been more or less afflicted with, and have foreshadowed, the evils being brought by scientific enlightenment. He then turns to examples of societies that have minimized the spiritual illnesses that attend all social existence. He thus provides concrete examples of the political standard by which he judges the emerging modern capitalist society to be so defective. The kind of society most in accord with or least distorting of human nature is exemplified by the ancient civic republics: republican Rome (before it became imperialist); original Persia (as a small civic society in the mountains, before it conquered Asia); and, above all, Sparta. At the start of the *Second Discourse* Rousseau lays out his standard more systematically, in the dedicatory letter addressed to his native city of Geneva (78ff.). Rousseau praises Geneva in a way that states the essential elements that are needed for the healthiest kind of human society; he uses Geneva as a kind of template for his conception of the best civil society. This means, however, that he idealizes Geneva, making it more perfect than it actually was. Most obviously, he drastically downplays the Calvinist Christian element in the Genevan republic and turns the Genevan religion into a purely civil religious spirit, akin to Roman paganism.

But we have obviously encountered a baffling paradox. How does Rousseau move from his new conception of virtue or freedom – as a deeply honest *individualistic* self-expression – to his contention that the best political situation for humans is full-time citizenship in an extremely *homogeneous* and *conformist* republic? The answer is found in asking correctly *the* basic political question. The correct question is not: "What sort of polity is best because it suits human nature?" That question has a null answer: No society suits human nature, or can. The correct question is: "What sort of polity is best because it artificially disfigures and corrupts human nature the *least*, by allowing its citizens to live lives that are the *least* dependent on competition to dominate one another, the *least* vain and deceptive and hypocritical, the *most* self-determining or independent, and the *most* honest and sincere and caring in their interdependency?"

Citizens of a small, conformist, participatory republic can, through their direct share in collective rule, be guided by what Rousseau calls in *The Social Contract* "the general will": a disposition that makes each person will, for public policy, only what each can understand that all the partner-citizens would join in willing. It is true that each thereby conceives of himself as a part, and hence only a partial individual. But each has a truly meaningful and respected partial share. The collectivity is one in which each citizen counts and is treasured by fellow citizens. The citizenry can, and must, genuinely sympathize with one another – truly knowing and feeling one another's simple, similar needs and concerns intimately. This requires that all live the same way, with the same needs and hopes and fears. They must live in substantial equality – economic and social as well as political. Their economic equality is, compared with modern society, a kind of equality in poverty, because they live with limited, very basic, and frugal property. Each family has just enough to be contented, as self-sufficient, small-scale farmers. They thus live free of need for all sorts of material goods and as a band of brothers and sisters – caring for and cared for by one another, while expressing and seeing one another for what they genuinely are, as similar citizens. They live in "a state where, all the individuals knowing one another, neither the obscure maneuvers of vice nor the modesty of virtue could be hidden from the notice and judgment of the public, and where that sweet habit of seeing and knowing one another turned love of the fatherland into love of the citizens rather than love of the soil" (78b–79t).

The government of such a society must be a "democracy," but one that is "wisely tempered." This means first and foremost that all must be "so subject to the laws that" none "could shake off their honorable yoke: that salutary and gentle yoke, which the proudest heads bear with all the more docility because they are suited to bear no other" (79b). But precisely because humans are *not* naturally political, or naturally obedient to the "yoke" of law, it takes a very long time to get people living reliably in conformity to the essentially artificial lawful habits that enable them to cooperate as fraternal republican citizens with a true general will: "A happy and tranquil Republic" is one "whose antiquity" is "in a way lost in the darkness of time." It is a republic that has no memory of civil strife, and has "experienced only those attacks suited to display and strengthen courage and love of fatherland in its inhabitants" (80–81). Rousseau goes on to describe something very close to what Aristotle described as the mixed democratic regime, where final legislative authority rests with the whole assembled citizenry, meeting occasionally, but where the administration of daily affairs is put in the hands of a small elected magistracy chosen for their superior political wisdom and public spirit (82b–83t). The regime needs to be supported by a shared, established "civil religion" (*religion civile*, a term invented by Rousseau – *Social Contract* 4.8), whose priests inspire and lead a piety that unqualifiedly promotes the civic virtues and patriotism; Rousseau claims that the example of Geneva shows that at least some version of Protestant Christianity can do so (88). But the fact that he even here reminds us that he honors pagan Rome (80) and Sparta (89) more than Geneva shows that he is viewing religion strictly as a means to fraternal civic virtue.

Even more important than "civil religion" is the civic role of women, as upholders and teachers of civic virtue and as models of chastity, allowing sexual pleasure only in marriage that supports the family, and thus preventing the erotic competition that breeds vanity, luxury, conspicuous consumption, and the slide into the worst social illnesses. Women, Rousseau insists, always dominate the men in deciding the moral tone of a society. Only if the women show that they have no use for vanity, or dishonesty, especially in love, and are dedicated to frugal and chaste family life, can the egalitarian simplicity, equality, and transparency of mores be preserved. The female citizens are "that precious half of the Republic which creates the happiness of the other and whose gentleness and wisdom maintain peace and good morals." Addressing his "virtuous citizenesses" (*vertueuses citoyennes*) Rousseau exclaims (89): "The fate of your sex will always be to govern ours. It is fortunate when your chaste power, exercised solely in conjugal union, makes itself felt only for the glory of the State and the public happiness! Thus did women command at Sparta and thus do you deserve to command at Geneva."

It is in the light of this political standard that Rousseau diagnoses in part two of the *First Discourse* the peculiarly terrible sickness of the emerging modern civil society, especially inasmuch as it is characterized by the popularization and authority of science.

The Evils of Scientific Enlightenment

Humans who live in a society that makes popular scientific enlightenment the heart of its education undergo three specific forms of degradation. In the first place, science induces in people a corrosive moral skepticism. Science promotes deep doubts about any grounding in nature for civic virtue and patriotism and for any self-transcendence of individual interest. By the same token, science induces deep doubts about all traditional religious beliefs that support civic virtue: "These vain and futile declaimers go everywhere armed with their deadly paradoxes, undermining the foundations of faith, and annihilating virtue. They smile disdainfully at the old-fashioned words of fatherland and religion, and devote their talents and philosophy to destroying and debasing all that is sacred among men" (50). Contemplating modern schooling, Rousseau laments: "I see everywhere immense institutions where young people are brought up at great expense, learning everything – except their duties." "Your children," he predicts, "will not even know what the words magnanimity, equity, temperance, humanity, courage are; that sweet name fatherland will never strike their ear; and IF they hear of God, it will be less to be awed by him than to be afraid of him" (56).

In the second place, science promotes, instead of virtue and religion, materialism and hedonism, or the false belief that what matters in life is ever-increasing economic power, prosperity, and even luxury: "Luxury rarely develops without the sciences and the arts, and they never develop without luxury" (50b). Science makes people think that the only reality is material, and that physical security or health and comfortable self-preservation are the only solid concerns. Science thus undermines the natural human capacity to risk life and limb for one's liberty as an individual or as a citizen. "While living conveniences multiply, arts are perfected and luxury spreads, true courage is enervated, military virtues disappear, and this too is the work of the sciences" (54m). Free people, Rousseau stresses, are always heroic fighters in the cause of their liberty, and free republics need spirited defenders because they are small and poor and hence mortally threatened by big, rich, imperialistic societies.

But there is a third, deeper and more corrosive, poison that afflicts people living in societies where scientific talent, ability to contribute to technology, and artistic talent are most highly honored. Respect for scientific ability and artistic talent necessarily feeds and intensifies the sick human desire to devote one's life to appearing superior to others in ways that do *not* express what one truly is; popular education in science and the fine arts *necessarily* encourages a culture of false vanity. Why? Because *genuine* scientific and artistic talents are *rare*. In truth, only a few people genuinely find deep spiritual satisfaction, find their true self-expression, in the pursuit of science and the arts. And as scientific and artistic talent become highly valued in a society, those few become drawn into a sense of superiority, while *most* people become infected with the desire and need to *pretend* to have and to enjoy the highly valued talents. This fuels the competition to have possessions, and to be able to talk and to act in ways that make one *appear* to share in the talents. Conspicuous consumption makes one appear to be good at, and to enjoy doing, what society honors. Money can buy the appearance of talents. Humans more and more lose sight of the deeper and more important sense in which they are truly by nature equal – which is in their capacity for *virtue*. All humans have the capacity to live and to express themselves as self-sufficient, economically modest, proud but not vain individuals; all have the capacity to live as virtuous fellow citizens in a participatory republic. But a society that values highly scientific and artistic talent is necessarily inegalitarian: "What brings about all these abuses if not the disastrous inequality introduced among men by the distinction of talents, and the debasement of virtues?" That "is the most evident effect of all our studies and the most dangerous of their consequences." We "have physicists, geometers, chemists, astronomers, poets, musicians, painters"; we "no longer have citizens" (58–59).

Artists, Rousseau stresses, are especially corruptible, on account of their hunger for popular applause (52–53). Artists very easily slip into a life dominated by vanity or the lust to appear superior through apparent artistic talent. But precisely because the artists are more dependent on public approval than are scientists, artists and the fine arts are not quite so intrinsically dangerous to civic health. Artists can to some degree be made to support civic virtue and religion, patriotism, and to respect civic traditions. Thus, in ancient Greek republics, artistic and theatrical festivals were embedded in the civil religion. Art and religion were partners in ancient Greece and Rome. But for this to work, the arts must be properly regulated and even censored or self-censored. Artists must be compelled – as they were in ancient Greece and Rome – to accept a sense of civic responsibility, to appreciate the grave dangers in their powers, and to recognize the benefit they can bring, by adorning and making more attractive the genuine and the civic virtues, while attacking the corruption brought by science.

The Outstanding Exception: Socratic Science

There is, however, one kind of science or philosophy that Rousseau praises, even in the midst of his attack on the pernicious consequences of the influence of science and philosophy. Rousseau presents *Socrates* as living in Athens at a time when that city was beginning to become corrupted by the rise of popular enlightenment. Socrates (as Rousseau presents him) responded by in effect turning philosophy against itself. Socrates, as Rousseau presents him, used his enormous philosophic talents to attack and to expose as ignorance the pretended wisdom of the sophists and the sophisticated artists. Socrates refuted these sophisticates in their claims to know things that cast doubt on or debunked the traditional civic virtues. Socrates upheld the wisdom of the traditional religious authority, the Delphic oracle, and advocated the unsophisticated, unscientific and un-philosophic wisdom of civic virtue. This, Rousseau claims, is the message of Plato's *Apology*, which he quotes at length (43b–45). This Socratic model, of the citizen-philosopher, is evidently what Rousseau presents himself as following.

Now as we know from our earlier study of Socrates' complex speech in Plato's *Apology of Socrates*, there is something very fishy about all this. If we compare what Rousseau claims he is quoting from the *Apology* with what Socrates actually says in the *Apology*, we see that Rousseau drastically misquotes, invents words, and thus completely transforms the Delphic oracle story. Rousseau changes the text so as to make the radical skepticism of Socrates totally disappear. He misquotes so as to make the *Apology* read as if Socrates were simply supportive of traditional civic virtue and religion. He completely drops the first and leading part of Socrates' cross-examinations; he leaves out Socrates' exposure of the ignorance of the democratic statesmen, the civic leaders. Rousseau likewise drops Socrates' cross-examination of the *artisans* or craftsmen, and substitutes instead a cross-examination of the *artists* – in addition to the poets! And Rousseau totally invents Socrates' cross-examining of the *sophists* – which is not in the *Apology*'s presentation at all.

What is Rousseau up to? Why introduce the Platonic Socrates, in his Delphic image, as *the* model, while so dramatically misquoting and changing the whole meaning of the passage as we find it in Plato?

We can begin to understand Rousseau's subtlety if we recall that in our study of Plato's *Apology*, we noted what Socrates himself does by giving *two contradictory* portraits of himself. Socrates *covers over* his first self-portrait given in the Delphic oracle story, as a radical skeptic, by giving a very different portrait, in the gadfly section, after the cross-examination of Meletus. If we bear this in mind, and everything it shows us concerning Socratic rhetoric, we can see that Rousseau is doing in his own way what the Platonic Socrates did. Rousseau is adopting a modified form of deceptive, Platonic-Socratic rhetoric. He goes a step farther than Socrates, by conflating the two accounts in the *Apology*, so as to hide even more completely the skeptical side of Socratic philosophy. Rousseau indicates that he is largely in agreement with Plato's Socrates on the major issue of how genuine philosophy should understand its relation to political society. He agrees that radical skepticism is indeed a core aspect of genuine philosophy, and of philosophic self-expression and self-discovery, but needs to be kept hidden. And if we next look through the *First Discourse* and bring together all the things Rousseau says or hints about himself, we see that Rousseau – imitating the Platonic Socrates – presents himself, and philosophy or science, in two contradictory ways.

On one hand, and most apparently, Rousseau presents himself, on the title page, as a nameless "citizen of Geneva," just as on the last page (64) he identifies himself as one of the "common men, not endowed by heaven with such great talents and not destined for so much glory." He presents himself as a simple, common person – a citizen. But on the other hand, he also says, in the preface (33) that he is writing because (as he puts it) he "wants to live beyond [his] century." In the foreword (32), he notes that this essay indeed made him "famous." And he says in the preface (33) that he is, as he puts it, "honored by the approval of a few wise men." In other words, he reveals that his truest audience, the audience that most gratifies him in its approval, is a tiny elite. On the title page (31), where he signs himself a nameless citizen of Geneva, there is also an epigraph – in Latin, the language of the sophisticated and learned. It is from the poet Ovid, who in these words is declaring and predicting that people will not understand him and therefore will call him a barbarian. Ovid became famous for all time as a poet of private erotic love, not of civic virtue, and he wrote under the corrupt empire, not the republic. In the poem from which Rousseau takes this epigraph,

Ovid is complaining about being exiled from the corrupt pleasures of
Rome and forced to live among simple people in the provinces.

But the most vivid manifestation of the fact that Rousseau is writing
on at least two levels, with different messages, is the frontispiece, the
engraving that Rousseau commissioned and directed in every detail.
It is, as Rousseau says, an allegory – which demands interpretation. In
the note in the text, to which he refers us (47–48), Rousseau stresses
that the mass of the Greek citizens understood Prometheus to be a god
unfriendly to mankind, because he brought the light of the sciences.
Rousseau stresses that the other, traditional gods were believed to have
punished Prometheus for bringing science to mankind. But Rousseau
also points out that in his own new version of the myth, as depicted in
this frontispiece, Prometheus is warning away an ugly satyr. And if we
look, we see that Rousseau leaves a key part of the allegory unexplained.
Prometheus is giving the torch to a beautiful human, who looks like a
statue ready to come to life. Who or what does this beautiful person
represent? Why is the one who is warned away a satyr – a subhuman
being? In a public letter written a few months later, defending himself
against attacks, Rousseau gives a thumbnail interpretation, in which he
presents himself as Prometheus, the god who brings true science to the
few true geniuses, while warning the masses away from it. Rousseau is not
a simple citizen – that is a role, a mask. Rousseau is in fact a god, higher
even than the geniuses, because Rousseau is the philosopher who truly
understands *both* the greatness of science *and* its limitations.

All of this helps us to understand the biggest contradiction in the *First
Discourse*, which crops up near the end (59ff.). Rousseau suddenly starts
to backtrack and to soften his attack on science and its effects. First,
he suggests that it is possible that it would be good for the sciences to
be promoted by academies led by scientists, *if* the scientists had a clear
sense of the dangers science poses to virtue – *if* they were scientists with
a deep sense of civic responsibility, who strove to avoid undermining,
and even strove to foster, civic virtue. It could seem that Rousseau is
here merely flattering the Academy of Dijon so as to soften the blow of
his earlier words and to help himself win the prize. Yet on the next page
(60) he returns to the attack on the present situation of science. We
thus begin to see that he is pointing toward an unrealized possibility – of
a far more politically responsible kind of science and philosophy. This
prepares for the startling denouement: "But if the development of the
sciences and arts has added nothing to our true felicity," if it "has corrupted our morals, and if the corruption of morals has impaired purity

of taste, what shall we think of that crowd of elementary authors who have removed the difficulties that blocked access to the temple of the muses and that nature put there as a test of strength for those who might be tempted to learn?" What shall we think of "those compilers of works who have indiscreetly broken down the door of the sciences and let into their sanctuary a populace unworthy of approaching it; whereas it would be preferable for all who could not go far in the learned profession to be rebuffed from the outset and directed into arts useful to society?" Those "whom nature destined to be her disciples needed no teachers. Verulam [Bacon], Descartes, Newton, these preceptors of the human race had none themselves." If "a few men must be allowed to devote themselves to the study of the sciences and arts, it must be only those who feel the strength to walk alone in their footsteps and go beyond them" (62–63). Rousseau here suddenly praises the fact that *ancient* science and philosophy were kept largely hidden from the mass of men, as a sacred thing that the masses are unworthy even to approach (see also 211). The reason Rousseau now gives why science needs to be kept hidden is not mainly that science corrupts society. Now the main reason is, rather, that *science* is corrupted *by* society; science is contaminated and debased by being made popular. Rousseau now discloses that he is at least as concerned for the true good of science or philosophy as he is for the good of civil society. By keeping science hidden, in books that are very hard to understand and decipher, obstacles are placed in the way of most people easily becoming involved in science. Those obstacles are a healthy "test of strength" that selects the truly talented, to whom the obstacles give the challenges that "teach them to exert themselves," to "feel the strength to walk alone."

In other words, in the closing pages of the *First Discourse*, Rousseau reveals that philosophy or science is the truest expression of the genuine and self-sufficient individuality of those very few who are gifted. Such geniuses, Rousseau goes on to say (63–64), should find a home in corrupt societies, in monarchies (i.e., *not* republics). Such geniuses can live well in such corrupt places and even become honored and powerful, without becoming corrupted themselves and while diminishing the corruption around them.

Is not Rousseau speaking of himself as exactly such a person? After praising such rare geniuses, he seems to answer that he is not. At the end, he identifies himself with the simple citizen, the unsophisticated, a follower of Sparta against Athens. But Rousseau implicitly identified himself earlier with Socrates, who never left Athens – although he always praised Sparta. Rousseau quietly indicates that he is in fact one of those who has the strength to walk alone, for whom philosophy and science *is* true self-realization. But he veils his own genius – thus setting an example for the way the philosopher should hide himself and do everything he can to honor un-philosophic civic spirit, to defend the dignity of ordinary people living simple, unpretentious, and maximally self-sufficient lives within corrupt modern society.

The Project of the Second Discourse

To see the fuller grounds for Rousseau's complex position, and to clarify his disagreement with classical political philosophy, we need to turn to the work in which – Rousseau says in his *Confessions* – his philosophical principles are "completely developed" and "are made manifest with the greatest boldness, not to say audacity": *The Discourse on the Origin and Foundations of Inequality among Humans*. At the outset, Rousseau makes plain his agreement with the moderns against the ancients; to understand human nature we need to conceive of humans as originally in a "state of nature" of radically disconnected individuals. But Rousseau criticizes his modern predecessors for failing to think through what is necessarily implied in this illuminating concept: "The philosophers who have examined the foundations of society have all felt the necessity of going back to the state of nature, but none of them has reached it" (102–103). If we are truly to understand human nature as not inherently directed to structured social existence, then we must think our way back to what strange kind of being the human animal must have been, for "thousands of centuries" (120t), *before* society came into being (by some long chain of *accidents*). Only by such imaginative reconstructive cogitation will we begin to uncover what is truly natural at our psychological core, under the layers that historically constructed convention and custom have imposed on us since childhood. Only thus can we begin to understand the deep reasons for, and character of, our social and psychological ills – the contradictions between our deepest natural impulses and needs, and the artificial needs and demands and repressions and distortions that society imposes on us. Only thus can we begin to obtain truly natural standards, standards of natural right or law – of what is right or best according to human nature (91–92, 95–96). This uncovering of our natural core is the task Rousseau executes in part one of the *Second Discourse*. In part two, he takes up a successor task: to speculate on what the accidental process was by which humans gradually acquired all the artificial psychological attributes that characterize us now, as social beings.

Rousseau stresses, however, that we immediately confront a massive problem: The true state of nature no longer exists anywhere that we know of. The human race appears everywhere entirely socialized. Rousseau admits and stresses that he can only initiate a very long investigation that needs to be continued by others (92b–93t). He means to launch a new scientific project (what came to be called "anthropology"). Especially in his crucial footnotes, he shows that he makes use of whatever empirical evidence he can find about primitive peoples, and also other primates – some of whom, he speculates, might even be humans still in the natural condition (204–209). Yet all primitive tribal peoples are already living in some form of society. And the fact that the apes cannot be humanized, even in captivity, seems to show that they belong to nonhuman species. We can see that humans must be a unique kind of apelike animal that is, paradoxically, naturally capable of a dramatic, artificial distortion or repression and restructuring of its original natural living conditions.

The most important and compelling, immediately available, body of evidence for the state of nature as presocial is the *pathology* that humans exhibit everywhere in society. All around us we witness humans desperately trying to *escape* their condition of existence – through alcohol and other narcotics, through so-called entertainments and vacations, through the "escapism" of thrills of risk, in gambling, in dangerous actions and relationships of all sorts. Every vigorous animal obviously longs and seeks to escape its *cage*, its *confinement*, its *trap*. Who ever heard of a vigorous animal that longed and sought to escape the environment that is naturally suited to it? How then can anyone seriously claim that society as we know it is the natural environment suited to the human animal? How can society be natural for humans, if in society humans act like neurotic animals trapped in cages? Rousseau contends that only something like the speculation he lays out is sufficient to explain this pervasive and profound empirical evidence of the terrible dislocation humans suffer in their social existence.

But before he can proceed, Rousseau must also confront another enormous practical as well as theoretical difficulty, in publishing his speculations: the powerful, punitive censorship exercised by the Christian churches, backed by the governments of every country of Europe. In Rousseau's time, prison, exile, or even death is dealt out to anyone who openly suggests that the Bible is not the literal truth, revealed by God. And as we have seen, the Bible has its own authoritative explanation of the reason for the agonized human awareness of dislocation, alienation, and inner contradiction in the way we are forced to live in society. The Bible teaches that all this is caused by the Fall: the contamination of original sin and God's condign punishment of the whole human race. Rousseau's state of nature teaching is profoundly contrary to this biblical teaching. Indeed, perhaps the deepest and most important purpose of Rousseau's teaching is the overthrowing of the biblical account and conception of the human condition. But in order to get his book published, and not immediately burned when published, and also, at the same time, in order to bring to the thoughtful reader's attention this most fundamental issue, Rousseau begins by claiming to disavow everything he is going to say and claiming to avow his acceptance of the biblical account in Genesis: "It did not even enter the minds of most of our philosophers to doubt that the state of nature had existed, even though it is evident from reading the Holy Scriptures that the first man, having received enlightenment and precepts directly from God, was not himself in that state"; and, "that giving the writings of Moses the credence that any Christian philosopher owes them, it must be denied that even before the flood men were ever in the pure state of nature" (102b–103). We see on close inspection that this wording suggests how ironical, not to say playfully impious, Rousseau is being, especially since he immediately goes on to indicate his true view. "I shall imagine myself in the Lyceum of Athens, repeating the lessons of my masters, with Plato and Xenocrates for judges"; "O man, whatever country you may come from, whatever your opinions may be, listen: here is your history as I believed it to read, not in the books of your fellow-men, which are liars, but in nature, which never lies" (103b–104t).

The Original State of Nature

Hobbes and Locke argue that the ugly truth about human nature, and about what the original state of nature must have been like, reveals itself when we witness the way humans behave when one removes the artificial constraints of civil society – when there is a breakdown of law and order: Then you see human nature in the raw. Rousseau exposes the fallacy in this reasoning. What we are observing in such situations, he submits, is what happens to beings who have been *artificially addicted* to social and political existence, and have then been *deprived* of that to which they have been *addicted*. To claim that such observation reveals the true nature of humans is as absurd as claiming that when you see a drug addict in withdrawal symptoms, you are seeing his true nature as a human. Besides, there is overwhelming empirical evidence in the rest of animate nature suggesting that we should *not* assume that the natural condition of humans was or could be "a state not to be endured" (as Locke asserts). Everywhere we look in nature, we find animals *well adapted* to their *natural* condition of *undomesticated* existence. Animals are found ill adapted only where humans have domesticated them (111). It is reasonable to proceed on the hypothesis that the same holds, or once held, for the human animal: That in its natural, wild state, the human was well adapted to the conditions of its existence (107–112). If this were not true, would it not become a mystery how the human race could have survived? Is this not a crushing problem for the whole outlook of Hobbes and Locke? If the state of nature is or was as dangerous as Hobbes and Locke say, how could the human species have lasted long enough to figure out and to construct all the artificial things it had to figure out – starting with language – in order to forge "social contracts" to overcome the natural state?

We must, Rousseau argues, think through the state of nature hypothesis much more carefully and consistently. We must stick intransigently to the hypothesis that humans survived for countless generations as independent and equal beings. This means that we need to conceive the state of nature as a state in which the human animal, like other animals, is well adapted to its environment. We must conceive of a condition in which there is not anything that leads or drives humans to need others. We must suppose that humans eventually became social only on account of a long series of "accidents" that were "the chance combination of several foreign causes which might never have arisen, and without which man would have remained eternally in his primitive condition" (140, 112). These accidents placed humans in *stressed* conditions, where they were compelled to change and *distort* their natural tendencies and behaviors.

On this more reasonable hypothesis, it follows that the original, presocial, individual state would *not* have been a condition of scarcity, anxiety, or frustration. It would not have been a state of unresolved tensions or contradictions that propelled humans toward constructing society. Each individual could meet his or her needs through his or her own independent efforts. The most important implication for human relations Rousseau makes explicit (at 134–135): There must have been *no family* by nature, and *no love* between the sexes. Reproduction would have been purely "physical"; copulation would have been casual and momentary, but also rare, since humans would have lived dispersed, not in groups, but more like wolverines or cougars or orangutans (119, 121, 137, 142, 222). There would be by nature nothing "moral" about sex. There would be no reason for any sense of exclusive attachments, or belonging to one another; no sense of fidelity or infidelity, no jealousy or competition; no special preference and no awareness even of beauty or merit or admiration. But Rousseau is still more radical: He draws into question most of the naturalness of motherhood. He suggests that if human females are naturally independent individuals, there would be by nature no mothering instinct or direct love of the offspring. Even a mother's care for her own children can be imagined to be not a strong natural drive or need but only a kind of incidental consequence of another natural need. Mothers who had given birth would at first suckle the child simply to relieve the pain in the breast, with no affection whatsoever for the child. Then purely by habit mothers would get used to having the baby around and become attached to it and its needs (121).

This goes with Rousseau's stress on natural man's (and woman's) likely hardiness and courage. Humans must have been quite capable of defending themselves from other animals, or running away, or climbing, or hiding. "Always near danger" (the state of nature is not paradise!), "his best-trained faculties must be those having as principal object attack and defense, either to subjugate his prey or to save himself from being the prey of another animal" (112; see also the long passage on 107–109).

It follows that the fundamental human experience by nature is not fear and anxiety (as Hobbes and Locke and Montesquieu claim). It is rather courageous self-sufficiency and sweet contentment in solitude, punctuated by very short-term desires, readily satisfied. Once they satisfied their modest needs, the human individuals would have lapsed into a state of repose, lightly napping most of the time, like cats, and suffused by a pleasant animal feeling of being alive – a feeling of their own satisfied, solitary existence. Prior to society and hence language, there would have been very little imagination, and hence almost no care for the future beyond the most immediate. Above all, and momentously, Rousseau contends that by nature humans would have no fear of death (116, 109) – because, like other animals, they would not have a conception of death (as opposed to pain). As we saw above (in the quote from 112), of course the human animal would, like all other animals, care for its "self-preservation." But the animal does so without thinking of preservation *from death*. Humans, like other animals, would preserve themselves by seeking the pleasures of satisfied natural needs and by avoiding the pains caused by the frustration of those needs.

Closely linked to the lack of knowledge of death is the most significant absence of all. There is nowhere in the state of nature any sign of any religious belief or experience of God or anything divine whatsoever. This is of course a teaching that it is not safe for Rousseau to put into plain words. He expresses this most important and dangerous dimension of his teaching on human nature by his conspicuous silence and by implication (see especially 96, 102, 110, 117 – the last two passages making clear that there is no natural human impetus toward thinking or philosophy) – and of course, in the midst of his footnotes: note O (222).

At the core of the natural human experience is what Rousseau calls the "sentiment of existence": The natural human's "soul, agitated by nothing, is given over to the sole sentiment of its present existence without any idea of the future, however near it may be, and his projects, as limited as his views, barely extend to the end of the day" (117). This deeply contented feeling of existence is closely linked to self-preservation: "Man's first sentiment was that of his existence, his first care that of his preservation" (142). Humans are drawn to preserve themselves partly or even mainly by the recurring sweet feeling of existence; the sweet sentiment is mentioned first, or is prior. Contrary to what is taught by Hobbes and Locke, humans are not naturally driven by fear of death, but instead attracted by the joy of feeling alive. In Rousseau's later autobiographical writing (the fifth promenade of the *Reveries of a Solitary Walker*), he contended that humans today *can* recover a version of this deepest, original, natural sense of wholeness and contentment. Rousseau tells us that he himself often experienced this. He suggests that this experience is the richest and most satisfying, the most in accord with our nature, that we can have. It is not the same experience as the original human would have, because we have and articulate it with all the mental development of historical culture. It is in that way a fuller, richer version of what the primitive human animal had.

What Distinguishes Humans from Other Animals

There are two respects in which human nature must always have been distinct from the nature of other life-forms. First, and most conspicuously, Rousseau claims that humans must always have had some experience, however dim at first, of free will. It is in this awareness of freedom, of acting on the basis of choice, rather than in any thinking, that the human is set apart from the other animals. Rousseau here takes his stand on the limits of modern mechanistic physics – which cannot account for

the direct experience every one of us has, of being free to choose how
one is going to act (114; see also 208t).

Yet as soon as he makes this claim about free will, Rousseau admits that
it is problematic or disputable; he goes on to offer in its stead a more
certain, undeniable, second distinction between the human and other
animals – "another very specific quality," about which "there can be no
dispute": *"perfectibility"* (*perfectibilité*), a "faculty which, with the aid of circumstances, successively develops all the others, and resides among us as
much in the species as in the individual." By contrast with a human, "an
animal is at the end of a few months what it will be all its life; and its species is at the end of a thousand years what it was the first year of that thousand" (114b–115t). We get some help in understanding what this means
if we recall an important passage near the beginning, in which Rousseau
stressed that humans are from the beginning distinguished by their lack
of fixed instincts, and hence their capacity to imitate: "Dispersed among
the animals," humans "observe and imitate their industry"; humans have
"the advantage, that whereas each species has only its own proper instinct,
man – perhaps having none that belongs to him – appropriates them all
to himself, feeds equally well with most of the diverse foods which other
animals share, and consequently finds his subsistence more easily than
any of them can" (105b–106t). "Perfectibility" seems to mean the mal-
leability that makes it possible for humans to adapt to circumstances with
a dramatic degree of plasticity, and hence to become, over time, radically
different from their original nature. To put it another way, Rousseau sees
that humans have an astounding range of unnecessary potentialities,
which can lie fallow and unrealized but can be triggered into action and
take on a fantastic variety of forms, in response to accidental pressures
of all sorts. Yet if this is what he means, the word Rousseau uses for this
adaptability is curious and thought-provoking. Why designate this plastic adaptability by the highly laudatory term "perfectibility," rather than
by some more neutral or even pejorative term? What is more, Rousseau
here characterizes the natural condition as one of "imbecility"! Does
Rousseau not suddenly raise the possibility that *leaving* the natural condition is a kind of ascent or "perfection" – rather than simply a corruption and degradation? Rousseau here certainly speaks of "perfectibility"
in ambiguous evaluative language: "Perfectibility" is "the source of all
man's misfortunes," by drawing him "out of that original condition in
which he would pass tranquil and innocent days"; "in the long run" it
makes him "the tyrant of himself and of nature." But in the process, perfectibility "brings to *flower* over the centuries" man's *"enlightenment and*

his errors, his vices *and his virtues*" (115, our emphasis). Rousseau thus begins to disclose that he is not unqualifiedly condemning the departure from the natural condition: There are large benefits, as well as perhaps worse costs, in that transition. We are thus introduced to a complexity and ambiguity in Rousseau's understanding of human nature, especially as norm or standard.

But before we get into that more complicated dimension of Rousseau's normative conception of human nature, we need to have more fully in view what Rousseau argues would characterize the relations that humans would have had when they did encounter one another in their original, purely natural, scattered state. First and foremost is something negative, that we have already stressed: Humans would have had *no* desire for superiority or domination. By nature they would not care what others think of them – except momentarily, when they get in a fight over food or a sexual partner and want to frighten one another. In a crucial note to his text, Rousseau elaborates, distinguishing *amour de soi-même*, or self-love, from *amour propre*, or vanity – "two passions very different in their nature and their effects." "Love of oneself" is a "natural sentiment which inclines every animal to watch over its own preservation, and which, directed in man by reason and modified by pity, produces humanity and virtue." In contrast, vanity is "only a relative sentiment, artificial and born in society, which inclines each individual to have a greater esteem for himself than for anyone else, inspires in men all the harm they do to one another, and is the true source of honor" (Rousseau's note O, 221b–222). The natural absence of vanity, as the chief emotional spring causing endless murderous struggle, is a major justification for Rousseau's asserting toward the end of the discourse (193) that he has "demonstrated" that humans are by nature "good." Rousseau does not mean by natural "goodness" strong mutual care, love, or moral virtue (129b–130t). Human "*goodness*" is found at its purest when humans are totally ignorant of and *lack virtue*, as morality.

Still, Rousseau goes on here (130) to speak in the second place of a more positive form of natural goodness. He contends that humans share with other animals a certain pity, or an aversion to the suffering of other animals, especially fellow members of the same species; this is the forerunner and natural root of what becomes compassion in society. Yet as one reads Rousseau's impassioned praise of pity or compassion as the one "natural virtue" (131), one can wonder if he is not exaggerating, in order to strengthen what he thinks is an important *social* virtue for his readers. He puts the matter most lucidly in the following formulation:

"In the state of nature," pity "takes the place of laws, morals, and virtue"; it "will dissuade every robust savage from robbing a weak child or
an infirm old man of his hard-won subsistence, if he himself hopes to
be able to find his own elsewhere." Instead of "that sublime maxim of
reasoned justice, *Do unto others as you would have them do unto you,*" pity
"inspires all men with this other maxim of natural goodness, much less
perfect but perhaps more useful": "*Do what is good for you with the least
possible harm to others*" (133). Like Hobbes, Rousseau replaces the golden
rule with a rule that is more selfish, but Rousseau traces the new, more
effective, natural substitute not (or not simply) to reason, but to the pre-
rational passion of pity.

The History of Our Humanity

In part two of the *Second Discourse*, Rousseau develops his conjectural
account of the long series of stages through which human existence
became alienated from its natural state. Throughout this process, and
still today, each of us remains at our core an animal that would find
true contentment in the original state that Rousseau sketches in part
one. In a sense, every baby, at the moment of birth, exists momentarily
in that state. But immediately after a baby is born, in developed society, it is subjected to terrific pressures that mold its "perfectibility" so as
to socialize it, repressing its natural animal individuality and forcing its
spirit into artificial habits that harness it to society and to artificial social
behaviors.

One can put Rousseau's thesis another way by saying that almost everything we call human, and certainly everything civilized, is a product of
history – of successive human constructions over time, in response to
accidental stresses. Human nature's "perfectibility" allows but does not
impel or guide historical human action that gradually constructs civilized humanity. The process occurs in ways that are almost never fully
self-conscious on the part of the humans who are reconstructing themselves through social changes. By tracing the major steps, Rousseau is
showing how mankind has acquired a kind of second nature, or a very
thick shell of ingrained habituation that overlays and hides the original
nature that remains deep within us.

Rousseau commences by leaping ahead to spotlight the most terrible
turning point: the "founding of civil society," or "the last stage of the
state of nature" – which is the moment when someone fenced off land
and thus invented private landed property. "What crimes, wars, murders,

what miseries and horrors would the human race have been spared by someone who, uprooting the stakes or filling the ditch, had shouted to his fellow-men: 'Beware of listening to this imposter; you are lost if you forget that the fruits belong to all and the earth to no one!'" Rousseau thus begins by directly opposing Locke and Locke's whole thesis. But Rousseau immediately adds a pregnant, deeply complicating qualification: "But it is very likely that by then things had already come to the point where they could no longer remain as they were" (141b–142). Humans must already have undergone vast changes in their ways, changes that had already made them dependent on all sorts of by nature unnecessary goods and relationships. Yet strangely enough, Rousseau here calls this moment "the last stage of the state of nature." He thus suddenly speaks as if the state of nature itself is *not* a static condition, but a mutating condition, with "stages." And, as he goes on (142b) to summarize what he has said in part one about original humanity and its condition, he now, curiously, calls the human described in part one *not* "natural man," but instead "*nascent* man." He thus opens up the possibility that the *original* state of nature is not the *whole* of the condition that is natural for humanity, that it is only the *beginning* of a process of change that is *as a whole* somehow natural, or at least not simply unnatural. The meaning of human "nature" for Rousseau becomes more explicitly ambiguous. In the pages that follow, the speculative account that Rousseau gives of the way humans might have been transformed over time surprises us by being less violent, or less wrenching, than we might expect. The account sounds in its early stages more like a gradual unfolding. This is true especially of "the first revolution" in human existence – the building of crude huts (146).

The Birth of Human Social Existence

This "first revolution" gave humans "a sort of property" and the beginnings of the family. "The first developments of the heart were the effect of a new situation, which united husbands and wives, fathers and children in a common habitation." The "habit of living together gave rise to the sweetest of sentiments known to men: conjugal love and paternal love." *The* "sweetest" sentiment is not, then, the original sweet sentiment of individual existence. The parental and conjugal joy of loving and being loved is not strictly natural, but it suits and delights humans. This first, familial, society is rooted in "affection and freedom," not compulsion. Yet this first society entailed the momentous division of labor, and differentiation in the way of life, and resulting interdependence, between the two sexes. And this primary loss of independence was soon followed by another: Since there was leisure, "they used it to procure many kinds of commodities unknown to their fathers; and that was the first yoke they imposed on themselves without thinking about it, and the first source of the evils they prepared for their descendants." For these commodities "degenerated into true needs," so that "being deprived of them became much more cruel than possessing them was sweet" (146–147; cf. 120b).

The second revolution grows out of this first. "Young people of different sexes live in neighboring huts; the passing intercourse demanded by nature soon leads to another kind no less sweet and more permanent through mutual frequentation." With the birth of extrafamilial erotic love, "people grow accustomed to consider different objects and to make comparisons; imperceptibly they acquire ideas of merit and beauty which produce sentiments of preference." The "tender and gentle sentiment" of erotic love becomes, "at the least obstacle, an impetuous fury. Jealousy awakens with love; discord triumphs, and the gentlest of the passions receives sacrifices of human blood" (148b–149t). Rousseau distinguishes between love within the family (even sexual love, which was originally simple and uncomplicated) and the very different, much more artificial and complex, romantic love between unrelated young people. The original, sweetest sentiment of affection is *not* romantic love, but rather a kind of bond of intimate familiarity between housemates, which one has not chosen, which one simply grows up with. But once sexual attraction and attachment becomes extrafamilial, then everything changes, and the erotic competition contributes to other forms of competitiveness that quickly emerge, linked closely to the emergence of the arts, primarily music: "People grew accustomed to assembling in front of the huts or around a large tree"; "song and dance, true children of love and leisure," became "the occupation of idle and assembled men and women." Each one "began to look at the others and to want to be looked at himself, and public esteem had a value." The one "who sang or danced the best, the handsomest, the strongest, the most adroit, or the most eloquent became the most highly considered; and that was the first step toward inequality and, at the same time, toward vice" (149, 134–135, 139t, 142).

Here is the original source of the *moral* life of man: Morality is born out of erotic vanity and contempt, shame and envy, and the concomitant demand for dignity and respect. "As soon as men had begun to appreciate one another, and the idea of consideration was formed in their minds, each one claimed a right to it, and it was no longer possible to be disrespectful toward anyone with impunity." From this "came the first duties of civility, even among savages," and from this "any voluntary wrong became an outrage, because along with the harm that resulted from the injury, the offended man saw in it contempt for his person which was often more unbearable than the harm itself." Thus, "everyone punishing the contempt shown him by another in a manner proportionate to the importance he accorded himself, vengeances became terrible, and men bloodthirsty and cruel." This is "precisely the point reached by most of the savage peoples known to us" (149b–150t).

Having thus shown how ambiguous is the evolution from what at first appeared a harmless and even sweet "revolution," Rousseau restates very strongly the standard he had established earlier, in his account of what he now calls the "*first* state of nature" or the "primitive state" – the condition of solitude described in part one, whose superiority he now ringingly affirms more than before. It was in that original state that man was "placed by nature at equal distances from the stupidity of the brutes and the fatal enlightenment of civil man" (150t).

But no sooner has Rousseau thus placed the original state on a spiritual pedestal than he shifts, in the midst of his *criticism* of nascent society, to a *praise* of nascent society: "[A]lthough men had come to have less endurance and although natural pity had already undergone some alteration, *this* period of the development of human faculties, maintaining a *golden mean* between the indolence of the *primitive* state and the petulant activity of our vanity, must have been the *happiest* and *most durable* epoch." "The more one thinks about it," Rousseau muses, "the more one finds that *this* state was the least subject to revolutions, *the best* for man, and that he must have come out of it only by some fatal accident, which for the common good ought never to have happened" (150b–151t, our emphasis). That the *Second Discourse* means to celebrate the state of "nascent society," the state of "savage *peoples*" (108, 110, 113, 132, 189) as much if not more than the "primitive," "true," original state of nature (the state of "savage man" – 102b, 106, 111, 112, 115, 117, 119, etc.), is also indicated by the frontispiece, designed by Rousseau, and explained in his note *P* (225–226): The engraving depicts a human renouncing today's developed society in order to return, not to the original state of nature, but rather to the savage social state.

Rousseau thus makes it clear that he is deeply ambivalent about the original pure natural state. After all, it was only when human life underwent the transformation into tribal existence that the mind and heart

developed, along with a heightened self-consciousness, an active imagination, the sweetest sentiments of family love, and bittersweet romantic love. Besides, Rousseau suggests that the savage social condition is
the most stable or durable, a sign of how well it suits the human being.
Moreover, this condition does still exist today, Rousseau stresses (179).
Many humans in many parts of the world, including North American
Native peoples, remain in this familial or tribal social state; this carries
with it major implications for modern culture. For one thing, it implies
that "savage peoples" still living in this condition will be better off if
they are left in it, that is, left alone by the "civilized" Europeans. The
whole *Second Discourse*, and especially the frontispiece, implies a severe
rebuke of European colonialism (see especially 223–260). Another and
still more telling implication is elaborated in Rousseau's novels. In them
Rousseau tries to show that even within commercial modern society, we
can and should strive to recover something of the more honest and more
intimate relations of the simple familial love that flourished in "nascent
society." Such a recovery *is* possible, for many people, whereas the original solitary condition seems, to say the least, much less retrievable.
Accordingly, *the* question with which Rousseau's novels wrestle is, to what
extent and in what conditions can (and cannot) romantic love lead to or
harmonize with, become consummated in, familial love. This question
becomes the chief theme of the novels of romanticism that dominate
nineteenth-century literature. We see here in this passage of the *Second
Discourse* the seed of that cultural movement, as inspired by Rousseau.
In this light, we may say that a major part of Rousseau's project as a
writer is exploring and clarifying which aspects of the historical overlay
of sociability are more, and which less, deeply set and essential, once the
human condition has left behind forever the original solitary and dispersed situation.

The Termination of the State of Nature

But of course, vast portions of mankind did leave behind the savage social
state – by undergoing a new, third, and far more devastating accidental
revolution: the twofold development of agriculture and metallurgy. The
creation of these arts went together with the development of exclusive
property rights in land, and the subsequent appropriation and enclosure, by a few, of all the good farm and mining lands. The vast majority
was thereby reduced to having to work for the few landholders and owners of the mineral resources. Why and for what reason did this happen?

Here again we see a massive disagreement with Hobbes and (especially) Locke. Rousseau presents the development of agriculture and metallurgy as something that was *not* necessary for human comfort and security. He repeats (at 151–152) his earlier suggestion (at 141–142) that there was nothing in the condition of savage society that made men truly need to acquire what agriculture and metallurgy provide. Rousseau even argues that agriculture must have come *after* the other arts, involving metalworking. For there was no need, he insists, for abundant food until many men were no longer hunting and gathering and instead had to spend their labor working in mines or in crafts involving metal and iron. Nonetheless, once agriculture and metallurgy were developed, there set in ever-growing inequality, caused most fundamentally by the unequal ownership of land and the division of labor, but fueled, above all, by the steadily increasing valuing of specific talents that are unequally distributed among humans.

Rousseau at this point (155–156) summarizes the key thesis of the *First Discourse*, according to which, as we've seen, the valuing of scientific talents goes together with an enormous pressure to appear to be other than what one truly is. The intensely dangerous competitive condition that results from the further development of this third stage leads to a general state of war. Rousseau agrees, then, that what Hobbes and Locke describe as the state of nature did and does come about – but only as the last stage of an eons-long development. Moreover for Rousseau, in contrast to Hobbes and Locke, the state of war that explodes in the final stage of the state of nature is less a war of all against all, as individuals or small gangs, than it is a *class* warfare: a combat between the small class of big property holders and the working-class majority, who have become slaves or who have to sell their labor power in order to survive (see especially 162). What Hobbes and Locke call the state of nature, Rousseau insists is already an organized social state, with economic classes and a class consciousness on the part of rich and poor. Consequently, while Rousseau agrees with Hobbes and Locke that the state of war is ended by a social compact, which constitutes the artificial justice devised by shrewd reasoning that constructs a way out of the state of war, Rousseau evaluates this contract and its justice very differently. The original social contract he decries as a swindle perpetrated by the clever among the conniving rich landowners: They persuaded the poor majority that in order to gain security and peace, and an end to dangerous violence, all must agree, consent, and contract to establish a "supreme power" that will protect everyone equally, and their property – *without redistributing* the property. "Crude" and "easily seduced," with "too many disputes among themselves," and "too much avarice and ambition," the poor majority "ran to meet their chains thinking they secured their freedom." The birth of lawful political society "destroyed natural freedom for all time, established forever the law of property and inequality," and "changed a clever usurpation into an irrevocable right"; "civil right" replaced the pure "law of nature" except in international relations, which descended into ever more heinous warfare and hostility, fueled by vanity or so-called honor (158b–161).

Natural Right

Having presented this account of the origin of political society, Rousseau acknowledges that there are other contrasting and not implausible accounts; however, "the choice among these," he declares, "is indifferent to what I want to establish" (161b). What, then, does he want to establish? That *actual consent* is the only sound and effective basis of government, because it is the only basis that is consistent with the passion to be free – which in political society means, having a significant role in determining the laws that govern one's own life, and not living under the arbitrary will of others. Rousseau proceeds to insist that there is a continuum from the wild animal's resistance to entrapment or domestication, through the savage's fierce love of freedom, to civilized people's demand for government by consent. Here we see the meaning of politically relevant "natural right"; here we see how the account of the prepolitical state of nature provides the natural basis and natural standard for all positive right, law, and government: "As an untamed steed bristles his mane, paws the ground with his hoof, and breaks away impetuously at the very approach of the bit," so "barbarous man does not bend his head for the yoke" but "prefers the most turbulent freedom to tranquil subjection." And "*therefore* it is not by the degradation of enslaved peoples that man's *natural* dispositions for or against servitude must be judged, but by the marvels done by all free peoples to guard themselves against oppression." "I see," Rousseau says, speaking empirically, "animals born free and despising captivity," who "break their heads against the bars of their prison"; "I see multitudes of entirely naked savages scorn European voluptuousness and endure hunger, fire, the sword, and death to preserve only their independence"; and similarly, "I see" that free peoples "sacrifice pleasures, repose, wealth, power, and life itself for the preservation of this sole good" – political *liberty* (164–165, our emphasis). Thus does original, integral human nature speak in and to political life, laying down the fundamental law of nature, which declares that liberty is the sole overriding political good and the only solid foundation of all the other political goods.

If we resist the temptation to be dazzled by Rousseau's eloquence here, if we mingle our appreciation for his eloquence with some critical reflection, we see that our political philosopher lends edifying rhetorical strength to the natural right basis of political liberty by blurring some very important distinctions – above all, between the kinds of freedom exemplified by (a) dutiful, patriotic, moral, and even pious Spartans, such as Brasidas, (b) tribes of "barbarous," naked "savages," and (c) wild animals. Besides, the closer we look, the more we may be provoked to wonder why Rousseau is silent here on the attachment to freedom that would have characterized *solitary* man in the *original* state of nature. Could it be because "nothing is so gentle as man in his primitive state" (recall 150, 139, 142b–143t, 195)? The link between the human's original, natural, and gentle attachment to personal liberty and the citizen's virile attachment to civil liberty would seem to be more tenuous than Rousseau's civic-spirited rhetoric here suggests.

Still, if the link is somewhat exaggerated here, it is far from being spurious. Original natural man may have asserted his freedom more often by running away or hiding than by fighting, but when necessary he fought for it because he loved it, or at least loved his sentiment of individual existence (107–108, 139–140, 179, 205, 207). The original social contract, even if it were a fraud perpetrated by the wealthy, must have promised to defend everyone's freedom to some extent. If this hadn't been so, early civilized man would have rejected the contract (161–164). "Even the wise" (who as such were not fooled by the fraud) "saw the necessity of resolving to sacrifice one part of their freedom *for the preservation of the other*" (160t, our emphasis; cf. 172). On this basis, Rousseau attacks existing political theories as well as governments for failing adequately to esteem and to defend freedom (164–168). He explains how "a true contract between the people and the chiefs it chooses for itself" obligates both parties "to observe laws that are stipulated in it and that form the bonds of their union" (169t). This sketch of the constitutional basis for civil liberty is richly improved in *The Social Contract* (especially 1.6–7, 2.1–6, 3.1).

But given the gulf between lawful liberty and the pre-civil forms of liberty that are more natural – whose remnants easily veer toward bloody anarchy when civil society breaks down – Rousseau speaks with reserve of the people's right to revolution. They do have such a right, but it is "fatal." The people's "right to renounce their dependence" on their rulers entails such "frightful dissensions," such "infinite disorders," that "human governments" need "a basis more solid than reason alone": It was "necessary for public repose that divine will intervened to give sovereign authority a sacred and inviolable character" (170b). While in *The Social Contract* Rousseau stresses how essential it is that the norms of reason be supported, in the best civil society, by the habitual piety of a "civil religion," here, toward the end of the *Second Discourse*, he stresses the importance of religious sanctions for all governments (see also 202–203).

Rousseau sees, however, two difficulties with religion as a basis for government in the modern world. The first is religious fanaticism, with the wars of religion to which it leads (171t). The second and now graver problem is the one Rousseau painted so vividly in the *First Discourse*; it is paradoxically the result of the recent attempt to solve the first. The success of the Enlightenment is causing traditional religion to atrophy. What is needed now is a new civil religion that will exalt and support the love of civil liberty – that will sanction no claims of superiority or inferiority and will instead present communal, lawful self-rule as the noble end in itself, favored and intended by God as the author of nature in its goodness (see especially 97, 201–202). In this way, vanity or *amour propre*, which cannot be removed from the souls of today's humans, will be directed against itself; it will not give rise to arguments for ruling over others, but will instead support government based on the general will. Such suprarational guidance is especially crucial at this historical juncture, because all forms of government have now degenerated into intolerable oppression (175, 177), and revolution may well be imminent and justified, as it has been time and again in the past (172–173, 177b, 180b–181t).

In the closing pages of the *Second Discourse*, Rousseau paints a gloomy picture of human political history, as largely the story of the exploitation of the vast majority by the few rich, who themselves fall continually into both international and civil conflict for prestige and power, leading usually to the final institution of one or another form of despotism, bringing a grim peace in servitude – the Hobbesian Leviathan state – followed by revolution and a new ruling class. There have been only a few islands in the dark sea of civilized history, islands where wise and public-spirited lawgivers have created totally different, small, participatory republics – exemplified by Lycurgus in Sparta, the ancient Hebrew republic of Moses, and the early Roman republic (163t, 164b, 171b, 173t).

The Puzzling Legacy

What is so deeply frustrating about Rousseau and his philosophy is the absence in his thought of any clear path to a political solution, or even an unambiguous mitigation, of the terribly deformed human condition as he describes it within modern "bourgeois" commercial society. Rousseau points in three very different directions for remedies – each of which has enormous difficulties.

First is his celebration of the small participatory republic such as the Geneva of his time. But this is a rare possibility, one that can and should be preserved and protected wherever it exists but that cannot be looked to as a practical remedy for most developed societies, most obviously because it requires slowly developed traditions.

Second and more widely available is something that Rousseau promoted not so much in his political writings as in his novels: a vastly deepened appreciation for the redeeming possibilities that may be found by retrieving some version of intimate family life, as the culmination of romantic love and as blessed by Nature's God. Rousseau, and the enormous influence he had, especially through the romantic novel, is the source of what are today called "family values," which are often associated today with Christian religious faith. In fact, the New Testament, as we have seen, has little talk of husband and wife as lovers of one another, and still less talk of romantic love. It was above all Rousseau's influence, as theologian and as artist, that profoundly changed Christianity, making it much more centered on the family and appreciative of romantic love leading to marriage.

Third, Rousseau through his autobiographical writings founded the cult of the lonely thinker as artist – as the conscientious objector against modern commercial, bourgeois society. He exalted the life of the bohemian artist as a rebel who uses his art to remind others of the pretensions and heartlessness of bourgeois commercial society, and who through his art gives to all those trapped in bourgeois commercial society some outlet and access to the appreciation and celebration of lost natural individuality. Rousseau is the founder of the modern cult of art or "aesthetics" as a kind of substitute for religion, as the source of a kind of escape from or transcendence of competitive commercial society.

But Rousseau always insisted on confronting the very grave limits on any possibility of solving the human problem. He remained convinced that we can understand only the reasons for – that we cannot hope to overcome – most of mankind's profound spiritual unhappiness. We are doomed to experience a profound sense of not belonging in this world in which history has placed us.

The leading thinkers in the subsequent century found much of Rousseau's diagnosis of the spiritual deficiencies of modern commercial, bourgeois society compelling, but could not rest satisfied with Rousseau's failure to show a way to overcome those deficiencies. The most important innovation in political theory was to suggest that what Rousseau had shown (see especially 178–180) was that since civilization as we know it is a product, not of our core and original nature, but instead of a historical development over time, then we should cease to look so much to *nature* and instead look to *history* for our fundamental standards and guidance.

12

Marx and Engels: *The Communist Manifesto*

Karl Marx (1818–1883) and his junior partner, Friedrich Engels (1820–1895), laid the theoretical foundation of modern communism, which aims to bring about a new world order born out of the overthrow of "bourgeois capitalism." The latter is the phrase Marx and Engels applied to the historically mature form of the system of competitive, acquisitive, commercial individualism that is articulated and defended in the thought of Hobbes, Locke, Montesquieu, and their revisers – including Hume and Adam Smith. The term "bourgeois" derives from Rousseau, who was the first to create and to make stick that pejorative label for the society and way of life designed and successfully promoted by the Enlightenment. In the century and a half after Rousseau, European thought was dominated by attempts to find a solution to the problematic that Rousseau had laid out.

History vs. Nature as Norm

The most important turn taken in post-Rousseauean theorizing was to "the philosophy of history": A new way of thinking, rooted in the contention that what Rousseau had discovered, without his fully realizing it, was that we must take our orientation in life, our positive normative standards, not from the idea of a permanent human nature but instead from a conception of humanity as coming into full maturation through history. If or since modern, civilized existence – and thus what we understand as human – is not a product of our original nature (which was that of a being close to an animal) but instead arises out of a historical development over a long time, then we should seek for standards for our *human* existence in that historical process and its outcome. Through history, humanity has gradually and painfully brought itself out of its *original* "natural" condition toward a fully *completed* "nature" or condition of being: "The entire so-called history of the world is nothing but the begetting of man through human labor, nothing but the coming-to-be of nature for man."*

The crushing rejoinder, implicit in Rousseau, to any such suggestion, is that the global condition humans find themselves in now is so obviously sick, contradictory, miserable, unjust, and even self-destructive that it is absurd to think that our species has "grown to completion" as such a mess. It is much truer to the evidence all around us, as well as the evidence of all past history, to proceed on the hypothesis that the historical state of our species represents a horribly accidental, monstrous degeneration from an originally harmonious, healthy, noncontradictory, and flourishing natural condition.

The "philosophers of history" confronted this objection seriously and responded in effect as follows. We grant that history cannot possibly be described as a process of growth, like that of a child into an adult; history is obviously one long record of terrible contradictions, strife, injustice, and suffering. But what if the process of the coming into being of humanity or the human essence is not at all like the processes of natural growth? What if history, as the key temporal dimension of *human* reality, is fundamentally different from nature and natural processes? What if history "progresses" in a much more paradoxical way than anything in nature "grows"? What if history "progresses" precisely through contradictions, conflict, war, injustice, exploitation, and rebellion?

This was the suggestion launched by Immanuel Kant and fully developed in the philosophy of Georg W. F. Hegel, Marx's teacher. Every decisive stage in the process of history, at least in Europe, can be seen to have been a mortal struggle between two or more competing cultural-civic visions, each of which claimed to be just, but each of which in fact had a very imperfect conception of the common good, involving considerable exploitation of opponents. In every stage of history, after a long protracted time of war, there has been a victory, but the side that has won has been deeply transformed by the struggle. The victors have had to recognize grave limits to their outlooks, and, in the attempt to remedy those limits, have had to incorporate major ideas and concerns of their

* Karl Marx, *Economic and Philosophic Manuscripts of 1844* (henceforth cited as *1844*), 92; quotations and citations from this and other writings are (with minor emendations) from *The Marx-Engels Reader*, ed. Robert Tucker, second edition (New York: Norton, 1978).

opponents. Each victorious civic culture "synthesized," or put together in an unprecedented, more comprehensive combination, crucial ingredients from the previously warring visions. Thus, successive new civic cultures have been born – each of which for a while has appeared more or less stable, but each of which eventually bred or discovered within itself a new set of contradictions, leading to a new set of wars, and then to yet another new synthesis. Now if this process appeared to be just continuing, on and on, Rousseau would be on very strong ground: Historical existence would manifest itself as an endless series of one ugly conflict after another, new exploiters taking over from the old. History in its injustice and cruel inhumanity would furnish overwhelming evidence that humanity's historical existence remains always revoltingly in contradiction with humanity's essence – with what humans most deeply are, and need, and long for. But, in the era after Rousseau, in the nineteenth century, a new dimension of history appears to be coming to sight, one that totally changes the entire picture. *Now* it can be demonstrated that history, as the coming into being of humanity, is arriving at what will be a beautiful and harmonious and just end. Rousseau has more or less correctly described the human condition as it looked in *his* time, when the end or goal of the process was still too far off to be seen. But with the advent of the industrial proletariat class, it can now be seen that we are on the verge of the final act in the drama, which is at the same time the prelude to what Marx calls "truly human" history. We can now see that hundreds of thousands of years stretch before us in which humans will live and continue to evolve, but in a way that is no longer tragically and desperately contradictory, conflict ridden, exploitative, unjust. We can now demonstrate that after one more final cataclysmic period of revolution there will soon begin to flower a genuinely communal existence of free and independent, mutually respectful and spiritually caring individuals. Humans will "return" to relating to one another in a sophisticated version of what was seen in primitive form in Rousseau's "savage" communal society – but now incorporating all the spiritual wealth that has been accumulated in and through history, and armed with modern science's Baconian, liberating mastery over nonhuman nature. "Communism, as the *positive* transcendence of *private property*," is "the complete return of man to himself as a *social* (i.e., human) being": a "return become conscious, and accomplished within the entire wealth of previous development." Communism, "as fully developed naturalism, equals humanism, and as fully developed humanism, equals naturalism." It "is the genuine resolution of the conflict between man and nature and between man and man – the true resolution of the strife between existence and essence." "Communism is the riddle of history solved, and it knows itself to be this solution" (*1844*, 84, original emphasis).

In the eighteenth century, the capitalist bourgeois system finally triumphed by momentous, violent revolutions – especially the American and French – which overthrew, destroyed, and eliminated what had become the totally contradictory, unjust, and self-destructive feudal-aristocratic-monarchic system. Those revolutions were inspired and guided by crucial new political and economic theories that offered a radically different form of society as the supposed solution to mankind's ills and needs. Now, in the nineteenth century, we can see that there is needed another, truly final, series of violent revolutions that will overthrow what has become the contradictory, hideously unjust, and self-destructive capitalist bourgeois society. But there is needed a new political and economic theory to inspire and to guide these revolutions. Marx and Engels provide that theory, in a nutshell, in their *Manifesto of the Communist Party*, which is the first published expression (in 1848) of their mature thought, and the most famous and influential of all their writings.

The Literary Distinctiveness of the Manifesto

The massive thing that first strikes us about this writing is how different it is from all the others that we have examined. Its peculiar nature is made clear by the authors in the opening preface. A "manifesto" is not a work simply or chiefly of theory or interpretation. It is instead a popular program, and justification, of a political party, in this case the Communist Party. This party, the *Manifesto* stresses from the outset, openly proclaims that it intends the violent overthrow of existing society and its legal order. This party is already in existence, and is posing an obvious, "haunting" threat to the governments of all European nations.

So the *Manifesto* is not at all the articulation of an "ideal" (as is, for instance, Rousseau's *Social Contract*), and still less a utopian thought experiment (as is, for instance, Plato's *Republic*). The *Manifesto* is a clarification – for the ordinary masses of mankind – of the urgent demands of the present political and historical *reality*. Here theory becomes completely reflective of and in service to practice of the masses of mankind whom the theorists educate. Here there is nothing subtle, nothing hidden, no sense that broadcasting anything in theory could be bad or dangerous for good practice: Good practice is revolutionary, aimed at destroying existing society, in order to rebuild from the ground up a wholly new order. That new order will be so totally "atheistic" that even the word "atheism" will become meaningless. So there is no need what-soever to be afraid of harming religion: Religion is to be thrown onto the rubbish heap of history, along with the traditional family and the state. One of the preeminent goals of the communist revolution is to liberate humanity from all religion, all gods, everything superhuman: "Communism begins from the outset (*Owen*) with atheism"; communism matures as "the return of man from religion, from family, from the state, etc., to his *human*, i.e., *social* mode of existence" (*1844*, 85, 72, 92–93; *Communist Manifesto* 487–89).

Marx continues, and pushes to its extreme, the anti-Socratic trans-formation, effected by the Enlightenment, of the understanding of the proper relation between philosophy and society, between theory and practice. Philosophy must no longer stand in any sense on the sidelines or above the fray. Philosophy cannot seek simply to understand the human condition. Philosophy must become the spiritual leadership and inspiration of a worldwide revolutionary movement to utterly transform human existence: "The philosophers have only *interpreted* the world, in various ways; the point, however, is to *change* it" ("Theses on Feuerbach" 145, original emphasis).

The Manifesto *'s Audience*

The chief audience for the *Manifesto* is the class of hourly, wage-earning laborers within the capitalist system who own and can market little except their own labor power. In adapting the Latin word "proletariat," which designated the propertyless working class in the ancient Roman repub-lic, Marx signals a deep sense in which his thought recovers a key aspect of classical political theory. Marx returns, from Hobbes's and Locke's stress on the individual, and on politics as a social contract among indi-viduals, to Aristotle's insistence that the struggle between the rich and the poor *classes* is *the* fulcrum of all actual politics. But Marx contends that Aristotle misunderstood the class struggle, even as it appeared in the Greek city. This failure is not Aristotle's fault; Aristotle completely lacked awareness of the philosophy of history, which can be apprehended only when a thinker lives at the time Marx and Engels live – when the end, the solution to the riddle, finally becomes visible in and through the mod-ern proletariat. Aristotle – like everyone prior to Marx himself – had a consciousness forged by the distorting class struggle of his time; without realizing it, Aristotle's thinking was aimed at justifying his own class's exploitative power over other classes (especially slaves). According to Marx, all past theorizing, all intellectual and cultural life of the past, has been a kind of justificatory self-deception on the part of intellectuals loyal either to the ruling class or to a rebellious class seeking to become the new ruling class. Marx employs the term "ideology" to designate this basic character of all past thinking. Ideology, as "the illusion of the class about itself," thus reveals something very important about humans: They cannot accept the fact that they are unjust or that they are driven, by economic scarcity and competition and hence necessity, to have to exploit others. Throughout the history of class struggle, humans have always desperately needed to believe in some myth, some false theory or religion, that veils from them their own ugly, exploitative domination. The universal phenomenon of "ideology" provides overwhelming historical evidence that humans are exploitative only because their terrible economic situation of scarcity compels them to be so (*Manifesto* 489; *The German Ideology* 163–175). Marx takes over from Rousseau, and makes even stronger and simpler, the thesis that humans are essentially good and wicked only when and because forced by desperate circumstances – but for Marx, essential human goodness is much more communal and much less individualistic than it was for Rousseau. Humans are in essence fraternal or what Marx calls "species beings" (*1844*, 75).

As Marx and Engels stress at the start of part two of the *Manifesto*, their theorizing is the articulation of the justification of the proletariat class's claim to deserve to dominate. As such, theirs is the first theorizing in history, the first "class-consciousness," that has no need for illusions, that can be purely "scientific" (Engels, "Socialism, Utopian and Scientific" 683ff.). For the proletariat is the first revolutionary class that cannot possibly wind up becoming a new exploitative ruling class. The cause of the proletariat is necessarily the cause of humanity as a whole.

What is the argument that proves that the proletariat is so totally different from every previous revolutionary class? This is the most important question raised and answered in the *Manifesto* – mainly in its first part.

Because it is written under the sense of an impending crisis, and directed to hardworking people who have very little leisure, the *Manifesto* is short, concise, and organized with simplicity. The first part explains the present historical situation, and the unique nature of the proletariat class, in the light of a comprehensive analysis of all human historical existence; it provides the theoretical foundation for the rest. The second part explains the relation between the proletariat and the Communist Party that is its vanguard of the workers. The third part explains the relation between communist theory and other competing critiques of capitalism – which Marx thinks are totally inadequate and in need of being exposed as such – especially noncommunist "socialism": "The Socialistic bourgeois ... wish for a bourgeoisie without a proletariat"; the "bourgeoisie naturally conceives the world in which it is supreme to be the best; and bourgeois Socialism develops this comfortable conception into various more or less complete systems" (496). Finally, the very short fourth part explains the relation of communists as activists to the other opposition activists.

The Opening, and the Question, of the Manifesto

The theoretical part one, entitled "Bourgeois and Proletarians," begins with a one-sentence paragraph: "The history of all hitherto existing society is the history of class struggles" (473). This sentence is explained in the next three short paragraphs, leading up to a massive implicit question. "Classes," Marx explains, are large groups brought together by their shared place, role, and interests in the economic system – which has *always* been a system of oppression. Every past society has had a "ruling class" exploiting and oppressing a range of classes beneath it. But no ruling class has ever succeeded in totally dominating the other classes. The struggle has *always continued,* even if "hidden." More than that: The ruling class has always been doomed, sooner or later – either by the rise of a new oppressor class from the oppressed or by war or a civil war that took the whole society down in ruins. One can say that Marx enlarges upon the conception of history that Rousseau presents at the end of the *Second Discourse,* except that Marx denies that there were ever any islands of nonoppressive republics. All political power has been and is essentially unjust. As Marx puts it near the end of part two (490), "[p]olitical power, properly so called, is merely the organized power of one class for oppressing another."

The first message, then, to the modern proletarians is: You feel oppressed, as a class, and you are right to so feel; but this is merely another chapter in what has been the story of all human history. The second part of the message, the good news, is: Your oppressors are doomed – as had been every previous oppressive ruling class. Yet might this be because all will be ruined in common? In effect, the *Manifesto* says to the proletariat: You are not doomed, you are saved, *if you, if we, act decisively:* your time is now; you can be the new, victorious, revolutionary class, which will dig the graves of the bourgeois capitalists. This raises at the outset, however, the acute question: Why then won't the proletariat become simply another oppressor ruling class? This question intensifies when we later hear, near the end of part two, what will be the first stage after the revolution: "The proletariat will use its political supremacy to wrest, by degrees, all capital from the bourgeoisie, to centralize all instruments of production in the hands of the State, *i.e.*, of the proletariat *organized as the ruling class*; and to increase the total of productive forces as rapidly as possible." And "[o]f course, in the beginning this cannot be effected except by means of *despotic* inroads on the rights of property and on the conditions of bourgeois production; by means of measures, therefore, which *appear* economically insufficient and untenable," but which "are unavoidable as a means of entirely revolutionizing the mode of production" (490, our emphasis).

The Uniqueness of the Bourgeoisie

The first clue as to why the proletariat or communist despotism will be different from all previous despotisms is given as the *Manifesto* next explains what makes our era different from all earlier eras. Every historical epoch is shaped by the character of its ruling class, and today's ruling bourgeoisie is an unprecedented ruling class. The bourgeois order is far and away the most productive and efficient, hence most powerful, most total, most ruthless system of exploitation ever seen. The clearest sign is that, as is stressed in the third paragraph, in all earlier historical epochs there were not simply one oppressor class and one oppressed class but many intermediate classes, each of which were to some extent oppressed and exploited (by the classes above), but to some extent oppressing and exploiting (of the classes below). "Our epoch, the epoch of the bourgeoisie," possesses "this distinctive feature: it has simplified the class antagonisms." Society "as a whole is more and more splitting up into two great hostile camps, into two great classes directly facing each other" (474). For the first time, there is no longer a complex hierarchy of *intermediate* classes, all of which *gained something* from the exploitative system, all of which had some *stake* in the system. In all previous societies, when there was – as there *always* eventually was – a revolutionary overthrow and transition to a new hierarchy and a new system, the revolutionary class rose up on the basis of *the power it had already accumulated* from its *own* exclusive and exploitative *property*. The revolutionary class always rose up to *enlarge* its own property, its own competitive economic advantage – which was always based on the exploitation of some class or classes beneath the revolutionary or new ruling class. Thus the economic power of the old feudal landed aristocracy (based on exploiting serfs) was eventually dwarfed by the new kind of economic power (based on exploiting wage laborers) of the rising capitalist bourgeois class (which had started out as merely serving the needs of the aristocrats). The bourgeoisie eventually was able to translate its superior economic power into military power, enabling it to rebel against and to destroy the economically outmoded aristocracy.

The *Manifesto* gives a brief history of the bourgeoisie that explains more precisely the source of its uniquely awesome economic power, while at the same time portraying the profound disfiguration – which is, paradoxically, also a liberation – of the human *consciousness* that the bourgeois capitalist system has brought about (474–481). By far the most important factor defining the bourgeois class is its devising of a new mode of *organizing* economic production – "the manufacturing system," with its intense division of labor and mechanization of work. This makes possible an enormous increase in productivity, achieved through ever increased splitting of manufacture into simple, repetitive, machinelike tasks that turn workers more and more into quasi-robotic operators. Such division of labor makes possible the assembly of workers in vast masses in factories, to produce on a vast scale, with less and less investment in the workers because the tasks the workers perform become so simple that it takes very little education or expense to train the worker. The factories allow intense centralization of management, whose members rule despotically over the workers and treat them more and more like ciphers, easily interchanged, fired, and hired: The "unceasing improvement of machinery, ever more rapidly developing, makes [the workers'] livelihood more and more precarious." At the same time, "the growing competition among the bourgeois and the resulting commercial crises make the wages of the workers ever more fluctuating" (480). And in proportion "as the repulsiveness of the work increases, the wage decrease." Nay, more: "In proportion as the use of machinery and division of labor increases, in the same proportion the burden of toil also increases, whether by prolongation of the working hours, by increase of the work exacted in a given time, or by increased speed of the machinery, etc." (479).

Meanwhile, "the lower strata of the middle class – the small tradespeople, shopkeepers, and retired tradesmen generally, the handicraftsmen and peasants – all these sink gradually into the proletariat, partly because their diminutive capital does not suffice for the scale on which modern industry is carried on, and is swamped in the competition with the large capitalists, partly because their specialized skill is rendered worthless by new methods of production." Thus "the proletariat is recruited from all classes of the population."

On the level of consciousness, because capitalism compels everyone to become caught up in the desperate economic competitiveness, everyone is compelled to see, as never before, the ugly truth about the historical human condition, which becomes so obvious that it can no longer be hidden by any myth, ideology, or religious illusion. Bourgeois ideology becomes the thinnest, the most transparent, or easily seen through of any ideology. All earlier ruling classes had much richer, more persuasive ideologies – religions, art forms, philosophies, doctrines about justice – that veiled and seemed to justify their rule, in ways that deceived especially the oppressors themselves. All ruling classes began as revolutionary classes fighting for what they deceived themselves into believing to be a more just society. This was true also of the bourgeoisie when they were fighting to overthrow the old aristocracies and church. But from the beginning, the bourgeois ideology (of Hobbes, Locke, Montesquieu) was quite openly centered on self-interest – with a very thin conception of justice. And once the bourgeoisie came into power, they and their system soon became so ruthlessly successful at creating conditions of fierce, cutthroat competition that they made their own and all previous ideology unbelievable. More and more, everyone is cynical about capitalism, even or especially the leading capitalists. The bourgeoisie has disenchanted human life: "Wherever it has got the upper hand, [it] has put an end to all feudal, patriarchal, idyllic relations" and "has left remaining no other nexus between man and man than naked self-interest." The bourgeoisie "has drowned the most heavenly ecstasies of religious fervor, of chivalrous enthusiasm, of Philistine sentimentalism, in the icy water of egotistical calculation." In short, "for exploitation, veiled by religious and political illusions, the bourgeoisie has substituted naked, shameless, direct, brutal exploitation" (475).

At the same time, the relentless forces of market competition tear apart every human connection and bond – except that of the market competition, leaving humans anxiety ridden and desperately isolated: "Constant revolutionizing of production, uninterrupted disturbance of all social conditions, everlasting uncertainty and agitation distinguish the bourgeois epoch from all earlier ones." "All that is solid melts into air, all that is holy is profaned, and man is at last compelled to face with sober senses, his real conditions of life and his relations with his kind" (476).

Both the new modes of production and the accompanying, agitated consciousness are spreading steadily throughout the entire earth, through the force of global trade and commerce, uprooting and destroying all local and nationalistic attachments and traditions. The bourgeoisie is creating the first truly global civilization and global consciousness. It is truly enlightening everyone – about the ugly truth underlying the whole system and all past human history.

But at the foundation of this awesome transformation is the ever more intensely oppressed and exploited working class, whose labor power is the ultimate source of all economic value and power. In shaping this class, the bourgeois system is compelled to do profoundly self-destructive things, which form the proletariat into a global revolutionary class. First, as we have seen, the system forces everyone who is not a big owner into the proletariat working class. Second, the system cannot avoid depriving the workers more and more of physical necessities and economic security. For as we've seen, competition intensifies among the big corporations, and so costs of production must be cut, and this eventually requires cutting real wages, making the workers work harder and longer for less and less. But this means the workers have *less to spend*, as well as *less leisure*, so they buy less. This cut in demand creates vast unsold inventories in the factories, which have to stop producing, and have to lay off workers, intensifying the drop in consumer spending, and bringing on crises – recessions, depressions. In each crisis, more and more companies fail, never to open up again, driving more and more owners and managers into the working class, and more and more workers out of work. This creates a "reserve army of the unemployed," even during boom times, which makes it easier for the remaining, bigger and bigger, companies to lower real wages more, forced by competition. This cuts the buying power of the workers still more, and leads back to still worse crises of overproduction. Marx was the first economic theorist who focused on this downward spiraling "business cycle" as an *essential* aspect of capitalism. What is most staggering, the *Manifesto* stresses, is the fact that the recessions and depressions are caused *not by scarcity*, but by *over*production (478). This signals the absurdity and irrationality of the whole system as it has matured. The age-old human economic dilemma – of scarcity – no longer exists. The problem is *too much* productivity! *Too much* wealth! Yet the masses are miserable! The system is obviously wildly out of control. "Modern bourgeois society with its relations of production, of exchange, and of property, a society that has conjured up such gigantic means of production and of exchange, is like the sorcerer who is no longer able to control the powers of the nether world whom he has called up by his spells." In the recurring economic crises, "there breaks out an epidemic that in all earlier epochs would have seemed an absurdity – the epidemic of *overproduction*." Society "suddenly finds itself put back into a state of momentary barbarism"; it appears "as if a famine, a universal war of devastation had cut off the supply of every means of subsistence; industry and commerce seem to be destroyed; and why? Because there is *too much* civilization, *too much* means of subsistence, *too much* industry, *too much* commerce" (478, our emphasis). The system has obviously become a Frankenstein monstrosity. The capitalist system emerged, in the eighteenth century, in a world of scarcity, where the historical need was indeed for the capitalist system and its enormous capacity for production through the conquest of nature. But the system has succeeded beyond anyone's dreams. Capitalism has ended scarcity. But now capitalism itself invents scarcity, artificially and *unnecessarily*. Capitalism has succeeded in totally transforming the human condition, in a way that makes capitalism itself totally inappropriate for the new conditions that it has created. "It becomes evident" that "the bourgeoisie is unfit any longer to be the ruling class in society." Society "can no longer live under this bourgeoisie": "Its existence is no longer compatible with society" (483).

But the third and most important thing that the bourgeois system creates is the class consciousness of the proletariat: "The more openly this despotism proclaims gain to be its end and aim, the more petty, the more hateful, and the more embittering it is." And "with the development of industry the proletariat not only increases in number; it becomes concentrated in greater masses, its strength grows, and it feels that strength more." The workers "begin to form combinations (Trade Unions) against the bourgeois"; "here and there the contest breaks out into riots." This happens not only because of the obviously terrible and irrational situation in which the proletarians are placed but also because, ironically, the bourgeoisie, in their internal political competition with one another and with the remnants of the old aristocratic order, are compelled to call upon the proletarians as political allies, as voters, and thus to educate the proletariat in political organization. "The bourgeoisie itself, therefore, supplies the proletariat with its own elements of political and general education; in other words, it furnishes the proletariat with weapons for fighting the bourgeoisie" (481).

The Uniqueness of the Proletariat

How has all this answered the fundamental question concerning what will distinguish the proletariat as a new ruling class? Why will its members not become the new exploiters? Marx and Engels can now give the answer, in these words: "All the preceding classes that got the upper hand sought to fortify their already acquired status by subjecting society at large to their conditions of appropriation." The "proletarians cannot become masters of the productive forces of society, except by abolishing their own previous mode of appropriation, and thereby also every other previous mode of appropriation." They "have nothing of their own to secure and to fortify; their mission is to destroy all previous securities for, and insurances of, individual property." All "previous historical movements" were "movements of minorities, or in the interest of minorities." The "proletarian movement is the self-conscious, independent movement of the immense majority, in the interests of the immense majority. The proletariat, the lowest stratum of our present society, cannot stir, cannot raise itself up, without the whole superincumbent strata of official society being sprung into the air" (482).

Because there are no intermediate classes, and because the proletariat is so totally dispossessed of private property within the system, it has no private property of its own to protect and enlarge. This means in addition that the proletariat is in a position to see and to accept that the whole system of competitive private property has reached a stage where it can and must be abolished. The proletariat, because it has no stake in the system, cannot be fooled or fool itself into thinking competitive private property can be reformed and made to work by simply changing the ownership, making the proletariat into bourgeois (that is the bourgeois socialist answer). The proletariat, being the total loser and oppressed, sees the system for what it is. This includes above all the proletariat's capacity to see or be taught that the problem is the absurd one, of *over*production. There is *no more real scarcity* – if the system were *reorganized, without the competition* that drives down wages, with rational cooperative planning, and factories and industry managed by the workers themselves, there could be production in *abundance* without exploitative and dehumanizing long hours of work. The proletariat can *see* that it has no one below it that it *needs* to exploit; *exploitation makes no sense* to and for the proletariat that grasps the beautiful new vistas opened up by the "problem" (for capitalism) of "overproduction." Besides, the proletariat correctly recognizes itself not as a minority, seeking something for a minority, but as the vast majority, which is practically the whole of humanity. For the first time in history, the problem is not how to create the goods, how to cook the pie: That has been figured out. The question now is how to divide up the pie: how to distribute, or to redistribute – rationally and fairly – the abundance we can easily produce. The working day could be vastly shortened, and creative leisure could flower. People no longer need to compete in mutually hurtful ways, but are in a position to see their competition, like good athletes, as expressing invigorating challenges of mutual concern and respect for one another's productivity. We need to take all productive power out of the hands of the outdated capitalist businessmen, who still think in terms of scarcity and the need for exploitative and mutually injurious competitiveness. It is time to replace the unplanned, and hence irrational, runaway competition and its basis, private property, with a new, rationally planned, cooperative, and fraternal system, where the advancement of each is *not* dependent on outstripping and dominating others. As the *Manifesto* puts it at the end of part two: "In place of the old bourgeois society, with its classes and class antagonisms, we shall have an association in which the free development of each is the condition for the free development of all" (491).

The Communist Intelligentsia

Yet there is one last complexity, one major component still needs to be explained. The proletariat is ripe for inspiration and direction, but it cannot give itself that inspiration and direction. The proletariat needs intellectual leaders and guides, people who have had the leisure to acquire the education that can allow them to see the big picture. Who accomplishes this task? The answer: "Finally, in times when the class struggle nears the decisive hour, the process of dissolution going on within the ruling class, in fact within the whole range of old society, assumes such a violent, glaring character that a small section of the ruling class cuts itself adrift and joins the revolutionary class, the class that holds the future in its hands." Just "as, therefore, at an earlier period, a section of the nobility went over to the bourgeoisie, so now a portion of the bourgeoisie goes over to the proletariat, and in particular a portion of the bourgeois ideologists, who have raised themselves to the level of comprehending theoretically the historical movement as a whole" (481). This of course is the self-description of Marx and Engels, and the vanguard intelligentsia of the Communist Party, which will not be made up mostly of workers or proletarians but of bourgeois intellectuals who have grown up in the wealth that provides the extensive leisure to acquire a rich education and a full philosophic training. These thinkers began, in their youth, by trying to justify the capitalist bourgeois system; they were originally "bourgeois ideologists." But they soon discovered the truth that the historical situation, and the proper understanding of the history of class struggle, makes so clear; they have now become the intellectual teachers of the proletariat and founding leaders of its vanguard Communist Party. Marxism elevates these bourgeois intellectuals to the leading role in human history.

After the Revolution?

What remains obscure is how the character of the postrevolutionary society will unfold *after* the revolution. In his published writings, Marx says very little about this crucial question. In the pages of the *1844 Manuscripts* immediately preceding the account of true communism, as the riddle of history solved (which we quoted at the beginning of this chapter), Marx gives a stark account of "primitive" and even "bestial" versions of communism – which he seems to concede will probably come as stages prior to the achievement of the true communism.

At first after the revolution, private property and wage labor will continue, but now the government will own everything and everybody will become a wage laborer working for the government. In this stage, the communist consciousness is crude and resentful: "On the one hand, the dominion of *material* property bulks so large that communism wants to destroy *everything* which is not capable of being possessed by all as *private property*. It wants to abstract *by force* from talent, etc." This "movement of counterposing universal private property to private property finds expression" in the "bestial form of counterposing to *marriage* (certainly a *form of exclusive private property*) the *community of women*, in which a woman becomes a piece of *communal* and *common* property," and "the woman passes from marriage to general prostitution." In "negating the *personality* of man in every sphere, this type of communism is really nothing but the logical expression of private property, which is this negation. General *envy* constituting itself as a power is the disguise in which *avarice* re-establishes itself and satisfies itself" (82–83). Then comes a second, intermediary, stage, where communism becomes more political, in some sort of benevolent democratic despotism, followed by the gradual "annulment of the state" (84). Then finally comes the third, fulfilled and fulfilling, stage, where "[n]eed or enjoyment" have "lost their *egotistical* nature, and nature has lost its mere *utility*"; where "activity in direct association with others, etc., has become an organ for *expressing* my own *life*, and a mode of appropriating *human* life"; where "through the objectively unfolded richness of man's essential being," the "richness of subjective *human* sensibility (a musical ear, an eye for beauty of form – in short, *senses* capable of human gratifications, senses confirming themselves as essential powers of *man*)" is "either cultivated or brought into being" (87–89). Here is the overcoming of both the possessive and the utilitarian consciousness. Humans will produce as makers, in order to enjoy and contemplate their works, like artists: but – since the work will no longer be alienated from them – with a communal, un-egoistical outlook, as "species beings." Not alienated from their labor, humans will not be alienated from themselves, and so will cease to be alienated from others. At this point communism itself is revealed to be not the goal, but a way to the goal: "Communism is the necessary pattern and the dynamic principle of the immediate future, but communism as such is not the goal of human development – the structure of human society" (93).

This of course raises the question of how Marx can be so sure that the communist revolution will transcend eventually the earlier crude forms of communism. How can we be confident communism won't get stuck at the second, or even the first, of the three stages? This is a source, within Marx's own writings, of the grave practical questions and doubts that appeared as Marxism was put into practice in the twentieth century. Does not the possibility or likelihood loom that a new class of oppressors will emerge precisely as the party minority, ruling over the workers – as indeed happened under Leninism, Stalinism, and Maoism? The heated debate within Marxism in the twentieth century became whether this was the betrayal of Marxism, or merely the necessary first stage, which does require severe and even despotic methods, for a few generations – partly in order to reeducate everyone and to exterminate the vestiges of the capitalist competitive spirit or consciousness, so that eventually the state, and oppressive coercion, can wither away, and a new form of society with a new fraternal and artistically contemplative spirit can emerge.

13

Tocqueville's *Democracy in America**

Alexis de Tocqueville (1805–1859) was raised in a conservative French aristocratic family, but as a young man he became a political liberal. After supporting the revolution of 1830, he was commissioned to go to America to study prison reform. But Tocqueville knew that there were vastly more important things to learn in and about America. He spent nine months traveling the country, getting to know people in many walks of life, questioning everything he saw – as an outsider, who took nothing for granted and looked with wonder at everything. Returning home, he studied his copious notes and many American documents, meditated on all that he had seen and learned, and crafted a treatise meant to teach present and future generations the deepest mainsprings and tendencies of the new kind of democracy he found emerging in the United States.

Tocqueville vs. Marx

Tocqueville lived at the same time as Marx, and like Marx was deeply influenced by the post-Rousseauean critique of the original Enlightenment and its bourgeois individualism. Tocqueville also shared with Marx a conviction that the history of the West in the previous centuries revealed itself as a process through which humanity had been gradually developing toward a final, decisive epoch, whose awesome challenge was coming to clear sight only in the early nineteenth century. Tocqueville parted company with Marx in that he takes with utmost seriousness two things that Marx does not take very seriously at all: God and American democracy.

---

* Our citations of *Democracy in America* are to volume, part, and chapter, followed by page numbers of the intelligently abridged and translated edition of Sanford Kessler and Stephen D. Grant (Cambridge, MA: Hackett, 2000).

As Tocqueville stresses in his introduction, he sees the history of the West for the past seven hundred years as revealing a progress, toward ever greater equality of conditions, that has all the marks of divine providence. Yet in the same introduction, and even more luridly in the closing pages of the entire work, Tocqueville portrays God's plan as deeply ambiguous and daunting. The divine historical process toward ever more equality is not guaranteed to have a good outcome. It appears that God is placing before the next few generations a staggering challenge and responsibility. Humanity must determine by and for itself whether history will issue in an equality and a democracy that is noble, uplifting, and fulfilling of the human spirit, or, instead, in an equality and a democracy that degrades humanity by leveling everyone into low herd animals living under a new, unprecedented form of despotism – what Tocqueville calls a "soft," paternalistic, despotism that treats everyone alike and reduces everyone to childlike dependency and spiritual conformity.

Tocqueville's diagnosis of the dangers haunting modern society is thus very different from Marx's. A major source of Marx's mistake, from Tocqueville's perspective, is that Marx focuses on Europe – which is not nearly as far along, historically, as is America. If one focuses on Europe, Tocqueville concedes, one can see class conflict predominating. In America, however, one sees that a new kind of society is emerging, where the vast majority is "middle class," without any real ruling class, and with only a minority hopelessly impoverished. There are indeed many poor in America, but most of them have a more or less realistic hope of rising, themselves or their children, into the middle class. *The* exception is the slave society of the South. But Tocqueville is certain that sooner or later that society will have to be abolished, as basically alien to the core spirit of democracy; after its abolition, he is convinced, the South will follow in the direction of the way of life one already sees in the northern and western states.

Tocqueville does agree with Marx in part: Industrial capitalism, if unchecked, has a tendency to develop oppressive concentrations of wealth and power that need to be policed with anxious vigilance (2.2.20). But Tocqueville insists that study of democracy in America reveals the gravest dangers to modern and future society to come from other sources, deep within democratic egalitarianism itself. In fact, a Frankensteinian democratic monstrosity is implicit in what Marx looks to as the solution: the socialist state, concentrating in its hands all the power and direction of society.

The Tyranny of the Majority

The most massive manifestation of the danger to human freedom and dignity haunting modern democracy Tocqueville christens "the tyranny of the majority." In the first volume, he explains in political terms what he means by this phrase. In the second volume, he explores in greater psychological depth the full implications of this new democratic threat to human dignity and freedom.

We can best begin to understand what Tocqueville means by "the tyranny of the majority" if we see it as an application, to modern conditions, of what we learned, from Aristotle's *Politics*, is the central moral problem of democracy. Democracy is defined by the principle of political equality: Each full citizen has one equal vote, and whoever or whatever wins the majority of votes has the final say. According to the democratic principle, there is no minority, no individual, that is justified in claiming to prevail over or against the majority, once the majority has made its most basic decisions. To defy the majority is essentially undemocratic. The majority is sovereign. This is felt *morally*, and not merely in a narrowly political sense. Inhabitants of democracy in America are brought up to think that what they call "public opinion" is morally as well as politically authoritative. "*Public* opinion" is the deceptively flattering name given in modern democracy to *majority* opinion: Whatever opinions are settled on by the *majority* are crowned the opinions of the entire "public" – despite whatever minorities are opposed. By the same token, inhabitants of modern democracy are brought up to think that once the majority has formed a settled opinion, or made a settled judgment, then "*the People* has spoken" – as if the majority is the same as, or always speaks for, the whole people. Still worse: The majority, flattered and deceitfully disguised as "the People," is held to be *never* fundamentally wrong. If "the People" are seen to be temporarily wrong, then it is assumed that some wicked agency has misled them – some minority, some leader or elite, is to blame. No politician in America can ever succeed by attacking, or blaming, or even criticizing, "the People." The majority as "the People" must always be flattered by its politicians, much more shamelessly than any monarch is flattered by his courtiers (1.2.7 [113–115]). Members of minorities who fail permanently to become part of the majority are made to feel that they have no right to refuse to go along with the majority's judgments: That would be to "defy the People's will," to be "undemocratic," to be "elitist" or "un-American." The result is that those who permanently fail to join or to get the support of the majority do not merely lose out.

They feel, and are made to feel, like "losers." They are excluded. This Tocqueville observes most starkly in the situation of free blacks in the northern states (1.2.7 [108–109, note 4]).

Tocqueville repeats the Aristotelian critique of this whole moral outlook. The authority of the majority in democracy rests on a perverted moral principle: Whatever the greater number wishes, simply because they are more numerous, ought to be advanced, even at the cost of the interests of the lesser number, no matter how deserving the fewer may be. But – Tocqueville moves us to ask – why should the good of those who are fewer in number be subordinated or sacrificed simply because they are fewer? If the democratic rule of the majority is not to be merely the tyranny of the stronger, the majority must always be required to explain why what it wants serves the interest, not only of the majority but also of the minorities: the *common* good, the good of the *whole* society, *including* the minorities that may more or less permanently disagree with, or be excluded from, the majority. There is a tidal tendency in democracy, however, for the majority to forget this deep moral truth. Whenever any individuals or groups wield power and authority without rivals, the result is almost always moral blindness and arrogance; this is at least as true of majority groups as of minority. Yet in democracy, the majority and its "public" opinion wield unrivalled power by the very principle of the political regime (1.2.7 [106–109]).

The resulting danger is not only moral: The majority, when lacking strong competitors, is not prudent, even about its own true good. In the absence of strong and forceful critics, the majority undergoes the same mental degradation, into practical stupidity, that humans always undergo when they never receive bracing criticism. The majority in modern democracy tends to be a vast disorganized mass animated by an amorphous group-thinking that lacks clear and firm direction. "Public opinion" is emotional, unpredictable, erratic, and fickle in what it focuses on as major problems and concerns. "Public opinion" lacks staying power, patience, the ability to fix attention on problems long enough to understand them and then to follow through on policies adequate to deal with the problems. The result is a tendency to instability and inconstancy in democratic public policy, and a tendency to try to cure problems with quick fixes, half measures, or very temporary remedies (1.2.7 [105–106]).

Tocqueville recognizes (1.2.7 [116–117]) that Madison and Jefferson were to some considerable extent aware of the problem: A key aspect of the genius of the founders was to embed in the Constitution some powerful aristocratic, or artificially aristocratic, institutions that were meant to counterbalance the power of "the People." This is most obvious in the independent judiciary, but also in the electoral college system for electing the president, and in the Senate devised as a legislative body whose members would have staggered and long terms and would be not popularly elected (a condition that obtained until the twentieth century). The founders also divided governmental power into different levels – federal, state, and local – whose friction with one another should make coalescence of an unchecked majoritarian force less likely, and might give minorities who felt threatened on one level of the government an avenue of recourse to another.

Tocqueville doubts, however, that these remedies are adequate to meet the problem. Above all, he stresses that the founders' institutions will remain strong checks on majority tyranny only if the majority itself has some real understanding of, and agrees with, the reasons for checking and thwarting its own power – only if "the People," only if "public opinion," agrees that "the People" and "public opinion" should *not* have too much power. Tocqueville fears that the founders did not devise very adequate means of giving to the populace the *civic education* that is needed to instill a widespread appreciation of the danger of the tyranny of the majority. Tocqueville tries through his book to offer leadership in such education.

To appreciate the magnitude of the difficulty of civic education in democracy, one must recognize how the power of "public opinion" seeps deeply into people's souls. One has to reckon with subtle but deep pressures on the individuals in a democracy to go along with and to adopt the outlook of "public opinion." One has to reckon with a profound undertow of conformity and loss of genuine diversity – diversity, that is, of *opinions and beliefs*. To be sure, there is diversity of opinions within a certain range, but the range is set by the options that are approved or tolerated by the majority. Once a way of living or thinking is truly condemned by the majority, it is set on the road to extinction from public discourse – except to be condemned (1.2.7 [104, 112]).

To see clearly what is threatened by modern democracy, and to begin to understand what sort of remedies need to be devised, one must compare spiritual life in the kind of aristocracy that used to rule in Europe. In that old aristocracy there was no tyranny of the majority; there was no power of public opinion. There was instead a tension-ridden structure of forces that produced and encouraged a much wider diversity of clashing, fundamentally contrary, opinions and ways of life. This is something, Tocqueville stresses, of which people living in American democracy have little idea, since they are so ignorant of what it was that held in European aristocracies the place held by public opinion in modern democracies.

In the old aristocracies, the majority tended to be oppressed and held in contempt: Its opinion counted for little. The opinions that counted were always opinions of rival minorities, led by powerful, proudly testy, individuals. As a necessary result, aristocracies tended to be hotbeds of vigorously competing centers of minority power and of clashing opinions about everything. The monarch, surrounded by a faction-ridden court, was locked in ceaseless struggle with the landed nobles, themselves divided into competing families and into regionally or religiously based coalitions. All the preceding contenders were in endless competition with the established Christian Church, which controlled the educational institutions and was endowed with immense property and hence economic power. But the established Church was (eventually) locked in spiritual battle with competing Christian sects, proclaiming and teaching antagonistic versions of Christianity. Meanwhile, all of these centers of power were challenged by the commercial bourgeoisie who dominated in the cities, advocating and fighting for freer trade and markets. And all this competitive diversity was further intensified by the hostility among nations and national identities. None of these competing powerful minorities owed its power to another. None was dependent on the majority, or public opinion. Each had a truly independent power base, deeply rooted in revered traditions.

But diversity was also encouraged at a deeper psychological level – among the upper classes and filtering down to the lower classes. Aristocrats were brought up being encouraged to distinguish themselves as individuals; they were bred to compete to appear superior and different. Nonconformity, challenging other powerful people, was a badge of honor. Aristocracies naturally bred eccentrics – idiosyncratic rebels on all levels, from the silly to the sublime. This means that in aristocracies, the tendency was exactly the contrary of what we see in modern democracy. Agreement, conformity, were marks of shame and weakness; defiance and disagreement were marks of pride and strength. Individuals or minorities defeated and persecuted by one mighty power often could find a rival power ready to take them in and to take up their cause. Censorship was everywhere but often fueled the flames of rebellious and even subversive expression. Under European aristocracy, Tocqueville points out, all sorts of antagonistic political regimes, economic systems, religious views, and styles of art and literature competed vigorously and circulated widely (1.2.7 [110ff.]).

In contrast, among Americans one finds no strong public expressions of support for any political system except democracy. Americans are only dimly aware of strong arguments for the superiority of monarchy, of aristocracy, of theocracy like the old Puritan regime, of un-American types of democracy like the Athenian. The result is that unlike citizens of aristocracy, Americans never hear profound criticism of their own regime – of modern democracy. But that means that Americans never really hear profound arguments *for* their democracy or democratic ideals. For one can have serious arguments for something controversial only if there is controversy – only if one first hears, and answers, the arguments on the other side – only if there is real debate over fundamentals.

Similarly, in their religious thinking Americans are less and less aware even of what the theological differences are between the different religions or sects. Americans never hear or read searching and profound theological debates. They thus grow more and more ignorant and shallow about religion and theology.

Similarly as regards popular thinking about science and its place: Most Americans have no idea that there are alternative conceptions of the nature and role of science – conceptions that reject the notion that science should be devoted to technological progress or to the practical betterment of material life. Americans rarely hear serious arguments that science should not be used for practical ends, or that science itself is corrupted by becoming popularized and will corrupt society – arguments advanced in different ways by classical philosophy, and Rousseau, and the Bible.

The big problem in aristocracy or with aristocrats is getting mighty minorities and individuals to compromise, to work together, to listen to ordinary people's opinions, to have some respect for the mass or the majority. The reverse is the big problem in democracy: What democracy desperately needs is some of that old aristocratic temperament and pride. Modern democracy needs more individuals willing to challenge and to criticize "the People" and public opinion, and democracy needs among the citizenry an appreciation for such individuals and their spirit.

In the second volume of *Democracy in America,* Tocqueville takes us to still deeper levels in his analysis of the peculiar new dangers that threaten modern democratic life in action as well as in thinking. On this diagnostic foundation, he builds his positive teaching about the important ways in which American democracy reveals and deploys resources to combat or to mitigate its peculiar ills.

The Spiritual Isolation of the Democratic Personality

Tocqueville begins his second volume (2.1.1) with an analysis of what he calls (with some irony) "the philosophic method of the Americans." No people, he observes, is more *un*-philosophic than Americans. Yet paradoxically, nowhere is a *single* philosophic outlook more completely *conformed to*, by everyone – without anyone being aware that they all are conforming to it or what it is. Americans are all imbued with the outlook of Descartes; they are all Cartesians, without knowing it.

Descartes was the most influential Enlightenment philosopher to advocate that everyone could and should doubt all authorities. Against Socrates and Rousseau, he promoted the spread of such radical doubt through society. Descartes spearheaded the modern cultural norm according to which everyone is urged to think out everything for oneself and to trust no one as a superior authority. This, Tocqueville finds, is the universal and unquestioned intellectual creed of Americans. One constantly hears from Americans that every individual should think for himself, and therefore take nothing on authority. This reflects or expresses on an intellectual level the fundamentally egalitarian ethos of democracy. Since no person is truly wiser than, or morally superior to, anyone else, there is no reason anyone should be listened to as if he or she were superior. This is applied to every important sphere – including morality, politics, and religion. Democracy makes people think everyone should interpret religion for oneself; that each of us should have his own "philosophy" and not follow the authority of any philosophers of the past.

Now, as Tocqueville goes on to explain in the next chapter (2.1.2), the deep paradox is that this overwhelming pressure in democracy to think for oneself does not lead to a wide diversity of vigorously competing, antagonistic ideas; it does not lead to profound public or private argument between opposed fundamental alternatives in morality, religion, politics, philosophy, or science. It leads instead to conformity, to a cultural world in which almost everyone thinks similarly, within a very narrow range, about most fundamental issues. For with regard to almost all truly important ideas and beliefs – about the existence and attributes of God; the nature and the fate of the human souls; the meaning of love and friendship and justice and freedom and happiness – truly to think through these complex issues requires enormous time and effort. There is needed, in *every* regime, years of mediation, extensive study, scientific research, and lengthy discussion, rooted in thoughtful reading and comparison of difficult books and works of art. Hence, as Tocqueville notes, human beings must accept on trust much of their most fundamental ideas. But this is especially true in modern democracy, where everyone has to work for a living – and where, as a consequence, unlike in aristocracy, there is no true leisure class, born and bred to a lifetime of uninterrupted spiritual preoccupation. In aristocracy, the vast majority thinks about authority in a manner exactly the opposite of the democratic way. The people are brought up to obey and follow superior authorities – not to think for themselves, except under the guidance of someone who is superior in wisdom. This leads to much docile obedience, especially in the majority. That is the big problem with aristocracy. But a leisured minority, bred to a lifetime of service as rulers, priests, artists, educators, is assigned the responsibility of being the guide to the greatest authorities – authorities who transcend anyone alive. For in aristocracy, the greatest authorities are certain specific great books and works of art from the past, whose interpretation and meaning become the subject of endless impassioned *debate*: the Bible, and its competing commentators; the poets (e.g., Homer, Virgil, Shakespeare, Milton, Racine); the classic theologians and philosophers and scientists (e.g., Aristotle and Plato and Thomas Aquinas, and their competing commentators). The demand in aristocracy that everyone obey and seek guidance from transcendent authority directs people to great books and works of art with an intense seriousness, looking to find wisdom from those works. This means that most people in aristocracy are followers, but of guides who are profound and thought-provoking, even if usually not well understood. Above all, there is deep disagreement among the highest authorities. The interpreters are constantly struggling to try to reconcile the authorities but compelled to keep alive their great disagreements. One sees a beautiful example of this in the way Thomas Aquinas writes, always beginning with authoritative opinions that disagree and then trying to resolve them – but showing the difficulties. The upshot is that paradoxically, the aristocratic demand to follow authorities is a demand that brings people to confront conflict among competing authorities, over the highest stakes. In contrast, modern democracy presents us with the vista of a mass whose members are taught not to look to great old books or to superior geniuses of the past for wisdom and guidance – but instead to think for themselves.

But to repeat, in modern democracy, where everyone is part of the working class, almost no one has the time or leisure to spend his life studying and thinking. And those who do are not supposed to be looked to as authorities. Where, then, do people turn to get their guidance about the fundamental questions? Whom do they trust, if everything in democratic culture tells each person not to rely on anyone else, as superior authorities?

The authority of public opinion, or the majority outlook, becomes the substitute for traditional authority. It is "not only" that "common opinion" is "the sole guide which remains for individual reason among democratic peoples." "In times of equality, because of their similarity," people have "an almost unlimited trust in the judgment of the public"; for "it does not seem plausible to them that when all have the same enlightenment, truth is not found on the side of the greatest number." Moreover, while "when the man who lives in a democratic country compares himself individually to all those who surround him, he feels with pride that he is equal to each of them," when "he comes to envisage the whole body of his fellows and place himself alongside this great body, he is immediately overwhelmed by his own insignificance and weakness." The democratic individual who starts to dissent has no spiritual basis on which to believe in the superiority of his dissident opinions to the conformist "public opinion" of the vast majority. "The same equality that makes him independent of each of his fellow citizens individually, abandons him, isolated and without defense, to the influence of the greatest number" (2.1.2 [176–177]).

The Syndrome of "Individualism"

This sense each individual in democracy tends to have of his or her own insignificance in contrast to the vast majority also expresses itself in a peculiar transformation in people's emotions or "sentiments." In this regard Tocqueville diagnoses another syndrome that haunts the life of democracy, a syndrome that he christens "individualism." In chapter 2 of the second part of volume 2, he characterizes "individualism" by once again employing the illuminating contrast with aristocracy. Democracy, by breaking the hierarchical ties that used to bind people to one another in aristocratic societies, leaves individuals more and more disconnected from one another. Individuals in modern democracy have no strong, lasting bonds except to their immediate nuclear families and to very small circles of friends and acquaintances – which, however, are unstable and not so lasting. The result is that individuals become deeply concerned with, and feel responsible for, a smaller and smaller circle of other individuals. Tocqueville stresses that in speaking of "individualism" he is not speaking of egoism or selfishness. Selfishness is "a vice as old as the world." It "scarcely belongs more to one form of society than another." "Individualism," in contrast, "is in origin democratic, and it risks growing as conditions become more equal." Individualism is "a reflective and peaceful sentiment that disposes each citizen to isolate himself from the mass of his fellow men and to draw himself off to the side with his family and his friends," so that "after having thus created for himself a small society for his own use, he willingly abandons the larger society to itself." Whereas selfishness "dries up the germ of all the virtues," individualism "at first dries up only the source of the public virtues," but "over the long term it attacks and destroys all the others" (2.2.2 [204–205]). Individualism is very comfortable and comforting – easy and untroubling. One can become entirely preoccupied in and with a kind of cocoon of existence. But this cuts humans off from the realization of their potentialities as politically active, truly self-governing, and thus genuinely free, adult beings. Individualism prepares and inclines people to accept being ruled like children by a paternalistic supervising bureaucracy that attends to their needs while depriving them of any important role in helping to direct the fundamental structure regulating their lives.

Equality vs. Liberty

This consequence of individualism is fed by yet another dangerous democratic syndrome: the greater love for equality than for liberty. By nature, humans love both liberty and equality, Tocqueville thinks, and when the two go together, both are healthy. But when they are pursued independently of each other, each becomes unhealthy. The love of liberty, without equality, haunts aristocracy and produces injustice and inhumanity. The love of equality, without liberty, haunts democracy and produces a resignation to, or despicably content acceptance of, a herdlike condition. The love of equality without liberty can be tempting because liberty, as active, participatory self-government, requires enormous effort, risk, and cost – of time, of economic opportunity. Political liberty requires transcending one's narrow circle of job and family and friends. Political equality, in contrast, can be enjoyed in individualistic passivity and strengthened by an envious resentment of those who do succeed in making themselves important and significant actors in government or in politics.

The Democratic Counterweights

What are the resources within modern democracy by which these unhealthy tendencies can be opposed? What are the contrary tendencies that wise democrats should constantly be trying to strengthen? Tocqueville spotlights a number of counterweights that he finds functioning within American democracy to save it from its worst proclivities. His goal is to try to make both American and European readers more aware of these fragile democratic virtues and of why they are so precious and so in need of being nurtured.

The first is the devolution of governmental power away from centralized authority to more decentralized and local government. If individuals are to be drawn out of their individualism into a fuller participatory citizenship, then government must be brought closer to the people. Wherever possible, authority and decision making need to be devolved to levels where policy making and execution can proceed on a smaller scale, within localities and neighborhoods, and neighbors can be brought to cooperate in community governance and the forming of political associations. This allows individuals to feel less insignificant, less lost in a vast herd or mass, and more capable of making a difference, making their arguments heard, influencing policy. "Local freedoms, which cause a great number of citizens to value the affection of their neighbors," constantly "lead men back toward each other," and "force them to aid each other" (2.2.4 [208]).

The last phrase is notable, and it introduces a second American virtue, closely intertwined with devolution of government: the reliance on and cultivation of what Tocqueville calls "interest" (self-interest) "rightly understood" (2.2.8 [219–224]). It is especially when key governmental decisions are made at a more local level that people can be made to see that their self-interest, especially their economic interest, impels them to become involved in governing. The genius of modern democracy in America is *not* that it appeals so much to people's self-sacrificing public spirit, or that it calls on people to get involved in government as a way of overcoming their self-interest. In modern democracy, what works best – Americans have shown – is drawing people into political participation by making it an imperative of their shrewd self-interest. The most reliable way to make people in a modern democracy more public-spirited is by doing it indirectly, or without expecting people to be mainly intending to become public-spirited. The outcome is often that individuals become, as it were, seduced into public spirit, drawn into the vocation of citizenship, without ever having intended to hearken to such a call. Statesmen in modern democracy need to have this goal more clearly in view. Democracies need to keep always in mind that *as* important as taking care of specific social problems is using those problems as occasions for getting people involved in the solving, and the thinking about how to solve, social problems. In other words, democrats need always to remind themselves that the biggest and permanent social problem in democracy is the drift toward passivity and incompetence, toward a childlike dependency on central government. This means that democracies ought to be ready to put up with considerable variation and diversity in the way problems are solved in different localities. Democracy has to resist the temptation to insist on uniformity of government and administration, and instead accept and protect diversity in the ways different localities deal with similar problems, even when this involves a lot of inferior, or less efficient, modes of proceeding.

Tocqueville concedes that decentralization does not by any means solve the problem of majority tyranny. In fact, decentralization entails the danger of tyranny of the majority at the local level. But this, he argues, is a lesser danger than the tyranny of mass public opinion, mass passivity, and paternalistic government. He concedes that the national or state government must exercise some supervision over local government, with a view to preventing local majority tyranny, and here the judiciary has an especially important role, along with the legal profession. A third virtue of American democratic society in Tocqueville's eyes is the way in which the legal profession forms a kind of aristocracy that is tolerated and even favored in democracy. The basis of the superiority of lawyers is their expert knowledge of the law and its prescribed forms and formalities; it is this expertise that gives lawyers a precious civic vocation in democracy. The members of this profession have the most responsibility to uphold the rule of law and to remind local government of the need to adhere to law and to the constitutional protection of minorities.

A fourth and crucial American virtue is the energy displayed by non-governmental, voluntary associations (2.2.5 and 2.2.7 [210–219]). Americans have developed a "habit" of forming what Tocqueville calls "civil associations" (in subsets of what has come to be called "civil society"). Some of these associations are fleeting, formed to meet a temporary problem or challenge in the neighborhood or across the country. Many others are quite permanent, with well-delineated missions – charity, education, sports, hobbies, business, labor, moral causes. The most important function that all these associations implicitly share is arousing

Americans from their lethargic individualism into collective action and discussion, which imbues Americans with the habits and the experiences and the satisfactions of working together for mutual accomplishments, both serious and lighthearted. Many or most Americans get their first taste, and often their only taste and experience, of collective action not in government but in these nongovernmental civil associations. Tocqueville goes so far as to designate "the science of association" as "the mother science" in democratic countries: the progress of all the others depends on its progress" (2.2.5 [214]). But Tocqueville stresses that the most enriching of American associations are those that get people involved in serious collective spiritual efforts: what he calls the "intellectual and moral associations" (ibid.).

This leads to a fifth American virtue – implied in the preceding but deserving separate treatment: the power in America of organized religion and churches. These are the most permanent and emotionally uplifting of the moral and intellectual associations. The churches, in their diversity and local authority, are preeminent among other sorts of associations in giving the mass of Americans experiences of invigorating and uplifting collective action and responsibility. But there is also something that sets church associations apart and above other associations. The churches are the associations that are least based on self-interest rightly understood and least dominated by material and economic concerns. They are the one enduring and pervasive sort of association that continually reminds Americans of self-transcendent spiritual meaning in life. The churches are the one sort of association that continually speaks to Americans about their deepest anxieties and concerns, as mortal beings who seek some link to immortality or eternity. The churches keep alive a kind of concern and reflection or thinking that was much more natural to aristocracy. They naturally counteract the overwhelming tendency in democracy to become fixated on material comfort and material acquisitions.

But Tocqueville stresses that the enormous benefit to democracy of religion depends very much on it being *organized* religion – what one finds in *churches*. It is this kind of religion – not private, personal religion – that makes for powerful social associations that bring people together in strong collective action. In contrast, nonorganized religious thinking and feeling in democracy has a tendency to make things worse – to intensify individualism. Nonorganized religiosity tends to make people satisfied with personal or private thinking and experiences. But still worse, to Tocqueville, is the fact that nonorganized religion tends toward various versions of pantheism, or the belief that the universe is all one or has one all-embracing being. This is a kind of transplantation, into the metaphysical realm, of the tyranny of the majority. This vague kind of spirituality intensifies the sense that the individual is an insignificant part of a vast whole in which one can and should be rather passive and withdrawn.

A sixth source of resistance to the dangerous tendencies of democracy is formal, and especially higher, school education. But the education that does the most good is of a specific sort, which is not what democrats naturally tend to favor or to like. In the first place, what democracy needs is schooling that teaches young people to be critical of democracy, in its dangerous proclivities – as Tocqueville has presented them. In the second place, democratic education needs to try to instill ways of thinking and feeling that oppose the drift toward individualism and tyranny of the majority. The general goal should be to stress the human potential for self-government and association and collective action that can make a major difference. Education in literature should focus less on contemporary democratic literature and more on classical and aristocratic literature. For that literature is more likely to give readers both an example of writing that was carried out in accord with difficult, strict codes refined sentiment and taste, and of writing that highlighted the kinds of civic virtues that are most lacking and most needing reinforcement in democracy: soaring ambition, pride, the desire to make a glorious mark through public service. Similarly, the education in history that democracy needs is education that focuses not on social and economic history, which tends to highlight the ways vast forces determine the lives of individuals without their being able to do anything about it. Instead, the healthy focus of democratic education in history should be on political and military history – battles and struggles in peacetime as well as war, where a few individuals working together made an enormous difference. History education in democracy should give to democratic citizens pride in their country, and thus a sense of responsibility to the past and mission for the future – resisting the overwhelming democratic tendency to live only in the present and for short-term goals.

This brings us to a seventh source of resistance to the syndromes of modern democracy. Tocqueville admires not only the decentralization of government but also the dynamism of national governmental action of a certain kind. What needs to be encouraged is not national bureaucratic administration. That will tend by itself to get all too strong. What is needed is leadership that seizes every opportunity to give to the whole nation projects and challenges that arouse the citizenry to a sense of high national purpose. Local government and civil associations are not enough, unless from time to time the whole citizenry has the experience of grand patriotic effort and achievement. Facing and meeting towering challenges is what most of all, if only temporarily, takes individuals out of their narrow lives and gives them a sense of belonging and contributing to something of enormous significance. The vast majority may have only a small role, but they can be aroused to take a keen interest in and to debate and listen to the debate that is provoked by the challenge. This means that a feature of the sort of national enterprise that is most constructive is considerable division and disagreement within the country. Tocqueville insists that in modern democracy, sharp disagreement and division are not paralyzing but energizing. It is times of clashing partisan politics that awaken vast numbers of people to the need to think and to argue and even to act, in order to advance one or another of the warring viewpoints. National debate impels vast numbers of people to rediscover a sense of self-transcending responsibilities, and to look for leaders in whom they can take pride and who will give to them a sense of dignity in being parts of a great nation meeting great challenges. Tocqueville argues that one of the worst dangers in democracy is people whining about how terrible it is to have the country divided and for there to be so much partisan politics. On the contrary, Tocqueville teaches, sharp division, fierce argument, and strong partisan conflict can be what arouses the sleepy citizenry and creates political vitality.

One can summarize all Tocqueville's foci by saying that in each case, he means to identify a source, in modern democracy, for the rebirth or the continuation of some major virtue that aristocracy possessed – and that is in danger of disappearing on account of democracy and its egalitarianism. In the next chapter we turn to Nietzsche – who is the greatest philosophic source of a new aristocratic radicalism, a revolutionary atheism of the right, born out of the conviction that democracy is incapable of correcting itself in the ways that Tocqueville had hoped.

14

Nietzsche and His *Zarathustra*

Friedrich Nietzsche (1844–1900) placed the whole tradition of political philosophy, founded by Socrates, in doubt. Prior to Nietzsche, the enterprise that Socrates started had been carried on for 2,500 years – by philosophers who disagreed with Socrates, on many fundamental points, and who of course disagreed with one another; but all their controversies proceeded on the basis of a fundamental consensus: Namely, that it is possible and necessary to make progress in discovering universal and abiding, rational standards of justice and of the good life. These standards were understood to be derivable either from insight into the permanently deepest needs of human nature, or from insight into the historical process through which humanity grows into completion. Nietzsche was the first philosopher to call radically into question this plane of agreement, and therewith the whole undertaking based on this plane.

The impact of Nietzsche's questioning has been devastating. In his wake, the preeminent philosophic thinkers in the twentieth century – Husserl, Bergson, Heidegger, Whitehead, Wittgenstein – abandoned or avoided political philosophy. In our time, political philosophy has largely been replaced by political "ideology," that is, high-level propaganda: the elaboration of sophisticated intellectual defenses for a presupposed, and never radically questioned, set of normative principles called "our values." The most influential and sophisticated political theorists – such as Hannah Arendt, John Rawls, Richard Rorty, or Jürgen Habermas – regard the original enterprise of political philosophy founded by Socrates, and continued through Marx, to be impossible. They are convinced that there is no knowable rational standard beyond or outside each historical culture on the basis of which one could independently judge between conflicting cultural "values." All "value commitments" are ultimately relative to and products of their specific historical culture. No thinker, however wise and profound, can ever really escape his culture. All thinkers are "children of their time." All past philosophers who believed themselves to be engaged in the Socratic project, who believed themselves to be making progress in discovering the universal and abiding norms of human nature or history, are detected to be victims of profound self-delusion. We today can claim to understand all of them better than any of them understood themselves. This astonishingly arrogant outlook – cultural or historical relativism – is *the* reigning intellectual dogma of our time. Socrates would say that it constitutes the "cave" in which we are imprisoned spiritually.

But relativism was originally not a cultural dogma. It began as a radical new philosophic challenge. It was Nietzsche who most profoundly and influentially raised this challenge. But Nietzsche did so in considerable agony and fear. He saw himself as bringing to light a chilling insight, which he saw as the fated historical destiny of the coming dark age. He predicted that a vast and destructive wave of relativism was going to sweep first Europe and then the world. The spiritual consequence of this relativism he christened *nihilism,* the "ism of nothing," the ism of spiritual emptiness. Nietzsche tried to think out, and then to show, a way through and ultimately beyond this spiritual crisis.

Nietzsche vs. Marx and Tocqueville

One can best approach Nietzsche's thought by recognizing that he is the heir of the philosophy of history, which, as we have seen, grew out of the problematic that was left by Rousseau. After Rousseau, as we have seen in Marx and Tocqueville, political philosophers turned away from nature toward history as the source of standards. They tried to interpret history as a meaningful process that eventually reveals itself as a progressive development toward a final completed human essence and condition, an "end of history" in the sense of a fulfillment of the process of growth. But we have witnessed in Tocqueville the shaking of this outlook. Tocqueville worries that the goal or end point, democracy, might turn out to be the source of a new, unprecedented, and bleak, if "soft," despotism. Tocqueville still tries to view or to present history as the manifestation of a divine providential wisdom, but he is compelled to admit that humanity has been led close to a kind of abyss, and that it us up to us whether or not we wander over it. Nietzsche in effect says that Tocqueville is on the verge of facing the real truth: That there is no God or quasi-divine reason detectible behind, or within, or emerging out of history. The human spirit is historical, yes, but it is *radically* historical: All important needs of the human spirit, and hence all important notions of right and wrong, good and bad, the divine itself, change from one historical culture to the next – and even within each culture, as each culture constantly mutates, in more or less subtle ways. This changing history is not as a whole an intelligibly meaningful process that can be understood as directed or aiming toward some highest, fulfilling end-state. There is no convincing evidence of a divine providence directing history from the outside, as Tocqueville suggested; nor is there, as Marx claimed, any emerging, previously hidden, solution to the riddle of history. There is no overall progress toward some fulfilling form of social existence or political society that resolves the clashing contradictions between competing cultural values. History is insuperably contradictory – a field of struggle, of war, between conflicting religions or gods, or of what Nietzsche taught the world to call "*values*" (*Werte*).

Nietzsche contends that our emerging age is privileged or cursed to be the first whose historical development has put it in a position to see this initially ugly or deadly truth – the truth that there are no moral truths, in the sense of transcultural standards. It is not simply the case, as Socrates thought, that we have *in*complete knowledge of our underlying spiritual nature and its permanent needs, and that therefore we know that we must strive to progress in learning more. Nietzsche contends, paradoxically, that we have, through our historical situation and experience, an exiguous kind of *complete* knowledge: We know the permanent truth that there is no permanent nature or set of natural needs such as would give us answers to the basic questions of what constitutes the most just and best life for all humans in all times and places. What is more, we can now see, by studying history from our privileged perspective, that all the standards of right and wrong, good and bad, beautiful and ugly, all the gods, that humans have ever had, have all been temporary, changing or mutating, *inventions* of different and clashing historical peoples, who were shaped and inspired by "creativity" – another key term in the new language of norms that Nietzsche taught us all to speak. Peoples or cultures are forged by law-giving prophets and statesmen and poets and artists of one kind or another, who *appear* to be "inspired" by gods or divine beings or insight into "nature" – but who in truth are the *creators* of the gods and "values."

But this mention of gods and prophets signals another and most troubling aspect of what Nietzsche teaches. All human ideals have been believed in, have had their inspiring power, only because they were believed to be *not* human creations, but instead permanent truths, either discovered by reason in nature or else (and much more usually) given to humans from outside – revealed by or from some divinity. Even or especially the most creative individuals, who became cultural founders and re-founders, have had to hide *from themselves* their own "creativity." Humans have always had to believe that they were, by their achievements, attaining to or partaking in something that was lasting, immortal, eternal. But now, our culture's two distinctive and newly created virtues – ruthless intellectual honesty or probity (*Redlichkeit*) and profound "historical sense" (*Beyond Good and Evil*, part 7, especially aphorisms 224 and 227) – will not allow us to avert our gaze from the truth about "creativity."

The realization of this truth is for humans initially paralyzing and destructive. Once we recognize that all our various ideals inherited from the past have been nothing but human creations, then we can no longer seriously believe in or live by any of these past ideals. No one can seriously believe in and live by the laws of a god who is believed to be merely the creation of some historical people's imagination – Zeus, or Thor. No one can seriously live by so-called natural law or natural right once it is known to be merely some culture's or epoch's imagined myth imposed on a purposeless and ever-mutating nature. The discovery of the underlying truth of "creativity" leaves humanity in a spiritual vacuum. Nietzsche expresses the void in his famous statement, "God is dead."

Nietzsche did not promote the death of God; he saw it as the terrible fate of mankind in our time. He intended to point the way out of the ensuing crisis of nihilism, to a radically new way of thinking and being, a new form of humanity – which he called the life of the "superman" or "over-man" (*übermensch*). We humans of today, or at least some among us, must transcend the limits of the hitherto "human-all-too-human"; we must create a new version of the human that has never before been seen on earth. The "over-man" will be unprecedented in the specific sense that, for the first time, these "over-humans" can have high and demanding ideals, gods, and heroes – for which they are willing to fight and to die and to kill and to make enormous sacrifices – while *knowing* that these ideals are their own creations.

Nietzsche is not at all sure that this transformation is possible. He calls it an experiment or "tempting attempt," sustained by the thought that since there is no fixed nature of the human spirit – since human spirituality is historical or constantly changing – there is nothing that makes it manifestly impossible that at least some humans might be transformed in this way and could become the spiritual leaders of the rest of humanity: a new cultural elite or cultural aristocracy. But Nietzsche admits that in the next few generations at least, nihilism will prove more powerful. And what is most terrible about nihilism is not the anguished spiritual emptiness. Something much worse is now emerging in the world around us. Since humanity is always mutating spiritually, today's humans are beginning to evolve into a horribly degraded new species, a species that is not only resigned to but welcomes or embraces nihilism – as if it were something good, a relief from agonizing struggle, choices, responsibilities. Humans are mutating into a species of beings each of whom has no deep self-contempt, no deep longing to go beyond what one already is, so as to become a better and higher person oneself, or so as to contribute to someone else's becoming such. Humans are becoming reconciled to a collective, leveling, herdlike, petty selfishness, and are losing their need for any vision of individual or communal excellences or virtues that rank humans according to their vastly unequal capacities for self-transcendence and self-transfiguration. Humans are becoming a species that is contented by mere physical comfort and sensual pleasures together with entertainment, sports, hobbies, easygoing companionship, and petty competitions of vanity. Humanoids are emerging who look a lot like past humans, physically (though prettier and a bit artificial on account of plastic surgery), but who have lost their souls: who have lost that uniquely human need and capacity to live for the sake of demanding spiritual challenges, involving transformative self-overcoming.

Nietzsche holds that Marx, and socialists in general, utterly fail to realize that their egalitarian, communal, pacifist goal will be in practice indistinguishable from the outcome of this species degeneration – what Nietzsche's Zarathustra calls "the last man" (*der letzte Mensch*). The socialist classless society of unalienated human beings with no felt need for radical overcoming or competitive struggle will conduce, Nietzsche insists, not to a new flowering of creativity but instead to the extinction of real creativity. Nietzsche presents as the *alternative* to Marx, and to socialism, the political and social experiment to which he aims to inspire the world: the project of "breeding" a new species capable of creating and then believing fervently in competing new gods, new heroes, new forms of virtue and excellence and love, and hence new *hierarchies* that are known (by their creators) to be human creations – but that, even or precisely as such, inspire devotion and sacrifice. The new self-consciously created values are to be not only diverse but contradicting and clashing with one another, and hence inspiring of invigorating new forms of spiritually based warfare and heroism; the values of the future do not promise peace and "wretched contentment" but instead a joy in recurring combat and recurring serenity achieved either through triumph or through the consolation of submission to acknowledged superiors.

Nietzsche agrees with Tocqueville that mass democracy, something like what one sees developing in America, is indeed the outcome of Western history, shaped especially by the egalitarianism of Christianity and the rationalism of the philosophic tradition rooted in Socrates. And Nietzsche agrees that in order to understand this democracy, one must constantly compare and contrast it with past aristocracy at its best. But Nietzsche is convinced that it is naively hopeful to think that the genuine greatness, noble freedom, and spiritual elevation – the sublime objects of devotion and self-overcoming – that were found in past aristocracy can survive in modern democracy.

Zarathustra's Prologue

Thus Spoke Zarathustra* is Nietzsche's most famous and influential writing, and the one in which he expressed most vividly what he meant by the hoped-for superhumanity, juxtaposed against the ugly subhumanity he saw developing in modern democracy. Nietzsche intends *Thus Spoke Zarathustra* to express his own creativity, through a new form of strange and haunting writing, embodying a new synthesis of poetry and philosophy, and centered on a new kind of hero-saint. Nietzsche himself rarely speaks in this book; almost everything after the opening drama consists of the speeches of Nietzsche's character Zarathustra. This of course reminds us of Plato and the way Plato wrote – through dialogues, with Socrates usually as the main (and rather playful or ironic) speaker. But Zarathustra is a very different character from Socrates. Zarathustra is rarely ironic or playful and engages in few dialogues. Instead, he characteristically delivers passionate sermons and allows us to overhear intensely emotional, even tormented, soliloquies. Nietzsche's Zarathustra is more reminiscent of the biblical prophets, and of Jesus, than of Socrates.

---

* We recommend either the translation by Walter Kaufmann (though it does not preserve Nietzsche's paragraphing), available in *The Portable Nietzsche* (New York: The Viking Press) or *Thus Spoke Zarathustra*, translated by R. J. Hollingdale (London: Penguin, 1974). Quotations in this chapter are from Kaufmann's *Portable Nietzsche*, with minor emendations. We will focus especially on "Zarathustra's Prologue" and the following speeches: "On the New Idol," "On the Friend," "On the Thousand and One Goals," "On the Gift-Giving Virtue," "On the Tarantulas," and "On Old and New Tablets."

Zarathustra is, if you will, a kind of atheistic prophet, the prophet not of a new god or supernatural being but instead of the superman or over-man, the higher type of human to be created by us in history. Nietzsche indicates what it would mean to put into a creative vision of a superhu-manity all that people in the past have put into their creations of gods. Zarathustra is the forerunner, the foretaste of the over-man.

In the opening section, called "Zarathustra's Prologue," we get a dra-matic, allegorical account of a drastic failure on the part of Zarathustra – who is at first not very prudent, not very worldly-wise, and has to learn a terrible lesson about present-day humanity. We meet Zarathustra, at the age of forty, outside his cave in the mountains, where he has spent ten years in solitude, together with his (allegorical) animals. His long, solitary meditations have finally reached maturity, and he is ready to go down again to human society to bring his revolutionary message. He descends to a city where the people are assembled in the marketplace at a kind of fair, waiting to watch a tightrope walker's performance. Zarathustra seizes the opportunity to make a public oration. He thinks and hopes that he can address the people, as a crowd, and that they will respond favorably to his vision. He thinks and hopes that the mass of modern mankind feels, as he does, the contemptible spiritual emptiness of contemporary existence and hunger in their souls for a way out of this emptiness. Zarathustra's goal is far more politically ambitious than that of Socrates. Like Jesus, Zarathustra seeks to revolutionize culture and everyone's way of thinking and living. The first stage in the drama shows how Zarathustra vastly underestimates the difficulty of this ambi-tious project. He suffers a deep disappointment. But it also transpires that the modern populace is by no means indifferent to his message; it turns out that, if not immediately, then at least within a few hours after hearing Zarathustra's oration, the crowd, and the entire city, became deeply hurt, angered, perhaps frightened or even ashamed; they plan to kill Zarathustra, and he barely escapes the city with his life.

The one thing Zarathustra worries about, at first, is that the people, in their spiritual emptiness, might be tempted to try to go back to the Christian religion. The first person Zarathustra had met, on his way down from the mountain, was a hermit, who was in a sense a kindred spirit but who still believed in God and was spending his life worshipping the old god. Zarathustra had expressed to himself his amazement that the her-mit did not realize that "God is dead!" But of course this means that God is not entirely dead. Zarathustra is surprised – and troubled; he did not expect to meet anyone like this. This is a problem. So Zarathustra begins his public oration by imploring the people to remain true to the earth, to seek purely earthly ideals: "I beseech you, my brothers, remain faithful to the earth, and do not believe those who speak to you of otherworldly hopes! Poison-mixers are they, whether they know it or not. Despisers of life are they, decaying and poisoned themselves." In the past, "impiety against God was the greatest sin; but God died"; now "to sin against the earth is the most dreadful thing" (125). In other words, Christianity did in the past indeed give people a profound challenge and meaning for their lives – that was its virtue. But it did so by leading people to put their energy into hopeful devotion to an eternal realm beyond the earth, a realm that does not really exist. And with a view to this nonexistent other world, Christianity created virtues that made people deny or resist the limited, mortal virtues possible in this earthly and transitory life, the only life that we really have. Christianity devalued the earth, and Zarathustra warns that we must not attempt to return to that devaluing. This is the first moral and religious commandment of Zarathustra's new, atheistic religiosity: remain true to the earth!

Then Zarathustra begins to give a foretaste of his vision of a new and higher kind of earthly human life: "Behold, I teach you the over-man." "What is the greatest experience you can have?" Zarathustra asks his audience, and he answers: "It is the hour of the great contempt. The hour in which your happiness, too, arouses your disgust – and similarly your reason, and your virtue." It is when you say, "What matters my happiness? It is poverty and filth and wretched contentment." It is when you say, "What matters my reason? Does it *crave knowledge as the lion his food?* It is poverty and filth and wretched contentment." It is when you say, "What matters my justice? I do not see that I am flames and fuel. But *the just are flames and fuel.*" It is when you say, "What matters my pity? Is not pity the cross on which he is nailed who loves man? But *my pity is no crucifixion.*" It is "not your sin, but your thrift" that "cries to heaven; your *meanness even in your sin* cries to heaven" (125–126, our emphasis). Zarathustra thus makes clear that he recognizes that modern democratic life does have what it calls its "virtues." But these virtues are too easy, too undemanding, too self-satisfied. Zarathustra wants to lead us back to the passionate and sacrificial kinds of happiness: to the hunger for knowledge that possessed Socrates; to the thirst for justice that enflamed revolutionaries; to a pity like that of Jesus on the cross – but now recognized as a *human* rather than a divine virtue. Zarathustra thus makes clear how very important the legacy of Christianity is to him, as a positive ingredient of and inspiration for the future superhumanity's "values": We must construct new values, but not out of nothing. Rather, we must construct them out of our historical legacy – and that includes an important role for trans-figured Christian together with Greco-Roman and Renaissance values. Christian pity is to be combined with classical pride and self-assertion, not with humility. We need to become able to put into human life and exis-tence everything that humans gave away to their imaginary conceptions of divinity. We need to make our descendants, as earthly beings, godlike. Sin takes on a new meaning. What is wrong or terrible is "thrift" – lack of generosity, lack of grandeur of ambitious responsibility for trying to shape ourselves and to inspire others.

But at this point Zarathustra pauses and witnesses the people respond-ing – in a shocking way: "When Zarathustra had spoken thus, one of the people cried: 'Now we have heard enough about the tightrope walker; now let us see him too!'" And "all the people laughed at Zarathustra" (126). The reaction of the people is incomprehension and ridicule. They think Zarathustra is some kind of comic warm-up announcer for the tightrope walker's performance.

But Zarathustra does not give up on his hope to start some kind of popular movement. He plunges desperately on, seeking to arouse the people by a second part of his oration, speaking more positively of what he "loves" in humanity – for which he offers a famous new definition: "Man is a rope, tied between beast and over-man – a rope over an abyss"; a "dangerous across, a dangerous on-the-way, a dangerous looking-back, a dangerous shuddering and stopping"; what is admirable in man is "that he is a bridge and not an end: what can be loved in man is that he is a *crossing over* and a *going under.*" Distantly echoing Jesus in the Sermon on the Mount, but speaking not of those who are "blessed" but rather (and more subjectively) of what "I love," Zarathustra proclaims: "I love those who do not first seek behind the stars for a reason to go under and be a *sacrifice,* but who *sacrifice themselves* for the earth, that the earth may some day become the over-man's"; "I love him whose soul *squanders itself,* who wants no thanks and returns none: for he always gives away and does *not* want to *preserve himself*"; "I love him who casts golden words before his deeds and always does even more than he promises." In sum, "I love all those who are as heavy drops, falling one by one out of the dark cloud that hangs over men: they herald the advent of lightning, and, as heralds, they perish. Behold, I am a herald of the lightning and a heavy drop from the cloud; but this lightning is called *over-man*" (126–128, our emphasis).

Again Zarathustra pauses, and again we see the popular reaction: Everyone laughs. They think he is crazy. Still Zarathustra does not give up; he essays yet a third part of his public speech – this time turning from the positive, from his hope, and from what is still lovable about humanity, to what is so disgusting about what is happening to humanity:

> I say unto you: one must still have chaos in oneself to be able to give birth to a dancing star. I say unto you: you still have chaos in yourselves.
>
> Alas, the time is coming when man will no longer give birth to a star. Alas, the time of the most despicable man is coming, he that is no longer able to despise himself. Behold, I show you the last man.
>
> "What is love? What is creation? What is longing? What is a star?" thus asks the last man, and he blinks.
>
> The earth has become small, and on it hops the last man, who makes everything small. His race is as ineradicable as the flea-beetle; the last man lives longest.
>
> "We have invented happiness," say the last men, and they blink. They have left the regions where it was hard to live, for one needs warmth. One still loves one's neighbor and rubs against him, for one needs warmth.
>
> Becoming sick and harboring suspicion are sinful to them: one proceeds carefully. A fool, whoever still stumbles over stones or human beings! A little poison now and then: that makes for agreeable dreams. And much poison in the end, for an agreeable death.
>
> One still works, for work is a form of entertainment. But one is careful lest the entertainment be too harrowing. One no longer becomes poor or rich: both require too much exertion. Who still wants to rule? Who obey? Both require too much exertion.
>
> No shepherd and one herd! Everybody wants the same, everybody is the same: whoever feels differently goes voluntarily to a psychiatric hospital.
>
> "Formerly, all the world was mad," say the most refined, and they blink.
>
> One is clever and knows everything that has ever happened: so there is no end of derision. One still quarrels, but one is soon reconciled – else it might spoil the digestion.
>
> One has one's little pleasure for the day and one's little pleasure for the night: but one has a regard for health.
>
> "We have invented happiness," say the last men, and they blink."
> (128–130)

The reaction of the crowd to this is deeply disappointing: They are *attracted* by this vision – they want to become these last men!

In the rest of the prologue, Zarathustra comes to see that he must get out of the city, that he must stop hoping to found a popular movement; if he stays and tries, he will be killed. So he becomes a wanderer, giving his speeches in semisecret or at the margins of modern society, not to crowds but to small groups and individuals. If there is to be hope for a future superhumanity, it must come much more slowly, and out of a process of gradual subversion of the existing order, whereby only a very few at first are convinced to join in the world-historical experiment.

Zarathustra's Disciples

At the end of part one, Zarathustra addresses his disciples, whom he has acquired in the meantime: "You that are lonely today, you that are withdrawing, you shall one day be the people: out of you, who have chosen yourselves, there shall grow a chosen people – and out of them, the overman." (77b). We see again the richly biblical language: "disciples," "a chosen people" (chosen by themselves, not by a god). Zarathustra goes on to speak of "salvation," and a "new hope" – not for personal immortality, but rather for a future, higher species of humans that we will help to create, and who will therefore be, in part, our continuations.

This is said, however, in a speech of leave-taking; Zarathustra must depart from his disciples because they must learn to rebel against him. They must cease to be disciples: "Now I bid you lose me and find yourselves; and only when you have all denied me will I return to you." On that return, he promises, "once again you shall become my friends and the children of a single hope – and then," he says, enigmatically, "shall I be with you the third time, that I may celebrate the great noon with you": "[W]hen man stands in the middle of his way between beast and over-man and celebrates his way to the evening as his highest hope: for it is the way to a new morning" (190–191).

We are now in a better position to understand the intended addressees of the work. Through the opening drama of "Zarathustra's Prologue," Nietzsche in effect retells the lesson he himself learned: What is needed in the immediate future is not a popular movement, but a new philosophic art and literature, with a new kind of hero-saint and a new way of speaking. To subvert existing democratic society, and to build a core of future aristocrats, what are needed are works of art and especially books that, as the subtitle of this one says, are "for none and for all." Nietzsche's writing is for "all" in the sense that it is available to all, but it is for "none" in the sense that the writing seeks out a small number of readers, the "chosen people," who will at first be disciples, but who must eventually become independent, creative, and competitive, even antagonistic, individuals bound together in a common cultural and political cause – the replacement or defiance of modern mass democracy by a new aristocracy. The "chosen people" will for a long time be marginal and even in a sense underground. They will be deeply alienated from, and threatened by, the vast democratic majority, whose future is the last men and who hate those who criticize them or that future. But precisely in this hatred and resentment, the modern mass and their intellectuals reveal their own abiding sense of self-contempt and their pained awareness of their spiritual barrenness. The crowd's laughter hides or represses the fact that they are *hurt* by what Zarathustra says; they want to stop him from speaking by eliminating him and his kind. This, paradoxically, is the source of hope for Nietzsche. It is a confirmation that Zarathustra and those like him are speaking to something that still beats in all or many hearts. Modern democratic people's hatred and fear of elitists who question the worth of democracy is a veiled and unselfconscious confession of modern democracy's deep vulnerability – its lack of self-confidence, its awareness of its own pettiness, its sense of shame at itself.

The Will to Power

The speech of Zarathustra that most clearly introduces the political dimensions of his teaching is entitled "On the Thousand and One Goals." Here we get a bird's-eye view of how Nietzsche understands all past civic idealism and disguised creativity – from which we must get our primary guidance in conceiving of future, undisguised creativity. This is Zarathustra's leading speech on power; it is Nietzsche's first explicit introduction to what he calls "the will to power," which his Zarathustra will later ("On Self-Overcoming") proclaim to be "*the* secret" of all life.

The speech begins with Zarathustra telling of his study of "many lands and many peoples," whereby he "discovered the good and evil of many peoples." And "Zarathustra found no greater power on earth than good and evil" – expressed in each people's "esteeming" or "treasuring" certain "virtues" as precious. Human communities cannot "live without first esteeming"; "esteeming" is the primary need of human existence. But "if they want to preserve themselves, then they must not esteem as the neighbor esteems. Much that was good to one people was scorn and infamy to another." "Never," Zarathustra proclaims, "did one neighbor understand the other: ever was his soul amazed at the neighbor's delusion and wickedness" (170). The supreme power of good and evil does *not* consist in there being a single, consistent moral code, the true morality. Rather, the power of good and evil is disclosed in the *clashing* moralities of peoples. Humans as moral beings do not conceive of themselves primarily as individuals, but rather as members of "peoples"

(*Volkёr*), sharply distinguished from one another by moral codes that violently contradict one another. Invoking the biblical image of Moses' tablet of Ten Commandments, Zarathustra elaborates: "A tablet of the good hangs over every people. Behold, it is the tablet of *their* overcomings; behold, it is the voice of *their* will to power. Praiseworthy is whatever seems difficult to a people; whatever seems indispensable and difficult is called good; and whatever liberates even out of the highest *need*, the rarest, the most difficult – that they call holy" (170). Each people gives itself severe and unique moral challenges, which require the "overcoming" of all sorts of inner and outer resistance. Distinct peoples are defined by moral challenges and virtues that are unprecedented and, as seen from the outside, extreme, even monstrous: Each people's morals appear to other peoples as "amazingly deluded and wicked" – but as thus awesome, in a terrible way. Each (genuine) people says, in amazement at its antagonistic neighboring people, "How *can* they *do* that? How *can* they live *that* way? How can they *endure* that?" The longing of each people to receive such awed and astonished reaction from other peoples is one aspect of what Nietzsche calls the "deepest need" that defines past humanity. But Zarathustra immediately adds that a people "needs" not only to astonish but to *rule over* other peoples: "Whatever makes them *rule* and *triumph* and *shine*, to the awe and envy of their neighbors, that is to them the high, the first, the measure, the meaning of all things" (170). Those qualities of character that allow a people to meet the new and unheard of challenges that it imposes on itself, and thereby to achieve apparent or acknowledged rule and supremacy over other peoples, is what the people calls its "virtues." At the peak of each people's virtues is its idea of the "holy," the divine, the sacred.

All of this complex "need" seen in peoples, taken together, is the primary meaning of Nietzsche's famous or infamous concept of "the will to power." Nietzsche is, like Hobbes, a philosopher of *power*. But Nietzsche understands the human preoccupation with power in a fundamentally anti-Hobbesian way. Hobbes tried to understand the urge to dominate others, and to have prestige, for its own sake, as a fundamentally confused expression of the deepest natural drive, which is to have power consistent with and as a means to security and comfort. Nietzsche contends that exactly the reverse is true. The "need" that humans feel most deeply is to shine forth as superior to others in the capacity to devise and to meet unique challenges that involve the *sacrifice* of safety and comfort. The need that has made humans human has not been a need for security and comfort; humans as human are most deeply concerned with finding (creating) moral challenges that inspire them to risk death, to enhance *in*security. Nietzsche in effect argues that what Hobbes tried to interpret as a distortion (as "vainglory") is more accurately and honestly interpreted as close to the core of the drive to power that expresses what has made humans human.

To be sure, this "need," this "will to power," is modified and shaped, Zarathustra goes on to say, by the physical environment – what Nietzsche calls the "land and sky of a people." The will to power is shaped like-wise by the neighbor or neighboring peoples. In other words, people's values are *partly* determined by utilitarian needs and are *partly* a *reaction* to neighboring peoples and their values: "Verily, my brother, once you have recognized the need and land and sky and neighbor of a people, you may also guess the law of their overcomings, and why they climb to their hope on this ladder" (170). This means that there is never a simply prudent reason, in a utilitarian sense, for a people's conception of good and evil. A people's "values" cannot be adequately understood by asking, "what does this people need for survival?" A people cannot survive if it lives for the sake of survival. A people's "values" answers above all the question: "What are we willing to die for?"

Zarathustra goes on to give four specific examples of past peoples and their unique codes of value: the Greeks, the Persians, the Jews, and the Germans. And then he pronounces the key point that makes *his* per-spective on these peoples and values, and on all the hundreds of other peoples and their antagonistic values, radically different from the peo-ples' *own* perspectives: "Verily, men *gave themselves* all their good and evil. Verily, they did not take it, they did not find it, nor did it come to them as a voice from heaven." But this involves further complexities: "First peoples were creators; and only in later times, individuals." Indeed, "the individual himself is still the most recent creation." The "delight in the herd is more ancient than the delight in the ego; and as long as the good conscience is identified with the herd, only the bad conscience says: I." But the creation of individuality is deeply ambiguous: "Verily, the clever ego, the loveless ego that desires its own profit in the profit of many – that is not the origin of the herd, but its going under." Good and evil, Zarathustra now proclaims, "have always been created by lovers and cre-ators. The fire of love glows in the names of all the virtues, and the fire of wrath" (171–172). Zarathustra identifies will to power with love, and love with will to power – which he will also designate "the gift-giving virtue." Will to power in its sublime form is a loving drive to re-create the human world in one's own image – the image of one's highest aspiration to what is most beautiful, most perfect, most supreme. Will to power is thus a drive to dominate in order to shape into perfection, as an artist with his canvas or as a strong parent with his child. For most of human history, peoples were not aware that it was in fact individuals who did most of this loving creation of values. In each people or culture there were a few of what Plato would call erotic geniuses, who possessed the truly generous souls, overflowing with loving visions of new challenges and virtues that would give vital meaning to the lives of vast numbers. The masses were given the meaningfulness of their lives by these very rare individuals. Yet even or precisely these magnificent individuals, Zarathustra teaches, were impelled to hide from themselves most of their own individuality, so that they could believe that their creations, their values, were coming from or rooted in what was beyond them. Only thus could they think that their creations might be eternal, and thus invulnerably powerful.

There is an additional grim fact that Zarathustra now discloses. Every creative genius and his shaped "children" or followers hid from themselves the fact that the people's distinctive values came into being only by destroying some previous created moral code that defined that people: "Whoever must be a creator always annihilates" (171). Creation of values is what Nietzsche elsewhere calls "re-valuation" or "trans-valuation." This has the major implication that all future, self-conscious creation of new values means not creating from scratch but instead comprehending and bringing together, into new grand syntheses, as many as possible of the most stirring challenges or values of the past. But this will have to be done from a radically new perspective that must destroy, in the sense of subduing and exploiting the old – that must view all previous, unselfconscious creativity and its creations as "monstrous," as something that now must be overcome and harnessed and forced to serve a new, fully aware or self-conscious, creativity. This overcoming of the thousand previous peoples and goals must become the goal of humanity as a whole, as it transfigures itself into a superhumanity: "Verily, a monster is the power of this praising and censuring. Tell me, who will conquer it for me, you brothers? Tell me, who will throw a yoke over the thousand necks of this beast?" The "yoke" is lacking: "The one goal is lacking. Humanity still has no goal" (172).

This "oneness" of humanity's goal is obviously paradoxical. The future unity will be a deeply conflictual, tension-ridden unity, because there cannot be a single, final, unifying, new "tablet of good and evil." There must instead be, at any time, a plurality of visionaries, each with many followers, forming new "peoples," elaborating sharply competitive alternatives. Each of these tablets gives, to those who follow it, scope for competitive interpretation and reinterpretation of the shared code of values. Genuinely vital values always promote competitive diversity *within* the people who share those values – as did the Greek values, above all others. Each people's code will be a source of war, among those within the code, as well as of war against other, external, competing peoples and moral codes. These will be wars fought spiritually, wars of ideas, but they will sometimes turn into military wars. For at the heart of real creativity, meaning creation of values, will be a passionate spiritual competitiveness for superiority, a passionate desire to do self-consciously what the peoples in the past did unselfconsciously: a striving to shine forth with a distinct and distinguishing moral code, a different way of life, by which one arouses the awe and envy of all other competing creators and their followers.

Justice vs. Equality

This analysis of a fundamental drive for rank, of a competition over superiority (and inferiority), is what most vividly puts Nietzsche at odds with modern democracy. Justice, Nietzsche insists, demands that we fight against equality. For equality is the denial of what makes us human. The equalization of all values, the end of passionate competition between clashing sets of values each seeking hierarchical superiority, is what the degraded last men, led by the socialists and democrats, stand for. Their historical victory would signal the end of competitive passionate love and creation of values: "I do not wish," Zarathustra insists, "to be mixed up and confused with these preachers of equality. For, to *me* justice speaks thus: 'Men are not equal.' Nor shall they become equal! What would my love of the over-man be if I spoke otherwise?" Zarathustra proceeds to give sublime expression to his inegalitarian vision:

> On a thousand bridges and paths they shall throng to the future, and ever more war and inequality shall divide them: thus does my great love make me speak.
>
> In their hostilities they shall become inventors of images and ghosts, and with their images and ghosts they shall yet fight the highest fight against one another.
>
> Good and evil, and rich and poor, and high and low, and all the names of values – arms shall they be and clattering signs that life must overcome itself again and again.
>
> Life wants to build itself up into the heights with pillars and steps; it wants to look into vast distances and out toward blessed beauties: therefore it requires height!

> And because it requires height, it requires steps and contradiction among the steps and the climbers! Life wants to climb and to overcome itself climbing.
>
> And behold, my friends: here ... the ruins of an ancient temple rise; behold it with enlightened eyes!
>
> Verily, the man who once piled his thoughts to the sky in these stones – he, like the wisest, knew the secret of all life!
>
> That struggle and inequality are present even in beauty, and also war for power and more power: that is what he teaches us here in the plainest parable.
>
> How divinely vault and arches break through each other in a wrestling match; how they strive against each other with light and shade, the godlike strivers –
>
> with such assurance and beauty let us be enemies too, my friends! Let us strive against one another like gods! ("On the Tarantulas" 213–214)

Precisely those who truly love and respect one another do *not* agree or wish to agree; nor do they make, or wish to make, one another comfortable. Instead they challenge and discomfit and fight with one another constantly – on the individual as well as social level: "In a friend one should still honor the enemy. Can you go close to your friend without going over to him? In a friend one should have one's best enemy. You should be closest to him with your heart when you resist him" ("On the Friend" 168).

Still, all the diverse and clashing new creative visions, and the future peoples who form around them, will be united politically in one crucial negative respect, namely, in their opposition to the last men, and hence to modern democracy and socialism, with their stress on collective pursuit of creature comforts and the de-emphasis of gripping spiritual challenges. The political expression of the historical drift toward the last men is the modern *state* – whose worship is for Zarathustra the modern form of idolatry.

The Monstrosity of the Modern State

"Somewhere," Zarathustra says with melancholy, "there are still peoples and herds, but not where we live, my brothers: here there are states. State? What is that?"

> State is the name of the coldest of all cold monsters. Coldly it tells lies too; and this lie crawls out of its mouth: "I, the state, am the people."
>
> That is a lie! It was creators who created peoples and hung a faith and a love over them: thus they served life.

> It is annihilators who set traps for many and call them "state": they hang a
> sword and a hundred appetites over them. ("On the New Idol" 160–161)

The modern state, in Zarathustra's eyes, is the death of true political
life. For the modern state convinces humans that they do not need to be
united by a single deep faith, opposed to other deep faiths. The modern
state teaches that society can be united merely by economic appetites
and the need for collective security. The modern state teaches that there
can and should be mere tolerance for diversity, without the genuine
diversity that arises only out of sharply antagonistic struggle for ranking.
Hence Zarathustra ends his attack on the modern state by calling on his
friends to stay out of the politics of the state: "Escape from the bad smell!
Escape from the idolatry of the superfluous! The earth is free even now
for great souls" – "for the lonesome and the twosome, fanned by the fra-
grance of silent seas." "There, where the state *ends*," cries Zarathustra,
"look there, my brothers! Do you not see it, the rainbow and the bridges
of the over-man?" (163). Zarathustra's teaching implores those who will
listen to live lives of withdrawal from state-centered politics, but with a
subversive attitude, laying the ground for a future "*great* politics," as he
calls it, which will arise out of the dismantling of the modern state and
the rejuvenation of "peoples" (*Volkër*).

Zarathustra admits that this dismantling of the state is fraught with
grave dangers: "a great despot (*ein grosser Gewalt-Herr*) might come along,
a shrewd monster who, according to his pleasure and displeasure, might
constrain and strain all that is past till it becomes a bridge to him, a
harbinger and herald and cockcrow" ("On Old and New Tablets" #11,
p. 314). Zarathustra recognizes the danger of a new kind of populist
despotism. But he is more worried by the progressive emergence of the
leveling disposition of the egalitarian last men: "This, however, is the
other danger and what prompts my further pity … one day the rabble
(*der Pöbel*) might become master and drown all time in shallow waters."
So, "my brothers, a *new nobility* (*eines neuen Adels*) is needed" – "to be the
adversary of all rabble," and "of all that is despotic," and "to write anew
upon new tablets the word 'noble' (*edel*)." For "many who are noble are
needed, and noble men of many kinds, *that there may be a nobility*. Or as I
once said in a parable: "Precisely this is godlike, that there are gods, but
no God!" (315, our emphasis). Superhumans, with heroic and saintly
virtues, are to become worshipped in place of the superhuman, otherworldly, old, and now dead god.

In a crucial passage in *Beyond Good and Evil* (aphorism #61) Nietzsche
makes clearer how important a role religions – of *created* "gods" – will

play in his vision of the future healthy civic society: "The philosopher as we understand him, we free spirits – as the man of the most comprehensive responsibility who has the conscience for the overall development of man – this philosopher will make use of religions for his project of cultivation and education, just as he will make use of whatever political and economic states are at hand." For those who are "strong and independent," who are "prepared and predestined to command, and in whom the reason and art of a governing race become incarnate, religion is one more means for overcoming resistances, for the ability to rule – as a bond that unites rulers and subjects and betrays and delivers the consciences of the latter, that which is most concealed and intimate and would like to elude obedience, to the former." For the "few individuals" who are "of such noble descent" that they "are inclined through lofty spirituality to prefer a more withdrawn and contemplative life, and reserve for themselves only the most subtle type of rule (over selected disciples or brothers in some order)," religion "can even be used as a means for obtaining peace from the noise and exertion of cruder forms of government, and purity from the necessary dirt of all politics." At the lower ranks, "religion also gives to some of the ruled the instruction and opportunity to prepare themselves for future ruling and obeying": The "slowly ascending classes – in which, thanks to fortunate marital customs, the strength and joy of the will, the will to self control is ever growing – receive enough nudges and temptations from religion to walk the paths to higher spirituality, to test the feelings of great self-overcoming, of silence and solitude." With a view to "educating and ennobling a race that wishes to become master over its origins among the rabble, and that works its way up toward future rule, asceticism and Puritanism are almost indispensable means."

Conclusion

With Nietzsche, here at the end of this volume introducing political philosophy, we return in a sense to where we began, or to what we spoke of in the introduction. One can now begin to see that this volume is in a sense a response to the icy challenges and questions with which Nietzsche has left modern humanity. All of us are compelled in one way or another to confront the problems Nietzsche diagnosed, and most people tend to think along *some* of the lines that Nietzsche identified, predicted, or laid down. Most sophisticated people today are in one way or another cultural relativists; most today cannot believe in the possibility of finding standards that transcend the different historical cultures and their merely human creations of value. Yet most relativists try desperately to resist the frightening political and moral and religious implications that Nietzsche drew.

Nietzsche's impact in the twentieth century was something like that of Rousseau in the late eighteenth and early nineteenth centuries. Rousseau left behind a legacy, for over a century, of thinkers striving to find a way to elevate and to enrich the Enlightenment so as to meet Rousseau's challenge. People could not find in Rousseau's own conception of human nature an acceptable set of guiding standards. The political movements that did try to build on Rousseau's critique of what he called "bourgeois" civilization wound up becoming frighteningly inhumane: the terrorists of the French Revolution, and then Marx, who elaborated a doctrine that was used or abused to justify even more horrific, nightmarish regimes of terror. Similarly, with Nietzsche, those who tried to apply his ideas in actual politics wound up creating right-wing, fascistic, and Nazi regimes and movements that were as horrific as those created by the followers of Marx. And today, Nietzsche is an important influence on radically militant Islamicist thinkers, as can be seen, for example, in the writings of the Shiite thinker Shariati, a major ideologist of Khomeini's revolution in Iran.

Nietzsche would have been disgusted by Hitler and Mussolini, and he would have been horrified to learn what they did with his teachings, just as Marx would have been horrified at what Stalin did with Marxism. We cannot accurately call Marx a Stalinist or Nietzsche a fascist. On the other hand, the hideous twentieth-century movements of the radical left and right did get important inspiration and guidance from these thinkers.

We are still living in the shadow of Nietzsche's legacy, even more than that of Marx – whose influence has waned since the demise of the Soviet Union. No one has yet found an adequate remedy for our syndromes as diagnosed by Nietzsche: most massively, the pervasive historical relativism that saps all our "values" and the "nihilism" or spiritual emptiness that haunts our culture as a consequence. Yet the horrors of twentieth-century elitist political experiments stifle any temptation to be seduced by the antidemocratic direction Nietzsche pointed to as the path toward overcoming our situation. The question on which we close is this: May there not be truths retrievable from the half-forgotten insights of past republican philosophers – ancient and early modern or pre-Nietzschean – that can guide us out of the bleak spiritual landscape in which we seem to have been left by Nietzsche?

Name Index

Subject Index

Academy of Dijon, 332, 344
acquisitiveness. *See also* luxury; money;
    property; wealth
  in Aristotle, 73–74, 84, 289
  in the Bible, 143, 149–50, 289
  in Hobbes, 252, 255–58, 267, 271
  in Locke, 279, 288–98
  in Marx, 365, 379
  in Machiavelli, 176–77, 178–79, 180–81,
    198, 203, 215, 221
  in Montesquieu, 316, 318–19, 324–27
  in Plato, 29–30, 32, 35, 40, 289
  in Rousseau, 335–36, 340–41
  in Thomas Aquinas, 168, 289
  in Tocqueville, 394
agape, 146. *See also* love
Agrarian law (Roman), 180
alienation, 336, 348, 380
ambition
  in Aristotle, 82, 85–88
  in the Bible, 127–28
  in Hobbes, 268–69
  in Machiavelli, 176, 178–79, 180–81,
    184–89, 190–95, 210–11
  in Montesquieu, 308, 313, 316–17
  in Plato, 62
America, United States of, 5, 35, 160, 223,
    273, 303, 315, 381–96, 402
amour de soi-même, 353
amour propre, 353, 362. *See also* vanity
anger, 93, 95, 121, 127, 143, 144,
    154, 403
  and courage, 74
  and law, 103
anthropology, 347

aristocracy
  in Aristotle, 83–88, 92–93, 97, 106
  in the Bible, 135
  in Locke, 298
  in Machiavelli, 177, 178, 184
  in Marx, 368, 373, 374, 376
  in Montesquieu, 313, 315–17, 321–22
  in Nietzsche, 401, 402, 407
  in Tocqueville, 385–96
Aristotelian(s), 160, 167, 177, 202, 208,
    224, 248, 250, 255, 278–79,
    280–82, 289, 384
ark of the covenant, 137, 139, 140
art(s), 5, 60–61, 64, 341–42, 356,
    358–59, 387
  in the Bible, 122, 123, 131, 258–59
  in modernity, 222, 225, 227, 235–36,
    236–39, 246, 291–98
  and nature, 56–58, 225, 227, 236–39,
    258–59, 291–98, 367
  of ruling, 60–61, 97
Asia, in Montesquieu, 313, 314, 315, 321,
    323, 326
associations, in Tocqueville, 393–94
Athens, 4, 14–15, 22, 24, 30, 33, 36, 53,
    67, 117, 206, 232–33, 332, 342,
    345, 348
Atlantis, 232–33, 236, 338, 339
authenticity, 335–36
avarice. *See* acquisitiveness

Babel, 123
Babylonian captivity, 142, 146, 230
barbarism, 69–71, 98, 315, 321
beatitudes, 143–44

Bensalem, 230–45
Bible, 8, 117–52. *See also* Christianity;
    god(s); Judaism; religion
in Bacon, 230–31, 238
books of:
  Acts, 148, 149, 150, 151
  Chronicles, 140
  Colossians, 147, 150
  1 Corinthians, 146, 147, 150
  2 Corinthians, 147
  Daniel, 145
  Deuteronomy, 118, 129, 130, 131,
    132, 133, 134, 135, 136, 142, 145,
    159, 162, 164
  Ecclesiastes, 141, 142
  Exodus, 118, 125, 131, 132, 133, 134,
    135, 159, 162, 164
  Ezekiel, 145, 168
  Galatians, 148
  Genesis, 118, 120, 123, 124, 125,
    126, 127, 128, 130, 131, 145,
    150, 348
  Isaiah, 125, 130, 134, 142, 146
  Jeremiah, 142
  John, 146, 147
  Joshua, 135–36
  Judges, 136
  Kings, 145
  Leviticus, 129, 130, 133, 134, 145,
    162, 164
  Luke, 145, 149, 150, 151
  Kings, 125
  Mark, 147, 149, 151
  Matthew, 142, 147, 149, 151
  Micah, 142
  Numbers, 129, 131, 133, 135, 164
  1 Peter, 146, 150, 152
  Proverbs, 141, 142
  Psalms, 141, 145, 146, 230
  Romans, 147, 152
  1 Samuel, 136, 137, 138
  2 Samuel, 140, 243
  Song of Songs, 141
  1 Timothy, 149, 150
  Zechariah, 142
and classical political philosophy, 8, 117,
    126–27, 129, 134–35, 142, 153–55,
    156, 159, 221
in Hobbes, 248, 250, 258–59, 271, 273,
    275, 289–90
in Locke, 277–80, 281–85, 289–97

in Machiavelli, 173, 179, 194–95, 207,
    221–22
in Montesquieu, 308, 312, 314
rhetorical character of, 153–54
in Rousseau, 347–48
in Tocqueville, 387
Bill of Rights, 14
  Fifth Amendment, 273
bourgeois, the, 267, 315, 335–36, 363–64,
    365, 368, 371–80, 381, 386, 416
business cycle, 375–76

Calvinism, 337
capitalism, 5, 8, 168, 222, 288–98, 336,
    365, 368, 371–80, 382
caritas, 146. *See also* charity
Carthage, in Aristotle, 76
censorship, 165, 222, 271, 319, 332, 342,
    347, 386
charity, 2, 146, 165, 169, 239–40, 281–82,
    289, 292, 297, 303
chastity, 339
China, in Montesquieu, 315
choice, 26–27, 69, 73, 120, 161–62,
    351–52
Christianity, 8, 142–52, 153–69.
    See also Bible; faith; god(s); religion
in Bacon, 228–32, 238–40
and classical political philosophy,
    153–69
and the Enlightenment, 331
and Hobbes, 248, 250, 252–53, 258–59,
    271, 289–90
in Locke, 277–80, 281–85, 289–97
in Machiavelli, 174–75, 179, 182–84,
    186–87, 192, 194–95, 195–98,
    199, 205–6, 210–11, 212, 215–16,
    221–22
in Montesquieu, 312, 314
in Nietzsche, 402, 403–5
in Rousseau, 332–34, 335, 337, 339,
    347–48, 363
sectarian conflict within, 246, 386
    (*see also* war: religious)
in Tocqueville, 386
Church of England, 279
citizenship, 3–5
in Aristotle, 73, 75, 77–78, 81–84, 91,
    97, 103, 105, 110–11
in the Bible, 117, 144–45, 150–52, 183
in Locke, 300, 302, 305
in Machiavelli, 183–84

Islamism, 416
Israel. *See* Jews
Italy, 187, 196, 200, 204–6, 209, 210–11, 216, 218–19

jealousy. *See* envy
Jerusalem, 117, 139, 140, 142, 146, 230, 244
Jews
    as chosen people, 124–30
    toleration of, 241, 243–45
Judaism, 117–42, 314
    and classical political philosophy, 153–54, 289
    toleration of, 243–45
Judges, regime of in the Bible, 136–37
judicial review, 303
judiciary, 303, 307, 322, 385, 393
jury, 95–96, 273, 322
justice, 1–5. *See also* law: natural; natural right
    as acquisitiveness, 288–89, 296–97
    as advantage of the stronger, 54–63
    as art, 44–45, 50
    in the Bible, 143–44
    and commerce, 324–25, 326
    as common good, 1, 74, 79, 90, 159
    contracts, as keeping, 41–42, 266–67
    democratic, 90–91
    as disadvantageous, 59
    dispute over among regimes, 79
    distributive, 1, 90, 102, 104–5
    as equality, 90, 97
    as friendship, 43–47, 47–52, 144–46
    in Hobbes, 247, 250, 261, 263–64, 266–67
    and law, 32, 54, 78, 159, 160–61
    in Locke, 277, 287–88, 288–89, 296–97, 303
    love of, 38, 41, 217
    and love's of one's own, 32
    in Machiavelli, 200, 202, 222
    in Nietzsche, 399, 404, 412–13
    and the noble, 47–49, 49–51
    as not self-destructive, 92–93
    oligarchic, 90–91
    passions, as rooted in, 250, 261, 277
    and philosophy of history, 366–68, 374
    retributive, 26–27, 133, 212, 268, 288
    and sacrifice, 2, 32, 45–46, 48–49, 50–51, 160

of Socrates, 30–31
Socrates's concern with, 20, 27, 32, 35, 37, 41
and the state of nature, 263–64, 287–88
as virtue, 2, 27, 49–51, 63–65, 90
of war, 320–21

king. *See* monarchy
knowledge. *See also* philosophy; science; wisdom
    in the Bible, 119–21, 140–42
    as an end, 112–13, 190–95, 199, 201, 225–27, 387
    extent available to reason, 156–57, 165, 168–69, 222, 227, 231–32, 238–39, 249–50, 399
    in Hobbes, 248–49, 251
    love of, 404
    as a means, 190–95, 225–27, 235–39, 255, 387
Koran, 153–54

language, 72, 80, 123, 251, 349–50
last man, 401, 402, 406, 413, 414
law, 3, 301–6, 348, 393
    and arms, 215
    as categorical, 100, 159, 167
    civil, 307, 322
    as commanding the advantage of the ruler, 54–55
    of concupiscence, 161–62
    criminal, 307, 322
    definition, according to Thomas Aquinas, 160–61
    divine, 3, 100, 103, 234, 238, 312, 314, 400
        in the Bible, 122–23, 125, 129, 130–35, 141, 142, 144–45, 148, 151, 152, 169, 285
        in Thomas Aquinas, 156, 159, 162, 168–69
    as educative, 102, 163–65, 166–67
    eternal, 160, 161–62
    ex post facto, 273
    habituation as source of strength of, 67, 163–65
    human. *See* positive law
    and justice, 32, 54, 78, 159, 160–61
    of nations, 311–12
    natural, 8, 100, 400. *See also* justice; natural right

law (*cont.*)
   in Bacon, 224–27, 231–32, 238–39
   in Hobbes, 263–64, 265–69, 270, 272,
      275, 280, 290, 336
   in Locke, 277, 282–85, 290, 292, 301
   in Montesquieu, 308–12, 320
   in Rousseau, 346, 360–61
   in Thomas Aquinas, 156–69
   nature, as distinct from, 126–27
   and passions, 73, 99–100, 103, 161–62,
      163–64, 259–60
   positive, 3, 161–62, 163–65, 166–67,
      168–69
   problem of, 99–102, 159, 166, 304
      (*see also* prerogative)
   rule of, 5, 73, 96–105, 130, 131–33,
      159, 161, 301–4, 306, 315, 325,
      339, 393 (*see also* prerogative)
   sumptuary, 165
lawyers, in Tocqueville, 393
legislature, 95–96, 301–5, 307, 322,
   339, 385
leisure, 6, 71, 83–84, 86, 88–89, 96,
   107–8, 109, 112–13, 176, 178,
   215–16, 356, 369, 375,
   378–79, 389
Leninism, 380
liberalism, 167, 222, 264, 271, 273, 276,
   323. *See also* democracy: liberal
liberty. *See* freedom
lie. *See* deception
love, 2–4
   in Bacon, 240
   as Christian virtue, 145–46, 152, 169,
      240, 281–82
   devotional, 125, 134, 141, 169
   divine, 146
   erotic, 39, 41, 119–20, 141–42, 327,
      339, 343, 349–50, 356–58, 363
   familial, 299, 349–50, 355–58, 363
   for God, 121, 124–25, 134, 140–42,
      145, 169, 212
   in Nietzsche, 401, 405–6, 410–11,
      412–13
   of one's own, 40, 144–45, 299
   romantic (*see* love: erotic)
   sexual, 119–20, 133, 134, 144, 310, 343,
      349–50, 353
luxury, 32, 108, 165, 176, 319, 324, 339,
   340. *See also* acquisitiveness; money;
   property; wealth
Lyceum, 67, 348

magnanimity, 224, 340
Magnificat, 212
manliness. *See* courage
Maoism, 380
marriage, 119, 275, 299, 339.
   See also family; love;
   patriarchy; women
materialism, 222, 226, 246–47, 248,
   250–51, 340
mercy, 125, 133, 134, 140, 141, 143,
   146–47, 259.
   See also compassion; pity
Messiah, 140, 142, 147–48, 150,
   152, 241
militia, 91, 109, 165, 302, 316
miracle, 129, 146, 158, 175, 195, 197,
   200, 229, 231–32, 238–39,
   308, 333
moderation, 32, 72, 176, 178, 222, 303,
   317, 325
modernity, 35, 58, 173, 222, 319–20, 337.
   See also Enlightenment; political
   philosophy: modern
monarchy
   in Aristotle, 68, 71, 74–75, 82, 88,
      97–105
   in the Bible, 128, 135, 136–37, 140–42
   in Hobbes, 249–50, 272–73
   in Locke, 279–80, 286, 299, 302, 303
   in Machiavelli, 198, 199, 202–14
   in Marx, 368
   in Montesquieu, 313, 315–17, 319,
      321–22, 323, 325
   in Rousseau, 333, 345
   in Tocqueville, 383, 386–87
money, origin of in Locke, 294–98.
   See also acquisitiveness; luxury;
   property; wealth
moral responsibility. *See also* free will; sin
   in the Bible, 120, 124–25, 133, 154
   in Hobbes, 253–54, 268
   in Plato, 26–27, 154
   in Thomas Aquinas, 161–62, 253–54
mortality, 2, 149–50, 229–30.
   See also immortality
   awareness of, 120–21, 124–25, 141–42,
      350–51
   concern with, 39, 40, 250–51, 258,
      260–62, 263–64, 265, 311, 394
   overcoming of, 147, 237, 261
motherhood, 275, 299, 350, 355.
   See also family; love; women

philosophy (*cont.*)
  and politics, 4–7, 14, 24–25, 27, 33–35,
    66, 67, 72, 74, 87–89, 98, 112–13,
    190–95, 200–2, 278, 331–32,
    342–43, 345–46, 368–69, 378–79
  Socratic, 7, 19–21, 23, 24, 66, 67,
    112–13, 117–18
pity, 143, 353–54, 404.
  See also compassion; mercy
Platonists, 248
poetry, 3–34, 140–42, 342–43, 402
poets, 21, 28, 31, 65–66, 70, 342, 389, 399
polis, 67, 68–69, 71–72, 369
political philosophy, 1–9, 117. *See also*
  philosophy; politics: and
  philosophy; science
  classical, 4, 7–8, 65–66, 87–88, 89, 201–
    2, 216–17, 221, 270, 331–32, 387
  and the Bible, 117–18, 153–55
  and Hobbes, 246–47, 247–50, 251,
    253, 255, 270–71, 289–90
  and Locke, 278–79, 280–81, 289–90,
    289–90, 293, 296, 297
  and Machiavelli, 173, 176–79, 184,
    186–87, 199–202, 215–18, 221–22
  and Rousseau, 331–32, 334, 336,
    342–43, 345–46
  and Thomas Aquinas, 155, 159–60,
    163–64, 165, 167, 169
  modern, 8, 223, 246–47, 247–50, 270,
    278–79, 331–32, 336, 369
  origin in Machiavelli, 173, 184, 194–95,
    217–18, 221–22
  Nietzsche's attack on the tradition of,
    397–98, 402
  publically defensive character of, 16,
    34, 72, 87–88, 154, 194–95, 201,
    247–48
  origin in Socrates, 13, 16–24, 66
  relation between classical and modern,
    8, 35, 91–92, 173, 176–79, 184,
    186–87, 189–95, 199–202, 215,
    217–18, 221–22, 224–27, 247–50,
    255, 270–71, 273, 277–82, 289–90,
    293, 296, 297, 317–18, 331–32,
    336, 342–43, 345–46, 368–69,
    369–70
politics
  artificiality of
    in Aristotle, 68, 72–73
    in Hobbes, 246, 259–60, 264,
      269–70, 336

    in Locke, 281, 285–86, 336
    in Machiavelli, 207–8
    in Montesquieu, 308, 310–11, 317–19
    in Rousseau, 336–37, 337–39,
      346–47, 348–50, 354–55, 359–60
  ends of, 1
    in Aristotle, 85–89, 91–92, 104–5,
      281, 297
    in Bacon, 228, 236–40, 242–43
    in the Bible, 151, 297
    in classical political philosophy,
      186–88
    in Hobbes, 246–47, 249–50, 252,
      259–60, 264, 270–71, 273, 274–75,
      277, 290
    in Locke, 280–81, 287, 290, 294,
      296–98, 301
    in Machiavelli, 176–77, 177–79,
      186–88, 219–22
    in Marx, 379–80
    in Montesquieu, 310–12, 318–19,
      321–22
    in Rousseau, 360–62
    in Thomas Aquinas, 162–65,
      166–67, 281
  limits of
    in Aristotle, 72, 74, 81–88, 89,
      97–105, 159
    in Bacon, 240, 243–45
    in the Bible, 151, 162
    in classical political philosophy,
      186–88
    in Hobbes, 246–47, 252, 270–71, 273
    in Locke, 280–81, 290
    in Machiavelli, 186–88
    in Montesquieu, 315
    in Nietzsche, 414–15
    in Plato, 33–35, 65–66
    in Rousseau, 363–64
    in Thomas Aquinas, 162, 166–67
  naturalness of
    in Aristotle, 68, 72–73, 85, 159–60,
      167, 208, 281, 336
    in Thomas Aquinas, 160, 162–65, 167
    in Plato, 33–34
  origins of
    in Aristotle, 68–73, 85, 101, 281
    in the Bible, 121–23
    in Hobbes, 246, 259–60, 264,
      269–70, 275
    in Locke, 281, 285–86, 294
    in Machiavelli, 207–8, 217–18

in Rousseau, 360–62
in Thomas Aquinas, 160
Roman Catholic Church, 155, 205–6,
   210–11, 215–16, 248, 321.
   See also papacy
Roman republic, 316, 337, 339, 369
in Machiavelli, 174–90, 192–94, 195–98,
   203–6, 206–7, 216
Romanticism, 333, 358

Salomon's House, 228, 231, 235–45
science. *See also* arts; knowledge; philosophy; wisdom
   aims of, 225–27, 235–36, 236–39,
      243–45, 387
   Aristotelian, 224–27
   atheism of, 16–18, 20, 236–40
   modern, 223–27, 247, 387
      in Bacon, 223–27, 235–36,
         236–39, 367
      in Hobbes, 246–47, 247–49
      modern scientific method,
         223–27, 247
      in Rousseau, 331–32, 340–42,
         342–46, 387
   in modern democracy, 388–89
   Socratic, 16–18, 19–20, 23, 226
   in Thomas Aquinas, 153, 156
security. *See* self-preservation
segregation, 160
self-expression, 335, 337, 338, 341, 345,
   346, 380
self-government. *See* freedom: civic
self-interest rightly understood, in
   Tocqueville, 392–93, 394
self-knowledge, 20–3, 51, 59–62, 64–65.
   See also knowledge; wisdom
self-preservation, 5. *See also* fear: of death;
   fear: as foundation of politics
   in Aristotle, 85, 91–92
   in Hobbes, 92, 258, 260–62,
      263–64, 273
   in Locke, 92, 282–88, 290–98
   in Montesquieu, 309–12, 313, 314–17,
      317–19, 319–21, 321–22, 324
   in Nietzsche, 405, 409–10, 414
   in Rousseau, 340, 350–51, 353
   in Thomas Aquinas, 163
senate
   American, 385
   Roman, 177, 181, 183
sentiment of existence, 350–51, 355, 361

separation of powers, 302–4, 307, 322
Sermon on the Mount, 143–44, 150, 151,
   169, 405
shame, 32–33, 53, 120, 123, 163–64, 356,
   403. *See also* honor; humility
sin. *See also* Fall, the; free will; moral
   responsibility
   in Bacon, 228, 233
   in the Bible, 120–21, 133–34, 140–41,
      147, 154, 258–59, 267–68,
      285, 293
   in Hobbes, 258–59, 267–68
   in Locke, 285, 293, 296
   in Nietzsche, 404–5
   in Plato, 27, 154
   in Rousseau, 333, 348
   in Thomas Aquinas, 158, 162
skepticism, 22, 29, 30–32, 34, 67, 201,
   247–48, 331, 340, 342–43
Skeptics, 248
slavery
   in Aristotle, 68–71, 73–75, 98
   in the Bible, 128, 131, 142, 146, 149
   in Locke, 278, 288
   in Machiavelli, 197
   in Montesquieu, 307, 323
   in Plato, 36, 59, 60–61
   in Rousseau, 359
   in Tocqueville, 382
social contract
   in Aristotle, 91–92
   in Hobbes, 246, 252, 264, 265–69, 272,
      274–75, 286, 300–301
   in Locke, 286, 299, 300–301
   in Montesquieu, 311
   in Rousseau, 349, 359–60, 361
socialism, 371, 377, 401, 412–13
Sodom, 124
sophists, 17, 18, 25, 37, 51, 52–53, 56, 342
sovereignty, 269–71, 272, 274–75, 304
Soviet Union, 416
Spain, 320–21
Sparta, 176–77, 178, 198, 206, 337, 340,
   345–46, 361, 362
speech, 72. *See also* language
Stalinism, 380, 416
state of nature
   in Hobbes, 259–64, 265–69, 272,
      280–88, 359
   in Locke, 279, 280–88, 290–96, 359
   in Montesquieu, 308–11
   in Rousseau, 346–60

For EU product safety concerns, contact us at Calle de José Abascal, 56–1°, 28003 Madrid, Spain or eugpsr@cambridge.org.

www.ingramcontent.com/pod-product-compliance
Ingram Content Group UK Ltd.
Pitfield, Milton Keynes, MK11 3LW, UK
UKHW020345140625
459647UK00019B/2304